SEARCH FOR THE AMERICAN RIGHT WING

SEARCH FOR THE AMERICAN RIGHT WING

AN ANALYSIS OF THE SOCIAL SCIENCE
RECORD, 1955–1987

William B. Hixson, Jr.

PRINCETON UNIVERSITY PRESS   PRINCETON, NEW JERSEY

Copyright © 1992 by Princeton University Press
Published by Princeton University Press, 41 William Street,
Princeton, New Jersey 08540
In the United Kingdom: Princeton University Press, Oxford
All Rights Reserved

Library of Congress Cataloging-in-Publication Data

Hixson, William B.
Search for the American right wing : an analysis of the social
science record, 1955–1987 / William B. Hixson, Jr.
p.   cm.
Includes bibliographical references (p.   ) and index.
ISBN 0-691-08623-0
1. Conservatism—United States—History—20th century.
2. United States—Politics and government—1945–1989. I. Title.
JA84.U5H59   1992
320.5′2′0973—dc20   91-36636

This book has been composed in Linotron Times Roman

Princeton University Press books are printed
on acid-free paper, and meet the guidelines
for permanence and durability of the Committee
on Production Guidelines for Book Longevity
of the Council on Library Resources

Printed in the United States of America

10 9 8 7 6 5 4 3 2 1

To the Memory of My Mother

Contents

Acknowledgments —————————————————————————

A PROJECT of ten years' duration entails many obligations: I can only begin to repay them here. At three key points Michigan State University helped this book along its way. I want to express my appreciation: first, to the All-University Research Initiation Grant program, which enabled me to go on leave and continue the project at a critical early stage; second, to the Library, which gave me access to a carrel quiet and spacious enough to allow me to do most of the work on it there; and finally, to the staff of Office Services for patiently retyping the final drafts. There are many individuals who have given me assistance, beginning with the historians, political scientists, and sociologists too numerous to name who know me only as a correspondent but who have made "the community of scholars" a reality. Beyond them, I wish specifically to thank William A. Gamson, who kindly read a much earlier draft; J. Morgan Kousser, whose comments on Parts One and Three were most helpful; and Stan Kaplowitz, whose statistical expertise was invaluable in helping me comprehend the ambiguities in survey data. Two friends helped determine the shape of this book: John F. Reynolds, who persuaded me to turn an unwieldy mass into a more focused analysis; and Theda Skocpol, who at a later point gave me shrewd advice as to how to make it more accessible to readers. Two of my colleagues in the Department of History at Michigan State played important roles in its creation: David T. Bailey, whose wise counsel and consistent support for my project helped sustain me in moments of doubt; and Emily Z. Tabuteau, who brought her meticulous scholarship to her reading of the text, saving me from errors both substantive and stylistic. I want to thank too my editor at Princeton University Press, Gail Ullman, for her encouragement and the two readers for the Press whose recommendations I have tried to incorporate. Finally, there is the one person without whom I simply could not have finished the book, my wife Vivian. Her steadfast sympathy for the book encouraged me to keep working on it during long periods of weariness and discouragement; her training as a sociologist forced me, in hundreds of conversations, to clarify my formulations and document my conclusions; and the literary skills she brought to her role as editor—a role she cheerfully assumed in spite of scholarly and artistic projects of her own—produced a far more coherent manuscript than I could have achieved alone.

East Lansing, Michigan   William B. Hixson, Jr.
June 1991

Introduction _____

IN DECEMBER 1954 sixty-seven of his fellow senators voted to censure Joseph McCarthy, effectively ending the career of the man who since the spring of 1950 had dominated so much of American public life. A year after the censure, a collection of essays entitled *The New American Right* appeared that attempted to explain the factors that had made "McCarthyism" possible. The essays, however, were less concerned with the senator himself than with what Daniel Bell termed in his introduction "the deeper-running social currents of a turbulent midcentury America." The contributors agreed, as Bell phrased it, that "McCarthy has to be understood in relation to the people behind him and the changed political temper which these groups have brought. He was the catalyst, not the explosive force. These forces still remain" (Bell 1955, 3, 19).* By the time the book was updated and reissued as *The Radical Right* in 1963, unrepentant supporters of McCarthy had already formed organizations ranging from the John Birch Society to the Young Americans for Freedom and were about to constitute the driving force behind Senator Barry Goldwater's successful campaign for the Republican nomination. It was clear that the "forces" that needed to be analyzed had an existence of their own transcending either the ambitions of one senator or the specific tensions of the early Cold War. Without perhaps realizing it, the contributors to *The New American Right* had set in motion one of the major scholarly investigations undertaken by American social scientists: the study of the American right wing.[1]

* The reader should be aware that frequently cited works, or works that in other ways are central to the analysis and argument, are given in abbreviated form in both the text and the footnotes; full citations appear in the Bibliography.

[1] Since the essays that triggered much of the subsequent research were collectively entitled *The New American Right*, one might think that by that point (1955) there were comparable studies of an "older" American right wing (of, for example, the forces that had come together to oppose the New Deal). Such, unfortunately, was (and still is) not the case. The respectable opposition to the Roosevelt administration's policies has been covered in part by James T. Patterson, *Congressional Conservatism and the New Deal* (Lexington: University of Kentucky Press, 1967) and by George R. Wolfskill, *The Revolt of the Conservatives: A History of the Liberty League, 1934–1940* (Boston: Houghton Mifflin, 1962). But what attracted the attention of observers at the time were the less respectable critics—men who trafficked in anti-Semitism, such as Father Charles Coughlin, William Dudley Pelley, Gerald B. Winrod, and Gerald L. K. Smith. That was one reason they were labeled "fascists." The most notable scholarly analysis written from that perspective is Morris R. Schonbach's 1958 dissertation published over a quarter century later as *Native American Fascism During the 1930s and 1940s: A Study of Its Roots, Its Growth, and Its Decline* (New York: Garland, 1985).

The most recent historical scholarship, however, tends to discount the concept of "native American fascism," not only for those spokesmen but even for the midwestern vigilantes in the

In the more than three decades since the publication of that book, political scientists, sociologists, psychologists, and historians—motivated in varying degrees by anxiety over the rise of right-wing organizations and by sheer intellectual curiosity—have tried to understand the phenomenon they were analyzing: specifically, by studying the activists who joined right-wing organizations and those segments of the public that supported right-wing candidates, or both; and, more generally, by locating the right wing in broader historical and societal contexts. Because many of the concepts these scholars formulated and tested in their analyses of the right wing—concepts such as "mass society," "status inconsistency," "symbolic politics," "relative deprivation," "critical realignment," and "modernization"—have been so influential within their disciplines, their studies shed light on the evolution of American social science since World War II. Because their findings have implications for a wide range of issues—the determinants of political attitudes and behavior, the complexities of American "populism," the relationship of racial prejudice to social structure, the influence of big business and organized religion, to name only a few—the debates among social scientists studying the right wing illuminate the contours of American society as well.

We are confronted, in other words, with a body of scholarship that because of the importance of its subject matter deserves to be investigated, that because of its bulk needs to be summarized, and that because of the controversies it has produced requires the closest possible critical analysis. In this regard, the scholarship on the American right wing that followed (and, positively or negatively, was shaped by) *The New American Right* bears a striking resemblance to the scholarly output by psychologists that was provoked by the publication of *The Authoritarian Personality* in 1950. As one well-known psychologist characterized that situation a decade and a half later, "the massive literature that followed upon it is by now quite indigestible." As a result, "political scientists, educators, historians, sociologists, and others outside the psychological fraternity are likely to throw up their hands, and accept or reject the original formulations as suits their fancy," while psychologists themselves "have become bored with the rather arid literature or methodologically oriented studies . . . and fashion has turned elsewhere, before many of the important substantive problems raised by *The Authoritarian Personality* have been properly resolved."[2]

The same set of problems—studies accepted or rejected on the basis of personal "fancy," a tendency to move from dull but methodologically rigorous

---

Black Legion: see Alan Brinkley, *Voices of Protest: Huey Long, Father Coughlin, and the Great Depression* (New York: Knopf, 1982); Leo P. Ribuffo, *The Old Christian Right: The Protestant Far Right from the Great Depression to the Cold War* (Philadelphia: Temple University Press, 1982); and Peter H. Amann, "Vigilante Fascism: The Black Legion as an American Hybrid," *Comparative Studies in Society and History* 25 (July 1983): 490–524.

[2] M. Brewster Smith, foreword to Kirscht and Dillehay 1967, p. viii.

approaches to more exciting speculations, the abandonment of lines of inquiry before the questions they raise have been fully answered, and (perhaps even more than in the case of the literature on the "authoritarian personality") layers of misinterpretation—has marred much of the scholarship on the American right wing.

This book is an attempt to overcome these problems. It is intended in the first place as a creative synthesis of major explanations of the American right wing, bringing together the hypotheses of scholars from a wide variety of disciplines over a period of three decades. In addition, this book is a critical analysis of the major explanations of the right wing and is structured as a continuing dialogue between the evolving concepts of the researchers and the patterns in the data that emerged over time. Its focus is not on changing paradigms in the social sciences as a whole, but on the way in which, in this specific body of research, the weight of accumulating evidence has stimulated new and more comprehensive explanations. Third, this book tries to document the extent to which the various discrete phenomena comprising the right wing can realistically be conceptualized as a continuous and interconnected political phenomenon, a task usually abandoned to journalists.

Finally, this book examines, as carefully as possible, the actual arguments and evidence produced by each social scientist. It is thus written as a corrective to the work of those who, instead of returning to the original text, rely on either the misrepresentations (or misunderstandings) of early critics or the oversimplifications of later summaries. My offering of a careful, point-by-point evaluation of the evidence for competing interpretations means that considerable space is taken up with detail; that detail is not extraneous but the essence of the book. As a result, the evaluations and syntheses I have produced are not perhaps as beguilingly simple as some others that are available, and researchers do not fall so neatly into prearranged categories. But the record that results is, I believe, more faithful to the actual dialogue between academic researchers and the evolving historical reality.

The organization of this book presented me with several major dilemmas. Because the amount of potentially relevant scholarship had reached such massive proportions, the first problem was how to decide what to include. Some decisions were relatively easy. To limit the topic to manageable proportions, I decided at the outset not only to exclude all unpublished material, whether doctoral dissertations or papers presented at conferences, but also to end my discussion with analyses of the "new right's" role in the 1980 election. I made that decision primarily because the interaction of the Reagan administration and the American right wing, however intensely examined by journalists, has not yet been the object of much attention by scholars. Finally, the pressures of finishing the writing—and rewriting—of the manuscript compelled me to cut off my research at the beginning of 1988; thus the scholarship covered runs from 1955 through 1987.[3] Within that span of time, however, I believe I have covered all the relevant scholarly material published by sociologists, psychologists, political scientists, and historians.

While these decisions on the book's scope were relatively easy to make, more difficult questions of inclusion confronted me as I was actually writing this book. Which individuals and organizations should be included as part of "the American right wing"? Conventional scholarly rules might dictate a single a priori definition. But as I gradually assimilated the massive literature on the right wing, I found that the subject of all this analysis was constantly assuming new forms. No single, rigid, a priori definition could do justice to this continually evolving and complex political phenomenon. A more intellectually honest approach, and the one I have adopted in this book, is to accept the fact that the best "definition" of the American right wing is the composite picture that has emerged from the accumulated efforts of scholars to adequately describe and analyze it. As readers will see as they follow my argument, it is only as researchers have examined one aspect of this phenomenon after another that they have begun to perceive the extent to which the right wing can be defined as a unitary phenomenon—and the extent to which it can be disaggregated into separate and unique historical developments.

[3] Of the scholarly works that have appeared in the last three years relevant to the subject matter of this book, seven in particular seem to me worthy of mention. In *The Party of Fear: From Nativist Movements to the New Right in American History* (Chapel Hill: University of North Carolina Press, 1988), David H. Bennett offers a suggestive model for understanding the right wing but has difficulty interpreting movements that are not clearly "nativist." Richard M. Fried, *Nightmare in Red: The McCarthy Era in Perspective* (New York: Oxford University Press, 1990) is especially sensitive to the relative impact of the elite initiatives and preexisting popular attitudes but tends to underestimate McCarthy's individual importance. Edward G. Carmines and James A. Stimson, *Issue Evolution: Race and the Transformation of American Politics* (Princeton: Princeton University Press, 1988) is the most persuasive argument yet made by political scientists on the permanent impact of Barry Goldwater and his supporters in 1964 in introducing into political discourse "racial conservatism" (i.e., a position neither overtly racist nor supportive of civil rights legislation).

In *To the Right: The Transformation of American Conservatism* (Berkeley and Los Angeles: University of California Press, 1990), Jerome L. Himmelstein presents a convincing statement of the continuity of the "new right" with its predecessors in the late 1950s and early 1960s but virtually ignores the Wallace campaigns and their significance for subsequent right-wing strategy. In their *Sex, Gender, and the Politics of ERA: A State and the Nation* (New York: Oxford University Press, 1990), Donald G. Mathews and Jane Sherron DeHart successfully convey the deep differences between the opposing sides in the conflict over the Equal Rights Amendment in North Carolina. Faye D. Ginsburg, in her *Contested Lives: The Abortion Debate in an American Community* (Berkeley and Los Angeles: University of California Press, 1990), in contrast emphasizes what the women active on both sides—at least in Fargo, North Dakota—have in common, especially their joint commitment to "women's values" such as nurturance. Finally, Steve Bruce's book, *The Rise and Fall of the New Christian Right: Conservative Protestant Politics in America, 1978–1988* (Oxford: Clarendon Press, 1988), moves beyond the simpler formulations of both "status politics" and "resource mobilization" to provide the most illuminating analysis yet written of the development of organizations such as the Moral Majority.

If scholars dealing with the American right wing strongly disagreed with each other as to which developments should or should not be included, such an approach might create intellectual and organizational problems. But this has not been the case. Rather like the Supreme Court justice who said that while he could not define pornography he knew it when he saw it,[4] social scientists, without in many cases explicitly defining the right wing, seem remarkably agreed as to what it constituted over this thirty-year period. Thus, to take some of the scholars I will consider as examples, in successive books and articles Seymour Martin Lipset has analyzed supporters of McCarthy, members of the John Birch Society and similar organizations of the early 1960s, the Goldwater backers in 1964, Wallace voters in 1968, and the mobilization in the late 1970s of right-wing evangelicals and fundamentalists.[5] In the collection of essays he edited, *The American Right Wing*, Robert Schoenberger included analyses of a number of organizations prominent in the early 1960s— the Conservative party in New York as well as the John Birch Society and the Christian Anti-Communist Crusade (Schoenberger 1969; Grupp 1969; Wolfinger et al. 1969). James McEvoy compared the Goldwater supporters of 1964 with the Wallace supporters of 1968 in his *Radicals or Conservatives? The Contemporary American Right* (McEvoy 1971). Finally, in the various studies he undertook in the first phase of his career, Michael Rogin wrote successively on the sources of support for McCarthy in the early 1950s, on support for Wallace in his first try for the presidency in 1964, and on Goldwater, Reagan, and other beneficiaries of a distinctive "right-wing" syndrome in southern California politics.[6]

Most of the individuals and groups that qualified for inclusion in these scholars' analyses had common ideological and organizational characteristics. On the ideological side, those who were identified as participants in right-wing political activity have typically maintained certain positions on public issues. They were hostile to the expansion of the welfare state and advocated the restoration of an unrestricted "free market"; they remained concerned with domestic "subversion" long after McCarthy had passed from the scene; they rejected the post–World War II foreign policy of "containment" in favor of various kinds of "rollback" of the power of Communist states and the "liberation" of their peoples; they generally opposed the civil rights agenda of the 1960s; and they much more sharply rejected the goals of the women's movement of the 1970s. On the organizational side, even though most of them have maintained some kind of affiliation with the Republican party, participants in right-wing political activity have developed a considerable degree of autonomy. These activists had differed with the party leadership on enough occa-

[4] Potter Stewart, in *Jacobellis v. Ohio*, 378 U.S. 184 (1964), at p. 197.

[5] Lipset and Raab, 1970, pp. 209–337; Lipset 1968, pp. 304–32; Lipset and Raab 1970, pp. 338–427; Lipset 1985, pp. 253–93.

[6] Rogin 1967; Rogin 1966; Rogin 1969; Rogin 1970b.

sions to create independent, "nonpartisan" organizations or—as in the case of the Conservative party in New York, or the Wallace presidential campaigns—to compete directly with Republicans. Over the span of thirty years right-wing activists therefore have not only linked themselves with the Republican party but with whichever other groups shared common ideological goals.

In this book, therefore, I have followed the evolving definition of the right wing made by the scholars whose work I assess, and have organized the material into four chronological segments: on McCarthy's supporters (1950–1954); on the right-wing organizations of the early 1960s (1958–1964); on George Wallace's constituents (1964–1970); and on the "new right" (1975–1980). This scheme has inevitably produced some omissions, which again are less mine than those of the scholars I follow. One is the development of those groups that openly appeal to racial or religious hostility and/or advocate violence: they simply have not attracted the interest of scholars, probably because (with the possible exception of the Ku Klux Klan) they have not proved particularly durable.[7] A second omission is the rise of a right-wing intellectual community, again because those writers have not attracted the interest of the political scientists and sociologists whose work constitutes the core of this study. Analysis of the "conservative intellectual movement" has, it is true, attracted a number of historians,[8] but their work has proven almost impossible to integrate into my discussion in this book. Although in some ways I, too, consider myself an intellectual historian, on this question I share the very different focus of social scientists, who insofar as they attempt the task at all try to infer right-wing ideology from interviews with activists rather than simply assume the influence of opinion-pieces in the *National Review*.[9] Third, although it is obviously hard to discuss the right wing (however defined) without mentioning the Republican party, much of the scholarly literature on the party

[7] The major exception is the massive study of Lipset and Raab, which does discuss the Klan (Lipset and Raab 1970, pp. 116–31, 276–82, 326–32). In addition, one historian has written a monograph on the Liberty Lobby, which has links both to the right-wing activists discussed in this book and to various racist and anti-Semitic spokesmen (Mintz 1985).

[8] See for example Ronald Lora, *Conservative Minds in America* (Chicago: Rand McNally, 1971); John P. Diggins, *Up from Communism: Conservative Odysseys in American Intellectual History* (New York: Harper and Row, 1975); and most of all George H. Nash, *The Conservative Intellectual Movement in America Since 1945* (New York: Basic Books, 1976).

[9] The problems entailed in using the methods of intellectual history to account for the development of the contemporary right wing are most clearly illustrated by the typical analysis of "economic libertarianism" and "moral traditionalism." Seeing the two streams of thought as moving in opposite directions, but noting that right-wing activists have embraced them both, historians (and not only historians) have spent most of their effort studying the few individual writers—William F. Buckley, Jr., but also Frank Meyer and M. Stanton Evans—who have tried to reconcile them. The historians, however, fail to specify either exactly whom these writers influenced, or (for me as a historian a far more important question) the way in which certain strains in the broader political culture could predispose activists toward accepting such a synthesis even without the benefit of the *National Review*.

and its recent leaders by historians and political scientists is irrelevant to the issues under discussion; and so party developments during this period will be considered only insofar as they relate to parallel developments in the American right wing.

Finally, there is the matter of terminology. Since its activists, intellectuals, and politicians by and large call themselves "conservatives," why do I insist on calling them "right wing"? I have two responses. In the first place, in the Orwellian world in which we live, where "people's democracies" have been imposed by armed force and electoral "mandates" used to justify keeping the public uninformed, it is a good rule not to grant final authority over the use of words to those whose interests are served by them. Second, after considerable reflection on the subject, I am not at all sure how "conservative" the contemporary right wing actually is. In my more inventive moods, I have considered making the argument that, as measured by many of the canons of classical conservatism—a reverence for the organic natural order of things and a deep sense of their interconnectedness, a keen awareness of the disastrous consequences that can follow upon the naive application of intelligence and goodwill, and above all the rejection of the idea that the earth belongs to the living—there is no more truly conservative movement in our time than the environmental movement. That movement has, however, not been notably supported by the American right wing, which responded to the issues environmentalists raised by making James Watt Secretary of the Interior.

For those who question the "conservative" credentials of the American right wing, an alternative designation is readily at hand. With very good company among American scholars, I could call them the "radical right." For a time in the late 1950s and early 1960s this was in fact the preferred designation; but while the phrase caught something important, it soon became freighted with all sorts of connotations borrowed from the horrifying record of the German Nazis. As a result, for too long a time social scientists occupied themselves with what now seem to be marginal issues: confirming or denying the psychological "health" of the "radical right's" adherents or the degree to which it constituted a "mass movement" outside the established party system. In its most precise meaning, of course—right-wingers who want "radical" changes—the term is still useful. In that connection it should be noted that the self-designation "radical" reappears regularly among right-wing spokesmen themselves: when Paul Weyrich said, "We are different from previous generations of conservatives. . . . We are radicals," he apparently forgot that two decades before William F. Buckley, Jr., had called himself a "radical reactionary."[10] Still, because of its other associations, I have tried not to use the phrase except where the immediate context renders it unavoidable.

[10] Paul Weyrich, as quoted in Saloma 1984, p. 49; William F. Buckley, Jr., as quoted in John

If the first major problem in writing this book was how to define (or whether to allow other scholars to define) the American right wing, the second was how to determine which scholarly disciplines to include, and whose work constituted relevant social science research. The inclusion of the work of political scientists and sociologists in this study does not, I think, need to be defended. Psychologists appear chiefly because the concepts in *The Authoritarian Personality* were so frequently applied to right-wing activists. Historians, who have been linked collectively with social scientists, distinguished collectively from them, or separated individually on the basis of their concepts and methods, have presented me with the most problems. Most historical work is of limited utility in a study such as this because historians tend to write specialized monographs on narrow, chronologically bounded topics—topics that (with one major exception) do not include most of those covered in this book. The exception is, of course, McCarthyism; and historians play the significant role they do in the first part of this book because so many of the questions scholars from other disciplines asked about McCarthy's support (Did it come disproportionately from "isolationist" constituencies? Was McCarthy the heir of the original Populists?) could only be answered by historians. With that exception, however, historians as a group play a minor role in this study.

But in the pages that follow some individual historians loom very large indeed. One very special case is Richard Hofstadter who—from the time his essay "The Pseudo-Conservative Revolt" first appeared to his book *The Paranoid Style in American Politics* ten years later[11]—framed so much of the argument about the historical antecedents of the American right wing that, even in a study centered on behaviorally oriented social scientists, it would be impossible to leave him out. My decision to include or exclude other historians turned on whether they developed models of American society that they then applied to the American right wing. Hofstadter developed such a model, without ever quite acknowledging it; so too, and more self-consciously, did Robert Wiebe and Richard Jensen, whose work will be considered. On the other hand, many of the historians who emerged in the 1960s and 1970s relegate the right wing to a very minor place in their depiction of a corporate-imperialist America. They therefore are simply not engaged in the same debate as the scholars covered in this book, who, whatever their other disagreements, take the right wing seriously as an independent force. In general, then, historians, like other scholars, have been included in the book to the extent that they have shaped, or can contribute directly to, the ongoing scholarly discussion about specific aspects of the American right wing.

B. Judis, "Savimbi: New Darling of the New Right," *In These Times* 10 (February 12–16, 1986): 3.

    [11] Richard Hofstadter, "The Pseudo-Conservative Revolt," *American Scholar* 24 (Winter 1954–55): 9–27 (reprinted as Hofstadter 1955a). See also Hofstadter 1955b; Hofstadter 1963a; Hofstadter 1963b; Hofstadter 1964; Hofstadter 1965a; Hofstadter 1965b.

Having indicated which political developments are (or are not) included in this book and what kinds of scholarship are (or are not) being analyzed, I want now to suggest the general approach I am taking to the subject matter, an approach shaped both by my own inclinations and by the configuration of the scholarly work to be analyzed. During the time span covered in this book, the political scientists and sociologists who studied the development of the right wing tended to ask three different sets of questions: Who are the members of right-wing organizations or worked for right-wing candidates, and why did they do so? Who voted for (or in public-opinion polls, indicated support for) right-wing candidates, and why did they do so? And, which segments of the economic, political, and intellectual elites funded or endorsed these right-wing organizations and candidates, and why did they do so? The reader of the book will undoubtedly be as disappointed as I was to find that neither of the first two sets of questions was asked all the time, and the third set was asked only intermittently. Combined with the tendency of historians to study some subjects more intensively than others, this unevenness in social science research has produced a body of scholarship that is far more impressive, both quantitatively and qualitatively, on some of the phenomena to be analyzed than on others.

The first part of this book, on the sources of McCarthyism, is the richest. Because of the initial monographs in political history and the ensuing syntheses, as well as studies of contemporary public opinion and electoral analyses of key states, we can reach some definitive conclusions about the historical antecedents of McCarthyism and who at the time supported the senator. The second part, on the so-called radical right of the early 1960s, is much more fragmentary and inconclusive. Some social scientists at the time raised the possibility of a significant connection between right-wing organizations, on the one hand, and big business and military leaders, on the other, but our third set of questions was never asked in any consistent way. Other scholars interviewed activists in right-wing organizations but reached inconclusive results. There are two good studies, based on survey data, of prenomination Goldwater supporters; but we know practically nothing about the backgrounds and motivations of the Goldwater delegates, and studies of voting behavior in the 1964 election are surprisingly few. So for what may be the single most significant period in the development of the American right wing—the six years or so ending with Goldwater's nomination that (in the words of one participant) "laid the foundations for everything that followed"[12]—scholars have still not provided a coherent picture.

Even though Wallace received only about a third as many votes as Goldwater, about his supporters we know a great deal more. This is so mainly because southern historians and historically oriented political scientists built

---

[12] William A. Rusher, *The Rise of the Right* (New York: Morrow, 1984), p. 161.

upon analyses of survey data to give us an exceptionally thorough interpretation of his base of support in his own region. And because of the work of political scientists like Rogin and Walter Dean Burnham, who portrayed the Wallace movement as a symptom of a broader societal crisis, we have an overall interpretation of Wallace support only slightly less developed than that of McCarthy's. In sharp contrast, even though over a decade has passed, the material on the "new right" remains disorganized. We have a number of studies based on interviews with "profamily" activists opposing abortion or the Equal Rights Amendment, which ask our first set of questions, and a smaller number of similar studies on politically mobilized evangelicals and fundamentalists. An exceptionally large number of studies ask the second set of questions: who voted for Ronald Reagan and right-wing congressional candidates in 1980, and did they do so either because of issues such as abortion or because of the mobilization efforts of the Moral Majority? A few studies asked the third set of questions, specifically investigating the degree of corporate support for right-wing political activity. Nonetheless, how each of these aspects of the "new right" relates to the other, how corporate contributors, "profamily" activists, and fundamentalist religious leaders were turned into a cohesive force, through an organizational infrastructure created by Richard Viguerie, Paul Weyrich, Howard Phillips, and others, has been largely left to journalists to explore.

It should be clear from the topical framework I have adopted that my primary interest in this book is to trace the development of the scholarly debate rather than to study the lives of the debaters. Thus I do not begin with an extended consideration of "the New York intellectuals" such as Bell, Hofstadter, and the other contributors to *The New American Right* who shaped so much of the subsequent debate. I have not written about the way they launched their careers in the paradoxical intellectual milieu that emerged out of the era of Hitler and Stalin, which simultaneously affirmed American institutions and doubted human perfectibility. (Nor for that matter have I tried to place younger scholars such as Rogin in their milieu, which, equally paradoxically, combined alienation with an almost millennial optimism.) Such topics have already attracted the attention of scholars studying American intellectual life after World War II.[13] Bell is the subject of at least two recent books,[14] and

[13] Most notably, Robert Booth Fowler, *Believing Skeptics: American Political Intellectuals, 1945–1964* (Westport, Conn.: Greenwood, 1978); Richard H. Pells, *The Liberal Mind in a Conservative Age: American Intellectuals in the 1940s and 1950s* (New York: Harper and Row, 1985); Alexander Bloom, *Prodigal Sons: The New York Intellectuals and Their World* (New York: Oxford University Press, 1986); Terry A. Cooney, *The Rise of the New York Intellectuals: "Partisan Review" and Its Circle* (Madison: University of Wisconsin Press, 1986).

[14] Nathan Liebowitz, *Daniel Bell and the Agony of Modern Liberalism* (Westport, Conn.: Greenwood, 1985); Howard Brick, *Daniel Bell and the Decline of Intellectual Radicalism: Social Theory and Political Reconciliation of the 1940s* (Madison: University of Wisconsin Press, 1986).

Hofstadter will undoubtedly receive even more attention from intellectual historians in the future.[15] I am not sure what I could add to their accounts.

This book is then a study of ideas rather than of individuals. But I have not organized the material by grouping the various scholars I consider into "schools" or "families," emphasizing the common assumptions of the members of those "schools," and treating the ensuing debates as clashes over the application of different "paradigms." As a matter of principle, I have no quarrel with such an approach. It would not, however, be a particularly productive way of organizing a book such as this, for a number of reasons. First, and most important, it would deflect the reader's attention from what scholarship can tell us about the American right wing to what scholarship can tell us about itself (an important question but not my primary concern).

Second, while their paradigms have undoubtedly helped shape the questions that scholars have chosen to ask, an emphasis on these broad "schools of thought" is often not very useful in clarifying the origins and evolution of the concepts discussed in this book. Having read and read closely the scholarly literature on the American right wing for over a decade, I have come away impressed with the relative narrowness of the debate, with the way researchers tended to ask essentially the same questions about what kinds of individuals joined right-wing organizations or supported right-wing candidates. As far as I can determine, the assumptions behind most of the work I analyze are what Robert K. Merton once called "theories of the middle range," theories lying between what he called the "minor working hypotheses" evolved in day-to-day research and "master conceptual schemes" with their "all-inclusive speculations."[16]

While changes in these "middle-range" assumptions certainly form a significant part of the development of the research covered in this book, they are best analyzed within the context of the historical events and research constraints in which they actually occurred. Any attempt to create sweeping categories can only obscure the extent to which analysts from very different political backgrounds found themselves asking similar questions and reaching similar conclusions. The idea, for example, that the newly affluent in the economically expanding South and West would be particularly predisposed to right-wing political activity has at various points been put forth by the Marxist editors of the *Monthly Review*, by the self-consciously centrist contributors to *The New American Right*, and, especially in the 1970s and 1980s, by right-wing strategists themselves.

---

[15] The first entries in what promises to be a wave of Hofstadter studies are Daniel Joseph Singal, "Beyond Consensus: Richard Hofstadter and American Historiography," *American Historical Review* 89 (October 1984): 976–1004; and Susan Stout Baker, *Radical Beginnings: Richard Hofstadter and the 1930s* (Westport, Conn.: Greenwood, 1985).

[16] Robert K. Merton, *Social Theory and Social Structure*, rev. ed. (New York: Free Press, 1957), pp. 5–6.

The recent tendency to classify scholars on the basis of their common assumptions—their "ideology," if you will—has in my view reached the point of diminishing intellectual returns. All too often, far from aiding the development of a deeper perspective on an individual's scholarship, the construction of such categories becomes a substitute for it. Since the polemical intentions behind such classifications are seldom hidden, scholars are sorted into "good" and "bad" categories on the basis of their theoretical assumptions, which in turn are reduced to positions on a crudely devised political spectrum.[17] As these categories are passed from one analyst to another, whatever connections they ever had with substantive reality become more and more tenuous. One notable example, taken from the material to be considered, is Rogin's onslaught on those he called "pluralists," whose assumptions, he charged, led them to misconceive the origins of McCarthyism. Anyone familiar with the wider literature will concur that those Rogin singled out did indeed share certain common assumptions. "Pluralism," however, was not what tied them together; and it is surely noteworthy that the two scholars whose conclusions about the sources of McCarthyism most closely agreed with Rogin were the two well-known "pluralist" political scientists Nelson Polsby and Earl Latham.[18] But that fact has been singularly ignored as one interpreter after another has echoed Rogin's denunciation of "pluralists."

At the same time, the debates between scholars covered in this book are often less "ideological" than methodological and reflect disciplinary rivalries as much as anything else. Much of the controversy over the interpretations of McCarthyism put forward in *The New American Right*, for example, can most easily be explained as arraying political scientists who emphasized partisan-

[17] Even considered only in polemical terms, it is not as easy to determine the ultimate thrust of these assumptions as some analysts have implied. Rogin, for example, has periodically observed that many of those scholars who denounced the "extremism" of the "radical right" in the late 1950s and early 1960s, subsequently attacked the "extremism" of student protests, the antiwar movement, and the other insurgencies in the late 1960s and after; for him, as for some other commentators, anti-"extremist" polemics ultimately had conservative implications (Rogin 1967, pp. 47, 300n; Rogin 1987, pp. 280, 352n).

As Alan Wolfe has pointed out, however, the major problem for those who used "extremism" was quite different: they "never came to recognize that while Communism *was* outside the postwar consensus, the ideas of the radical right *were not*" (Wolfe 1981, p. 12). Insofar as that is so, the concepts developed by these social scientists were hardly necessary to discredit the left-wing insurgencies of the 1960s in the eyes of either politicians or the general public. Rather, if it had any independent influence on the course of American politics at all, their use of "extremism" *may*—contrary to the assumption of Rogin and others—actually have had a mildly progressive impact by temporarily delegitimizing the activities of the right wing, most notably in the presidential election of 1964.

[18] See especially Nelson W. Polsby, *Community Power and Political Theory* (New Haven: Yale University Press, 1963), pp. 112–38; and Earl Latham, *The Group Basis of Politics: A Study in Basing-Point Legislation* (Ithaca, N.Y.: Cornell University Press, 1952), pp. 1–53.

ship as a key explanatory variable against sociologists who similarly emphasized social mobility.

It might be argued that an investigation of assumptions is essential to any
analysis of social science scholarship because they determine the questions
researchers ask. As an abstract proposition this can hardly be denied; but its
actual importance in determining the contours of scholarly discourse is quite
another matter. Let us take as an example our third set of questions: which
segments of existing economic, political, and intellectual elites funded or endorsed right-wing organizations and candidates, and why did they do so? It is
almost certainly true that one of the reasons such questions were seldom asked
in the early 1960s was that social scientists assumed that the right wing was
so peripheral it could not possibly have close connections with the institutional
centers of American life. The problem, however, is that such assumptions
were far less common—indeed they were widely challenged—in the early
1980s. Yet studies exploring the relationship between corporations and right-
wing organizations were still relatively few and far between, and the relationship between the right wing and the national-security bureaucracy remained
almost totally unexplored.

That situation reminds us that factors other than ''ideology'' determine research agendas, and even a moment's reflection on the day-to-day exigencies
of academic life suggest what they can be. Specific research topics and meth-
odologies tend to be popular not only because they conform to dominant ''paradigms'' or suit the ''ideological'' preferences of mentors or peers but because
they are relatively inexpensive in time, money, and effort. The demand in so
many American universities for production of the greatest possible quantity of
scholarship in the shortest possible time has probably had more to do with the
topics researchers have or have not chosen than any combination of ''ideological'' considerations. As an academic myself, I can appreciate the constraints
under which many of the scholars whose work I discuss were forced to operate. I am not retrospectively about to blame them for not undertaking different
research strategies.

Nonetheless, because this is a study of what the accumulated research can
tell us about the American right wing, I can only regret the absence of data
and conclusions on certain key issues, an absence that will never be remedied.
Ironically, that what is past can never be recovered is an axiom far more relevant to the work of quantitatively oriented social scientists than to that of the
more traditional historians, who can always turn to newspapers, private cor-
respondence, and official documents. It is true that the aggregate data on specific elections has been compiled, so that those trying to locate the 1968 Wallace supporters can scrutinize county returns for the next half century if they
so choose. It is also quite possible that within the survey data periodically
gathered by national polling organizations there are still nuggets of relevant
information waiting to be uncovered. But many of the questions left unan-

swered by the scholarly work covered in this book—particularly those concerning the kinds of individuals who belonged to right-wing organizations at specific points in time—can never be answered because those points in time have passed (and so in many cases have the individuals and the organizations). Throughout the book, therefore, I have tried to draw conclusions from the evidence that does exist, because—except in a very few cases—no more will be forthcoming.

I want to conclude by emphasizing something that, in view of the foregoing discussion, might not be immediately obvious. The analysis of the aspects of the contemporary right wing in this book—the support for Senator McCarthy, the "radical right" organizations of the early 1960s, the presidential campaigns of George Wallace, and the mobilization of the "new right" in the late 1970s—contains more than partially answered questions and significantly qualified conclusions. There are definite themes that run through the book and that, at least in my view, point toward the historically oriented interpretation I offer at its end. (Readers who wish to gain a quick overview at the outset of the major research problems discussed in the book are encouraged to turn to the "Summary of the Research So Far" section of the concluding chapter.) What follows is a brief guide to those themes.

First of all, readers will find the book far more cohesive if they keep in mind my effort to emphasize, as far as possible, the role of activists in the developments covered. Such an emphasis may seem obvious but my attempt to achieve it has often been thwarted because at a number of points, as I have already indicated, the social science research on the particular topic ignored the activists and concentrated on responses from the general public. That tension, between my interests and the direction of the existing research, did not (by definition, could not) arise in the case of either the right-wing organizations of the early 1960s or those of the late 1970s. But it was a problem in the case of McCarthy, where the activists were difficult to locate, and in the case of Wallace, where the activists were easy to locate but attracted a minimum of scholarly attention. Unable to solve the problem directly, I approached it indirectly in the way I framed my analysis. My concern with McCarthy, for example, is not with his personal contribution to the emotional anticommunism of the early Cold War years (a question that scholars continue to debate) but rather with why it was he who inspired a generation of right-wing activists and what the accumulated evidence on the sources of his support can tell us about the possible future constituencies for right-wing anticommunist appeals. Similarly with Wallace I am not as interested in either assessing his motives or locating him politically as I am in looking at his campaigns to find out why so many right-wing activists found him attractive and at his popular support to investigate the extent to which those who voted for him might continue to be available for right-wing mobilization.

Under my definition, then, the right wing consists, first of all, of activists and, second, of the constituencies to whom they appeal. Just as the constituencies will vary in their socioeconomic level, so at any one point will the backgrounds of the activists. And that is the second theme in this book: in spite of the massive amount of effort social scientists have invested in trying to find it, there is no single socioeconomic base for right-wing activism. That conclusion is, I believe, amply confirmed by the data analyzed throughout this book. It is not, however, one that will go unchallenged because many scholars continue to try to fit the right wing on a procrustean bed of their own making. Their consequent squeezing and stretching of the evidence typically takes one of two forms. Those who see the right wing as "top dogs" spend much time showing the continuity between the upper-middle-class activists who joined the John Birch Society and/or nominated Barry Goldwater and those most active opposing the Equal Rights Amendment a decade later; stress economic concerns; put special emphasis on corporate funding of the right wing; and in general disparage right-wing claims to "populism." Those who see the right wing as "bottom dogs," on the other hand, concentrate on the support given George Wallace; are especially sensitive to religious concerns; tend to focus on grass-roots opposition to legal abortion, homosexual rights, and curricular changes in the public schools; and not only see the right wing as "populist" but in potential conflict with corporate interests.

Those in both camps tend to dismiss phenomena that do not fit their model. But surely the events of the last decade and a half have revealed the degree to which the right wing fits both: we live in an era in which some of the country's largest corporations fund writers and research institutes dedicated to the promotion of the "traditional family"; and one in which many voters not themselves affluent nevertheless vote for self-styled disciples of the "free market." What is happening here? There are of course many possible explanations— and no intelligent observer of American politics can ever rule out the possibility of manipulation. But there do appear to be two common attitudes that bring together the various right-wing activists and the constituencies they hope to attract. The first (the third theme in the book) is what might broadly be called "anticosmopolitanism" and is perhaps the most consistent note struck by right-wing leaders since World War II. In that connection one thinks not only of Joe McCarthy's attack on the "young men born with silver spoons in their mouths" in the State Department but also of Barry Goldwater's bewilderment at those who refused to acknowledge that "the answers to America's problems are simple," of George Wallace's anger at "those overeducated ivory-tower folks with pointy heads," and of Jerry Falwell's lament about a "secular humanist" establishment dominating American culture. As the most discerning analysts of this kind of rhetoric have noted, it may sound like the rhetoric of class resentment but is in fact something else for it bridges different socioeconomic backgrounds. This is so because, whatever the influence of those "cosmopolitans'' has been in the universities and in the media, it is their role in the Federal Government that has produced the most impassioned right-wing responses. Thus businessmen fighting economic regulations could be (indeed have been) joined in common cause with community leaders fighting mandated changes in race relations and religious spokesmen opposed to similar changes in the legal status of women—all policies, in their minds, spawned in the same alien (''Communist,'' ''secular humanist,'' ''elitist'') cosmopolitan environment.

The second attitude is positive; and to locate it one must begin with the proposition, increasingly accepted among scholars, that there are certain worldviews that transcend socioeconomic position, most notably those arising from a common religious orientation. It was suggested in the early 1960s— first by various journalists, then by small-scale studies of clergy and laity, and most of all in the essays of Bell and Hofstadter—that that common religious orientation might well be fundamentalist Protestantism. That possible connection between right-wing activism and religious fundamentalism constitutes the fourth underlying theme in the book. Never systematically pursued in the early 1960s, challenged and then ignored in the subsequent decade, that possible connection became an object of renewed scholarly interest at the end of the 1970s when ''new right'' strategists created an alliance with like-minded fundamentalist and evangelical ministers to form organizations such as Christian Voice and the Moral Majority. I have no desire to substitute a narrow kind of religiosity for an inadequate concept of economic interest as *the* explanation for the development of the American right wing; and the bulk of the research certainly suggests that the impact of the Moral Majority in 1980 was greatly overrated. But it does seem to me that the fundamentalist-evangelical role in the right wing, slowly growing over time, better accounts both for its ideology (notably its commitment both to the ''free market'' and to the ''traditional family'') and for its relatively diverse social base than do alternative explanations.

Finally, the durability of the right wing raises doubts about the validity of the idea, most forcefully articulated by Lipset but maintained by many other scholars, that the right wing is essentially reactive, a response to threats to the prestige (or ''status'') of particular groups and the values they uphold, so that historically it represents forces in retreat. That the right wing represents forces in retreat is perhaps less clear in the 1990s than it was in the 1960s; in any case Rogin is surely right to insist that the right wing's durability comes from its articulation of values that lie at the core and not at the periphery of American political culture. That is the fifth theme in the book, which I explore in chapter 10 (in which I analyze Rogin's work on right-wing politics in southern California) and in chapter 15 (where I contrast his model of the right wing with Lipset's). In the concluding chapter (chapter 16) I offer a synthesis combining Rogin's emphasis on a ''liberal-capitalist'' core with various historians' applications of modernization theory to the American experience. I suggest at the end of this book that the American right wing may best be understood not as reactive but as proactive and not as vaguely traditionalist but specifically as the heirs of the nineteenth-century ''modernizers,'' promoting Victorian values in a late twentieth-century world.

Part One ―――――――――――――――――――――

THE SOURCES OF ''McCARTHYISM''

BY THE TIME he was censured by his fellow senators, Joseph McCarthy had the distinction of being one of the very few politicians in American history to have a movement (or more precisely, in his case, a particular political style) named after him. Conceived originally by his critics as a term of opprobrium, "McCarthyism" was soon adopted by him and by his supporters as a badge of honor. But as the years recede and memories grow dim, scholars are having difficulty in defining exactly what "McCarthyism" was, and many would now deny McCarthy's singularity and see "McCarthyism" as simply another expression of the emotional anticommunism of the early Cold War years. It is true enough that during the years McCarthy sat in the Senate other prominent Americans—politicians in both parties, government bureaucrats, business leaders, writers, and educators—made similar accusations of "subversion," and some of them may have been even more responsible for the actual repression of radicals and dissenters. But it does not follow that McCarthy himself was an insignificant figure. As many perceived at the time, the junior senator from Wisconsin was in important ways unique; and, as we can now see, it would be his most active supporters and not his opponents, however intense their anticommunism, who would shape the contemporary American right wing. To understand how that was possible it is necessary to reconnect McCarthyism with McCarthy.[1]

From the moment he propelled himself onto the national stage in the spring of 1950 until his fateful encounter with the Army four years later, McCarthy devoted his efforts primarily to uncovering Communist "subversives" in the executive branch of the United States Government. Much to the annoyance of the Eisenhower administration, he kept at his self-appointed task even after the political party of which he was ostensibly a member had returned to power. McCarthy may have distinguished himself in his exceptional disregard for truth and in his ability to hold the public's attention through a steady stream of charges. What distinguished "McCarthyism," what seemed to bind the senator to his supporters, was a preoccupation with the foreign policy apparatus, particularly that in the State Department. It was there (so the "McCarthyites" believed) that Communist "subversives" had occupied positions of importance, and because of their influence the Soviet Union dominated Eastern Europe and the Communist forces had won the Chinese civil war.

The State Department, at that point in our history, was exceptionally vulnerable to political attack. If one wanted a central figure about whom to ar-

---

[1] In the discussion of McCarthy that follows, I am especially indebted to the historical analyses of Griffith 1970; Fried 1976; O'Brien 1980; Reeves 1982; and Oshinsky 1983.

range those of his rhetorical attacks that made McCarthy seem so formidable, Truman's Secretary of State between 1949 and 1953, Dean Acheson, would do as well as anyone else. The son of the Episcopal Bishop of Connecticut and the product of a Groton, Yale, and Harvard Law School education, Acheson was brilliant and arrogant, with the clothes and manners of a British aristocrat. In truth he was far removed from radicalism: he had resigned from the Treasury Department in the early Roosevelt years in protest against what he regarded as its excessive financial experimentation, and until his death he remained intensely anticommunist. But it was his critics' juxtaposition of two of his remarks in early 1950 that made Acheson such an easy target.

On January 25, a federal judge sentenced Alger Hiss, a former State Department official, to prison for perjury, for denying that he had passed government documents to an admitted Soviet agent. Upon hearing the news, Acheson, probably as much out of friendship as anything else, remarked, "I will not turn my back on Alger Hiss." Two weeks before, however, in a major speech on January 12, Acheson had outlined American strategy in Asia. Predicting that China and Russia would eventually come into conflict over Soviet expansionism, he argued that the United States had no strategic interests on the Asian mainland. Instead, he maintained, the United States should hold to a "defensive perimeter" along the offshore islands stretching from the Aleutians to Japan and the Philippines. Later, in the wake of the Sino-Soviet confrontation and the American debacle in Vietnam, Acheson's remarks might seem prescient; at the time, he was blamed for the North Korean incursion into South Korea which followed his speech by five months.

McCarthy simply linked Acheson's support for Hiss to his "defensive" strategy in Asia, and put them in the worst possible light. Certainly the senator left no doubt in the minds of his audiences that he had only deep contempt for the Secretary of State: "I have studied Acheson's public utterances sidewise, slantwise, hindwise, and frontwise; I have watched the demeanor of this glib, supercilious, and guilty man on the witness stand; I have reflected upon his career, and I come to only one conclusion: his primary loyalty in international affairs seems to run to the British Labor government, his secondary allegiance to the Kremlin, with none left for the country of his birth."[2]

Acheson, however, turned out to be merely a piece in a much larger puzzle that, McCarthy announced, he had solved. "At war's end," he would recall, "we were physically the strongest nation on earth and, at least potentially, the most powerful intellectually and morally," but now, less than five years later, "we find ourselves in a position of impotency." McCarthy may have exaggerated the decline of American power, but at least he addressed a real prob-

---

[2] Joseph R. McCarthy, speech in the Senate, June 14, 1951, reprinted as *America's Retreat from Victory: The Story of George Catlett Marshall* (New York: Devin-Adair, 1951), p. 132.

lem. Then, in a breathtaking leap of logic, he offered his own explanation for the decline:

> How can we account for our present situation unless we believe that men high in this Government are concerting to deliver us to disaster? This must be the product of a great conspiracy, a conspiracy on a scale so immense as to dwarf any previous such venture in the history of man. . . .
>
> What is the objective of the conspiracy? I think it is clear from what has occurred and is now occurring: to diminish the United States in world affairs, to weaken us militarily, to confuse our spirit with talk of surrender in the Far East and to impair our will to resist evil. To what end? To the end that we shall be contained and frustrated and finally fall victim to Soviet intrigue from within and Russian military might from without.[3]

McCarthy was not sure who, besides Acheson, "constitutes the higher circles of this conspiracy," but on its general social composition he was quite clear: "It has not been the less fortunate or members of minority groups who have been selling this nation out, but rather those who have had all the benefits that the wealthiest nation on earth has had to offer—the finest homes, the finest college education, and the finest jobs in Government we can give. This is glaringly true in the State Department. There the bright young men who are born with silver spoons in their mouths are the ones who have been worst."[4] Perhaps McCarthy was thinking specifically of Hiss, the product of Baltimore gentility, Johns Hopkins, and Harvard Law School, a man who had clerked for Supreme Court Justice Oliver Wendell Holmes and served on the legal staff of the Agricultural Adjustment Administration before going on to the State Department. In any case, the line led back to Acheson; and in drawing it McCarthy not only explicitly linked Communist expansion to Democratic foreign policies but attributed both to men of a certain social background: eastern, upper- or upper-middle class, and Ivy League–educated.

If this was the heart of McCarthy's rhetoric, then what lay behind its appeal, not only to millions of ordinary Americans but to those politicians, businessmen, and journalists who defended his actions and urged him on? Seeing this appeal, historians and social scientists at the time wanted to know what made "McCarthyism" possible. The first and simplest answer came to them when they located the senator's career, and the support he received, against the backdrop of world events. In this view, McCarthyism was a logical (if not necessarily justifiable) response to the decline in America's fortunes in the

---

[3] McCarthy, speech at Wheeling, West Virginia, February 9, 1950, as inserted into Senate debate, February 20, 1950, and reprinted in *Major Speeches and Debates of Senator Joe McCarthy Delivered in the United States Senate, 1950–1951. Unabridged Reprint from the Congressional Record* (Washington, D.C.: n.p., n.d.), p. 8; McCarthy, speech of June 14, 1951, pp. 171–72.

[4] McCarthy, speech of June 14, 1951, p. 168; speech of February 9, 1950, p. 9.

years after World War II, and especially in 1949, "the year of shocks": the Communist victory in China, the Soviet atomic bomb, and the conclusion of the Hiss case.[5] Attractive though it was (and it is impossible to understand McCarthy without *some* attention to those events), this argument is insufficient: among its other weaknesses is its total lack of comparative perspective. The British, too, were forced between 1945 and 1950 to confront Soviet espionage at home and Communist expansion abroad; and nothing in the American experience compared with either the economic devastation wrought by wartime bombing or the loss of the Empire. Yet Britain produced no McCarthy.

Thus, on second look, perhaps it was not world events alone but a peculiarly American reaction to them that produced McCarthyism. Was it not perhaps the result of an unwillingness on the part of Americans to adjust their fantasies about a malleable world to the harsh realities of great-power conflict and revolutionary change? Did it not reflect what the visiting British scholar D. W. Brogan, in a famous article, called "the illusion of American omnipotence . . . the illusion that any situation which distresses or endangers the United States can only exist because some Americans have been fools or knaves" (Brogan 1952, 21)? Brogan's argument would play a major role in subsequent interpretations of McCarthyism; yet, while possessing more explanatory power than the first simplistic analysis, it too was insufficient. For one thing, not all Americans supported McCarthy; even at the peak of his popularity, almost a third of those interviewed were critical of his conduct. Were there then certain tensions within American society that predisposed certain groups toward a pro-McCarthy stance; and if so, what were they?

Of the several different attempts to discover specific sources of McCarthy's support made during the period of his greatest influence, two seemed especially promising.[6] One came from Samuel Lubell's path-breaking interpretation of the breakdown of the New Deal coalition, *The Future of American Politics*, which appeared in 1952. Differing from those who had seen American "isolationism" as the result of emotional distance from the affairs of Europe, Lubell argued that, on the contrary, "isolationism" sprang from the most intense emotional involvement. Specifically, he argued that the core of modern isolationism consisted of ethnic groups such as the German- and Irish-Americans opposed to the dominant foreign policies that had placed the United States alongside Great Britain in the two world wars. Insofar as these ethnic isolationist voters were able to link Roosevelt's diplomacy in World War II with the subsequent expansion of Communist power, now in the changed climate of the Cold War they sought vindication (Lubell 1952, 129–57). Though Lubell did not single out McCarthy as a leader of this "politics of revenge"

[5] The phrase is Eric F. Goldman's, in *The Crucial Decade* (New York: Knopf, 1956), p. 112.

[6] For a survey of the various analyses of McCarthyism during its ascendancy, see Wrong 1954.

until his second book on the subject in 1956 (Lubell 1956, 52–74), in *The Future of American Politics* he already made it clear that Republicans as a whole sought such a role: "Even a cursory study of the dominant Republican propaganda line in Congress reveals a consistent effort to develop an emotional chain reaction between the frustrations of the Cold War and the German wars. No opportunity is let slip to harp on the alleged mistakes of Teheran, Yalta, and Potsdam or to blame the rise of world Bolshevism on the way the last war was conducted" (Lubell 1952, 152).

One interpretation of McCarthy's appeal, therefore, was as a leader of this ethnic isolationist coalition. Though in retrospect it is hard to see McCarthy as the leader of anything, his concentration of foreign policy issues, on the linkage between what he saw as "appeasement" abroad and "subversion" at home, made the Lubell interpretation attractive to those analyzing the sources of McCarthy's popularity.[7] Still, the isolationist hypothesis did not explain much of his prominent support. McCarthy himself may, in the words of one of his recent biographers, have "had no ideology or program of any significance" beyond a simplistic belief in an all-encompassing "Communist conspiracy" (Reeves 1982, 675), but many of his most avid supporters possessed developed ideologies—and reactionary ones at that. McCarthy had in the ranks of his supporters, for example, the true economic extremists such as those who advocated the repeal of the income tax amendment to the Constitution.

Far more significant, however, was the warm response he received in segments of the respectable business community; some businessmen, it appeared, had no difficulty reinterpreting McCarthy's attacks on the State Department as attacks on the New Deal. As one business reporter observed, "Among businessmen who approve of McCarthy's war on subversion there is a satisfaction, subconscious perhaps but very strong, over his incidental licks at *all* the longhairs, eggheads, professors, and bright young men of the 1930s and 1940s. Only one was named Alger Hiss. But the others, in NLRB, REA, TVA, etc., etc., were scarcely less dangerous—or so it seemed to some businessmen."[8]

No group of businessmen was more supportive of McCarthy than the nominally Democratic oil men of Texas, millionaires such as H. L. Hunt, Hugh Roy Cullen, and (until the senator's fight with the Army) Clint Murchison (see Murphy 1954b). To journalists and social scientists observing this phenomenon, it was obvious that these individuals—who took up a collection to buy McCarthy a Cadillac for a wedding present and repeatedly asked him to speak at fund-raising dinners in Texas—were simply the most flamboyant representatives of a larger group of "self-made men" emerging out of the prosperity

[7] For an early effort to use Lubell's argument to explain McCarthy's sources of support, see Glazer 1953.

[8] Murphy 1954a, p. 180; for evidence suggesting general business opposition to McCarthy, see Oshinsky 1983, pp. 302–5.

brought about by World War II. As the Marxists editing the *Monthly Review* were among the first to argue, it was also possible that these men supported McCarthy in part out of their "feelings of jealousy and even hatred for the aristocracy" which refused to accept them socially and their consequent "longing to humiliate" their adversaries (Huberman and Sweezy 1954).

By the mid-1950s there were thus at least two different, possibly complementary ways of locating and analyzing support for Senator McCarthy, either by focusing on certain ethnic groups or by focusing on the newly rich. McCarthy's attacks on Acheson and the State Department may, as Lubell emphasized, have brought him support from those ethnic groups that disliked his targets' pro-British sympathies; or, as the *Monthly Review* editors suggested, some of the newly rich may have rallied behind him because they resented Acheson and the others as representatives of "old wealth" and eastern snobbery.

Today scholars might argue that such efforts to uncover the base of McCarthy's support had already lost their relevance because McCarthy had been simply a soldier in the Republican campaign to regain power, and after 1952 that campaign had been won. That was not, however, the view of the senator's contemporaries. Not only in the year before his censure but *for some time afterward*, many observers (including the president himself) saw McCarthy and his allies as actively challenging Eisenhower for control of the Republican party.[9] By 1955, then, many observers believed that while McCarthy had been damaged he was not necessarily eliminated as a major political figure; and various analysts had already suggested that he had drawn his support disproportionately from ethnic isolationists and/or from the newly rich. That year the first major scholarly attempt to analyze McCarthyism appeared: a collection of essays entitled *The New American Right*.

[9] On this point compare Murphy 1954a, p. 146, and Huberman and Sweezy 1954, pp. 426–29, with Reeves 1982, pp. 474–75, 494–98, 555–56, and Stephen E. Ambrose, *Eisenhower: The President* (New York: Simon and Schuster, 1984), pp. 219–22.

One _____

The New American Right: "McCarthyism" as "Status Politics"

IN 1955 A COLLECTION of essays appeared that attempted to locate support for McCarthy in a broad social and historical perspective. Entitled *The New American Right*, it was primarily designed as a series of answers to the question of who supported McCarthy and why. The seven contributors to the book were men on the threshold of major intellectual influence: Daniel Bell, former managing editor of the *New Leader* and at the time labor editor of *Fortune* and lecturer in sociology at Columbia; Richard Hofstadter, professor of history at Columbia and author of *Social Darwinism in American Thought* and *The American Political Tradition*; David Riesman, at the time professor of social science at the University of Chicago and author of *The Lonely Crowd, Faces in the Crowd*, and *Individualism Reconsidered*; Nathan Glazer, associate editor of *Commentary* and collaborator with Riesman on *The Lonely Crowd*; Peter Viereck, professor of history at Mount Holyoke and author of *Metapolitics: From the Romantics to Hitler* as well as of books of poetry, one of which had received the Pulitzer Prize in 1949; Talcott Parsons, professor of sociology at Harvard, one of the leaders of the dominant functionalist school in American sociology and author of *The Social System, Towards a General Theory of Action*, and other books; and Seymour Martin Lipset, at the time associate professor of sociology at Columbia and author of *Agrarian Socialism*.

The above descriptions, adapted from the biographical notes at the beginning of the book, would seem to suffice for the authors' backgrounds. But we cannot begin to account for either the influence the book exerted, or the controversies that continue to surround it, without pursuing the matter further. For a book that would become one of the seminal works in the study of contemporary American social movements and political behavior, it is remarkable that none of the authors was a political scientist, that at the time only two of the contributors (Parsons and Lipset) had Ph.D.s in sociology, and that only one of the historians (Hofstadter) specialized in American history. Bell and Glazer would receive their doctorates within a few years and eventually end up as professors at Harvard, but at the time the world in which they moved was not primarily that of the university and scholarly monographs, but that of the political/literary weeklies and quarterlies. And Riesman had never been trained as a sociologist at all: he was a graduate of Harvard Law School who had served as clerk for Supreme Court Justice Louis D. Brandeis and as deputy assistant district attorney in New York.

What these men had in common and what gives the book its power is a certain style, far more characteristic of freewheeling intellectuals than of specialized scholars, which Irving Howe has acutely described as "the style of brilliance," a style characteristic of those he was among the first to call "the New York intellectuals." Unlike the traditional article in the social sciences which moves steadily, if not always gracefully, from a statement of the problem and review of the existing literature, through the author's hypothesis, a description of methodology, and an explication of the data, to a conclusion, the articles in *The New American Right* moved in a somewhat different direction. They bear far more resemblance to the kind of essay Howe saw as the product of the "New York intellectuals": one "wide-ranging in reference, melding notions about literature and politics, sometimes announcing itself as a study of a writer or literary group but usually taut with a pressure to 'go beyond' its subject, toward some encompassing moral or social observation." Reading Viereck's identification of the McCarthy supporters with the French Jacobins of 1793, or even Hofstadter's relocation of the concept of "the authoritarian personality" in immigrant families struggling for social acceptance, one is reminded of Howe's discussion of the implications of this "style of brilliance": "a certain view of the intellectual life: freelance dash, peacock strut, daring hypothesis, knockabout synthesis. . . . the idea of the intellectual as anti-specialist, or as a writer whose speciality was the lack of a speciality: the writer as dilettante-connoisseur, *Luftmensch* of the mind, roamer among theories."[1]

It is true that the focus of Howe's essay was primarily on the literary critics associated with *Partisan Review* and *Commentary*, but it is also true that the essays in *The New American Right* all appeared in whole or in part elsewhere, and that the journals in which they appeared—not only the *Partisan Review* and *Commentary*, but the *American Scholar, Encounter*, and the *Yale Review*—were more closely associated with literary criticism and with the New York intellectual community in general than with specialized scholarship in the social sciences. (Significantly, only one essay—Lipset's—had appeared in a "scholarly" publication, the *British Journal of Sociology*.) It is not too much to say that the strengths and weaknesses of this "style of brilliance" associated with New York intellectuals determined the reception of the essays in the book: their conceptual confusion and lack of empirical data in support of their conclusions made them easy targets for scholars of more conventional academic backgrounds; but at the same time, their sweep, their brilliance,

---

[1] Irving Howe, "The New York Intellectuals," in *The Decline of the New* (New York: Harcourt, Brace, and Jovanovich, 1970), pp. 240–42.

what Howe would call their "dazzle," continued to attract and inspire other scholars eager for new angles of perception.

As Bell noted in his introductory essay, although the other essays in *The New American Right* had already appeared in print, "they showed a remarkable convergence in point of view." "To an extent, then," he wrote, "this is a 'thesis' book" (Bell 1955, 16, 4). Can we extract such a "thesis" from the book? If so, it might run as follows:

1. Senator McCarthy's career represented more than simply one demagogue's exploitation of fears about domestic Communists against a background of high tension with the Soviet Union and open warfare with China. Such an explanation, according to Bell, "fails to account for the extensive damage to the democratic fabric that McCarthy and others were able to cause on the Communist issue—and for the reckless methods disproportionate to the problem." Nor did calling him a demagogue explain his unusual choice of targets: "intellectuals, Harvard Anglophiles, internationalists, the Army." Implicit in all the essays was the idea that "McCarthy has to be understood in relation to the people behind him and the changed political temper which these groups have brought. He was the catalyst not the explosive force. These forces still remain" (Bell 1955, 14, 17).

2. The forces behind McCarthy were not truly conservative, as their increasingly open hostility to the Eisenhower administration made clear. They constituted a movement of the "radical right": radical both because "it desires to make far-reaching changes in American institutions, and because it seeks to eliminate from American political life those persons and institutions which threaten either its values, or its economic interests."[2] As individuals, members of this "radical right" expressed

---

[2] Lipset 1955, p. 166. The origins of the concept of the "radical right" are not altogether clear; but it appears to have been first used in the aftermath of the ascendency of Fascism in Italy and National Socialism in Germany. As early as 1933, for example, one self-styled disciple of Mussolini and Hitler, the writer Seward Collins, began publishing his *American Review* to provide a forum for those he called "revolutionary conservatives" or "radicals of the right," by which he meant all those attacking society from a traditionalist basis (Arthur M. Schlesinger, Jr., *The Politics of Upheaval* [Boston: Houghton Mifflin, 1960], p. 70). Thus the simplest meaning of the "radical right," and the meaning Lipset gave it in the passage quoted, was that of extreme reaction.

As the events of the 1930s heightened the interest of American scholars in European fascism, however, another meaning was added to the concept. What sociologists like Talcott Parsons saw as "radical" in German Nazism and Italian Fascism was the mass base of their "right-wing" (i.e., anticommunist) movements: "large masses of the 'common people' have become imbued with a highly emotional, indeed often fanatical, zeal for a cause." Because they are "mass movements, which are in an important sense revolutionary movements," he concluded, they had little in common with "ordinary conservatism" (Parsons, "Some Sociological Aspects of the Fascist Movements," *Social Forces* 21 [December 1942]: 138). Thus, following Parsons, Lipset might have argued that McCarthy was leading a comparable mass movement and thereby creating a "new" American right. But in his 1955 essay he was considerably more cautious, at the most *implying* the existence of such a movement (notably at pp. 209–10); and he subsequently stated flatly that "McCarthyism was not a political movement" (Lipset and Raab 1970, p. 220). In any

"a profound if largely unconscious hatred of our society and its ways"; as such they conformed to the psychologists' model of the "pseudo-conservative," the person who "in the name of upholding traditional American values and institutions and defending them against those more or less fictitious dangers, consciously or unconsciously aims at their abolition."[3]

3. The most suggestive way to account for the social origins of these "pseudo-conservatives" was through adaptation of the idea of "status politics."[4] Thus the famous dichotomy of the book: between "interest politics, the clash of material aims and needs among various groups and blocs" (Hofstadter) or "class politics, . . . the discord between . . . those who favor redistribution of income, and those favoring the preservation of the status quo" (Lipset), on the one hand, and "status politics" on the other. "Status politics" represented "the clash of various projective rationalizations arising from status aspirations and other personal motives" (Hofstadter) and took the form of "political movements whose appeal is to the not uncommon resentments of individuals or groups who desire to maintain or improve their social status" (Lipset).[5]

4. "In the United States, political movements or parties which stress the need for economic reform have usually gained strength during times of unemployment and depression." On the other hand, "status politics" becomes salient "in periods of prosperity . . . when many individuals are able to improve their economic position," and characterizes both those rising groups "frustrated in their desire to be accepted socially" and those groups believing their superior status to be in jeopardy (Lipset 1955, 168).

5. Since "the basic aspirations that underlie status discontent are only partially conscious . . . it is difficult to give them a programmatic expression. . . . Therefore,

---

case, far from definitively stating what the "radical right" really was, Lipset left to successive scholars the task of defining it for themselves. Few who did so bothered to specify whether they thought the movement or organization they were analyzing was "radical" because of the far-reaching changes it advocated, or because of its ability to develop a mass following, or both.

[3] T. W. Adorno, as quoted in Hofstadter 1955a, p. 35; for the original, see Adorno et al. 1950, p. 676.

[4] It has been generally assumed by scholars that Hofstadter, Lipset, and the other contributors in *The New American Right* fleshed out their concept of "status politics" from the few fragmentary suggestions made years before by Max Weber (see, for example, Brandmeyer and Denisoff 1969, p. 5). Insofar as that is so, it should be noted that Weber, while distinguishing between "classes" (those similarly situated in their control over goods and skills) and "status groups" (those similarly situated in the social estimation of their honor or prestige), did not directly link "status" concerns to social mobility (as do Lipset, Hofstadter, and the others) and did not imply (as Hofstadter especially does) that "status" concerns are somehow irrational.

For Weber's original references, see his *Economy and Society*, ed. Guenter Roth and Claus Wittich (New York: Bedminister Press, 1968), pp. 302–7, 926–40. For a general critique of the way American sociologists translated and conceptualized Weber's *stand* as "status groups," see Morton G. Wenger, "The Transmutation of Weber's *Stand* in American Sociology and Its Social Roots," *Current Perspectives in Social Theory* 1 (1980): 357–78.

[5] Hofstadter 1955a, p. 43; Lipset 1955, p. 168.

it is the tendency of status politics to be expressed more in vindictiveness, in sour memories, in the search for scapegoats, than in realistic proposals for positive action'' (Hofstadter 1955a, 44). Notable American examples of past political movements based on "status politics" were the Know-Nothings of the 1850s and the Ku Klux Klan of the 1920s.

6. Not surprisingly, then, the 1950s, like the 1850s and the 1920s a period of prosperity, saw the reappearance of "status politics" in the form of support for McCarthy, or what might better be called "McCarthyism." "The intense status concerns of present-day politics are shared by two types of persons who arrive at them, in a sense, from opposite directions. The first are found among some types of old-family, Anglo-Saxon Protestants, and the second are found among many types of immigrant families, most notably among the Germans and Irish, who are very frequently Catholic. The Anglo-Saxons are most disposed toward pseudo-conservatism when they are losing caste, the immigrants when they are gaining" (Hofstadter 1955a, 44; see also Lipset 1955, 195).

7. "Both the displaced old-American type and the new ethnic elements that are so desperately eager for reassurance of their fundamental Americanism can conveniently converge upon liberals, critics, and nonconformists of various sorts, as well as Communists and suspected Communists," who thus take the place of racial and religious minorities scapegoated by earlier movements expressing "status politics" (Hofstadter 1955a, 50–51).

Stated in this manner the arguments in *The New American Right* have a certain attractive simplicity about them, which would account for the hold of "status politics" on subsequent scholars. Many of them further concluded that the book's "thesis" was that McCarthyism was the expression of the "status" anxieties of specific groups in the population. That may be true of the book as a whole; it is not necessarily true of the individual contributions. Upon closer examination it would be fair to say that among them only Hofstadter had such a coherent theory. For him at least the sources of McCarthyism lay in the anxieties experienced by the upwardly mobile descendants of recent immigrants, intensely pressured individuals who turned their suppressed rage against imagined "subversive" adversaries, including the leaders of their own government.

The application of "status politics" by the other contributors to *The New American Right* was far less focused. As the above quotations suggest, Lipset also utilized "status politics" as an explanation of McCarthyism; but he added so many other factors in his discussion—including the economic situation of small businessmen, the ethnic origins of isolationists, and the traditional anticommunism of the Catholic hierarchy—that the reader is left wondering whether he believed "status politics" was the central explanation of McCarthyism or merely one of a number of explanations. Parsons saw McCarthyism as representing not only the "status politics" of the upwardly mobile but also a more diffuse resentment on the part of the business community at having its leadership challenged by politicians and intellectuals.[6] In the hands of Riesman and Glazer, "status politics" was broadened to include all those who, whatever their ethnic background, had undergone "a fast race from humble origins, or a transplantation to the city, or a move from the factory class to the white-collar class" (Riesman and Glazer 1955, 67). With Viereck, on the other hand, the concept was narrowed to its crudest component, making it almost synonymous with envy: "McCarthyism is the revenge of the noses that for twenty years of fancy parties were pressed against the window pane" (Viereck 1955, 93). Not surprisingly, therefore, the chief *conceptual* problem of the book (even aside from the *empirical* problems raised by the authors' interpretation of historical and behavioral evidence) soon became clear: "status politics" was so variously interpreted that it became a catch-all, leading one exasperated reviewer to protest that this was "multidimensionality run riot. *When we know so much we know scarcely anything.*"[7]

Only two published studies tested the hypotheses of *The New American Right* through empirical investigations of patterns of support for McCarthy, and both provided only a partial confirmation of those hypotheses. The first was a study of attitudes toward McCarthy in Bennington, Vermont, undertaken by Martin Trow at the height of the senator's visibility in 1954 (Trow 1958). From his sample he concluded that, insofar as "authoritarian" attitudes revealed themselves in opposition to freedom of speech for radical leftists (a connection assumed by Hofstadter and some of the others), the correlation between such attitudes and support for McCarthy was largely a statistical artifact—the supporters of McCarthy were simply less educated than his opponents. Once education was held constant, however, his opponents were as "authoritarian" as his supporters: they simply preferred to ferret out "subversives" within an established framework and tended to identify with McCarthy's targets, "responsible" officials in the federal bureaucracy.[8]

Trow's major argument was that McCarthy supporters in Bennington were disproportionately self-employed, and that a McCarthyite response on the part of small businessmen came from their allegiance to what he called "nine-

[6] Parsons 1955, pp. 122–24, 135–36. Indeed, as a number of commentators have pointed out, Parsons' major theme—that "McCarthyism is best understood as a symptom of the strains attendant on a deep-seated process of change in our society" (ibid., p. 138), a process most clearly revealed in the Federal Government's assumption of large-scale domestic responsibilities after 1933 and international responsibilities after 1939—stands largely outside the "status politics" emphasis of the other essays. For that reason, it will not be considered further here.

[7] Bernard Rosenberg, "The 'New American Right,' " *Dissent* 3 (Winter 1956): 47.

[8] Unlike Trow, Lipset found in his later review of survey data that "authoritarianism" was of some utility in explaining McCarthy's support: that those who scored high (i.e., gave "authoritarian" responses) on the measures originally developed by the authors of *The Authoritarian Personality* were at all educational levels (but especially at the college-educated level) more likely to be pro-McCarthy (Lipset 1963a, pp. 341–43; Lipset and Raab 1970, pp. 234–35).

teenth-century liberal'' ideology, hostile both to unions and big business. That ideology in turn reflected their fear of trends toward economic concentration, bureaucratization, specialization, and their lack of organization in meeting those threats.[9] By implication, however, the threat posed by the trends Trow described were to the income and power of these small businessmen far more than to their prestige, and so status considerations were not applicable. On two key points, then, Trow challenged the specific arguments in *The New American Right*: he found that ''authoritarianism'' did not automatically translate into support for McCarthy, and that class considerations, not status considerations, determined the support of small businessmen. On two other points, however, the general tone of *The New American Right* was confirmed: McCarthy's support was due in part to his image as defender of ''the little guy,'' and in the case of the most prominent group of supporters in Bennington, the small businessmen, his support was clearly reactionary, opposing the dominant trends in social and economic organization.

The second case study, of attitudes in Winchester, Massachusetts, based on interviews conducted in 1958 by Robert Sokol, was not initially intended to uncover support for McCarthy per se. Rather, it was designed as a general test of the ''status politics'' model or, more precisely, the effects of what other sociologists were now calling ''status inconsistency''—the strains, for example, experienced by a self-made millionaire with only a grade-school education. Able to discover no single pattern of response to any of his questions (including those dealing with McCarthy) on the part of those with ''inconsistent statuses,'' he reorganized his material around sources of support for McCarthy and had it published a number of years later (Sokol 1968). What he found was that the most effective predictor of support for McCarthy among all social strata was ''power orientation,'' far more than either of the ''status politics'' models.

Using an index devised earlier by another sociologist (''Which groups do you think have influence?'' ''Which would you like to have influence?''), Sokol found that those respondents desiring the most change in the national power structure were the most likely to support McCarthy. In other words, McCarthy supporters thought that certain sectors of the power hierarchy—those they saw as ''liberals who are soft on Communism, as misguided intellectuals, as misdirected members of the American aristocracy, etc.''—should be downgraded and that McCarthy was the man to do it (Sokol 1968, 449). In this way, the McCarthyites described by Sokol resemble those described by Trow, who found that McCarthy was seen as attacking those ''authorities and

---

[9] In his subsequent examination of survey data, Lipset was unable to confirm Trow's hypothesis that ''nineteenth-century liberal'' ideology correlated with support for McCarthy (Lipset 1963a, pp. 340–41).

institutions—the 'big shots,' the 'stuffed shirts,' and 'bureaucrats'—against whom many of his supporters felt anger and resentment" (Trow 1958, 273).

In the long run the major contribution of the authors of *The New American Right* was their introduction of the concept of "status politics" into the discourse of social scientists and historians. However loosely applied at the onset, the concept would over time be refined and lose both its overtones of irrationality and its links to social mobility; by the 1980s it (or its synonyms) would be used to embrace a wide variety of political conflicts not clearly reducible to class or economic interest. Oddly enough, however, the question of the relevance of the concept to the specific phenomenon of "McCarthyism"—emphasized by *The New American Right* authors—was soon forgotten. The case studies of Trow and Sokol (the only ones published) pointed in a different direction. What one remembers from their research is that, at least in Bennington, Vermont, and Winchester, Massachusetts, support for McCarthy represented a protest against the perceived holders of power. One might even conclude from this (though Trow and Sokol did not) that McCarthy was in some sense a "populist" hero, an argument that had already appeared in *The New American Right* and elsewhere. As we shall now see, whether McCarthy was a "populist"—either in the general sense, or in the specific sense that he appealed to the same constituencies as the Populists of the 1890s—would become far more productive of scholarly debate than "status politics" had ever been.

Two

Hofstadter, Viereck, Shils: "McCarthyism" and the "Populist Heritage"

BY FAR THE GREATEST scholarly controversy occasioned by *The New American Right* arose from the attempt of some of its authors (and those influenced by them) to link McCarthy to what might broadly be called "the populist heritage." Though they did not always carefully distinguish between the phrase's two meanings, those making this argument seem to have been referring *both* to the specific ideology, style, and constituency of the Populist movement in the late nineteenth century as well as to the much more diffuse tradition of "direct democracy" and legislative supremacy and of a distrust of political, economic, and intellectual elites that went back to the American Revolution.

"The populist heritage," in the first and more specific sense, was bequeathed by the "movement of political and economic protest that rose out of the Farmers' Alliances about 1890, made its vehicle the Populist or People's party in several southern and western states in the nineties, reached a high point nationally in the Bryan-McKinley campaign of 1896, and then went rapidly downhill."[1] In this sense, it should be noted, only two of the contributors to *The New American Right* decided to explore the possible connections between the Populists of the 1890s and the McCarthyites of the 1950s: Hofstadter and Viereck. Hofstadter, however, developed his argument not in his contribution to that book but in *The Age of Reform* which appeared the same year. In it he indicated that his "interest has been drawn to that side of Populism and Progressivism . . . which seems very strongly to foreshadow some aspects of the cranky pseudo-conservatism of our time. Somewhere along the way a large part of the Populist-Progressive tradition has turned sour, become illiberal and ill-tempered." This "deconversion from reform to reaction," Hofstadter argued, "did not require the introduction of anything wholly new into the political sensibilities of the American public but only a development of certain tendencies that had existed all along, particularly in the Middle West and the South" (Hofstadter 1955b, 19–20).

Of all the beliefs and attitudes that the Populists and McCarthyites might have shared, none struck Hofstadter and Viereck as more important than their common isolationism. Along with many of their contemporaries, the two his-

---

[1] Walter T. K. Nugent, *The Tolerant Populists: Kansas Populism and Nativism* (Chicago: University of Chicago Press, 1963), p. 4.

torians saw those who had opposed American entry into World War II as McCarthy's prime constituency and their support for his linkage of American diplomacy and Communist expansion as part of their collective search for vindication. And like most other historians at the time, Hofstadter and Viereck located the center of isolationism in the Midwest, which was also the ancestral home of Populism. Though he was never particularly precise about how this happened, Hofstadter seemed to suggest that the very insularity of the region's environment, which brought with it a tendency to perceive complex sequences of events in terms of simple conspiracies and an oscillation between pacifism and bellicose nationalism, had shaped a midwestern isolationist tradition that connected the Populists at one end with the McCarthyites at the other.[2]

Viereck, on the other hand, drew more specifically on Lubell's argument, that "the hard core of isolationism in the United States has been ethnic and emotional, not geographical." If so it followed that the constituency the Republicans were trying to reach was primarily the German-Americans (but also the Irish-Americans) who had opposed American intervention in 1917; and that had interesting implications. For two decades after 1917, Lubell had maintained, a coalition between progressives concerned with economic issues and these isolationist voters had developed in a number of places, notably in Wisconsin under the leadership of the LaFollette family, and in North Dakota, home of the Non-Partisan League, Senator Gerald Nye, and Representative William Lemke. With the approach of war in the late 1930s, however, this coalition split, with the progressives moving behind Roosevelt's foreign policy and the isolationists becoming Republicans (Lubell 1952, 132). In 1936, McCarthy himself had run the Roosevelt Ball in Waupaca, Wisconsin, on be-

[2] Hofstadter 1955b, especially pp. 70–73, 85–87. Hofstadter's view that the Midwest had been historically isolationist for other than ethnic reasons owed much to Ray Allen Billington, "The Origins of Middle Western Isolationism," *Political Science Quarterly* 50 (March 1945): 44–64. For an early dissent, expressing the view that the strength of isolationism in the Midwest had been exaggerated, see William G. Carleton, "Isolationism and the Middle West," *Mississippi Valley Historical Review* 33 (December 1946): 377–90; and for a subsequent quantitative effort to break apart the identification of "the Midwest" and "isolationism" through an analysis of congressional roll calls, see Ralph H. Smuckler, "The Region of Isolationism," *American Political Science Review* 47 (June 1953): 386–401. Although he cited Billington (Hofstadter 1955b, pp. 85–86n), Hofstadter seems to have overlooked Carleton's and Smuckler's critiques.

In the 1960s the political scientist Leroy N. Rieselbach challenged both Lubell's interpretation and (by implication) that of Billington: "The Basis of Isolationist Behavior," *Public Opinion Quarterly* 24 (Winter 1960): 645–57; and Rieselbach, *The Roots of Isolationism: Congressional Voting and Presidential Leadership in Foreign Policy* (Indianapolis: Bobbs-Merrill, 1966), pp. 106–26. Analyzing roll-call votes in the years after World War II, he found that Republican identification was a far stronger predictor of "isolationist" voting behavior in the House of Representatives than either the degree of rurality or the percentage of German-American and Irish-American constituents in the district. In the Midwest, moreover, "isolationism"—as measured by votes on foreign-aid and foreign-trade legislation—was wholly a Republican phenomenon, midwestern Democrats being among the least "isolationist" members of the House.

half of local Democrats; by 1944 (and most probably between 1939 and 1941) he had become a Republican.[3]

In his essay in *The New American Right* and at length in several chapters of his subsequent book, *The Unadjusted Man*, Viereck elaborated on Lubell's argument with great enthusiasm. "The missing link," he announced, "between the often noble idealistic Populist-Progressives (like that truly noble idealist, LaFollette) . . . and something so different, so bigoted as McCarthyism" was Father Coughlin. "All liberals know that Coughlin ended by defending Hitler in World War II and preaching the vilest anti-Semitism. They sometimes forget that Coughlin began his career by preaching social reforms to the left of the New Deal." Similarly Senator Nye (who had campaigned for LaFollette in his presidential race of 1924 and, after his own election to the Senate in 1926, had become something of a liberal hero) was part of the movement from reform to reaction. On closer examination, Viereck argued, men like Coughlin and Nye had "never changed at all: throughout they remained passionately Anglophobe, Germanophile, isolationist, and anti-eastern-seaboard" (Viereck 1955, 94). Behind Coughlin and Nye stood LaFollette; his role as the precursor of McCarthy was clear. "LaFollette denounced the New York internationalists as capitalistic, reactionary, and pro-British; McCarthy denounced them just as strongly but as Red, liberal, and pro-British" (Viereck 1956, 188).

With Viereck we also come to the second meaning of "the populist heritage." There was, he claimed, an American populist tradition running "from Tom Paine through Jackson, Weaver, Bryan, LaFollette" that "rested squarely on faith in the natural goodness of man, the infinite perfectibility of the masses." This faith had clear and pernicious consequences: "If you deem evil external, if consequently you deem utopia just around the corner, then you cannot blame human nature or the masses for the failure of utopia to arrive. Instead, you are then tempted to blame some small aristocratic or plutocratic 'conspiracy.' The next step, while still believing in democracy and 'the people' is to set up an undemocratic terrorist dictatorship in order to purge these 'unnatural' aristocrats or plutocrats (British snobs, Jewish bankers), sole obstacles to the mass utopia inherent in 'nature' " (Viereck 1956, 208–9). In America—fortunately—these purges were bloodless, but even so had produced McCarthy and the collateral committees on "un-American activities." The tradition running from Paine through McCarthy, Viereck asserted, favored "direct democracy, . . . government by direct, unfiltered mass pressure, government by referendum, mass petition, and popular recall of judges" as opposed to the "indirect democracy" he himself favored, which "likewise

[3] The most detailed account of McCarthy's career as a Democrat can be found in O'Brien 1980, pp. 19–25. O'Brien surmised that McCarthy changed parties as a way of advancing his political career: the predominantly Irish Catholic Democrats were clearly the third party in Wisconsin, typically running well behind both the Republicans and the LaFollette Progressives.

fulfills the will of the people but by first filtering it through the people's representatives, through the parliamentary, judicial, and constitutional sieve'' (Viereck 1956, 131).

The most important work stressing the relationship of "the populist heritage" to McCarthy appeared the same year as Viereck's *The Unadjusted Man*—Edward A. Shils's *The Torment of Secrecy*. Shils's specific concern was the background and consequences of the Federal Government's loyalty-security program, begun under President Truman and expanded under Eisenhower, in part as a response to the demands of McCarthy and his allies to root out "subversives" in government positions. Paralleling many of the themes in *The New American Right* but in some ways going beyond them, Shils developed his own analysis of the current obsession with "secrecy" and "subversion" at three different levels. At one level there was the "democratic" emphasis on publicity, not only as a curb on the official abuse of power but as a good in itself, an emphasis that both threatened individual privacy and made the society as a whole identify secrecy with the unfolding of malevolent conspiracies rather than with the necessities of statecraft.

At a second level, America's adjustment to the threatening world situation after 1945 was made more painful by various aspects of what Shils called "the traditional American outlook": anxiety over the assimilation of ethnic groups, which produced tendencies toward both hyperpatriotism and xenophobia; a resulting isolationism and suspicion of Europe; a deep strain of fundamentalism and rejection of "modern" culture; and finally what he, defining it much the same way as Viereck, termed "populism." At a third level, the social origins of American legislators, self-made men from provincial backgrounds, made them the natural adversaries of cosmopolitan intellectuals, and the insecurity of elected office made them exceptionally vulnerable to the pressure of small groups of constituents convinced that the country was caught in a web of subversion. By giving intellectuals positions of administrative responsibility (and later by bringing theoretical scientists into government), the Roosevelt administration triggered the reaction that followed.

The consequences of these interrelated developments were that countless lives and reputations had been ruined, that the integrity of science was seriously threatened, and that the autonomy of the private sphere, the basis of a liberal society, was put in jeopardy. Such a disaster had been brought about— on this Shils was clear—by "the populist heritage." He held "populism" in the relatively narrow sense responsible, because so many of the villains in the drama were midwesterners, and Shils did not hesitate to call McCarthy the heir of LaFollette.[4] He also concluded, however, that at every level—the con-

---

[4] For other references to the "midwestern" component, with its supposedly isolationist overtones, its Anglophobia, and its fears of conspiracy, see Shils 1956, pp. 31, 83–84, 88, 91, 101, 103.

cern with publicity, the emphasis on legislative supremacy and impatience with procedural restraints, and the insecurity of the representatives of "the people"—"the populist heritage," in the second broader sense, was directly or indirectly responsible for the hysteria of the 1950s.

McCarthyism and the "Populist Heritage": Early Reexaminations

As the 1960s progressed, however, a number of scholars subjected the analyses of Viereck and Shils to a barrage of criticism, arguing that those propounding them misunderstood both the historical past and the McCarthyite present. First, historians attacked the idea of continuity between the Populists and/or LaFollette supporters and the McCarthyites. The most important criticism in this regard was by C. Vann Woodward in his article, "The Populist Heritage and the Intellectual," a criticism made all the more persuasive by its gentleness of tone (Woodward 1960). Woodward had already written not only the standard history of the late nineteenth-century South but also the major biography of that most illiberal of Populists, Tom Watson, whose career slid downward to the lowest depths of racial and religious bigotry. So it was with special authority that he wrote in defense of the Populists against their recent critics. The first of the critics' problems, Woodward argued, was that they located Populism in the wrong region; whether measured by the strength of the true Populists (the supporters of the People's party) or the successes of opportunistic Democrats who adopted some of their positions on issues, the South not the Midwest was the center of Populism. The Populist stronghold of the South was also, in the judgment of all observers, the least isolationist and the most interventionist part of the country on the eve of World War II; and after the war, as measured by survey data, the most anti-McCarthy section of the country.[5] Thus the Populist-isolationist-McCarthyite continuum did not exist.

[5] Woodward was surely right on southern opposition to McCarthy (see Glazer and Lipset 1955, p. 160), but when he tried to trace foreign policy attitudes he fell into the same logical trap as those he criticized, confusing partisan and regional variables. To make his argument stick, he would have to show that southern interventionism on the eve of World War II (and ultimately southern opposition to the "isolationist" McCarthy) sprang from some kind of deep-rooted regional commitment to "internationalism" and not simply from Democratic partisanship. The only empirical study that might cast light on this question is George Grassmuck's analysis of congressional roll calls on foreign policy measures between 1921 and 1941; but he found that southern congressmen supported military appropriations, to take but one example, only after the Democrats regained the White House in 1933. It was eastern congressmen (regardless of party), not southerners, who were the consistent "internationalists" over the entire period. George L. Grassmuck, *Sectional Biases in Congress on Foreign Policy* (Baltimore: Johns Hopkins University Press, 1951), pp. 41–42, 151–52.

Even more, in order to confirm his argument, Woodward would have to show that Populist

Woodward concluded by noting that if the Populists had their share of conspiratorial theorists and economic simplifiers, so too did their opponents, "the
spokesman of the educated, successful and privileged classes of the urban
East" (Woodward 1960, 68). It was thus possible that other, non-Populist
sources might have contributed to the tensions of the recent past.

At about the same time another historian, David Shannon, addressed himself specifically to the question, "Was McCarthy a political heir of La-
Follette?" and concluded that he was not (Shannon 1961). The close ties
LaFollette established with the University of Wisconsin during his years as
governor refuted any attempt to make him a simple-minded defender of "the
people" against the experts, Shannon argued, and he could find little if any
evidence of conspiratorial imagery in his writings. Further, LaFollette and Mc-
Carthy had very different political positions and styles—LaFollette consistently attacking what he saw as corporate privilege in long, heavily documented speeches; McCarthy slinging unsubstantiated charges at those he
deemed subversive. Finally, McCarthy enjoyed the support of the regular Republican organization in Wisconsin and the support of businessmen throughout the country, while LaFollette had neither; and at the electoral level, the
voting patterns for the two were almost diametrically opposed except for a few
German-American counties that came late to the LaFollette coalition.

In their criticism of *The New American Right* the political scientists concentrated on the immediate context of McCarthy's career. In "Towards an Explanation of McCarthyism," Nelson Polsby took aim at a good part of the edifice
of the book. In the first place, he argued, most of its contributors had speculated about the sources of support for McCarthy without bothering to check
their predictions against the available survey data: had they done so they
would have found that they ignored some groups that the data indicated were
pro-McCarthy while emphasizing others whose pro-McCarthy sentiment was
not so clearly supported by the data. Working through the data (especially that
supplied by the Gallup organization), Polsby found that while Lubell's "eth-
nic-isolationist" hypothesis was simply insufficient to explain McCarthy's
support at the national level, the data partly confirmed the "status-politics"
hypothesis. However, even that confirmation was "unimpressive when set
against comparable figures describing the two populations [McCarthy supporters and opponents] by their political affiliations" (Polsby 1960, 262). Put
another way, McCarthy was disproportionately supported by Republicans and

---

constituencies within the South (however measured) were "internationalist." Though given the
time span it is hard to see how empirical work could be done on this question, it may turn out, as
Charles O. Lerche, Jr. has implied, that the Populist constituencies (i.e., lower-class whites) remained isolationist and that "internationalist" sentiment in the South was largely the creation of
their antagonists, the upper-class planters and their business allies. Lerche, *The Uncertain South:
Its Changing Patterns of Politics in Foreign Policy* (Chicago: Quadrangle Books, 1964), pp. 52–56.

disproportionately opposed by Democrats, both in his home state of Wisconsin and in the country as a whole.

Of greater importance was Polsby's attack on the assumption that underlay the essays in *The New American Right* as well as a good deal of unrelated journalistic commentary: "that McCarthy was in fact uniquely powerful at the grass roots; that he had a vast following which crosscut party lines and loyalties, which he could call upon to defeat his enemies." Examining the returns from the 1952 senatorial race in Connecticut, in which Democratic incumbent William Benton was supposedly defeated because of his outspoken opposition to McCarthy and McCarthy's "retaliation," Polsby found no such effect. Benton's vote rose and fell with the shifting fortunes of his party; he was done in by Eisenhower's landslide, not by McCarthy's vendetta. McCarthy's power, then, did not need to be explained by constructing a grass-roots movement: it was only necessary to note that he "was, at first, the weapon of a desperate Republican Party," a member of the Senate with "protection of immunity from libel suits . . . and the powers to hold hearings and issue subpoenas" and an extraordinarily effective "political entrepreneur who exploited the mass media" and intimidated two successive presidents. Far from leading a mass movement, McCarthy was "more deeply a political phenomenon" in the narrow sense, more a product of partisan and institutional roles than politicians, journalists, or social scientists had realized.[6]

The first attempt to provide a historical explanation for the rise of McCarthyism that took into account the partisan and institutional factors Polsby had mentioned was by another political scientist, Earl Latham. Toward the end of his massively detailed *The Communist Controversy in Washington: From the New Deal to McCarthy*, Latham began his explanation by noting that it was Congress, of all the branches of the Federal Government, that showed the greatest concern about domestic Communism. Unable for a variety of reasons to direct its investigations of those believed subversive toward a specific legislative end, Congress resorted to what he called "prescriptive publicity": "a form of public notice intended to instruct, and deter. . . . The sanction of prescriptive publicity was social disapproval and whatever personal consequence (like loss of employment) that might follow public exposure" (Latham 1966, 381–82).

At this point in his argument Latham might seem to be echoing Shils, except that Latham did not regard Congress as representative of "the people" in the way that Shils did. Skewed as Congress was at the time "in favor of white, Protestant, nonurban, better-off elements," it was not necessary to evoke

---

[6] Polsby 1960, pp. 264, 263, 271. Polsby was not the first political scientist to note that, however frosty McCarthy's relationships with individual senators were, his career was greatly enhanced by the prerogatives he enjoyed as a senator and by the rules and customs of that body: see Aaron Wildavsky, "Exploring the Content of McCarthyism," *Australian Outlook* 9 (June 1955): 88–104.

"populism" to explain its responses. Rather, the impetus behind the congressional inquisitions of the late 1940s and early 1950s came from frustrated conservatives in both parties who had assumed control of Congress after 1939 but were not in control of the White House. Truman's surprise victory in 1948 blocked "a decisive change in office for which the impulse had been building for a decade" and particularly infuriated the Republicans who in their entire history had never been out of power for so long. With his fixation on the single issue of subversion, McCarthy was the perfect front for all those Republicans whose real dissatisfaction lay with the social and economic changes wrought by twenty years of Democratic rule. McCarthy did indeed represent a segment of midwestern opinion, Latham concluded, but it was not the heritage of Populism that he embodied. Instead, it was a "fundamentalist conservatism embodied in the Republican Party," which "believes with profound faith in free enterprise, reacts to symbols which threaten it, is suspicious of welfarism and other social reform, tends to stand pat, and is moved only by exigency" (Latham 1966, 376, 394, 423).

For Latham, then, the origins of McCarthyism could be found institutionally among congressmen and politically among Republicans. Plausible though this argument would come to seem, especially to other political scientists, it did not go unchallenged. Only a few years after his book appeared, some younger historians relocated "the origins of McCarthyism" in the White House. For them it was President Truman not Senator McCarthy who played the major role in shaping "the emotional anticommunism of the post-war years" since it was his administration that conceived of "radicalism, whether at home or abroad, as potentially subversive" and of "Communism as monolithic, alien, and unpopular"; and it was his administration that failed to set critical standards for defining "subversion," "disloyalty," or "aggression."[7] Few would disagree that Truman bears some of the responsibility for what followed: even sympathetic historians concur that his Federal Employee Loyalty Program as implemented after 1947 denied civil servants vital procedural safeguards, expanded the bureaucratic empire of J. Edgar Hoover, and helped legitimate in the public mind the nebulous concept of "subversion."[8] The

[7] Though this interpretation has been utilized by a number of historians, its major initial statements remain two works by Athan Theoharis: "The Rhetoric of Politics: Foreign Policy, Internal Security, and Domestic Politics in the Truman Era, 1945–1950," in Barton J. Bernstein, ed., *Politics and Policies of the Truman Administration* (Chicago: Quadrangle, 1970), pp. 196–241; and Theoharis, *Seeds of Repression: Harry S. Truman and the Origins of McCarthyism* (Chicago: Quadrangle, 1971). Also influential in formulating this interpretation was Richard Freeland's close analysis, *The Truman Doctrine and the Origins of McCarthyism: Foreign Policy, Domestic Politics, and Internal Security, 1946–1948* (New York: Knopf, 1972). (The quotations are from Theoharis, "The Rhetoric of Politics," p. 201.)

[8] See for example Alan D. Harper, *The Politics of Loyalty: The White House and the Communist Issue, 1946–1952* (Westport, Conn.: Greenwood, 1969), pp. 34–53, 232–46; Alonzo L. Hamby, *Beyond the New Deal: Harry S. Truman and American Liberalism* (New York: Columbia

larger implication that Truman somehow planted "the seeds of repression" that McCarthy would later harvest nonetheless remains dubious.

Even before Harry S. Truman uneasily assumed the presidency in 1945, Roosevelt's opponents were already busy identifying the New Deal with Communism. As early as the midterm election of 1938, for example, the newly formed House Committee on Un-American Activities intervened in several key races to charge Roosevelt supporters with Communist affiliations. In the presidential election of 1944, Republican spokesmen repeatedly alluded to connections between the Communist party, the CIO's Political Action Committee, and Roosevelt's reelection campaign. By 1946 an emphasis on the Communist issue (however defined) had become a major element in the Republican offensive; and, insofar as that offensive resulted in a landslide at the polls, it was hard for frightened Democrats not to conclude that the issue was politically potent.[9] In such circumstances (as one of the revisionists' critics has pointed out), "to assume that McCarthyism grew naturally out of Truman's actions . . . ignores the problem of what might have happened had Truman done nothing."[10] Considering all the evidence, it is difficult to avoid the conclusion that however much the Truman administration's rhetoric or its policies aggravated the situation, the sources of "McCarthyism" lay elsewhere. Latham's argument that it was in the first instance an expression of the frustration of congressional Republicans remains compelling.

Latham's interpretation of course should also be seen as part of the growing scholarly criticism during the 1960s of the earlier efforts on the part of Hofstadter, and especially on the part of Viereck and Shils, to link McCarthy and his supporters to the agrarian insurgents of the late nineteenth and early twentieth centuries. Those critiques moved along two lines. Historians like Woodward and Shannon argued that in style, ideology, and constituency, McCarthy

University Press, 1973), pp. 388–90, 467–68; and Francis H. Thompson, *The Frustration of Politics: Truman, Congress, and the Loyalty Issue, 1945–1953* (Rutherford, N.J.: Fairleigh Dickinson University Press, 1979), pp. 44–64.

[9] On the "Communist" issue in 1938, see Richard Polenberg, "Franklin Roosevelt and Civil Liberties: The Case of the Dies Committee," *Historian* 30 (February 1968): 165–67, and Sidney Fine, *Frank Murphy: The New Deal Years* (Chicago: University of Chicago Press, 1979), pp. 502–12; on 1944, Leon Friedman, "Election of 1944," in Arthur M. Schlesinger, Jr., ed., *History of American Presidential Elections, 1789–1968*, 4 vols. (New York: Chelsea House, 1971), 4:3033–35; on 1946, James Boylan, *The New Deal Coalition and the Election of 1946* (New York: Garland, 1981), pp. 135–39.

[10] Alonzo L. Hamby, "The Clash of Perspectives and the Need for a New Synthesis," in Richard S. Kirkendall, ed., *The Truman Period as a Research Field: A Reappraisal, 1972* (Columbia, Mo.: University of Missouri Press, 1974), p. 134. One recent regional study strongly suggests that, given the mobilization of conservative elites, Truman's options were narrower than Theoharis is willing to admit. In his *The Red Scare in the Midwest, 1945–1955: A State and Local Study* (Ann Arbor: UMI Research Press, 1982), James Truett Selcraig makes clear that at the state and local level the hunt for "subversives" *preceded* Truman's actions at the federal level and were initiated by conservative Republicans, *not* by Democrats (ibid., pp. xi–xii, 42–44, 96–100).

bore little resemblance either to the original Populists or to midwestern progressives such as LaFollette. Political scientists such as Polsby and Latham,
on the other hand, concentrated on the immediate context in which McCarthy
gained influence; and they concluded that his career was furthered not by the
diffuse anxieties of the mass public but by the specific needs of Republican
partisans. None of these men attempted a fully developed historical explanation of the relationship between Populism and LaFollette progressivism and
McCarthy's support; that would come in 1967 with the publication of Michael
Rogin's *The Intellectuals and McCarthy: The Radical Specter*. The possibility
of Rogin's gaining acceptance for his onslaught on the ''Populist'' image of
McCarthy was, however, undoubtedly enhanced by the work of these other
scholars.

In narrowing the issue to the connections between the historic Populists (and
comparable midwestern progressives) and McCarthy, these historians and political scientists made it more amenable to scholarly analysis, but in doing so
ignored the larger thrust of the arguments of Viereck and Shils. For ever since
the 1940s one of the implications of the concept of the ''radical right'' had
been that right-wing mass movements were possible; not only had they developed in Europe between the world wars but under different auspices could do
so in postwar America. Insofar as the American right wing could build a mass
movement it could thus lay claim to being ''populist'' in the broad sense and
reinforce that claim (as Viereck and Shils had stressed) by attacking political,
economic, and intellectual elites. And so, even after scholars had denied Joseph McCarthy his Populist credentials and shown that ''McCarthyism,''
whatever else it was, was not a mass movement, the larger questions remained
unanswered. The possibility of right-wing populism in America would continue to confront analysts of the American right wing.

Three

Rogin: "McCarthyism" as Midwestern Conservatism

WITHOUT QUESTION the most influential critic of the interpretations of Mc-Carthyism offered in *The New American Right*, *The Unadjusted Man*, and *The Torment of Secrecy* was the political scientist Michael Paul Rogin. His 1967 book *The Intellectuals and McCarthy: The Radical Specter* was, as the full title would suggest, not so much about McCarthy as about those interpretations, which saw the junior senator from Wisconsin not as the enemy of radicalism but as in some sense its fulfillment, "challenging, like earlier radicals, the established institutions of American society." "In this new view," Rogin continued, "McCarthyism was a movement of the radical right that grew out of movements of the radical left," specifically out of what he called the "agrarian radical" tradition of the Upper Middle West or what we have called "the populist heritage."[1]

The empirical core of *The Intellectuals and McCarthy* consisted of three chapters on voting behavior in states with a strong "agrarian radical" tradition—Wisconsin, North Dakota, and South Dakota—and one chapter analyzing survey data on the sources of popular support for McCarthy at the height of his career. To investigate the claim that McCarthy and his senatorial allies had "agrarian radical" roots, Rogin analyzed "county voting returns in [each of these states in] approximately seventy elections between 1886 and 1960," the point being less "to compare the vote for a single county for two candidates widely separated over time" than to relate certain factors—"urbanization, acreage in wheat, percentage of foreign stock, and so on—to the political behavior of the counties."[2]

Rogin's analysis of the political behavior of Wisconsin and North Dakota led him to conclude that in both states progressivism before World War I was economically based, a movement of poor farmers. This progressive movement was sustained in the interwar years in North Dakota by the Non-Partisan League and in Wisconsin by the LaFollettes' Progressive party of the 1930s (which also included the working class of a more urbanized state). Though

---

[1] Rogin 1967, p. 3. That is not quite what those Rogin was attacking had argued. Viereck, for example, had noted that McCarthyism had *both* a "reactionary root" in conservative Republicanism (which he felt was so obvious as not to warrant further discussion) *and* a less obvious "left-wing root" in "the western radicalism of the former Populist and Progressive Parties," which he wanted to explore further (Viereck 1956, p. 165).

[2] Rogin 1967, pp. 60–61. For our purposes here, Rogin's analysis of Wisconsin and North Dakota are more important than his analysis of South Dakota, so that state will not be considered.

coming out of the Republican party, these progressive coalitions foreshadowed, both in their broad economic appeal and in their specific constituency,
the contemporary Democratic party in both states. The continuity of this progressive tradition was the basic pattern; where Viereck and the others went
wrong was in focusing on minor factors such as the aberrant behavior of one
ethnic group, the Germans (or in North Dakota, the Russian-Germans). In
both states, the Germans had opposed progressivism before World War I and
came to support progressive candidates largely because they found their isolationism attractive after 1917. When a second conflict with Germany approached in the late 1930s, they again expressed their isolationism, but not in
the progressive coalition. Instead, quite possibly because of their relative prosperity, they moved into the right wing of the Republican party.[3]

In Wisconsin, McCarthy's appeal was primarily to the traditional conservative Republican counties (now including the Germans) that had opposed
progressivism. He also appealed to Catholic farmers of eastern European ancestry, traditional Democrats; but this, Rogin argued, could be explained simply by the exceptional appeal to them of his "anticommunist" posture. Significantly, he was opposed by Catholic workers who found his economic
conservatism more salient than his anticommunism. In the case of North Dakota, contrary to Hofstadter's implication, there was no general "deconversion from reform to reaction": politicians influenced by the old Non-Partisan
League did not uniformly follow Nye and become right-wing Republicans.
Some moved into the Democratic party; and the most notable product of the
NPL, Senator William Langer, although remaining a Republican and an isolationist, was a progressive to the end (Rogin 1967, 84–86, 91–96, 133–34).

Although Lubell had also emphasized the tenuousness of the interwar coalition of progressives and ethnic isolationists, Rogin faulted him for overem-
phasizing the degree to which isolationism had been the product of ethnic
resentment in the first place. On the contrary, he pointed out; the isolationism
of both the LaFollettes and the Non-Partisan League preceded American intervention in 1917 and came from quite different, nonethnic roots, the old
"agrarian radical" suspicion of international finance and European imperial-
ism.[4] This was a tradition quite different from the right-wing kind of isolationism, onto which the resentments of the Germans could so easily be grafted,
which feared the contagion of European "radicalism." Thus, as the last major
representative of this left-wing isolationist tradition, Langer could consistently

[3] Rogin 1967, pp. 69–70, 116–17; 120–23, 75–78; 65, 84, 133–34; 72, 120; 75, 84, 128–29.

[4] Rogin 1967, pp. 79–80, 133–34. The most detailed exposition of the "agrarian radical"
origins of this kind of isolationism is the work of Robert F. Wilkins: see especially his "Middle
West Isolationism: A Re-Examination," *North Dakota Quarterly* 25 (Summer 1957): 69–76; Wilkins, "The Non-Ethnic Roots of North Dakota Isolationism," *Nebraska History* 44 (September
1963): 205–22; and Wilkins, "The Non-Partisan League and Upper Midwest Isolationism," *Agricultural History* 29 (April 1965): 102–9.

oppose American participation in the United Nations, military alliances, and foreign aid, but publicly rejoice in the British Labour party victory of 1945, argue that the United States should have befriended Mao Zedong and champion nationalist movements in Africa and Asia.[5]

In his analysis of public support for McCarthy, Rogin challenged the arguments that McCarthy was another manifestation of "populism" standing outside political elites; that he "mobilized feelings of uneasiness over a sophisticated, cosmopolitan, urban, industrial society"; and that he "split apart existing political coalitions." In the specific historical context in which McCarthy had risen to power, Rogin maintained, he represented not a radical break, but continuity with the immediate past. Within the Republican party he was the agent of midwestern conservatives battling for control of the party against eastern moderates and liberals who had come to accept the main outlines of Democratic foreign and domestic policies. For these midwestern conservatives, secure in their small-town bailiwicks but fearful of larger bureaucratic and cosmopolitan trends, "Communism" had long symbolized everything alien and hence undesirable. It was their good fortune that the Communist victory in China followed by open warfare in Korea gave them a nationally receptive audience, an audience they began to lose, however, once the war ended. Second, Rogin argued, it was unwise to accept McCarthy's "populist" rhetoric at face value. The midwestern conservatives he represented had consistently opposed all forms of "agrarian radicalism" (including the original Populists); and McCarthy's attacks on elites represented simply a tactic in their fight against moderates within the party and in their bid to regain national power.[6]

Third—and here Rogin turned to survey data—McCarthy did not lead a mass movement in the sense of enjoying unstructured political support cutting across existing alignments. Rather, his following was disproportionately Republican, and support for him was highly correlated with conservative stands on economic and foreign policy questions. Lipset, however, had emphasized that survey data also revealed that McCarthy was supported by groups that did not come from this expected constituency, and Rogin felt that he had to take into account Lipset's evidence: "When the influence of party is eliminated and often even when it is not, the lower socioeconomic groups, the more poorly educated, and the Catholics tended to support McCarthy, the big business and professional classes, the better educated, and the Protestants to oppose him." The simplest reason for this kind of support for McCarthy, Rogin suggested, was that the senator received public approbation insofar as he was linked to "the fight against Communism," and his lower-class supporters

---

[5] Glenn H. Smith, *Langer of North Dakota: A Study in Isolationism, 1940–1959* (New York: Garland, 1979), pp. 115, 199–200, 221–23; and in general, Robert Griffith, "Old Progressives and the Cold War," *Journal of American History* 66 (September 1979): 334–47.

[6] Rogin 1967, pp. 217–18, 221, 223, 222, 228, 230–31.

were either unaware of or unconcerned with his violations of civil liberties. "The evidence did not suggest that the Communist issue preoccupied the lower classes," nor did it suggest that this lower-class support for McCarthy had translated into voting behavior.[7]

If McCarthy's career could not be explained by mass mobilization, what then accounted for it? The answer, Rogin believed, lay in "the actions and inactions of various elites." At the core of McCarthy's elite support were "conservative politicians and publicists, businessmen, and retired military leaders discontented with the New Deal, with bureaucracy, and with military policy," the "occasional ex-agrarian radical" or "former Marxist intellectuals" occupying essentially peripheral roles. But even outside of the right-wing core, McCarthy enjoyed a good deal more elite support than was commonly recognized. "Eastern and moderate Republicans and their allies desired political power and were also genuinely concerned about the Communist question," so some of them supported McCarthy's early charges. And "large numbers of newspapers, particularly outside the major metropolitan centers, actively supported him." Finally, even those elites who were "uninvolved in or opposed to the politics motivating his ardent supporters"—senators unwilling to interfere with a fellow senator's prerogatives, unsympathetic newspapers looking for sensational stories, for example—contributed to McCarthy's success by their passivity. When, however, these elites "turned against him, and when with the end of the Korean War his political issue became less salient, McCarthy was reduced to insignificance."[8]

The two decades that have elapsed since the completion of Rogin's book has given other scholars ample time to review and challenge his empirical findings. Relatively little criticism has emerged, however; most of what there is has been devoted to his historical analysis of voting behavior. The increasingly sophisticated quantitative techniques of what has come to be known as "the new political history" have thrown into glaring relief the inadequacy of Rogin's approach. One methodological weakness is peculiarly his own. In spite of his promise at the beginning of *The Intellectuals and McCarthy* that he was going to emphasize the relationship between voting behavior in the counties under study and economic and demographic variables over time, what in fact he did was present data simply correlating *elections*. His implication was that this uncovered the voting patterns of specific ethnic and economic *groups*; but, as two historians tartly commented, "how this approach generates insights about voting continuities for discrete groups within the state remains a mystery to all but the author."[9]

---

[7] Rogin 1967, pp. 233–34, 239 (referring to Lipset 1963, pp. 330–38), 243–45.

[8] Rogin 1967, pp. 248, 250, 252–53, 255–57, 217.

[9] Robert R. Dykstra and David R. Reynolds, "In Search of Wisconsin Progressivism, 1904–1952: A Test of the Rogin Scenario," in Joel H. Silbey, Allan G. Bogue, and William H. Flani-

Rogin's other problem came from his reliance on ecological correlation, looking at election returns to see where the votes came from and matching the voting patterns with their physical and social environment. The problem was that such methods led inevitably to the "ecological fallacy," in which conclusions about individual behavior patterns (in his case voting behavior) were drawn from ecological data (such as the proportion of Catholics, the average value of a farm, etc.).[10] To give a blatant example of the ecological fallacy, taken from material we have yet to consider, suppose in a given southern state the percentage of the vote received by a militant segregationist candidate in each county correlated positively with the percentage of blacks in each county. Even those with the most rudimentary political knowledge would challenge any conclusion that therefore blacks supported the segregationist and would strongly suspect that the votes came from the neighboring whites. Substitute "percentage received by LaFollette" and "percentage of poor farmers"— which is more or less what Rogin does—and the fallacy is the same, even though it might not be so obvious.

Insofar as the ecological fallacy weakens Rogin's work, he stands in very good company; indeed, until the 1970s it was the inevitable accompaniment of practically all historical analyses of voting behavior. At first historians thought they could overcome the problem by analyzing smaller units such as townships, villages, and city wards, ostensibly more homogeneous than the counties Rogin chose. One, who utilized election returns from these units to analyze Wisconsin voting behavior over the first half of the century, corroborated Rogin's overall analysis.[11] Two others, using many of the same methods, were unable to do so, finding, for example, no clear "progressive" continuity (i.e., from LaFollette to the contemporary Democrats) on the part of Scandinavian farmers.[12]

By that point, however, another group of historians was rejecting the methods of ecological correlation entirely and proposing in their place more complex techniques of ecological regression, in which a number of possible variables were measured against each other.[13] One of the leaders of this group

gan, eds., *The History of American Electoral Behavior* (Princeton: Princeton University Press, 1978), p. 301.

[10] Charles M. Dollar and Richard J. Jensen, *Historian's Guide to Statistics: Quantitative Analysis and Historical Research* (New York: Holt, Rinehart, and Winston, 1971), pp. 97–99, 276.

[11] David L. Brye, *Wisconsin Voting Patterns in the Twentieth Century, 1900 to 1950* (New York: Garland, 1979).

[12] Dykstra and Reynolds, "In Search of Wisconsin Progressivism," pp. 299–326.

[13] The historians most active in making this argument have been J. Morgan Kousser and Allan J. Lichtman: see particularly Kousser, "Ecological Regression and the Analysis of Past Politics," *Journal of Interdisciplinary History* 4 (Autumn 1973): 237–62; Lichtman, "Correlation, Regression and the Ecological Fallacy: A Critique," *JIH* 4 (Winter 1974): 417–33; Laura Irwin Langbein and Lichtman, *Ecological Inference* (Beverly Hills: Sage, 1978); Kousser and Lichtman, "New

took a dim view of the attempts to retrace Rogin's steps in Wisconsin, both on methodological grounds and on those of common sense. "It has always seemed to me," he wrote,

> that the best answer to Michael Paul Rogin's question—whether the Populists and Progressives voted for Joe McCarthy or not—was the simplest: they couldn't have, since most of them were long dead. To expect to find continuity in the voting records of the same rural precincts over a forty-eight year period (1904–52) which contained two world wars and a depression and which witnessed large changes in the state's economic and social structures, a major shift in governmental agricultural policy, and no doubt a great deal of population growth and many shifts in population, is simply nonsensical.[14]

Be that as it may, one can say with reasonable assurance that Rogin accomplished what he set out to do, at least in the minds of most historians and social scientists: to show that there was no significant continuity between La-Follette's progressive coalition and the supporters of McCarthy. Probably the ultimate vindication of this part of Rogin's argument came from Lipset himself, who in 1970 admitted that "McCarthy did not receive the electoral support of the LaFollette stream" in Wisconsin or elsewhere. Rather, "his support in the Midwest came from the economic conservatives" (Lipset and Raab, 1970, 232–33).

While some scholars have criticized Rogin's historical analysis of voting behavior, others have raised questions about the explanatory power of his interpretation of the public support for McCarthy. Two historians of the Truman era, for example, who agree on little else, find his interpretation insufficient.[15] Specifically, their doubts revolve around Rogin's statement that "McCarthy's popular following" apparently came from two distinct sources: the "activists and elites" within "the traditional right wing of the midwestern Republican Party" supplemented by a broader group of "citizens mobilized because of Communism and the Korean War," who, Rogin himself admitted, tended to come from "traditional Democratic ethnic and social groups" (Rogin 1967, 247, 236).

Part of the problem here, and what made much of the initial scholarly debate on "support for McCarthy" so nebulous, is defining what exactly one means by "support." As Lipset noted in 1970, a "distinction must be made between

---

Political History: Some Statistical Questions Answered," *Social Science History* 3 (Summer 1983): 321–44.

[14] J. Morgan Kousser, "History − Theory = ?," *Reviews in American History* 7 (June 1979): 160.

[15] Hamby, "The Clash of Perspectives and the Need for a New Synthesis," in Richard S. Kirkendall, ed., *The Truman Period as a Research Field: A Reappraisal* (Columbia, Mo.: University of Missouri Press, 1974), pp. 134–35; and Barton J. Bernstein, "Commentary," in Kirkendall, ed., *The Truman Period as a Research Field*, pp. 186–87.

support for McCarthy and for McCarthyism''—the former as measured by "electoral endorsement," either directly in Wisconsin or indirectly in those contests in which McCarthy intervened; the latter as measured by survey data (Lipset and Raab 1970, 233). Fortunately, subsequent analyses of voting behavior have made it possible to find out who actually "supported" McCarthy. Probably the most important finding concerns Catholic voters, who Rogin (like many of those he criticized) had seen as especially susceptible to McCarthy's "anticommunist" appeal. The most recent analyses of voting behavior in Wisconsin during this period suggest, however, that McCarthy received less Catholic support in 1952 than even Rogin had assumed and that (to take the most dramatic case) the most anti-McCarthy ethnic group in the city of Milwaukee were the Polish-Americans![16] Similarly, recent studies underscore the limits of McCarthy's appeal to Catholics in contests outside Wisconsin, even though he directly intervened in Maryland in 1950 to defeat Millard Tydings and in Connecticut in 1952 to defeat William Benton. Both Tydings and Benton were indeed defeated, but scholars are still unable to locate any distinctive Catholic role in their defeat.[17] The evidence so far accumulated, then, would appear to strengthen Rogin's argument: while pro-McCarthy sentiments certainly did exist among the lower classes as measured by survey data, they were not a significant influence on their voting behavior.

Explaining Midwestern Support for McCarthy: Some Unresolved Issues

Successful as he has been in convincing most other scholars that McCarthy did not inherit the traditional "agrarian radical" constituency in the Middle West and that he did not "split apart existing political coalitions" by mobilizing hitherto Democratic lower-class voters, Rogin is less persuasive in showing where McCarthy's support *did* come from—though, strangely, on this point he has received almost no criticism at all. The thrust of his positive argument, it will be remembered, was that the core of "McCarthy's popular following" came from "the activists and elites" in "the traditional right wing of the midwestern Republican Party." This argument is highly plausible, but Rogin did not substantiate it: on this crucial point he relied not on survey data but on deductions from arguments he had already made. And so, in the absence of data clearly confirming the statement, we are left with some unanswered questions.

[16] Oshinsky 1976, pp. 148–49; Crosby 1978, pp. 96–98. An earlier study focused on the way Catholics who *publicly* took a position on McCarthy created the impression of "Catholic support of McCarthy" (Vincent P. DeSantis, "American Catholics and McCarthy," *Catholic Historical Review* 51 [April 1965]: 1–30).

[17] Fried 1976, pp. 138–39, 248–49; Crosby 1978, pp. 73–74, 102–3.

Take, for example, the first part of his argument, that "McCarthy's appeal had its greatest impact upon activists and elites, not upon the rank-and-file voters" (Rogin 1967, 247). How he reached that conclusion is difficult to determine. It is true enough that, as the classic study of contemporary public opinion on the subject concluded, the issue of Communist "subversion" did not preoccupy very many Americans: only 1 percent in a national sample stated that the issue of "Communists in the United States" was their chief concern.[18] It would seem to follow that those rallying to McCarthy's one-man crusade because of their concern about "subversion" were a very small minority. We also know, from a study conducted shortly after McCarthy's demise, that (at least as measured by those who served as delegates to the national convention) Republican activists were distinctly more conservative than Republican voters as a whole (McClosky 1960, esp. 422–23). Thus, Rogin could have merged the small minority concerned about "subversion" with the relatively conservative delegates to compose his picture of pro-McCarthy activists. Until we know more about the reasons *these* Republicans supported McCarthy and more about Republican rank-and-file attitudes on *this* question (were they as unconcerned about "subversion" as the population as a whole?), however, this conclusion must remain only speculative.

Like Latham (whose book appeared too late for him to use) Rogin also located these pro-McCarthy attitudes among Republicans in "the traditional right wing of the party" in the midwestern states. But is this linkage correct? Was McCarthy more popular among midwestern Republicans than among Republicans in other parts of the country? We simply do not know. And if so, why? In his analysis Latham had posited a durable "fundamentalist conservatism" in the Republican party going back to the Civil War era which had as its stronghold "the Middle and Rocky Mountain West" and which was dissatisfied "with the moderate conservatism of the eastern states" (Latham 1967, 423). But surely he was reading the present into the past: almost any informed observer between about 1900 and about 1940 would have located unyielding conservative Republicanism in the East, not in the "progressive" Middle West.[19]

In contrast to Latham and more consonant with the historical and demographic record, Rogin implied in his book that the Republican party in several midwestern states *became* conservative because its progressive base, the poorer farmers, moved away, leaving the more conservative Republicans in the small towns and cities in positions of dominance. Even if it could be con-

---

[18] Samuel A. Stouffer, *Communism, Conformity, and Civil Liberties: A Cross-Section of the Nation Speaks Its Mind* (Garden City, N.Y.: Doubleday, 1955), p. 59.

[19] This point is confirmed by two quantitative analyses of congressional voting: Howard W. Allen and Jerome Clubb, "Progressive Reform and the Political System," *Pacific Northwest Quarterly* 65 (July 1974): 134; and Barbara Sinclair, *Congressional Realignment, 1925–1978* (Austin: University of Texas Press, 1982), pp. 58–59, 63–64.

firmed, however, that hypothesis raises other questions: *why* were midwestern small-town Republicans so attracted to McCarthy? What recent events would have made them so angry? One possibility, Rogin suggested, was the New Deal, which "as social legislation and trade unions became prominent and the power of the national government increased . . . created a balance of forces more opposed to Midwest conservatism than this country had seen since the Civil War." Still, one wants to ask, did not this "new balance of forces" threaten conservatism elsewhere as well? Perhaps, as he seems at one point to imply, the more complex bureaucratized corporations of the East could more easily accept New Deal reforms and the rise of mass-production unionism than could the individualistic entrepreneurs of Ohio—or of Wisconsin (Rogin 1967, 222). Nonetheless "the Midwest" he was concerned about in his book was (with the obvious exception of Wisconsin) the states on the west side of the Mississippi,[20] and we are left unsure what exactly it was that led Republicans in the Plains states, still dominated by agricultural interests and far removed from the CIO, to support McCarthy so enthusiastically.

Further—to make the point for the final time—while McCarthy's voting record indicated that he shared economic positions with other conservative Republicans in Congress, he did not spend very much time criticizing either the social legislation or the unions supported by the New Deal. He built his public career on foreign policy issues, attributing Communist gains abroad to domestic "subversion" at home. That, and the amount of attention commentators gave to his "isolationist" support, suggest the need for a broader analysis of the way changes in foreign policy as well as domestic policy were perceived by conservative Republicans (in the Midwest and elsewhere) and why these individuals rallied behind McCarthy in response. Such an analysis has subsequently been offered by Michael Miles, whose *Odyssey of the American Right* builds upon Rogin's work while at the same time answering some questions Rogin had not addressed.

In spite of the massive changes wrought by the Roosevelt policies at home and abroad, Miles noted at the beginning of his book, "the late nineteenth- and early twentieth-century world of hegemonic Republicanism did not abruptly or entirely disappear in 1932. Stripped of many of its working-class and black allies, uncertain even of the allegiance of the metropolitan upper class and many farmers, classical Republicanism retained the loyalties of un-

---

[20] In spite of recurrent references to "the Midwest" in his book, it is not always clear what area of the country Rogin is talking about. In his initial formulation (Rogin 1967, pp. 4–5), he uses as indicators of "agrarian radicalism" the presidential vote cast for the Populist candidate in 1892 and for LaFollette in 1924, in which case the region of "agrarian radicalism" included the Rocky Mountain states and even extended to the Pacific Coast. And on the crucial censure vote in 1954, it may be significant that "midwestern" Republican senators were less pro-McCarthy (voting 10–6 against censure) than were "western" Republican senators (voting 10–2 against censure).

reconstructed Republicans in the provincial Midwest'' (Miles 1980, viii).
These men and women retained earlier partisan commitments to ''true liberalism'' (the nineteenth-century, laissez-faire variety) and to a nativist, anti-
radical ''Americanism''; both in their minds dictated uncompromising opposition to the policies of the New Deal and to the coalition Roosevelt had
amassed behind them.[21] The foreign policy attitudes of these conservative Republicans, like their other attitudes, represented their allegiance to tradition—
in this case, perhaps, that of William McKinley and the early Theodore Roosevelt. Insofar as their attitudes were ''isolationist,'' it was of the unilateralist,
nationalist variety. Unlike LaFollette and some of his progressive allies within
the party, these conservatives were not even close to being pacifist: they had
never criticized the informal American empire in the Caribbean, and some
favored an active American role in the Pacific.

Where these conservatives joined with progressive ''isolationists'' was of
course in their opposition to entering a second war in Europe, an opposition
(in their case) stemming from a long-standing fear of ''entangling alliances,''
from disillusionment with the results of World War I, and (after June 1941)
from a belief that a ''war against Hitler on the side of Stalin could only contribute to the expansion of Communism'' (Miles 1980, 59). This reluctance to
assist Western Europe hurt them politically on two important occasions. Gains
made by conservative Republican politicians in 1938 and again in 1946—
gains that led many of their supporters to see the possibility of repealing the
New Deal—were soon reversed by Presidents Roosevelt and Truman, who
adroitly exploited crises in Western Europe to regain control of the national
agenda and help assure their reelection.

The change in conservative Republican fortunes, according to Miles, came

[21] For another recent attempt to classify conservative Republicans and define their position, see
Reinhard 1983. He defines the ''Republican right wing,'' especially in the 1940s and 1950s, as
follows:

> They opposed a strong chief executive like FDR and a powerful federal government that over-
> regulated business and meddled in the affairs of state and local governments. They supported
> only limited government intervention in America's capitalistic economy. Federal budgets
> should be kept low (and in balance), along with federal taxes. In foreign affairs, right-wing
> Republicans generally favored a strong American defense that relied heavily on air and sea
> power, and a foreign policy that allowed the United States to ''go it alone'' in pursuit of its own
> national interest. Fierce anticommunism was also a hallmark of conservative Republicanism,
> and this influenced their foreign and domestic programs. Right-wing Republicans consistently
> argued that the Republican party had to offer a real choice to Democratic domestic liberalism
> and internationalism. (Reinhard 1983, vii)

In Reinhard's view it was this unyielding opposition to Roosevelt's policies at home and abroad
that set ''conservatives'' off from party ''moderates,'' who accepted the New Deal as a fact of
political life but showed no interest in extending it, and who although ''internationalists'' were
quick to criticize foreign policy ''blunders.'' Even more, ''conservatives'' differed from the small
number of Republican ''liberals,'' committed in principle to the welfare state and far more re-
strained in their criticism of Democratic foreign policy (Reinhard 1983, pp. 3, 8, 9).

with the Communist victory in China. For on China—unlike Europe—the entire Republican party stood united in opposition to Administration policy; and the concurrent revelations of Soviet espionage provided abundant opportunities for ambitious politicians to enlist in the war on "subversion." But, even more than that, Mao's victory—following as it did upon the 1948 defeat of the moderate, "internationalist" Dewey—appeared to vindicate the party's traditionalists. Individuals such as textile importer Alfred Kohlberg may have been the first to argue for a connection between the "loss of China" and "subversion" in the State Department, but it would be McCarthy who would dramatize the connection not only for the general public but for these party conservatives. McCarthy shrewdly appealed to their grievances, and soon his "speeches and charges were the standard ideological fare of the Republican right" (Miles 1980, 129).

The very framework in which Miles developed his argument—his linkage between economic conservatism, a certain kind of "isolationism," and "McCarthyism," his placing these in a partisan context—suggests the way Rogin's book marked a turning point in the scholarly debate (see Reeves 1976). Even a cursory glance at the literature on "McCarthyism" written since 1967 suggests that the arguments he attacked no longer find much of a sympathetic audience. In part, as we have seen, this is because "revisionist" scholars have attempted to shift the responsibility for "the emotional anticommunism of the postwar years" from McCarthy and his allies to the Truman administration; whether their arguments have convinced others or not, they have certainly changed the terms of the debate. Even those working within a more conventional framework have also largely abandoned the argument that McCarthy was somehow heir to the "agrarian radical" tradition of the Middle West. The best reply Lipset could make in 1970 was to raise the possibility that a vaguely defined "midwestern political tradition," which included "such tendencies as opposition to the effete eastern elite and attraction to the concept of direct democracy," somehow "affected the nature of McCarthyism" (Lipset and Raab 1970, 233).

Since the publication of his book, most scholars studying McCarthy's support in Wisconsin have followed Rogin's framework.[22] In a larger sense, whatever else may be said about voting patterns, Rogin seems to have made his major point: the "agrarian radicals" and the McCarthyites appealed to substantially different constituencies, represented at least two different kinds of isolationism, and thus showed only superficial continuity. However much lower-class support he ultimately attracted—less, it turns out, than Rogin had assumed—in the first instance McCarthy was the agent of midwestern conservative Republicans in their attempt to regain national power.

[22] See, for example, Oshinsky 1976, pp. 147–55; O'Brien 1980, pp. 143–46; Reeves 1982, pp. 453–57.

Four

Beyond Rogin: "McCarthyism" as the Revenge of the "Locals"

"THERE ARE FASHIONS in theories as there are in clothes or domestic architecture," one political scientist has remarked, and so interpretations of "populism" have swung between two extremes, populism as "a rising of the irrational and dangerous masses" and populism as "the grass-roots rediscovery of what democracy means" (Canovan 1981, 166, 51). There can be little doubt that in the two decades since the appearance of *The Intellectuals and McCarthy* the historical analysis of the Populists of the 1890s has moved in the latter direction. To a considerable extent this has been the result of generational replacement, as the places of older scholars, permanently traumatized by the horrors of the 1930s and 1940s, have been taken by younger men and women. To the latter, more hopeful generation it is the American civil rights movement of the early 1960s and not German National Socialism of the early 1930s that is the quintessential "mass movement," and it is Martin Luther King, Jr., not Adolf Hitler, who is the quintessential "charismatic leader."

Obviously this shift in scholarly paradigms, and in the attitudes that underlay them, not only assured the success of Rogin's book but further hampered any attempt to link Senator Joseph McCarthy to "the populist heritage." But it by no means eliminated such attempts, even on the part of those who might otherwise sympathize with Rogin's broader concerns. The persistence of those attempts was due in part to other changes in the political climate (surely the recurrent presidential campaigns of George Wallace had something to do with the survival of the concept of "right-wing populism"), but mainly to Rogin's failure to resolve some important conceptual issues. He spent most of his effort, it will be recalled, in showing the absence of any connection between McCarthy and the earlier agrarian insurgents in the Middle West, whether Populists or comparable groups of progressives. He therefore devoted relatively little attention to confronting the other meaning of "populism"—that developed by Viereck and Shils—"populism" with a small *p*, populism as advocacy of direct democracy and legislative supremacy, populism as the exploitation of popular impatience with procedural restraints.

What Rogin wanted to show in his book was that neither McCarthy nor his supporters were in any sense former "leftists" but instead represented traditional conservative elements in the Republican party. But even if he achieved that objective, there were still two possible readings of the relationship between McCarthy and "populism" in the broad sense. McCarthy might have had a "populist" appeal even though he was a conservative; such a conclusion would certainly suggest the future possibility of a "right-wing" populism even if the senator himself led no movement at all. Alternatively, it might be that real "populism" could only be "leftist" or "progressive" in orientation, in which case McCarthy's appeal could at most be labeled "pseudopopulist." Without specifically saying so, Rogin seemed to move toward the latter conclusion in his book; but he omitted so much in order to get there that he failed to make a conclusive case.

One can conceive of several ways in which conservatives could invoke the authority of "the people," the most obvious being the repression of dissident minorities. As the travail of abolitionists, religious sectarians, labor organizers, and (in our own time) Communists makes abundantly clear, when it comes to repression in America, a "populist" conservatism is not simply rhetoric but the real thing. Surprisingly, however, Rogin did not discuss such repression as a general phenomenon in his first book. What he did emphasize in *The Intellectuals and McCarthy* was the way in which "since the decline of the Federalists, American conservatives have used 'populist' rhetoric" against various elites to achieve their specific objectives. "In America this rhetoric is essential" for political victory but it "does not necessarily reflect a reality of popular enthusiasm and power; often it disguises the power resting in the hands of [other] local and national elites. 'Populism' is often an ideological formula used to gain legitimacy, not a factual description of reality" (Rogin 1967, 230).

If McCarthy's attacks on elites—in the State Department, at Harvard, and at points in between—had historical precedents in earlier conservative attacks on elites, then Rogin should have been able to produce them. What he came up with instead were two examples, one of which was almost completely inapposite: nineteenth-century lawyers arguing that "the people" had imposed constitutional limitations on legislative power. In the context of legislative attempts to regulate the railroads this was indeed a conservative use of "populist" rhetoric, but it hardly constituted an attack on elites; indeed, insofar as it revealed a broader defense of an independent judiciary, it was a defense of such elites. Far more relevant was his other example: southern planters using "grass-roots" rhetoric to counter the redistributive tendencies in the New Deal agencies that affected them.[1] But he did not place this particular example in historical context. And so while Rogin correctly recognized that attacking elites has always been a *potential* conservative tactic, he failed to give full weight to the possibility that it has become an *actual* one in the last half cen-

---

[1] Rogin 1967, pp. 50–52. Rogin drew his latter example from Philip Selznick's classic study, *TVA and the Grass Roots: A Study in the Sociology of Formal Organization* (Berkeley and Los Angeles: University of California Press, 1949).

tury because more than ever before the conservatives' adversaries were in elite positions:[2] the 1930s brought liberals into key positions in domestic policy-making; the 1940s brought them into comparable positions (at least by conservative standards) in the foreign policy apparatus; the 1950s marked the ascendancy of liberal activists on the Supreme Court, and so on.

Though Rogin may have doubted it, he did not successfully refute it; and so the possibility of a "populism" that could have both "right-wing" and "left-wing" manifestations survived his book. Thus, it is not surprising that, only a few years after the publication of *The Intellectuals and McCarthy*, one political scientist put together a collection of documents entitled *American Populism* and included in it not only the expected selections from Thomas Paine, William Jennings Bryan, and Huey Long—but also a speech by Joe McCarthy. He justified his inclusion by arguing that "populist egalitarianism" has always had "two halves . . . one economic and the other cultural," and it was only scholars' arbitrary distinctions that made the former "left-wing" and the latter "right-wing." What McCarthy's attacks on the State Department had in common with earlier attacks on business monopoly, he explained, was that both assume that the majority, "the 'plain people' of America . . . are in agreement with one another," that problems arose because "an elite has indeed taken power, and that the remedy is 'to restore' the Republic back into the hands of the majority." "This means that we must first throw the rascals out, the rascals being the economic royalists, the Harvard intelligentsia, the effete snobs, or the Communists."[3] One can imagine Rogin responding to all of this by saying that those—like McCarthy—who attacked the latter three groups were not real "populists" at all; far from trying to enhance the power of "the people" they were simply conservative spokesmen for elites trying to regain power. Such a response, however, only underscores the paradoxes of "the populist heritage," even in its "left-wing"/"economic" variants: few of the "populist" movements in America—and probably none since the Civil War—have enjoyed the support of the majority of the people.[4] And thus the task of the scholar studying "populism" is somewhat more complicated than Rogin's formulation would suggest: to determine not whether a given leader or movement represented "the people" but how many of them, and where in each particular case "elite" influence ended and "popular" influence began.

[2] Though Rogin does not mention it, the post-1933 conservative attacks on elites were foreshadowed in McCarthy's home state. In the 1914 election, according to LaFollette's major biographer, "conservatives charged that the 'tax-eating commissions' that constituted the Wisconsin Idea formed an elitist, unresponsive 'bureaucracy.' In the name of democracy and lower taxes, the conservatives blasted the rising costs of state government." David P. Thelen, *Robert M. LaFollette and the Insurgent Spirit* (Boston: Little, Brown, 1976), p. 118.

[3] George B. McKenna, ed., *American Populism* (New York: Putnam, 1974), pp. 210, xiii, xiv, xviii.

[4] McKenna, *American Populism*, pp. xvi–xvii; see also Canovan 1981, pp. 274–75.

Wiebe and McCarthyism as "Localism"

What now seems to be the most fruitful alternative to Rogin's interpretation, one that puts McCarthy back into at least one kind of "populist" context, was not formulated as an explanation of the sources of McCarthyism at all. It would arise, rather, out of one of the most influential historical undertakings of recent years, the series of books in which Robert Wiebe sought to understand what he called "the meaning of America." At the very outset of the first book in the series, *The Search for Order*, Wiebe introduced the reader to the American small town in the mid-1870s which together with its counterpart urban "neighborhood" constituted the environment in which most Americans then lived, a social world of face-to-face contacts and a political unit with a remarkable degree of autonomy in what was still—the Civil War notwithstanding—a decentralized republic. As the forces unleashed by capitalist industrialization steadily eroded the autonomy of these "island communities" throughout the late nineteenth century, their inhabitants tried to comprehend the world in terms of their traditional morality and struck out "at whatever enemies their view of the world allowed them to see. They fought . . . to preserve the society that had given their lives meaning." Their responses, Wiebe deliberately emphasized, could not be neatly classified on a political spectrum: "any distant threatening power was alien to the beleaguered communities"; it could equally well be the giant railroad corporation or the Roman Catholic Church. The major reform movements that came out of this era—Wiebe singled out the Knights of Labor, Edward Bellamy's Nationalism, and the Farmers' Alliances with their Populist offshoot—were all at their deepest level conservative because all aimed to preserve the autonomy of the "island communities" from which they arose (Wiebe 1967, 44, 54, 66).

In formulating this argument that late-nineteenth-century reform was the response of communities striving to resist the consequences of industrialization, Wiebe was indebted to other historians; but Wiebe went beyond them, making the claim that such defensive "community" responses to "modernizing" elites constituted the central dynamic of American society. In *The Segmented Society*, for example, he argued that "the enduring qualities of American society" lay in its "persisting segmentation." By "segmentation," he went on, he meant "a configuration of small social units—primary circles of identity, values, associations, and goals—that have sufficient authority to dominate the terms of their most important relationships with the world outside." He included in these "segments" kinship networks, occupational groups, ethnic groups, and of course geographically defined "communities" (Wiebe 1975, x).

The centralizing consequences of industrialization, paradoxically, reinforced this "segmentation." Public policy increasingly appeared to be determined through the interaction of corporate, governmental, and professional elites, and individual success measured by admission to their ranks; but those unable to gain membership in those elites were forced to fall back on "some version of the old-fashioned cultural norms, personal networks, and attachments to place as their defense against the national system's demeaning evaluation of their lives" (Wiebe 1975, 25). Therefore the kinds of responses he had first noted in the "island communities" of the 1870s and 1880s Wiebe found persisting throughout the twentieth century; and he emphasized these "localist" tendencies in his 1977 contribution to a textbook survey of American history. One such example was the resurgent Ku Klux Klan of the decade from 1915 to 1925. Unlike the first Klan of the Civil War era which frankly attempted to subordinate the recently freed black people, this "second" Klan—all observers agreed—had a multiplicity of targets: Catholics, Jews, bootleggers, radicals, and other assorted violators of "traditional" morality, as well as blacks. Wiebe interpreted this multiplicity of targets to mean that "the Klan was a collection of local organizations that adapted their purposes to fight the particular enemies of each community" but in every case aimed to restore "a lost unity and lost virtue." Similarly the movements led by Coughlin and Long in the 1930s represented community-oriented impulses: they "spoke the language of local politics, where the appeal of a popular, common-sense economics had always remained strong"; and as in the case of their predecessors in the 1880s, they "promised at a strike to give ordinary Americans a decent life without elaborate laws or government regimentation" (Wiebe 1977, 1060–61, 1085).

Wiebe portrayed "McCarthyism" in very similar terms. Unlike the revisionists who blurred the differences between President Truman and Senator McCarthy, Wiebe stressed the superficiality of the "anticommunist" consensus that both men seemed to share. Truman's anticommunism "expressed the natural preoccupations of national politics," the concerns of the governing elite, and as such developed specific strategies for dealing with the problem, not only the containment of Soviet power abroad but the elimination of Communists in government. McCarthy's kind of anticommunism, however, ultimately drew on very different impulses, "the fears and frustrations of locally oriented Americans." Communism, as they defined it, "was a pervasive web of dangers that might appear in the guise of atheism, sexual freedoms, strange accents, civil rights, or whatever most threatened a particular group's sense of security. Although this anticommunism also spoke of national defense and international conflict, it equated these issues with threats to a locality's cultural and moral standards. The actual sources of danger might well be some of the leaders in national politics." "The key to McCarthy's success," Wiebe continued, was his ability to exploit "the national issue of communists in government" as a way of achieving initial prominence while continuing to conjure up the dangers of "subversion" as a way of maintaining his support at the grass-roots level. It was in his latter role, as leader of this "localist" anticommunism, that McCarthy "invariably identified communism as 'Godless' and usually discovered its American disciples among the well-born, well-educated, and well-placed" (Wiebe 1977, 1120–21, 1122).

Another book, Mona Harrington's *The Dream of Deliverance in American Politics*, followed Wiebe in attempting to explain McCarthyism as one example of "localism," but she defined "localism" more narrowly as representing the sentiments of farmers and small-town entrepreneurs. From the era of the Farmers' Alliances, she argued, these "localists" had believed that since "no essential interest divided person from person, class from class, or even nation from nation . . . disharmony is caused by deliberate, wrongful power-seeking behind the facade of large, legitimate-seeming institutions." In 1900, such institutions were "monopolies and big business generally"; in 1950, the executive branch of the United States Government, presiding over the intricate network of military alliances, foreign-assistance programs, and international organizations created as a result of world war and the Cold War. Increasingly uncomfortable with the Truman administration's escalation of international commitments, "localist" congressmen easily moved from vague "suspicions of executive wrongdoing" to a sharper perception of a "hidden but deliberate influence of Communists in various parts of the Federal Government" (Harrington 1986, 34, 36–37, 150–52, 153).

Assessing the "Localist" Model: Community, Power, and Culture

Particularly in its emphasis on the fear of elites who represented "alien" forces, this "localist" interpretation of McCarthyism bears certain resemblances to those we described earlier that saw it as an expression of "populism," and indeed for both Wiebe and Harrington the Populists of the 1890s were spokesmen for similar "localist," "community"-oriented impulses. At the same time, however, there are subtle but important differences from those earlier interpretations. Unlike the "populism" that so worried Viereck and Shils, Wiebe's "populism" was not so much an aggressive majoritarianism as a reactive impulse, a defense of the community against external political and economic forces. And unlike Hofstadter, Wiebe (and those influenced by him like Harrington) found no "deconversion," no "left-wing" constituencies becoming "right-wing" constituents. Indeed for Wiebe and those historians influenced by him the impulse underlying "localism," what one of them called "the fear of concentrated power, . . . can, under different circumstances, lead either to the left or to the right or . . . to both simultaneously."[5]

---

[5] Alan Brinkley, *Voices of Protest: Huey Long, Father Coughlin, and the Great Depression* (New York: Knopf, 1982), p. 283.

The ways in which Wiebe's model differs from that offered by Rogin are more obvious. By making the "community" one of the protagonists in his historical drama, Wiebe tends to overlook conflicts within the "community" itself. This omission can result in serious misreadings of the evidence. In the case of the Klan of the 1920s, for example, at least in Oklahoma (where it was exceptionally strong) it represented community *division*, specifically the reaction of small-town elites to the militancy of local tenant farmers.[6] In the case of support for McCarthy, one would like to know exactly who the McCarthyites in a particular community were and which *local* individuals or groups they saw as threatening. To what extent did the "localist" themes detected by Wiebe and Harrington serve primarily (as Rogin had suggested) "to protect the power and conservative interests of locally powerful groups?"[7]

Additional problems arise from Wiebe's and Harrington's attempts to tie these "localists" to specific places, whether in geographic regions or in the social structure. Harrington's identifications of "localism" with predominantly agricultural states recalls Hofstadter's less than successful efforts to locate reactionary impulses in the hinterland. Wiebe, on the other hand, found his "locals" occupying the bottom layers of the social structure, without access to power except on those rare occasions when they rallied behind a self-appointed tribune such as Joe McCarthy. Yet his evocative portrayal of the way sexual and racial fears lay underneath many Americans' fear of "subversion" suggests no single individual so much as the most powerful bureaucrat in the twentieth century—J. Edgar Hoover. As the most detailed account of Hoover's harassment of Martin Luther King, Jr., makes clear, the FBI director was as obsessed with what he thought were the sexual activities of a black man as with what he feared was the potential radicalism of a civil rights leader, and at a deeper level probably made no distinction between them. While these were certainly the embodiment of white Protestant "small-town" prejudices, neither Hoover nor the agency he shaped in his image can be called powerless.[8] As Wiebe's comment about the differences between Truman and McCarthy would seem to imply, moreover, a common commitment to fight

[6] Garin Burbank, "Agrarian Radicals and Their Opponents: Political Conflict in Southern Oklahoma," *Journal of American History* 58 (June 1971): 5–23.

[7] Rogin 1967, p. 51. One case study that does try to explain support for McCarthy and anticommunist repression in general in terms of local conflicts is Don E. Carleton's analysis of Houston: *Red Scare! Right-Wing Hysteria, Fifties Fanaticism, and Their Legacy in Texas* (Austin: Texas Monthly Press, 1985). Carleton's book weaves together *The New American Right*'s emphasis on the social insecurity of the newly rich with Rogin's concern with the way the actions of elites establish the context for right-wing activism.

[8] David J. Garrow, *The FBI and Martin Luther King, Jr.* (New York: Norton, 1981), pp. 152–56, 171–72, 208–13. In fairness to Wiebe, it should be noted that Hoover began his ascendancy in the bureaucracy during World War I, the point (Wiebe argues) at which elite and "localist" fears of radicalism converged (Wiebe 1967, pp. 286–93).

"Communism" only superficially covered deep splits between "locals" and "cosmopolitans" at the highest levels of the Federal Government.

Once we put aside the image of united "communities" and powerless "locals," however, the strengths of the Wiebe-Harrington interpretation reveal themselves. In the first place, that interpretation underscores—as Rogin had not yet done in his first book—the role of culture, not clearly reducible to economic interests, in shaping support for McCarthy. Most observers have detected a clear anticosmopolitan component in McCarthy's rhetoric (Miles 1980, 146–47, 222–25); and the mutual hostility that developed between McCarthy's supporters and "Wall Street" almost certainly had less to do with the easterners' control of resources than with their educational backgrounds, aesthetic inclinations, and global interests. Right-wing activists have never forgotten what others have overlooked, that the nation's financial center and its most influential intellectual community are right next to each other, on a little island between the East River and the Hudson.

As Miles pointed out, McCarthy's anticosmopolitanism also said something important about his political base. Previous analysts of McCarthy's support had been perplexed by an apparent anomaly: the accumulated survey data showed that the senator was disproportionately supported by Republicans but also disproportionately supported by the less-educated, including blue-collar workers. What Miles concluded from his review of the data was "that the metropolitan wing of the party, which included the bulk of well-educated Republicans, was skeptical of McCarthy, while the provincial wing, based in areas less developed economically," and including "manual workers [who] in such areas often voted Republican," supported him. These "cultural traditions of political Republicanism and white Anglo-Saxon Protestantism," even more than economic interest, were decisive in creating this "provincial" support for McCarthy (Miles 1980, 141, 45, viii). In the final analysis it was the cultural fears of these "localists," their sense that their America was being destroyed—far more than the direct interests of manufacturers resisting union demands—that best explains the ferocity of the McCarthy era and gives new meaning to Lubell's "politics of revenge."

Finally, Wiebe's model has another great strength in that it points toward the future, toward seeing what would follow McCarthy's demise. On the much-debated question of who supported McCarthy and what difference it made, Rogin was surely correct when he concluded that McCarthy had no long-range impact on voting patterns. The question of "working-class support" for McCarthy will always to some extent remain an academic question because no worker—or anyone else for that matter—outside of Wisconsin ever had a chance to vote for him; and in Wisconsin, we now know, he received much less of the working-class vote than had previously been assumed.

Nevertheless, Rogin considerably overstated the case when he concluded that, at the time of his censure, with the Administration and much of the congressional party against him, McCarthy was left only with "anomic 'masses'," individuals "basically hostile to American society" (Rogin 1967, 259). On the contrary: McCarthy's censure marked not only an end but a beginning, something that should have been apparent by 1967. What followed the censure, in the late 1950s and early 1960s, was a major burst of energy on the part of his most dedicated supporters. In 1955, for example, the small number of intellectuals who had defended McCarthy's activities had regrouped around a new, unabashedly "conservative" journal of opinion, the *National Review*. A few years after that, its editor, William F. Buckley, Jr., presided over the creation of a nationwide right-wing youth organization, the Young Americans for Freedom; and he then went on to challenge the very center of liberal Republicanism by supporting the formation of a New York Conservative party.

In 1958, a retired candy manufacturer, who had already privately expressed the opinion that President Eisenhower was a "dedicated, conscious agent of the Communist conspiracy," persuaded other businessmen to join him in forming a militantly anticommunist organization to be called the John Birch Society. In 1960, an Australian doctor who had discovered a new vocation as a right-wing evangelical pastor, Dr. Fred C. Schwarz, transformed the little-known Christian Anti-Communist Crusade into a formidable presence: the following year his anticommunist "school" in Los Angeles grossed over $300,000 and his Hollywood Bowl rally was televised in various cities across the country. In 1964, the Republican party gave its presidential nomination to Senator Barry Goldwater, who was not only one of McCarthy's staunchest supporters in the Senate but soon became known for his uncompromising opposition to what he termed the "collectivism" of domestic policy since the New Deal and for his call for a foreign policy of "victory" over Communism.

Looking Back: McCarthy and the Development of the American Right Wing

Considered in the context of the development of the American right wing, McCarthy's importance takes on a new dimension, not only because of what he said but because of who he was. In several important ways he foreshadowed the right-wing strategy that would follow. He was, in the first place, an Irish Catholic whose two most notable aides were Jews; the support he received from self-styled defenders of "Americanism" indicated the way "the postwar right [had] converted 'Americanism' from virtually a genetic trait to a creed which receptive minds from all backgrounds could absorb and embody."[9] Second, McCarthy "appealed" to the working class in the sense that

[9] Mintz 1985, pp. 199–200. Among the first to notice this was of course Viereck (Viereck 1955, pp. 97–100).

he *appealed for* their support in a particular way. As Miles noted, his references to "the bright young men who are born with silver spoons in their mouths" may have been the "rhetoric of provincial resentment" but "it sounds like working-class rhetoric" (Miles 1980, 143). The extent to which the working class found McCarthy *appealing* is quite another matter; but his decision, conscious or not, to de-emphasize unacceptable conservative positions and stress noneconomic issues would prove an attractive model for subsequent right-wing candidates and activists.

Third, McCarthy had never really been an "isolationist." And so in the short run he was able to contribute to the larger Republican effort which sought to win over Americans of eastern European origin by talking vaguely about the "liberation" of their relatives from the Stalinist yoke. In the long run the campaign for "liberation" that he and his allies helped shape revealed changes in the foreign policy orientation of conservative Republicans, away from their earlier skepticism about foreign commitments toward a projection of American power in the world far more extensive than even that proposed by Democrats.[10]

Fourth, historians newly attuned to the social construction of sexuality, and to sexual conflicts within society, are rediscovering what his contemporaries discerned but did not always articulate about McCarthy: the unmistakable sexual polarity he conveyed between his own uninhibited macho image and the ostensible lack of manliness on the part of his opponents. One did not have to follow McCarthy's rhetoric very far before noticing that his targets in the State Department included not only suspected Communists but suspected homosexuals. Many of his supporters already believed in an all-encompassing "Communist conspiracy" and had no trouble accepting an all-encompassing "homosexual conspiracy"; they saw both as equally "subversive" and (for some of them at least) as largely interchangeable.[11] The implications of McCarthy's rhetoric—that real men were right-wing Republicans—would continue to play a major role in subsequent political discourse long after he had passed from the scene.

Polsby, Latham, and Rogin were correct to stress that McCarthy arose in a particular historical context, as the agent of a frustrated opposition seeking to regain national power; as a result, the base of his support remained Republican. For the same reason, his opposition was also historically conditioned; and one of the advantages of the Wiebe-Harrington emphasis on "localism" as an explanation of McCarthyism is that it is relevant not only to what might have happened then to change the base of the American right wing, but to what

[10] Miles 1980, pp. 84–85, 144–45, 183–85, 188–89, 193–94.
[11] For McCarthy's macho image, see Oshinsky 1983, pp. 56–57; for the McCarthyites' belief in a "homosexual conspiracy," Miles 1980, pp. 225–26; and for the devastating consequences, John D'Emilio, *Sexual Politics, Sexual Communities: The Making of a Homosexual Minority in the United States, 1940–1970* (Chicago: University of Chicago Press, 1983), pp. 41–49.

would in fact happen in the near future. The South, according to survey data contained in polls, was the most anti-McCarthy region in the country, and not surprisingly: it would be hard conjuring up a figure less attractive to southerners than an Irish Catholic Republican who climaxed his career by attacking senior officers in the United States Army and senior members of the United States Senate. The motivations behind this southern rejection were hardly "cosmopolitan," however, and one can speculate about the implications for McCarthy's career of the fact that the Supreme Court declared racial segregation unconstitutional just as the Army-McCarthy hearings were reaching their end. Though not a defender of segregation himself, he was too shrewd not to know that among white southerners "Communism" had already become a code word for civil rights and black mobilization and that after 1954 attacking the Supreme Court was a sure way of attracting support from these segregationist Democrats (Oshinsky 1983, 497–98). Had McCarthy peaked later, or the Court decided earlier, it is not unreasonable to assume that the junior senator from Wisconsin could well have split existing coalitions and launched a genuinely "new American right."

That brings us back to the beginning, to the book that launched the scholarly debate on McCarthyism. Had the scholarly career of *The New American Right* been determined solely by its analysis of the sources of support for McCarthy, the book might well have fallen into obscurity. "Status politics" was not only vaguely defined but did not seem particularly helpful in understanding McCarthyism, while the image of McCarthy as some kind of offspring of the original Populists did not withstand close scrutiny. The book survived for two reasons. First, as social scientists began searching for a framework to account for the surge of right-wing organization in the late 1950s and early 1960s, they naturally turned to whatever models they could find; and the most influential by that point were those contained in *The New American Right* (updated and reissued in 1963 as *The Radical Right*). Beyond that the book continued to exert a major influence because, whatever their other errors, its contributors recognized that McCarthy's significance transcended his immediate historical context. They saw, in Bell's words, that "McCarthy has to be understood in relation to the people behind him and the changed political temper which these groups have brought. He was the catalyst, not the explosive force. These forces still remain."

Part Two

THE "RADICAL RIGHT" OF THE EARLY 1960s

AT THE HEIGHT of Joseph McCarthy's career it was easy to identify the right-wing presence in American public life with the junior senator from Wisconsin; and so, as we have seen, scholarly analysis of the "radical right" began with a series of efforts to locate the sources of support for "McCarthyism." Few at the time thought the right wing would survive the senator's fall. But not only did the right wing survive the 1950s, in the early 1960s it appeared to flourish; and it reached its first significant consummation in the Republican presidential nomination of Senator Barry Goldwater. The right-wing organizations that appeared after McCarthy's career had ended—the John Birch Society, the Christian Anti-Communist Crusade, the Young Americans for Freedom, to name a few—attracted far more attention from journalists and social scientists than McCarthy's supporters had ever done.

Most of those who studied the right wing of the late 1950s and early 1960s concentrated their efforts on describing and analyzing the supporters of Goldwater and the members of those organizations. But it is one of the contentions of this book that in order to fully understand the American right wing, one must understand the specific historical context within which such spokesmen and organizations appeared, and the way that context determined their political views and strategies. The first question that should be asked, therefore, is why the right wing took the particular shape it did at that point in our history. The question seems hard to answer now because, in view of the tribulations that would follow, the years after McCarthy's demise retain a certain sweetness in the memory. It is tempting to remember those years as a golden age of consensus—in the words of a perceptive British commentator, as an era in which "a strange hybrid, liberal conservatism, blanketed the scene and muffled debate" and "few fundamental disagreements . . . were aired in either presidential or congressional politics."[1]

On closer examination it is not hard to see that the "consensual" decade of 1954–1964 was in fact an era of rising social tension. These were the years, after all, in which the Supreme Court's desegregation decision produced first a grim determination on the part of southern whites to preserve the institutional structure of white supremacy and then an even more impassioned commitment on the part of southern blacks to end it. On other matters the Court under Chief Justice Earl Warren took an equally activist role, monitoring a wide variety of established procedures, ranging from the apportionment of legislatures to the prosecution of "subversives" and from open prayer in the public schools to the interrogation of criminal suspects. Furthermore, the world that Americans

[1] Godfrey Hodgson, *America in Our Time* (Garden City, N.Y.: Doubleday, 1977), pp. 72, 73.

confronted was becoming more complicated and in some ways even more threatening than it had been in the early Cold War years. Revolt against colonial rule had spread out from Asia to encompass sub-Saharan Africa (and to Americans' shock) Latin America as well; and that acceleration in turn led both to bitter rivalry between the Soviet Union and Communist China, as to who could more effectively champion "wars of national liberation," and to renewed tension between the Soviets and the United States. The result, or so it seemed to many Americans, was that more and more effort was required simply to hold the line against the spread of what most still saw as an undifferentiated "Communism."

It is even more important to remember something else about the decade lasting from McCarthy's censure to Goldwater's presidential campaign. In recent years it has become fashionable to indict the Democratic presidents of the era, Kennedy and Johnson, for allowing the rhetoric of what they hoped to achieve to run ahead of what they could realistically accomplish and in the process to allow popular expectations to get out of control. With equal justification the same charge can be leveled against Eisenhower: frustrated conservatives—not radicalized liberals—were the first and most vociferous challengers of the decade's consensus. One major source of right-wing disillusionment, frustration, and anger with Eisenhower was his foreign policy, which turned out to resemble the Democratic policy of "containment" far more than the dynamic "liberation" about which Republican campaigners had talked in 1952. Right-wing disappointment with Eisenhower was probably even greater, however, in the area of economic policy. In his postconvention gestures of reconciliation with Robert Taft in 1952, the general had agreed with the senator that the fundamental issue in the campaign should be the defense of "liberty" against "creeping socialism."[2] Yet when he left the White House, the Tennessee Valley Authority still operated as a public enterprise, labor unions had suffered no major new curbs, the minimum wage had been raised and Social Security benefits extended. What seems to have happened was that Eisenhower's personal conservatism was checked by his assessment of what the public would accept, and he repeatedly warned that any party that repudiated the New Deal legislation already on the books would be committing political suicide.[3]

In spite of periodic expressions of resentment at what he saw as the negativism of right-wing Republicans, Eisenhower left his party as divided as he found it. Republicans remained split along two lines: among elected officials,

[2] James T. Patterson, *Mr. Republican: A Biography of Robert A. Taft* (Boston: Houghton Mifflin, 1972), pp. 577–78.

[3] Fred I. Greenstein, *The Hidden-Hand Presidency: Eisenhower as Leader* (New York: Basic Books, 1982), pp. 50–52; Gary W. Reichard, *The Reaffirmation of Republicanism: Eisenhower and the Eighty-Third Congress* (Knoxville: University of Tennessee Press, 1975), pp. viii, 234–35.

between "moderates" (and a few "liberals") primarily from the East and West Coasts and "conservatives" concentrated in the Midwest and Rocky Mountain states; and, in the population at large, between "conservative" party activists and "moderate" Republican voters.[4] The conservatives, many of whom had never reconciled themselves to New Deal economic policy, still occupied key positions in the legislatures and in the party's organization. With considerable influence within the party but unable to persuade the Administration to institute the far-reaching changes in either foreign or economic policy they desired, these conservative Republicans would constitute a natural core for the emerging right-wing organizations.[5] Thus many of the organizations that would attract the attention of journalists and social scientists—the John Birch Society, the Christian Anti-Communist Crusade, the Young Americans for Freedom, even the first stirrings of a Goldwater-for-President campaign—began during the Eisenhower years. They were not, as some have assumed, primarily a reaction to the new directions of the Kennedy administration.[6]

The second question confronting anyone examining right-wing individuals and organizations of the late 1950s and early 1960s is what ideology they shared, what made them seem, by the presidential election of 1964, to constitute a coherent right wing. Many of the journalists (and some of the scholars) who studied them at the time convinced themselves that the emerging right-wing constellation was "extremist." In spite of the fact that much of this literature was transparently polemical, it can still guide us toward seeing some of the characteristics the right wing of the era seemed to share. Three specific charges made by these writers were particularly notable: first, that the right wing developed tightly organized, centrally controlled "cadres" which then "infiltrated" or disrupted more moderate organizations; second, that right-wing leaders were obsessed with an all-encompassing "Communist conspiracy"; and third, that they advocated "radical" change, including the repeal of most of the major domestic reforms of the previous three decades and the pursuit of a far more aggressive foreign policy.

Those thinking of "cadres" and "infiltration" surely had in mind the best-known and most controversial organization of the era, the John Birch Society.[7] Created by retired candy manufacturer Robert Welch in 1958, by the early

[4] The best-known statement of this activist-voter cleavage is McClosky 1960, especially pp. 422–23.

[5] For right-wing Republican frustration during the Eisenhower years, see Reinhard 1983, pp. 121–51.

[6] It is often forgotten that the very first journalistic exposés of the John Birch Society, which brought it national attention, *preceded* the Kennedy administration—those by the *Chicago Sun-Times* in the summer of 1960 and by the *Santa Barbara News-Press* in the winter of 1960–61.

[7] Of the immense journalistic literature on the right-wing organizations of the late 1950s and early 1960s that appeared at the time, four books—Dudman 1962, Janson and Eismann 1963, Sherwin 1963, and Forster and Epstein 1964—have been most useful for details, and the subsequent analysis follows them.

1960s the Society had a membership estimated at between 20,000 and 100,000, a membership most notably described, by California Attorney-General Stanley Mosk, as consisting "primarily of wealthy businessmen, retired military officers, and little old ladies in tennis shoes."[8] Every month, the members of each chapter, under the direction of their appointed leader (who in turn was supervised by a coordinator appointed by national headquarters), would review the "plan of action" for the last month to see what they accomplished and discuss the coming month's plan of action as sent out from national headquarters. The plan of action might involve disrupting meetings and heckling speakers believed to be "Communists" or "Communist sympathizers" ("Comsymps"), engaging in mass letter-writing campaigns to elected officials, boycotting stores that sold goods made in Communist countries, or creating "front organizations" with a broader base.

While the John Birch Society was still attracting attention, Arizona Senator Barry Goldwater received the Republican presidential nomination. Since he had never been the consistent first choice of Republican voters in the polls, and had fared badly in the 1964 primaries, the question immediately arose: *how* had he gained the nomination? The much-praised Goldwater organization was as fallible as any other; as one of its leaders candidly admitted, "The only reason we came out all right is the people at the grass roots."[9] Who were these "people at the grass roots"? Goldwater's moderate Republican critics were sure they had the answer: the Goldwater organization in key states had in fact been "infiltrated" by right-wing activists, particularly from the John Birch Society, and in California there were angry charges of "takeovers."[10] Whether that opinion simply reflected the bitterness of losers or something more substantial is hard to determine, in part because Goldwater had encouraged the participation of rank-and-file Birchers in his campaign by calling them "good, sincere" people, "the kind we need in politics."[11]

Those who identified conspiratorial modes of thought with the right wing of

[8] Stanley Mosk and Howard Jewel, "The Birch Phenomenon Analyzed," *New York Times Magazine*, August 20, 1961, p. 12.

[9] John Ashbrook, as quoted in Robert D. Novak, *The Agony of the G.O.P., 1964* (New York: Macmillan, 1965), p. 468.

[10] George F. Gilder and Bruce K. Chapman, *The Party That Lost Its Head* (New York: Knopf, 1966), pp. 161–91.

[11] At the time Goldwater coupled his praise for Society members with criticism of Welch, whom he wished would resign (Goldwater as quoted in Janson and Eismann 1963, p. 200, and in Dudman 1962, p. 29). In his memoirs written almost twenty years later, however, Goldwater was more charitable toward Welch, writing that "no man should be judged by a single act. Robert Welch has done much to alert people to the dangers of Communism." He reiterated his earlier praise for Society members ("Most of the John Birchers are patriotic, concerned, law-abiding, hardworking, and productive) and remained outraged that his Republican opponents of 1964 would have considered them "comparable to the Commies, the Nazis, and the Ku Klux Klanners." Goldwater, *With No Apologies: The Personal and Political Memoirs of United States Senator Barry M. Goldwater* (New York: Morrow, 1979), pp. 119, 189.

the era could also begin with Robert Welch. Even before he founded the John Birch Society, he had circulated an essay among his friends that called President Eisenhower "a dedicated, conscious agent of the Communist conspiracy." Thereafter in publications issuing from Society headquarters in Belmont, Massachusetts, Welch and his colleagues charged not only that "Communists" or "Communist sympathizers" controlled most of Western Europe but that within the United States "Communist influences now are in almost complete control of our Federal Government," and are "very powerful in the echelons of our educational system, our labor-union organizations, many of our religious organizations, and almost every important segment of our national life."[12]

Similar conspiratorial thinking could be found in the statements of other prominent right-wing spokesmen. There was, for example, Rev. Billy James Hargis, a Disciples of Christ minister who had broadened his interests from fundamentalist religion to right-wing politics. He had founded what became known as "Christian Crusade" in 1947, but his publications, weekly radio broadcasts, and National Anti-Communist Leadership Schools attracted attention only in the early 1960s. Like Welch, whom he repeatedly praised, Hargis argued that the all-encompassing "Communist conspiracy" was increasingly within sight of its goal. "So clever has been the Communist intrigue and so successful has its subversion within America been," he announced in one of his pamphlets, "that the capture of the world's freest and richest nation lacks only another shove or two." All this happened, he claimed, because "America's daily newspapers are promoting the Communist line," because Congress is also "leaning heavily to the left-wing, pro-Communist side," and because the Communists are receiving much of their funding from American business.[13]

A third right-wing spokesman, whose career attracted more attention than did Hargis's (although it did not last as long), was the former doctor and Baptist preacher Fred C. Schwarz. Having moved from his native Australia in 1950, he decided to become an "expert" on Communism and by 1960 had assumed complete control over the Christian Anti-Communist Crusade which he had helped found. His Crusade was notable for the five-day "schools" he and his "faculty" conducted, "schools" justified on the ground that the Federal Government was not meeting the Communist threat. At such gatherings Schwarz would use his considerable oratorical powers to impress upon his audiences the danger they confronted: unless stopped in time, by 1973 Communists would take over the United States. Unlike Welch and Hargis, Schwarz tried to avoid connecting the "conspiracy" to all aspects of domestic politics and policy and preferred calculated ambiguities such as telling

[12] Robert Welch, as quoted in Dudman 1962, pp. 71, 72.
[13] Billy James Hargis, as quoted in Janson and Eismann 1963, pp. 76–77.

his listeners that not everyone fighting racial discrimination was a Communist.[14] Some of his "faculty members," however, were considerably more outspoken, including the man who announced that he didn't want to impeach Earl Warren, he wanted to hang him. Although Schwarz tried to dissociate himself from Welch, moreover, he offered no objection to those of his speakers who followed the John Birch Society in condemning the courts, public education, the Protestant clergy, and the labor movement.[15]

For Welch, for Hargis, even for Schwarz, an all-encompassing "Communist conspiracy" was central to their rhetoric and organization, as indeed it was for many of the other 232 "militantly anticommunist" organizations operating in the United States in the early 1960s.[16] Could such thinking be said to characterize the right wing as a whole? There are several possible answers, depending on one's categorization of conspiratorial thinking. If one regards someone like Welch as the exemplar of conspiratorial thinking then obviously many other right-wing spokesmen would be excluded: few of them were willing to follow him in maintaining that Communists were in control of practically all American institutions. But, as critics like Peter Viereck noted, they had not drawn back from the far more formidable McCarthy: indeed, they had defended him.[17] The intellectuals at the *National Review* had actively championed his cause, the best-known of them, William F. Buckley, Jr., describing McCarthyism as "a movement around which men of good will can close ranks."[18] In his eulogy in 1957 Goldwater had told those assembled that "because Joe McCarthy lived, we are a safer, freer, more vigilant nation today."[19] In their statement of principles in 1962, the founders of the New York Conservative party still felt it necessary to resolve that "the Communist drive to infiltrate and undermine our institutions must be prosecuted with every resource of our laws."[20]

Not only was the spirit of the late senator from Wisconsin present in the general right-wing conviction that "subversion" constituted a clear and present danger, but his rhetoric or something close to it was never far beneath the surface. In his *Conscience of a Conservative* of 1960, for example, Goldwater had charitably exonerated past policymakers for setbacks in foreign policy:

---

[14] Fred C. Schwarz, as quoted in Janson and Eismann 1963, p. 68.

[15] Sherwin 1963, pp. 117–18; Forster and Epstein 1964, pp. 57–58.

[16] The figure is the Anti-Defamation League's estimate, as cited in Janson and Eismann 1963, pp. 126–27.

[17] Peter Viereck, *Conservatism Revisited* (New York: Free Press, 1962), p. 145.

[18] William F. Buckley, Jr., and L. Brent Bozell, *McCarthy and His Enemies: The Record and Its Meaning* (Chicago: Regnery, 1954), p. 335.

[19] Barry Goldwater, as quoted in Jack Bell, *Mr. Conservative: Barry Goldwater* (Garden City: N.Y.: Doubleday, 1962), p. 102.

[20] Declaration of Principles Issued upon First Public Announcement of Formation of Conservative Party in February 1962, in J. Daniel Mahoney, *Actions Speak Louder* (New Rochelle, N.Y.: Arlington House, 1968), p. 377.

"Our national leadership over the past fourteen years has favored neither surrender nor treason."[21] Nonetheless, four years later, in the heat of his presidential campaign, he was willing to accept "treason" as an explanation for
the "softness" of the Democrats' foreign policy when it was offered by an
enthusiastic crowd.[22] Welch may have been considered extreme in his views
and divisive in his tactics, but his assumption that the "Communist conspiracy" was still engaged in "subversion" within the United States characterized
the right wing of the era.

The last characteristic attributed to right-wing spokesmen—that they proposed dramatic, "radical" changes in domestic and foreign policy—is by far
the easiest to document. One does not need to base the argument on idiosyn-
cratic characters such as Welch, who wanted to repeal all the major legislation
of the preceding half century beginning with the income tax amendment of
1913. The principles behind the course most of these spokesmen proposed
were most clearly enunciated in the founding statement of the leading right-
wing youth group of the era. The Young Americans for Freedom believed
"that the market economy, allocating resources by the free play of supply and
demand, is the single economic system compatible with the requirements of
personal freedom and constitutional government" and "that when government interferes with the work of the market economy, it tends to reduce the
moral and physical strength of the nation; that when it takes from one man to
bestow on another, it diminishes the incentive of the first, the integrity of the
second, and the moral autonomy of both."[23] In order to defend these principles against what they saw as "the subtle tide of bureaucratic socialism," the
New York Conservatives called for "a return of all possible activities to the
several states; of all possible activities of the states to the local communities;
and of all possible governmental activities at every level to the private energies
of individual and non-governmental associations."[24]

What was "possible"? As the man most likely to turn those principles into
policies, Goldwater felt he had to be specific. In *The Conscience of a Conservative*, the statement that gained him a national audience, he took a strict-
constructionist view of the Constitution, arguing that the Federal Government
had no power to regulate agricultural production, no power to impose progressive taxation, no authority to intervene in educational matters—and as a corollary that the federal courts had no authority to order the desegregation of the
public schools. (He added that he personally favored desegregation as policy

[21] Barry Goldwater, *The Conscience of a Conservative* (Sheperdsville, Ky.: Victor Publishing,
1960), p. 89.

[22] E. W. Kenworthy, "Goldwater Says Johnson 'Doesn't Understand' Job," *New York Times*,
October 21, 1964, p. 1.

[23] The Sharon Statement, as quoted in Forster and Epstein 1964, p. 228.

[24] Conservative Party Declaration of Principles, in Mahoney, *Actions Speak Louder*, p. 377;
and in general Kolkey 1983, pp. 45–53.

but was "not prepared to impose that judgment of mine on the people of Mississippi or South Carolina.") His own proposals included the end of all farm
subsidies, the use of antitrust laws to prohibit industry-wide bargaining by
labor unions, a constitutional amendment reaffirming the states' exclusive jurisdiction in the field of education, and the suggestion that all federal welfare
functions be transferred either to state and local authorities or to private char-
ity.[25]

If in domestic policy right-wing spokesmen called for retrenchment, in foreign policy they were paragons of activism. To counter the threat of "the
Communist enemy of all mankind," the New York Conservatives called for
"a total reassessment of American foreign policy so that . . . we place the
achievement of victory over this menace as the lodestar of all our international
action."[26] To meet those goals, Goldwater proposed, among other things, that
the United States should withdraw recognition from the Soviet Union and all
other Communist governments, "thereby serving notice on the world that we
regard such governments as neither legitimate nor permanent." The United
States should also actively encourage "the captive peoples to revolt against
their Communist rulers" and, specifically referring to possible efforts by the
Nationalist regime to recover mainland China, assist "friendly peoples . . . to
undertake offensive operations for the recovery of their homelands." Should
the Soviets resist these actions or for whatever reason repress rebellions within
their orbit, the United States should deter such reaction by threatening nuclear
war.[27]

What makes it possible, then, to speak of *the* right wing during this period—as opposed to a number of different organizations—was a common ideology and a common view of history. However unsettling the implications
they drew from it, that ideology was classically American.[28] Right-wingers
saw themselves as defenders of an earlier individualism, sanctified by the Declaration of Independence and the Constitution (and, for preachers like Hargis,
by God himself),[29] against a newer collectivism that had gathered momentum
in the earlier part of the twentieth century and dominated American politics
and policy after 1933. Their adherence to the principles of nineteenth-century
liberalism and their concomitant defense of "states' rights" against the Federal Government placed them in opposition to the dominant trends of the last
half century. That adherence, obviously, accounts for their opposition to spe-

[25] Goldwater, *The Conscience of a Conservative*, pp. 39, 61–62, 77, 34; 37; 42–43, 56–57,
36, 73–74.

[26] Conservative Party Declaration of Principles, in Mahoney, *Actions Speak Louder*, p. 377.

[27] Goldwater, *The Conscience of a Conservative*, pp. 120, 121.

[28] This paragraph is heavily indebted to the analysis of right-wing ideology in Ellsworth and
Harris 1962, especially pp. 10–25.

[29] For Hargis's conviction that the Constitution was divinely inspired and that it, like true Christianity, mandates laissez-faire economics, see Redekop 1968, pp. 74–84.

cific public policies. But it also accounts for their intense dislike of those non-governmental influences that they saw as encouraging this collectivist trend: not only the political power of labor unions, but also the intellectual influences of modern social science, progressive education, and the Social Gospel in religion.

At the same time—and this cannot be stressed too often—their classically American defense of individualism differentiated the American right wing of this era from possible European counterparts, such as the fascist movements that some worried liberal and leftist critics saw as analogous. A test given members of a discussion group affiliated with Schwarz's Christian Anti-Communist Crusade is suggestive in this connection. Asked to construct a political spectrum and locate themselves on it, they not only put "no government at all, a state of natural chaos" on the right and "the American system" (with themselves as its defenders) in the middle, but they placed all forms of what they saw as "collectivism" (not only social democracy and Communism but also fascism) on the left.[30] Hargis, too, saw the enemy as a hydra-headed collectivism. "Socialism inheres in the Nazi ideology as it does in Communism and liberalism," he wrote. "American liberals and American Nazis [both] derive from Karl Marx."[31]

The major intellectual problem for the right wing was to account for the waning of the earlier individualism and the rise of the newer collectivism. Rejecting the desirability of the welfare state on principle, the right wing also rejected the possibility that it was in some sense an inevitable response to the evolution of industrial capitalism. While it was still possible for right-wingers to see recent American history as the result of a number of forces which had all converged in the wrong direction, it was easier and far more comforting to see the recent past as the result of a conspiracy. The Bolshevik Revolution and the rise of an international Communist movement guided by the Soviet Union gave considerable substance to right-wing fears; thenceforth they could argue, with at least a superficial plausibility, that the tendencies in modern America that they disliked were the results of an "alien conspiracy" of "Communistic" collectivists.

Although the point has seldom been commented upon, the right wing's view that they were facing an all-powerful "Communist conspiracy" also shaped their attitudes on specific policy questions, preventing all but a small minority from becoming pure libertarians. Their belief in conspiracy, for example, goes far toward solving the riddle that perplexed many of their critics: how could these self-styled defenders of individualism be so cavalier about the protections of the Bill of Rights, how could these opponents of the Federal Government cheer on the FBI and congressional investigating committees? The an-

[30] Chesler and Schmuck 1963, pp. 21–23.
[31] Hargis, as quoted in Jorstad 1970, p. 139.

swer, in their own minds at least, seems to have been that the danger of the conspiracy was so great that extraordinary measures had to be taken before traditional freedoms could be restored.

Similarly, the right-wing belief in conspiracy may help us understand their changing foreign policy views. Because of their quite valid suspicion that continual foreign intervention and the domestic expansion of government were closely connected, right-wingers had tended to oppose what an earlier age called "foreign entanglements." Then, as the ensuing Cold War heightened fears of an encircling "Communist conspiracy," they turned in a far more aggressive direction.[32] The older isolationist tradition did not disappear all at once: Welch could still argue, for example, that a large defense budget was unnecessary so long as Americans kept their unrestricted right to obtain firearms,[33] and right-wingers generally remained hostile to the United Nations and foreign aid and ambivalent toward multilateral alliances. During the 1950s, however, individual right-wing spokesmen increasingly began to advocate a strategy that would end the "Communist conspiracy" once and for all by striking at its source. As two analysts noted, there was an inner logic to this shift in thinking: only if Americans regained "unchallenged world supremacy" would they have the "freedom to return to the relatively uncomplicated life of the nineteenth century." It therefore became necessary to advocate "winning the cold war immediately."[34] This new aggressive posture, linked as it often was to the conspiratorial view of history, helps explain why many of those who were primarily interested in restoring economic laissez-faire described themselves as "militantly anticommunist," or conversely why organizations such as Schwarz's Christian Anti-Communist Crusade, which ostensibly had no connection with domestic politics and policy, could be so warmly supported by right-wing activists with unambiguous domestic agendas.

[32] My argument here has been influenced especially by Justus N. Doenecke, *Not to the Swift: Old Isolationists in the Cold War Era* (Lewisburg, Pa.: Bucknell University Press, 1979); John B. Judis, "William F. Buckley, Jr.: The Consummate Conservative," *Progressive* 45 (September 1981): 25–33; Ronald Lora, "A View from the Right: Conservative Intellectuals, the Cold War, and McCarthy," in Robert Griffith and Athan Theoharis, eds., *The Specter: Original Essays on the Cold War* (New York: New Viewpoints, 1974), pp. 40–70; and Miles 1980.

[33] Janson and Eismann 1963, p. 36; Miles 1980, p. 249.

[34] Janson and Eismann 1963, pp. 239–40; see also Kolkey 1983, pp. 113–18.

Five

Bell and Riesman: The "Radical Right," American Society, and the Cold War

THE APPEARANCE of a panoply of right-wing organizations in the late 1950s and early 1960s, and the increasing coverage given them by journalists, forced social scientists not only to pay attention to the developments at hand but to consider what aspects of American culture and society had made the apparent resurgence—more probably, the steady persistence—of the right wing possible ten years after McCarthy. It is important to remember in that connection that in the first few years after its publication the most damaging criticism leveled against *The New American Right* came not from those seeking alternative explanations for right-wing political behavior but from those who argued that the book's theses were simply unnecessary to explain McCarthy's rise. In his generally critical review of the book, for example, Samuel Lubell had maintained that "much of McCarthy's appeal was generated by the frustrations of the Korean War" and that by the time the book appeared, "moderation rather than vindictiveness has become the dominant political quality of the whole country."[1] However, against the background of the right-wing efflorescence of the late 1950s and early 1960s, which seemed to climax in the Goldwater campaign of 1964, journalists and social scientists were unlikely to be impressed by Lubell's argument that the sources of McCarthyism were ephemeral. They were more likely to remember Daniel Bell's cautionary tone in the book's introductory essay: "McCarthy has to be understood in relation to the people behind him and the changed political temper which these groups have brought. He was the catalyst, not the explosive force. These forces still remain" (Bell 1955, 17).

In this context of the growth of right-wing organizations, and of the increasing attention paid to them by the media, Bell and the other contributors to *The New American Right* were encouraged to bring out a new edition of the book, supplemented with additional essays by themselves and two new contributors, and now entitled *The Radical Right*. The new edition attracted much less attention than its predecessor, most probably because it lacked coherence: the

---

[1] Samuel Lubell, review of *The New American Right*, ed. Daniel Bell, *New York Times Book Review*, December 11, 1955, p. 8; see also Margaret Mead, "The New Isolationism," *American Scholar* 24 (Summer 1955): 378–82.

supplementary essays moved in several different directions, and the contributions of Richard Hofstadter and Seymour Martin Lipset were outlines of arguments they would develop in later, more important works. Nevertheless, two of the new contributions to the 1963 edition—those by Daniel Bell and David Riesman—deserve consideration because they attempted to put the growth of the right wing in a broader historical perspective, Bell emphasizing the changes in society that facilitated the growth of the "radical right" and Riesman the way in which those changes occurred in the context of the Cold War.

In his essay, "The Dispossessed," Bell touched upon many of the areas that would engage social scientists studying the right-wing activity of the era; at the same time, however, he attempted to cover a wider range of phenomena than most of those who followed him. In spite of its occasional ambiguity, his essay (in both of its published versions) remains a compelling piece of analysis.[2] At the outset he noted the contrast with the early 1950s: "McCarthyism . . . was never an organized movement; it was primarily an atmosphere of fear"; while "the radical right of the 1960s has been characterized by a multitude of organizations." Using for purposes of illustration *National Review* editorials, Birchite literature, Schwarz's speeches, and *Dan Smoot Reports*, Bell emphasized certain recurrent themes: a belief in the breakdown of American moral fiber, a conspiratorial view of history, and a detailed forecast of Communist takeover. Moreover, the right wing's continued emphasis on an internal Communist threat and its identification of Communism with liberalism suggested to him that "what the right wing is fighting, in the shadow of Communism, is essentially modernity." By "modernity," at least judging from the two versions of his essay, Bell appears to have been referring to two closely related but not identical developments: "the belief in rational assessment, rather than established custom, for the evaluation of social change" (Bell 1963, 4, 12) and "the new nature of decision-making, with its increased technicality" necessitated by the growing functional complexity of organizations (Bell 1962, 12).

Various segments of the population felt threatened by these aspects of modernity, and the "radical right" of the late 1950s and early 1960s was in some sense their response. The broadest reaction came from those Bell called variously "the generational dispossessed," or representatives of "the small-town mind." What these individuals shared, he went on, was "the life-style and values of Protestant fundamentalism—the nativist nationalism, the good-and-evil moralism through which they see the world" (Bell 1963, 18; Bell 1962, 6). Since this general argument, first raised by Bell in his 1962 essay, would

---

[2] Since the point here is to summarize Bell's thinking, the reader should note that I am combining the two versions in which his essay appeared, first in the *Columbia University Forum* (Bell 1962) and then somewhat differently in *The Radical Right* (Bell 1963).

loom so large in subsequent analyses of the American right wing, it will be useful to put it into some perspective.

Looking backward from the 1980s, the identification of fundamentalist religion with right-wing politics may seem obvious; but in fact this assumption became widespread only about the time Bell wrote his essay. Many earlier analysts had tended to differentiate the two. In his detailed study of right-wing activity within the major Protestant denominations during the McCarthy era, for example, Ralph Lord Roy had concluded that, with the possible exceptions of the Baptists and the Disciples of Christ, the right-wing critics who objected to the political stances taken by their denominations' leadership had no clear theological profile: they were not, in other words, clearly fundamentalist.[3] As journalists began investigating the proliferating right-wing organizations of the early 1960s, however, they began to uncover evidence that suggested that at the mass level one major source of right-wing activity was indeed what one of them called a "fearsome evangelical fundamentalism."[4] In early 1962, a writer in *Commentary*, David Danzig, made the first forceful statement of the connection.

In "The Radical Right and the Rise of the Fundamentalist Minority," Danzig defined fundamentalism in the usual religious terms, as "a rigorously orthodox point of view which completely dominates some Protestant denominations and has adherents in many others, including even the Episcopal Church. Among its basic doctrines are the inerrancy of the Bible, salvation by faith alone, and the premillennial return of Christ. On religious questions, it takes a stand against any attempts at revisionism and modernism." Moreover, he continued, fundamentalist doctrine also predisposed its adherents to a certain kind of political outlook: its emphasis on literalness made them suspicious of "pragmatism in the social world" while its commitment to Biblical prophecy resulted in "an anti-historicist perspective which readily supports the conspiracy theory of social change." In the past these conservative tendencies

---

[3] Ralph Lord Roy, *Apostles of Discord: A Study of Organized Bigotry and Disruption on the Fringes of Protestantism* (Boston: Beacon Press, 1953), especially pp. 308–67. Roy reiterated his position that analysts needed to separate theological and political positions even after Bell's essay appeared: "Conflict from the Communist Left and the Radical Right," in Robert Lee and Martin E. Marty, eds., *Religion and Social Conflict* (New York: Oxford University Press, 1964), p. 62.

A subsequent student of the conflict over the newly formed National Council of Churches was even more specific, concluding that "fundamentalists often failed to reconcile their religious and social beliefs with their more theologically liberal political allies. While a conservative political rationale and a common antipathy to the Social Gospel united many conservative business executives and professional men with theologically fundamentalist ministers, their often divergent religious views and social activities weakened the union." E. V. Toy, Jr., "The National Lay Committee and the National Council of Churches: A Case Study of Protestants in Conflict," *American Quarterly* 21 (Summer 1969): 208. (See also Warren L. Vinz, "Protestant Fundamentalists and McCarthy," *Continuum* 6 [Fall 1968]: 314–25.)

[4] Willie Morris, "Houston's Superpatriots," *Harper's* 223 (October 1961): 54.

were held in check by the economic hardship of the mass of fundamentalists in the South and West, and so, during the half century between 1890 and 1940, fundamentalists could support the economic radicalism of a William Jennings Bryan or a Huey Long. The economic boom following World War II brought affluence to these fundamentalists, however, without (at least from Danzig's perspective) bringing enlightenment. The result was a powerful reinforcement of theological conservatism by the economic self-interest of the newly prosperous: it was not coincidental, he wrote, that "the states that repudiated Darwinism and Al Smith are today prominent among those nineteen that have passed 'right-to-work' laws" (Danzig 1962, 292, 293).

Though Bell was obviously influenced by Danzig's essay, in using the term "fundamentalism" he meant something more than even the political consequences of a particular theological tendency. For him fundamentalism was part of a wider effort to retain the dominance of the middle-class values that had characterized American society in the early twentieth century. As "the gradual cultural ascendancy of metropolitan life over rural areas . . . began to threaten established customs and beliefs," the middle classes in the small towns of America had responded by trying to impose intellectual orthodoxy and repress "alien" minorities (Bell 1963, 21, 20). Since the 1930s the fundamentalists had seized upon "the emotions generated by foreign policy conflicts [symbolized by 'anticommunism'] to confuse domestic issues" (Bell 1962, 7). Bell agreed with those who maintained that the "radical right" represented certain traditional American values; but, he argued, in the increasingly complex world of the twentieth century their attempts to implement those values were quixotic. Their peculiarly American kind of moralism ("if anything was wrong, the individual was to blame") led the "radical right" toward both punitive attitudes toward social deviants and conspiratorial explanations of failures in foreign policy (Bell 1963, 8, 14).

In so broadly portraying the mass base of right-wing organizations, however, Bell had achieved only part of his purpose; he had yet to account for the financial support they received from the business community or their connection with various officers in the armed forces. What specific factors would account for the appeal of the "radical right" to what he called "the managerial dispossessed" and "the military dispossessed"? At this point Bell sketched out a theme with which he would soon become closely associated; in the later 1960s it would form one of the major arguments for his thesis that America had become a "post-industrial society." The "new nature of decision-making," he argued, necessitated "a new system of recruitment for power" in which "technical skill rather than property" had become one of the bases from which power was wielded and education had become "the major way to acquire the technical skills." Later critics would charge that Bell had overestimated the degree to which technical skill had in fact replaced property ownership as a base of power, but that criticism does not necessarily vitiate his point in this essay: that a trend in that direction was occurring and that "those who are the products of the old system understandably feel a vague and apprehensive disquiet" over these changes.[5]

This "displacement of the older elites" was clearest in the business world. Unlike "the old family firm [which] was securely rooted in the legal and moral tradition of private property," the modern corporation and the managers who administered it lacked any legitimating ideology. Unable to justify their control they now found themselves challenged within and outside their firms not only by labor unions but by "the new technical and professional intelligentsia." "Within a business enterprise, the newer techniques of operations research and linear programming almost amount to the 'automation' of middle management, and its displacement by mathematicians and engineers, working either within the firm or as consultants. In the economy, the businessman finds himself subject to price, wage, and investment criteria laid down by the economists in government." The managers' response to their sense of displacement was, Bell suggested, to push their corporations into an aggressive posture—"by taking a public stand on political issues, by sending out vast amounts of propaganda to their employees and to the public, by encouraging right-to-work referendums in the states," and by "contributing financially to the seminars of the radical right evangelists" (Bell 1963, 22, 17, 24).

The dispossession of the military, Bell believed, showed certain striking parallels to that of the managers, though here of course the new technical and professional intelligentsia was challenging not the prerogatives of property but the traditions associated with the military: "The problems of national security, like those of the national economy, have become so staggeringly complex that they can no longer be settled simply by common sense or past experience." "Trained in older notions of strategy," the military were simply "ill-equipped to grasp modern conceptions of politics, or to use the tools . . . of strategic planning." As a result, "the old military elites find themselves challenged in the determination of strategy by scientists, who have the technical knowledge on nuclear capability, missile development, and the like, or by the military intellectuals whose conceptions of weapon systems and political warfare seek to guide military allocations" (Bell 1963, 24, 17).

Since the end of World War II, Bell pointed out, the military had been involved "in a number of battles to defend its elite position," beginning with the conflict over the control of atomic energy and continuing through the debates over the construction of the hydrogen bomb and the strategy of massive retaliation. The affinity of retired military officers not only for groups such as the Institute for American Strategy, which advocated a far more aggressive

[5] Bell 1963, p. 17. For his subsequent development of this argument, see his preliminary "Notes on the Post-Industrial Society," in *Public Interest* 6 (Winter 1967): 24–35, and 7 (Spring 1967): 102–18; and his major statement, *The Coming of Post-Industrial Society: A Venture in Social Forecasting* (New York: Basic Books, 1973).

American posture in the world, but for Schwarz and other "radical rightists" came from "the rancor of an old guard that now finds its knowledge outdated and its authority disputed or ignored, and that argues, bitterly, that if only 'their' advice had been followed, America would not be on the defensive" (Bell 1963, 25–26, 29).

In his contribution to *The Radical Right*, David Riesman concentrated on the interaction between the "radical right," the policymakers, and the course of international conflict. By 1963 he was increasingly preoccupied with the threat of nuclear war. He liked the term the "radical right," he wrote the following year, because it was "an effort to combat the notion of the right as inherently conservative." His own position, he added, was "quite conservative in some ways, since I want to conserve America as a going concern and the rest of the world with it, and am opposed to nuclear and other experiments and adventures, from whatever side, that seek to upset the status quo with which we must live and work."[6]

Eisenhower's second term was a period of disquiet, Riesman wrote, in which many Americans "had become uneasy at the growing signs that the United States could no longer play world policeman with impunity, and that we might someday be unable to roll back the tide of Communist advance while going about our business as before." The increasingly bellicose "radical right" was one response; but so was the Kennedy campaign of 1960, "fought . . . on the basis of ascetic insistence on sacrifice, reminiscent of Theodore Roosevelt's belief in strenuousness, in American destiny, and in the responsibility owed the nation by patrician intellectuals." Moreover, he provocatively suggested, it was not always possible to distinguish the two: "Kennedy during his campaign shared the right-wing picture of an America pushed around by Khrushchev and Castro, and suffering defeat after defeat in the Cold War" (Riesman 1963, 122, 117, 121).

Riesman remained ambivalent about Kennedy. He granted that the new president had "broken out of the limits imposed on American policy" by his predecessor, and he appreciated Kennedy's commitment to civil rights and civil liberties. Nevertheless, he warned, "his rhetoric of activism speaks to the mood of many in the discontented classes, and since he has in some measure freed himself from his predecessor's budgetary and other controls, the anti-Communism of the radical right can always appear to be an extension of the administration's doctrine to its logical conclusion—a conclusion from which, as the right would say, the administration itself draws back only from softness, inconsistency, treason, or incompetence." "The effect of this pressure from the radical right" was unmatched "by anything like comparable pressures from the left" because "a number of the most influential spokesmen

---

[6] Riesman, *Abundance for What? And Other Essays* (Garden City, N.Y.: Doubleday, 1964), p. 12.

for liberalism within the Democratic Party are now part of the administration'' and intellectuals who were more critical hesitated to express themselves because they feared the prospect of becoming powerless (Riesman 1963, 124, 117, 128).

For Riesman, therefore, the long-run effect of the "radical right" was "to shift the whole climate of political contest and discussion toward the right." He feared most the consequent rise of a spirit of militancy in the administration. "Older, more tolerant, or more acquiescent men who are not themselves militant may be influenced more than they realize by militant subordinates or critics" and in turn "press the administration toward policies . . . of responding to the nuclear stalemate by energetic non-nuclear military actions, whether in Cuba, or in South Vietnam." Such actions would moreover "antagonize much of the rest of the world." "Indeed, it may well be that this administration, far more cosmopolitan and world-minded than the country at large, may serve to isolate us from the world more than did an administration dominated by the fiscal conservatism and small-mindedness of men like George Humphrey and 'Engine Charley' Wilson." In view of the convulsions that would follow the American intervention in Vietnam, it was a prescient analysis.[7]

The Corporations, the Military, and the Radical Right

These essays of Bell and Riesman should engage our attention because they raised issues that are still largely unanswered; they opened up lines of inquiry about the "radical right" that no other social scientists at the time chose to pursue. Plainly, when Bell referred to "the managerial dispossessed" and

---

[7] Riesman 1963, pp. 124, 125. In making these criticisms Riesman prefigured much of the left-wing revisionist criticism of Kennedy's foreign policy: compare his conclusions, for example, with Richard J. Walton's in *Cold War and Counterrevolution: The Foreign Policy of John F. Kennedy* (New York: Viking, 1972), especially pp. 229–34; or with Bruce Miroff's in *Pragmatic Illusions: The Presidential Politics of John F. Kennedy* (New York: McKay, 1976), especially pp. 12–21, 36–48.

There are, however, important differences between Riesman and these subsequent critics. Unlike their portrayal of Kennedy as a virtually free agent in foreign policy, a president for whom public opinion was something to be manipulated (Miroff, *Pragmatic Illusions*, 288–92), Riesman was far more concerned with the Administration's naiveté about the depth of bellicose anticommunism in crucial segments of the public. In his account of the policymakers who led the country into Vietnam, David Halberstam tells a revealing anecdote about Riesman in this regard. At a 1961 lunch with two Administration officials who talked knowingly of the applicability of "limited-war" concepts to Vietnam, Riesman asked if they had ever been to Utah. Why Utah? they asked. He replied that "he had read a great deal about the Church of the Latter-Day Saints, and it occurred to him that his friends did not know much about America, about how deep the evangelical streak was: 'You all think you can manage limited war and that you're dealing with an elite society which is just waiting for your leadership. It's not that way at all' " (*The Best and the Brightest* [New York: Random House, 1972], p. 42).

"the military dispossessed" as key elements in the development of the contemporary American right wing, he was not basing his analysis on their numbers but on their influence; and many of Riesman's observations directly revolved around the interaction of the right-wing spokesmen on "the outside" with the policymakers of the Kennedy administration on "the inside." Both men, in other words, were emphasizing the role of elites in shaping public discourse. That was not the direction most social scientists would follow. Instead, whether they concentrated on how specific right-wing organizations attempted to achieve their objectives or on what the participants in those organizations thought, most social scientists ended up defining the significance of the right wing in terms of the organizations they studied. While the data they accumulated answered most of the questions they asked, their methods shifted the scholarly focus almost completely away from the role played in the emergence of the "radical right" by wealthy individuals and corporations, on the one hand, and by national-security bureaucrats (most notably senior military officers) on the other.

As a result of this methodological approach, a number of the important questions raised by journalists at the time were simply left unanswered in the scholarly literature appearing shortly afterward. As far as corporate links to the right wing were concerned, journalists were already pointing out the extent to which Schwarz's Christian Anti-Communist Crusade was dependent on Patrick Frawley, the head of the Schick Safety Razor Company and Technicolor, and to a lesser extent on the executives of Richfield Oil (Janson and Eismann 1963, 66–67). They further noted the number of right-wing radio commentators, notably Wayne Poucher and Dan Smoot, whose careers had benefited from the financial backing of Texas oil millionaire H. L. Hunt.[8] In response, some might argue that Hunt—and even Frawley—were isolated in their support of right-wing organizations and not representative of the larger business community. But what about the case of George S. Benson and his National Education Program?

In the twenty-five years since he had assumed the presidency of Harding College, Benson transformed a hitherto obscure fundamentalist institution in Arkansas into one of the leading centers of right-wing propaganda in the United States. By the early 1960s his National Education Program was producing high school course outlines for teaching "Americanism" that had been adopted by 300 schools, a *National Program Letter*, and perhaps most notably movies such as the widely shown *Communism on the Map*, in which, according to two journalists, "the entire world is shown turning pink and red. Only Spain and Switzerland hold out against the tide. The United States, red arrows

---

[8] Janson and Eismann 1963, pp. 132–34; Forster and Epstein 1964, pp. 133–37. For more on Hunt's political activities, see Jerome Tuccille, *Kingdom: The Story of the Hunt Family of Texas* (Ottawa, Ill.: Jameson, 1974).

circling it menacingly, bears an enormous question mark at the climax'' (Janson and Eismann 1963, 94).

There was more to Benson's operations than militant anticommunism, however. When he became president of Harding College in 1936, he had just completed missionary work in China. Upon his return to the United States he was shocked to discover that Americans had, in his words, "lost their Christian convictions and their sense of moral purpose and were listening to all manner of false prophets" (Sherwin 1963, 83). One such group of "false prophets" were the leaders of an expanding labor movement, and for the next decade Benson threw himself into various efforts to curb union power, such as the movement to prohibit the closed shop.[9] Those efforts in turn attracted the attention of industrialists from across the country. The National Education Program, which would couple its attacks on unions with denunciations of the welfare state and "democracy" in general, was launched with a personal grant of $300,000 from General Motors chairman Alfred M. Sloan. Not counting further grants from corporate-sponsored foundations (including another $300,000 from the Sloan Foundation), the NEP received major contributions from the Republic and United States Steel Corporations, Gulf Oil, and Olin-Mathieson. Finally, Benson himself enjoyed close relations with the executives of Monsanto, Swift, and perhaps most notably, General Electric.[10]

In the case of the National Education Program, then, it would be hard to disagree with the conclusion of a journalist who studied it closely: "much of the most radical right-wing literature in the country is the considered and calculated achievement, not of the lunatic fringe, but of some of the largest, most powerful, and most eminently respectable of our corporate giants."[11] Because it was not a participatory organization, however, Benson's operation attracted practically no attention from social scientists except from Bell (Bell 1963, 6, 36–37n). And the idea that sizable segments of the business community could still, after more than two decades, be fighting the moderate unions and limited welfare state created by the New Deal was an idea that few scholars at the time, regardless of their ideological perspective, were willing to accept. As a result most of them portrayed firms actively supporting the "radical right" as somehow marginal to the larger business community: family-operated enterprises, small and middle-sized manufacturers, companies located in the Midwest and the South, and so on.[12] Such conclusions simply overlooked the Na-

[9] Fred J. Cook, "The American Ultras: Aims, Affiliations, and Finances of the Radical Right," *Nation* 194 (June 30, 1962): 590.

[10] Cook, "The American Ultras," pp. 591–92; Forster and Epstein 1964, pp. 93–94.

[11] Cook, "The American Ultras," p. 589.

[12] This was certainly Lipset's view. See both his specific analysis of the membership of the national council of the John Birch Society (Lipset and Raab 1970, pp. 310–12) and his more general comments on the kinds of businessmen attracted to right-wing politics (Lipset 1964, pp. 18–19).

tional Education Program's corporate sponsors: Alfred Sloan, General Electric, and the big steel companies.

Similarly, the relationship between military officers and the "radical right" had dimensions that were seldom examined by social scientists. Most of the right-wing organizations of the late 1950s and early 1960s featured at least one retired admiral or general on their letterheads, and several such men were popular as speakers at rallies.[13] But the most sensational incident involved a military officer still on active duty, Major General Edwin A. Walker. To all appearances Walker was a model career officer: he had served with distinction in World War II and Korea, had commanded the U.S. Army troops sent by Eisenhower to maintain order in the 1957 desegregation crisis in Little Rock (ironically, in view of his subsequent activities), and by 1960 was commanding general of the 24th Infantry Division stationed in Germany. What no one yet knew was that he had joined the John Birch Society shortly after its inception. Even more ominously, Walker was using his position as commander to distribute Society literature on the base, to invite spokesmen affiliated with the Society to appear as speakers, and to launch his own attacks on various public figures including Truman, Acheson, and newscasters Eric Sevareid and Walter Cronkite.

Journalists' exposure of his activities in the spring of 1961 led directly to an investigation by the Inspector General of the Army who found that Walker had overstepped both Army regulations and the Hatch Act's prohibitions on civil servants engaging in partisan politics. He was relieved of his command and resigned from the Army in late 1961; he thereupon decided to enter the race for governor of Texas. In the spring of 1962 Walker was invited to appear before a Senate committee investigating charges that military officers were being censored. Stumbling and inarticulate in his presentation, he did not help his case by vague references to a "hidden control apparatus" within the government that was dictating a "no-win" foreign policy (Janson and Eismann 1963, 180–81). Defeated though he was in the subsequent Texas Democratic primary, he still had enough zeal to harangue the mob resisting the desegregation of the University of Mississippi in the fall of 1962 and then go on a nationwide speaking tour organized by Hargis, called "Operation Midnight Ride," in 1963. Although most commentators soon relegated Walker to the category of eccentric, President Kennedy was not quite so dismissive, one of

---

[13] At the time, both journalists critical of the military establishment and sociologists studying it agreed that, while retired officers active in politics were disproportionately right-wing, they were minor exceptions to the dominant military tradition of avoiding partisan politics. See, for example, Tristram Coffin, *The Passion of the Hawks* (New York: Macmillan, 1964), p. 189; Morris Janowitz, *The Professional Soldier: A Social and Political Portrait* (Glencoe, Ill.: Free Press, 1960), p. 347.

the reasons he privately aided the filming of *Seven Days in May* which depicted an attempted military coup.[14]

Bringing in the Kennedy administration opens up yet another largely unexplored dimension of the relationship between the professional military and the right wing, a dimension brought to the fore by the controversial Fulbright memorandum of 1961.[15] That summer, as chairman of the Senate Foreign Relations Committee, J. William Fulbright sent a memorandum to Defense Secretary Robert McNamara detailing incidents in which right-wing speakers had participated in programs either organized by officers or using the facilities of the armed forces. These had occurred because of a 1958 National Security Council memorandum that called on commanders to utilize the personnel and facilities under their direction to "arouse the public to the menace of Communism." A broad interpretation of the directive had led, to take only a few examples from 1960 and 1961, to a series of "strategy-for-survival" conferences at various cities in Arkansas featuring Benson, which were attended by members of the National Guard and Reserve units; to Project Alert, organized by the chief of naval air training at the Pensacola base, which featured a variety of speakers from Benson's National Education Program; and to a Schwarz school held at the Glenview, Illinois, naval air station with the cooperation of base commanders. The result of the Fulbright memorandum was a directive from McNamara that (1) forbade officers to speak on partisan topics or express views "contrary to established national policy," (2) forbade them from appearing at programs where others were expressing such views, (3) forbade the use of facilities or personnel for such programs unless they were sponsored "by responsible organizations," and (4) forbade the sponsorship of such programs unless authorized by the Secretary of Defense. At the same time, however, McNamara delegated to local commanders the responsibility for meeting these criteria.

Even ignoring the point that each local commander could use his discretion in interpreting it, the McNamara directive contained fundamental ambiguities: What views were "contrary to established national policy"? What was a "responsible organization"? McNamara himself tried to make clear that the Defense Department did not oppose military participation in programs that met its standards, and he specifically praised the work of the Institute for American Strategy (IAS) and the Foreign Policy Research Institute of the University of Pennsylvania. But it was the role of both those organizations in conducting

[14] Arthur M. Schlesinger, Jr., *Robert Kennedy and His Times* (Boston: Houghton Mifflin, 1978), p. 450.

[15] The fullest account of the Fulbright memorandum and its implications, on which my interpretation is based, can be found in Fred J. Cook, *The Warfare State* (New York: Macmillan, 1962), pp. 263–65, 268–71, 310–19.

seminars at the National War College under the auspices of the Joint Chiefs of Staff that helped trigger Fulbright's memorandum in the first place.

Bell was quite right to point out that in their presentations neither the IAS nor the Pennsylvania group discussed domestic politics and policies, nor did they resort to conspiratorial theories to explain setbacks to American foreign policy (Bell 1963, 5). Fulbright was equally correct, however, to emphasize that both groups did take a view of the world that precluded the possibility of any meaningful coexistence with Communist states and instead emphasized the necessity for preparing for a period of "protracted conflict." They favored a "forward strategy" including the use of covert operations inside Communist-held territory and the use of nuclear weapons to ensure an eventual Communist defeat. Was there not therefore a danger, the senator inquired, in having such organizations operate with the endorsement of military leaders at the highest levels, since such "relationships may give one particularly aggressive view a more direct and commanding influence upon military and civilian concepts of strategy than is desirable?"[16] Fulbright must have wondered (as Riesman certainly did) about the degree to which that "forward strategy" had become "established national policy" under the Kennedy administration. If it had not, why were its advocates allowed to continue their programs under the auspices of the Joint Chiefs of Staff? Was the entire relationship the result of a national-security bureaucracy "out of control"? Or was it instead the result of a bureaucratic trade-off between liberal civilians and conservative military leaders with their powerful business and political allies?

The issues raised by the financial support major corporations gave the National Education Program and the various ways the military endorsed right-wing organizations come to the very heart of the scholarly analysis of the American right wing. Throughout the entire period covered by this book, many social scientists have noted the tendency to exaggerate the right wing's importance, whether on the part of anxious liberals, trendy journalists, or of course right-wing activists themselves. It might at first seem that in no other period was such exaggeration greater than in the late 1950s and early 1960s, at least as measured by the criteria social scientists typically used. Most of the organizations of the period soon collapsed; the John Birch Society survived but at the price of virtual isolation from the political mainstream; and Barry Goldwater was overwhelmingly repudiated at the polls. Yet the briefest glance at the political phenomena of the 1980s—the personnel of the Reagan administration, the leadership of various right-wing interest groups and political-action committees, the institutionalization of a right-wing intellectual community—would suggest that in a more profound way the "radical right" of the late 1950s and early 1960s had tremendous durability. The durability of the right wing in turn has had many sources, not the least of which has been

---

16 J. William Fulbright, as quoted in Cook, *The Warfare State*, p. 310.

its access to funding from wealthy individuals and corporations and the continuing respect it has received from segments of the national-security bureaucracy, including the military, intelligence agencies, and law-enforcement officials. Unfortunately, the social scientists who interviewed members of now-defunct organizations or extrapolated from survey data the narrowness of Goldwater's support shed little light on those crucial developments. To their credit, Bell and Riesman did. With their focus on elite interaction and institutional bases of power, both scholars provided a framework for understanding the remarkable persistence of the American right wing.

Six

Sociological and Psychological Profiles
of Right-Wing Activists

THE PUBLICATION OF *The Radical Right* in 1963 was followed by the appearance of two more collections of essays on the right wing: the April 1963 number of the *Journal of Social Issues*, "American Political Extremism in the 1960s," edited by Harold M. Proshansky and Richard I. Evans; and the 1969 volume, *The American Right Wing: Readings in Political Behavior*, edited by Robert A. Schoenberger. Together with a scattering of other books and articles, these collections constitute the existing scholarly literature on the right-wing activities of the late 1950s and early 1960s. Unlike most of those writing in *The Radical Right*, almost all the subsequent contributors to the literature based their conclusions on primary research they themselves had conducted. Perhaps because of that, their methods and conclusions—unlike the generalizations in *The Radical Right* that attracted swarms of critics—have largely gone unexamined. In a number of cases, moreover, subsequent analysts have selected one or two of these studies for citation (and disregarded the rest) not because they were better designed but because their conclusions were more agreeable. The justification for the close analysis that follows, therefore, is that only by intensively examining each study and comparing it with the others can we begin to see the variation in the way these social scientists gathered their data, a variation that makes it difficult to reconcile their conclusions and in some cases impossible to regard these studies as more than merely suggestive.

These difficulties, it must be emphasized, reflect less on the scholarly competence of the various authors than on the unique problems they faced in gathering data. In the first place they were aware, as one of them noted, of "the ambiguities both in abstract a priori definitions of ideological propensity" (such as had, for example, characterized much of the early work on personality and political behavior) and "in the passive self-definition occasionally employed by pollsters." So they tended to adopt an alternative approach: an examination of "the membership and/or known supporters of organizations which exist to aggregate and channel the actors themselves" (Schoenberger 1969, 281). Such empirical examinations of the beliefs of members of organizations had the further advantage of avoiding another error: the assumption (as another researcher put it) that "what the organization stands for is . . .

representative of the views of the membership'' so that ''the individual member is assigned an 'ideology by proxy' '' (Grupp 1969, 84).

Given the suspiciousness of many of the members of right-wing organizations, however, and their particular hostility toward academic social science, it was often impossible for the researchers to sample the members systematically. In one study, of those attending one of Schwarz's anti-Communist schools, ''about forty people refused to be interviewed'' and ''since these refusals often were accompanied by invective and accusations of subversive intent, it is likely that the most extreme members of the audience are underrepresented in our sample'' (Wolfinger et al. 1969, 16). In another case, the researcher was forced to use an intermediary to distribute and collect questionnaires addressed to members of the John Birch Society (Grupp 1969, 85). Rather than distribute questionnaires, of course, the researchers could study the organization from within by themselves becoming participants, but this created further dilemmas. One scholar who became a participant-observer put it this way: ''If you want the good will of the people you are studying, you must adopt portions of their rhetoric and style. In my particular case, this meant I had to pretend to believe in political dogmas that I did not believe in, and participate in activities that I had not participated in before'' (McNall 1975, 8). For many scholars, apparently, the psychological strain of such duplicity was too high a price to pay.

To make some sense out of these empirical studies of supporters and/or members of right-wing organizations in the early 1960s and to see whether they confirmed any of the hypotheses in *The Radical Right*, let us divide the material into two categories. The first emphasizes *sociological* variables: not only the usual background variables (age, sex, income, occupation, education, partisan affiliation, and so on) but also the factors specifically mentioned in *The Radical Right*—religion (to see to what extent a ''fundamentalist'' connection could be confirmed), ''status'' (however defined), and residential mobility (to explore any possible links between right-wing activism, population growth, and social disorganization). Under the second category fall those studies that emphasize *psychological* variables: the attitudinal variables associated with personality structure, especially those associated with the ''authoritarian personality'' (punitive feelings toward deviants, racial and religious prejudice, alienation from the political system); and finally the role of their families in the early socialization of these right-wing activists.

The Right-Wing Activists of the Early 1960s: Sociological Profiles

Turning first to the analyses that focus upon sociological variables, all of the studies concur that the members of right-wing organizations of the early 1960s

were disproportionately white. Of the two other obvious demographic categories, sex and age, no researcher empirically tested whether men or women
were more likely to participate in right-wing activity although J. Allen
Broyles, who studied the John Birch Society at close range, estimated that
two-thirds of its membership was female (Broyles 1964, 46–47). The widespread impression that right-wing activists were if not elderly at least in advancing middle age was confirmed in four studies: by Raymond Wolfinger and
his associates, in their sample of participants in Schwarz's anti-Communist
school in the Bay Area; by Mark Chesler and Richard Schmuck, who as par-
ticipant-observers sat in on a small discussion group affiliated with Schwarz's
Crusade; by Scott McNall, in his analysis of the members of the Freedom
Center, a local right-wing organization in Eugene, Oregon; and by Ira Rother
who found his sample of "rightist" activists in the Pacific Northwest to be
older than his sample of "nonrightist" activists.[1]

On the other hand, Fred Grupp found his sample of national members of the
John Birch Society to be surprisingly young—"the average Bircher is forty-
one years old"; and Barbara Stone reached very similar conclusions in her
study of members in California (Grupp 1969, 86; Stone 1974, 188). Though
much of this data is nonsystematic and other investigators did not ask the question, Stanley Mosk's impression of the foot-soldiers of the "radical right" as
"little old ladies in tennis shoes" received general empirical confirmation—
though, ironically, not in the case of the John Birch Society!

The study of the possible correlation of the closely related variables of income, occupation, and education—what might in shorthand be described as
the "class" variables—with right-wing activism began with Lipset's essay
written for *The Radical Right*. Because the activities of the John Birch Society
were just breaking upon the national consciousness at the time he was preparing his essay, he was unable to analyze the members themselves. Instead,
Lipset relied on survey data to uncover public attitudes toward the Society;
and he found that, at least in California, the tiny minority who "supported"
the Society were not only more likely to be Republicans and live in the southern part of the state but were also more educated and with higher incomes than
were "opponents": indeed, among Republicans greater education correlated
positively with support for the Society (Lipset 1963a, 354, 357).

Although they had far more data at their disposal, the scholars who followed
Lipset disagreed among themselves, reaching several different conclusions
about the socioeconomic base of the right-wing activism of the early 1960s.
Here, perhaps more than in any other case, methodological problems made it
difficult for researchers to be convincing. If the optimum research design was
to interview a random sample of participants in right-wing activities or mem-

[1] Wolfinger et al. 1969, pp. 17–18; Chesler and Schmuck 1963, p. 18; McNall 1975, p. 140;
Rohter 1969, p. 220.

bers of right-wing organizations, then none of these studies achieved it. In his analysis of New York Conservative party members in the Rochester area, Robert Schoenberger came closest, though he arbitrarily restricted his sample to male Conservatives. The Wolfinger group could never be quite sure that their undergraduate interviewers had interviewed participants at random or that their returned questionnaires were representative; even though the demographic characteristics of both samples matched, it is possible that both contained a bias in favor of upper-income, highly educated respondents (Wolfinger et al. 1969, 16). The same problem confronted Sheilah Koeppen, one of Wolfinger's students, who conducted her own study of another Schwarz "school" (Koeppen 1969a, 51). Grupp was dependent on a third party who distributed and collected his questionnaires for him; he had no control over the sample; and the validity of his response rate (35 percent) could not be confirmed by cross-checking it against interviews, as could that of the Wolfinger group (Grupp 1969, 8). The other studies had other problems: the group in which Chesler and Schmuck participated, for example, consisted only of ten to fifteen people, possibly too small to be representative of anything (Chesler and Schmuck 1963, 18). McNall's control group of "rightists" not affiliated with the Freedom Center had for unexplained reasons a very different profile from Rohter's sample, taken in a very similar environment in the Pacific Northwest (McNall 1975, 139; Rohter 1969, 200, 220).

Where does all this leave us? In terms of solid evidence pointing in any one direction, not very far. Taking the various studies together, and without attempting to reconcile the data further, we are left with the following disparate conclusions. Participants in right-wing activities were broadly "upper middle class" in the following areas: in California, members and supporters of the John Birch Society (Lipset and Stone), and nationally, members of the Society (Grupp); in California, those attending Schwarz's anticommunist schools (Wolfinger et al., Koeppen); in New York, members of the Conservative party (Schoenberger).[2] On the other hand, participants in right-wing activities were broadly "lower middle class" in the following areas: in the Midwest, those attending a discussion group affiliated with Schwarz's Crusade (Chesler and Schmuck); in Oregon, participants in the Freedom Center (McNall); in the East, members of the John Birch Society (Grupp).[3] Some of these contradictory conclusions may be the result of regional variations; but two studies using similar measurements and conducted in similar areas reached opposite conclusions (McNall and Rohter).[4]

Amid all this confusion, the reader may be heartened to be told that there was one characteristic of these individuals—a characteristic often correlated

[2] Lipset 1963a, pp. 354–57; Stone 1974, pp. 189–90; Grupp 1969, pp. 93–96; Wolfinger et al. 1969, pp. 17–19; Koeppen 1969a, pp. 53–54; Schoenberger 1969, p. 295.

[3] Chesler and Schmuck 1963, pp. 18–19; McNall 1975, p. 144; Grupp 1969, p. 101.

[4] Compare McNall 1975, pp. 143–46, and Rohter 1969, pp. 219–20.

with income, occupation, and/or education—on which all of those studying them agreed, and that was their partisan affiliation. The participants in these right-wing organizations were overwhelmingly, massively Republicans.[5] The problem was that, aside from the increasingly obvious point that the Republican party organization would be more susceptible to "radical-rightist" influence than would that of the Democrats, it was not at all clear where this conclusion led. While political scientists liked to stand on it in a morass of unsubstantiated hypotheses and conflicting data,[6] sociologists and historians were more skeptical of its overall utility. Hofstadter in fact dismissed it as one of those truths that will "go ringing down the corridors of time unchallenged and unimpaired . . . but do not offer an arresting new idea to our store of understanding." "What would be most pertinent," he continued, "would be to find out just what characteristics divide those Republicans who have joined the extreme right from those who believe that it is a menace to the body politic" (Hofstadter 1965b, 86n).

Let us now turn to the hypotheses raised directly (or indirectly) in *The Radical Right*. Though he was more interested in examining "the life-style and values of Protestant fundamentalism" than in locating it theologically, Bell had certainly suggested that participants in right-wing activities in the early 1960s might be disproportionately fundamentalist Protestants. In general, the empirical studies validated this putative right-wing fundamentalist connection. Whether they measured "fundamentalism" doctrinally or denominationally, most researchers found fundamentalists to be significantly overrepresented among members of right-wing groups.[7] The major dissent came from Broyles, who found no distinctive fundamentalist component, or for that matter much active religious affiliation, in the members of the John Birch Society he interviewed.[8]

Fundamentalist doctrine, it will be recalled, was linked by Bell to a broader worldview once held by the middle classes. What "the radical right" seeks to defend, he added, "is its fading dominance, exercised once through the institutions of small-town America, over the control of social change" (Bell 1963, 12). To test that observation empirically, several researchers asked their samples of right-wing activists the place of their birth: were they disproportionately from small towns? The Wolfinger group found no difference between

[5] Wolfinger et al. 1969, p. 19; Koeppen 1969a, p. 55; Grupp 1969, p. 99; McNall 1975, p. 151. The obvious exception would of course be the New York Conservatives at this time (though subsequently there would be a Republican-Conservative rapprochement in that state).

[6] See, for example, Koeppen 1969b, p. 78.

[7] Wolfinger et al. 1969, pp. 38–40; Grupp 1969, pp. 90–93; Stone 1974, p. 191; Chesler and Schmuck 1963, p. 19; Chesler and Schmuck 1969, p. 183; Rohter 1969, pp. 208–9.

[8] Broyles 1964, pp. 121–22. In addition, Koeppen minimized the point, remarking that the number of fundamentalists the Wolfinger group had uncovered was "small" (Koeppen 1969b, p. 79); and McNall found that while the Freedom Centerites were fundamentalist, his sample of other "rightists" was difficult to classify (McNall 1975, pp. 147–50).

their sample and one drawn from the general population (Wolfinger et al.
1969, 36–37). On the other hand, Chesler and Schmuck, in a second study of
midwestern activists, found these "superpatriots" to have come disproportionately from farm families; and McNall found that about 70 percent of both
his Freedom Centerites and his contrasting sample of other "rightists" had
been raised on farms or in small towns. He added quite sensibly that this may
have been due to the advanced age of his Centerite sample, and he doubted
that if a sample of the general population in the same age range were taken,
the proportions would have been much different (Chesler and Schmuck 1969
189–90; McNall 1975, 141).

The overrepresentation of fundamentalist Protestants in right-wing organizations was matched by the underrepresentation of adherents of theologically
liberal Protestant views and of Jews (see, for example, Grupp and Newman
1973). On those points the existing studies are clear; what is less clear is the
role of Roman Catholics. Welch had claimed that half of the John Birch Society was Catholic, and in his analysis of the Society included in *The Radical
Right*, Alan Westin was among the first to raise the possibility of "an unprecedented coalition of Catholic and Protestant right-fundamentalists" (Westin
1963, 210, 218). Lipset had found Catholic Republicans in California more
supportive of the Society than Protestant Republicans or any religious category of Democrats.[9] Grupp concluded that, nationally, Catholics were represented in the John Birch Society membership in almost exact proportion to
their percentage of the population; but closer analysis of this data reveals that
in both the East and the Midwest they were overrepresented, and in the East
considerably so.[10]

On the other hand, the Wolfinger group found Catholics underrepresented
among those attending the Bay Area School (Wolfinger et al. 1969, 18). Since
Catholics in California were overwhelmingly Democratic while those attending the school were predominantly Republican, however, the proper test
would seem to be to see whether Catholic *Republicans* were overrepresented
at the school. It may also be, however, as the Wolfinger group suggested, that
the militant Protestant style of the Christian Anti-Communist Crusade, like
that of other overtly fundamentalist organizations, antagonized Catholics in a
way that the vaguer religiosity of the John Birch Society did not.[11] Finally, for

[9] Lipset 1963a, p. 357; for his final thoughts on the Catholic role in the John Birch Society, see
Liset and Raab 1970, pp. 261–63, 297, 300.

[10] In fact Catholics, who comprised 38 percent of the eastern region's total population, constituted 48 percent of Grupp's sample (Grupp 1969, pp. 92, 101). My computations of the Catholic
percentage of each region's population as of 1965 (the year in which Grupp collected his data) are
based on the statistics in the *1966 National Catholic Almanac* (Garden City, N.Y.: Doubleday,
1966), pp. 474–76.

[11] Wolfinger et al. 1969, p. 19. Similar observations are made in Broyles 1964, pp. 121–24,
and McNall 1975, pp. 96–99.

the two organizations in which impressionistic evidence suggests a significant Catholic role—the Young Americans for Freedom and the New York Conservative party—the researchers studying them did not ask the question.

Except perhaps for Bell's concept of "the dispossessed," "status politics" did not play a prominent part in the 1963 additions to *The Radical Right*.[12] But, as we have seen, it certainly formed the core of the original 1955 essays written for *The New American Right*. Never very precisely defined, "status politics" was supposed to differ from "class politics" or "interest politics" insofar as (in Hofstadter's words) it represented "the clash of various projective rationalizations" rather than "the clash of material aims and needs," or insofar as (in Lipset's words) it involved the "resentments" of those "who desire to maintain or improve their social status" rather than efforts to advocate or oppose the redistribution of income (Hofstadter 1955b, 43; Lipset 1955, 168). The major emphasis in the original volume, it should be added, was on the "protective rationalizations" and the "resentments" of those moving up, not down, the social scale.

In the years following the appearance of *The New American Right*, other social scientists tried to redefine the general concept of "status" to make it more easily subject to empirical proof. The first such attempt conflated "class" (as measured by income and occupation) with "status" and tried to measure social mobility by placing it in an intergenerational context. Was there, in other words, any correlation between whether an individual exceeded (or failed to achieve) his father's occupational prestige level and/or income, and his participation in right-wing activity? Of the five empirical studies mentioned here that undertook such an analysis, the Wolfinger group and Schoenberger did not find any such correlation, Chesler and Schmuck and Rohter did, and McNall was inconclusive.[13]

A second, more promising approach replaced the vague "status politics" model with the somewhat more precise "status inconsistency" model already developed by sociologists.[14] "Status" here referred to any of a number of vertical hierarchies of prestige: income, occupation, education, ethnicity, and so on. There was a tendency, so this argument held, for these "statuses" to be consistent, to "crystallize" (in the words of one author) as in the obvious example of the Harvard-educated president of a large corporation whose ancestor had signed the Declaration of Independence. But what about those in-

[12] Even Bell was moving toward a broader definition of "status" than he and the others had formulated in the mid-1950s. The year after *The Radical Right* appeared, for example, he defined "the dispossessed" as "those who have lost not wealth, or even immediate political power and status, but a comfortable sense of historical position in the world." Daniel Bell, in the symposium "Some Comments on Goldwater," *Partisan Review* 31 (Fall 1964): 586.

[13] Wolfinger et al. 1969, p. 32; Schoenberger 1969, p. 294; Chesler and Schmuck 1969, pp. 189–90; Rohter 1969, pp. 221–22; McNall 1975, p. 32.

[14] For our purposes here, the key work is Lenski 1954.

dividuals whose statuses had not (yet) crystallized: the Italian immigrant who had become a millionaire with only a smattering of education, or conversely the scion of an established family who ended up as a salesman? What were the behavioral consequences of the psychological strains that such individuals experienced? As it developed the "status inconsistency" model came to be used to account for a very wide range of behavior; at the same time, the model was criticized for explaining very little.[15] How useful was "status inconsistency" as an explanation for participation in right-wing activity?

Studies that raised this question reached no single conclusion. The Wolfinger group found no greater status inconsistency among those attending the Bay Area School than in a sample of the general population (Wolfinger et al. 1969, 35). Schoenberger also found no significant level of status inconsistency in his sample of New York Conservatives (Schoenberger 1969, 295). On the other hand, Chesler and Schmuck found that their sample of midwestern "super-patriots," especially at the middle-income level, tended to have incomes higher than their education might seem to warrant (Chesler and Schmuck 1969, 188). The possible implications of such "inconsistency" between education and occupation were further developed by Gary Rush, whose analysis of a sample of Oregonians suggested that low educational levels combined with high occupational and income levels might predispose individuals to what he called "right-wing extremism."[16] In 1970 Lipset approached the problem from a different direction. Even if right-wing activists were more affluent and had more education than the general public, he noted, that did not eliminate the possibility of status inconsistency. He pointed out that, as compared to their liberal-activist adversaries, right-wing activists had typically spent fewer years in school, attended less prestigious institutions, and were more likely to major in "technical" subjects. Such differences, he speculated, might well give them feelings of inferiority and thus the sense that their education was "inconsistent" with their occupation and income (Lipset and Raab 1970, 322–24).

Another possible "status inconsistency" is between occupation and income, on the one hand, and ethnicity on the other. David Westby and Richard Braungart found that members of the Young Americans for Freedom were far more likely to come from low-income, low-occupational status but high-eth-

[15] The sociological literature on "status inconsistency" is immense. See, as examples of early critiques, William F. Kenkel, "The Relationship between Status Consistency and Politico-Economic Attitudes," *American Sociological Review* 21 (June 1956): 365–68; Dennis Kelly and William J. Chambliss, "Status Consistency and Political Attitudes," *ASR* 31 (June 1966): 375–81; and Donald J. Treiman, "Status Discrepancy and Prejudice," *American Journal of Sociology* 71 (May 1966): 651–64.

[16] Rush 1967. For a more complex model of the relationship between "status inconsistency" and right-wing attitudes, see the study based on 1964 Survey Research Center data on public attitudes toward the John Birch Society: Hunt and Cushing 1970.

nic status backgrounds (British, German, Scandinavian) than were a comparable sample of Students for a Democratic Society, whose parents made more money and held more prestigious jobs but were disproportionately of eastern European ancestry (Westby and Braungart 1970).

No scholar of this period tried more conscientiously to apply the various status hypotheses to the "radical right" of the early 1960s than did Ira Rohter; in that sense his work represents the most important empirical confirmation of the "status politics" model of *The New American Right*. Attempting to avoid previous definitions of the "radical right" that tried to "combine ideologies, appeals, and sociological characterizations," he made his own precise definition: it consisted of those who believed that "the United States is deeply in the grip of a massive Communist conspiracy which has significant influence" (Rohter 1969, 194, 195). He then administered a series of structured interviews to samples of "rightist" and "nonrightist" letter-writers and petition-signers. His findings were, first, that rightists were overwhelmingly committed to traditional values against modernity; and second, that they were far more mobile in status, both upward and downward, than the comparable group of "nonrightists," though the overall trend was downward (Rohter 1969, 223–26). It thus seemed logical to Rohter that these individuals participated in activities that emphasized anti-Communism to regain the status they felt they were losing.

In fairness to Rohter it should be noted that he regarded neither traditionalism nor status frustration as sufficient explanations for right-wing behavior and, as we shall see shortly, emphasized the importance of psychological variables. He did not, as had the original contributors to *The New American Right*, simply create hypotheses and then deduce who would be "radical rightists" from them without the benefit of corroborative data; and his use of "status" explanations bore a clear relationship to the data he had collected. Still, while there is no reason to question his evidence, its usefulness is another matter; and in reviewing his work it is hard to forget the doubts expressed over the original *New American Right*. Rohter included not only those who were measurably, "objectively," rising or falling in status ("the newly arrived" and "the decliners," in his words), but also those who *felt* themselves losing status, including within that group those who saw their traditional values threatened, since "a dispute over values also becomes a contest for prestige and social position" (Rohter 1969, 213–14, 215–17). He thus succeeded in covering all possible contingencies, but weakened the explanatory power of his model.

The final sociological variable to be considered is residential mobility. In *The Radical Right* Lipset was impressed by the fact that right-wing activity seemed to be greatest in areas of rapid population growth. Journalists had already observed that fast-growing states such as California, Texas, and Florida contained a disproportionate number of members of the John Birch Society and of right-wing activists in general. As a sociologist Lipset was also influenced by the general theoretical perspective coming to be known as the "mass society" thesis, which (in the words of McNall) maintained that "the movements or organizations which people join are a means of handling the disorganizations in their environment. In the mass society those old settings in which the individual has received support for his ego . . . are fragmented. The intermediate groups which spring up in the mass society are a direct response to the social needs of the isolated person."[17] Further, those advocating this thesis argued that "extremist" politics were characteristic of areas experiencing the social disorganization with which rapid population growth was closely connected.[18] Thus it was tempting for social scientists to use the "mass society" thesis to account for the concentration of right-wing activity in California in the fast-growing southern portion of the state.

In his contribution to *The Radical Right*, Lipset did exactly that. He not only attributed southern Californians' relatively greater support for the John Birch Society to their region's rapid growth but also raised the possibility that Birch supporters were more likely to be recent migrants to the state (Lipset 1963a, 362–63). The empirical studies that immediately followed Lipset agreed with him there might well be a correlation between rapid growth and right-wing activity but were unsure exactly what it was. The Wolfinger group, for example, had no data showing whether rightists in fast-growing areas were "rootless newcomers" (as Lipset had implied) or "discomfited old-timers" (Wolfinger et al. 1969 [but originally published in 1964], 45). Several years later (after 1964), in an article coauthored with another political scientist, Wolfinger concluded that neither new arrivals to California nor those moving around within the state were disproportionately right-wing, and that there was in fact no clear correlation between areas of population growth and areas of right-wing activity (Wolfinger and Greenstein 1969, esp. 79–80). Lipset then backed away from his original argument.[19]

[17] McNall 1975, p. 125. McNall here was rephrasing the arguments of the best-known synthesis of this view: William Kornhauser, *The Politics of Mass Society* (Glencoe, Ill.: Free Press, 1959).

[18] Kornhauser, *The Politics of Mass Society*, pp. 143–50. The early and influential critique of this thesis—Joseph R. Gusfield, "Mass Society and Extremist Politics," *American Sociological Review* 27 (February 1962): 19–30—does not deal with this aspect.

[19] Lipset and Raab 1970, pp. 303–4. Outside of the case of California, attempts to confirm Lipset's hypothesis were suggestive but inconclusive. In another study they conducted, for example, Chesler and Schmuck found a disproportionate number of right-wing letter-writers from states with fast-growing populations and from middle-sized communities that were "experiencing the greatest percentage of recent influx from more rural areas and from central cities" (McEvoy, Chesler, and Schmuck 1967). McNall also found that, in the case of a Birch Society–sponsored letter-writing campaign, the residences of the writers did correlate with various indicators of "social disorganization." In his larger study of the Freedom Center, on the other hand, he found that such indicators were insufficient to explain membership in the organization (McNall 1975, pp. 121–38).

The Right-Wing Activists of the Early 1960s:
Psychological Profiles

Turning now to analyses utilizing psychological variables—and many of the
studies discussed here used them as well as sociological variables—one is
struck again by the difficulty of comparing studies that employed what were
often very different methods and by the divergence in their conclusions. It
would seem, for example, that one of the unifying characteristics of members
of the "radical right" of this period was their fear of internal "subversion,"
of a supposed Communist movement secretly operating within the United
States and controlling major institutions; indeed, for Rohter as for others, such
convictions defined the "radical right." Not surprisingly, most of the empirical studies mentioned here—Wolfinger's, Koeppen's, and McNall's, for example—found such convictions in those they sampled.[20] But Schoenberger
found that his sample of Conservative party members was not particularly concerned about internal "subversion" (Schoenberger 1969, 287–90). And, in
what is perhaps the single most astounding finding in all these studies, Grupp's
sample of members of the John Birch Society were not that concerned about
"subversion" either (Grupp 1969, 106)!

Probably because of its salience in the study of the "radical right," attitudes
toward internal "subversion" were measured by more researchers than attitudes on any other subject. The research on attitudes (which remains to be
discussed), therefore, while suggestive, is fragmentary. On the question of
tolerance for dissent, for example, the results are quite mixed. Wolfinger and
his associates could draw no firm conclusions about their sample; Koeppen
found less support for "democratic procedures" among those attending
Schwarz's school than among samples of the general public in two cities; but
Schoenberger found his Conservatives more civil-libertarian in general than a
matched sample of Republicans and not much different from a sample of
Berkeley students.[21]

In an interesting reversal of their attitudes on internal "subversion,"
Grupp's Birchers appear to have been more bellicose, more willing to intervene with military force elsewhere in the world, than the participants in
Schwarz's Bay Area School studied by the Wolfinger group (Grupp 1969,
106–7; Wolfinger et al. 1969, 22–23). As one might expect, Grupp's Birchers,
Schoenberger's Conservatives, and Chesler's and Schmuck's "superpatriots"
were hostile to most of the social and economic legislation passed since the

[20] Wolfinger et al. 1969, pp. 21–22; Koeppen 1969a, p. 55; McNall 1975, pp. 151–52.
[21] Wolfinger et al. 1969, pp. 25–26; Koeppen 1969a, pp. 67–69; Schoenberger 1969, pp. 285–
86.

1930s.[22] McNall's Freedom Center participants, on the other hand, undoubtedly because of their greater age and lower economic position, were more
sympathetic than those others to government programs in specific areas such
as medical care, housing, and employment (McNall 1975, 152–53). And
while Wolfinger's sample expressed generally conservative views, surprisingly large minorities expressed liberal views on specific measures, such as
federal aid to education (Wolfinger et al. 1969, 24).

During the years in which these studies were conducted, few topics produced a greater quantity of research in the social sciences in general, and psychology in particular, than did "authoritarianism." Though simply witnessing
the horrors perpetrated by the authoritarian regimes of the first half of the
twentieth century provided sufficient incentive to study the problem, the specific intellectual stimulus came from one of the classics of social science, *The
Authoritarian Personality*. It would take (indeed, it has taken) a small book to
describe the research inspired by that work in the fifteen years after its publication in 1950 (Kirscht and Dillehay 1967). For our purposes here, only a few
need be mentioned. Those who wrote *The Authoritarian Personality* were primarily concerned with uncovering the psychological roots of anti-Semitism.
They administered both fixed-alternative questionnaires and free-response interviews to a diverse but not necessarily adequate sample of individuals, including students, teachers, prison inmates, mental patients, members of veter-
an's organizations, and unionists.

As a means of measuring their responses, the researchers of *The Authoritarian Personality* developed their famous scales. Three of them—the Anti-
Semitism (A-S) Scale, the Ethnocentrism (E) Scale, and the Political and Economic Conservatism (PEC) Scale—measured political ideology. The most
famous of them, the Potentiality of Fascism (F) Scale, however, measured
certain personality characteristics such as conventionalism, submission, extrapunitive attitudes, tendencies toward stereotyping, preoccupation with
"toughness," cynicism, and so forth. What they found (as even many who
have never read their book know) was, first of all, that those scoring high on
the A-S Scale also scored high on the E Scale (i.e., those who were prejudiced
against Jews were also prejudiced against blacks); and second, that there was
a correlation, far lower but still positive, between high scores on either the A-
S Scale or the E Scale and on the PEC Scale.[23] And of course, those scoring

[22] Grupp 1969, pp. 104–6; Schoenberger 1969, pp. 291–93; Chesler and Schmuck 1969, pp.
171–72.

[23] In fairness to the authors of *The Authoritarian Personality*, it should be emphasized that
while they did argue that "the more conservative an individual is, the greater the likelihood that
he is ethnocentric," they also noted that "this is a probability and not a certainty. . . . The correlations are far from perfect" (Adorno et al. 1950, p. 180). Indeed, the existence of conservatives
(i.e., high scorers on their PEC scale) who were *not* ethnocentric or potentially "fascist" permit-

high on any of the three ideological scales also scored high on the F Scale. Thus, they concluded, anti-Semitism and right-wing ideology generally correlated with the "authoritarian personality" as measured on the F Scale.

The book quickly came under attack for three interrelated reasons. The research methods employed suffered from a number of glaring—in the minds of many social scientists, fatal—methodological weaknesses. In the most famous critique along these lines, Herbert Hyman and Paul Sheatsley pointed out that, among other flaws, not only were their samples unrepresentative of the population (even of the white Christian middle-class segment the authors had hoped to investigate), but the unrepresentativeness of their sample produced the very correlations they found significant. Thus, for example, a comparable group of white southerners scored high on the E Scale but not on the A-S Scale, suggesting that in their case antiblack racism was dependent not upon individual personality structure but upon regional cultural norms (Hyman and Sheatsley 1954).

Hyman and Sheatsley also noted that the researchers who produced *The Authoritarian Personality* did not control for formal education, which leads us to the second major objection of the book: that the authors' psychoanalytic training blinded them to the structural component of prejudice and "authoritarianism." It might have been, in other words, that their scales could not measure the prejudice of the educated and that the consistent association of low status and low education with prejudice and "authoritarianism" reflected responses to the subject's immediate environment rather than the dynamics of a personality structure formed in early childhood.

Finally, Shils presented the most notable ideological critique of *The Authoritarian Personality* (Shils 1954). At the time the book was written, the still-vivid memories of the Holocaust made its authors' identification of anti-Semitism, right-wing ideology, and authoritarianism eminently plausible. By the mid-1950s, however, ten years of Cold War had led most Americans to equate the Soviet Union with Nazi Germany as a threat to the nation's security and Communism with fascism as equally endangering the democratic way of life. At a more rarefied level, social scientists were increasingly impressed by the similarities between German Nazism and Soviet Communism and had begun to subsume both under the entity "totalitarianism." It was in this context that Shils challenged the biases of the authors of *The Authoritarian Personality*. They still adhered, he maintained, to an outworn nineteenth-century dichotomy of "left" and "right," ignoring what he saw as the more fundamental distinction between democracy and totalitarianism. Thus, he charged, they constructed their questionnaires and scaled them so that proto-Nazis fell at one end (he had few problems with that) but at the other end the "low scorers"

---

ted Adorno to formulate his famous distinction between "real" conservatives and "pseudo" conservatives, which of course influenced Hofstadter (see ibid., particularly pp. 675–85).

could include both sincere social democrats and advocates of totalitarian Communism.[24] These last, Shils surmised, revealed in their slavish devotion to the changing party line some of the same "authoritarian" tendencies as their "rightist" counterparts; and he complained that the researchers had ignored some of their own data and lacked the imagination to devise other measures to test this hypothesis.

During the late 1950s and early 1960s various researchers followed his suggestion. As late as 1965, various studies (admittedly using small samples) more or less confirmed *The Authoritarian Personality*'s correlations between anti-Semitism, right-wing ideology, and the "authoritarian personality." It is remarkable, however, that few left-wing "authoritarians" (even among samples of Communists) could be located. Either the F Scale simply could not measure the putative "authoritarianism" of the left, or at least in democratic countries (studies of Communist party members in Soviet-bloc countries might well have shown different results) "authoritarians" of the left did not exist.[25] In an effort to resolve some of these problems, Milton Rokeach developed a new scale—the D or Dogmatism Scale—which concentrated on cognitive style rather than ideological substance. He argued, most notably in his 1960 book *The Open and Closed Mind*, that it was the rigidity with which beliefs were held that was crucial rather than the beliefs themselves.[26]

By the time the empirical studies of the "radical right" of the early 1960s were undertaken, then, researchers had at hand not only the scales developed in *The Authoritarian Personality* but also Rokeach's alternative. They also had a choice of strategies: they could continue to pursue Shils's line of argument, accept "right-wing authoritarianism" as a valid entity and seek to locate its counterparts on "the left," or they could raise the question whether there was a correlation, at least among the individuals they were studying, between right-wing ideology/activity and "authoritarianism." Of the studies surveyed here, only one, by Edwin N. Barker, followed the first strategy. Administering a variety of tests to samples of graduate students in the New York City area and undergraduate activists at Ohio State, several years apart, he partially substantiated Shils's critique of *The Authoritarian Personality*. Yes, he concluded, there were more "authoritarians" on the right, probably because the F Scale does only measure right-wing "authoritarianism"; and, yes, using Rokeach's scales as well as a number of others one could uncover "dogmatic" leftists and centrists. But there were still far more "dogmatists" on the right,

[24] The authors of *The Authoritarian Personality* were not quite as naive on this issue as Shils implied (see particularly Adorno et al. 1950, pp. 721–23, 772–73).

[25] See the discussion in Roger Brown, *Social Psychology* (New York: Free Press, 1965), pp. 523–41.

[26] Rokeach 1960. Rokeach's book was in turn criticized as suffering from some of the same weaknesses as the earlier work: it was not clear, for example, how different his D Scale was from the earlier F Scale.

especially when the sample consisted of activists and the spectrum was widened to include both the "extreme left" and the "extreme right" (Barker 1963, 70–71). All the other researchers considered here, however, followed the second strategy and tried to find out whether the right-wingers they were studying were "authoritarian" or "dogmatic."

Before turning to the studies that uncovered particular "dogmatic" or "authoritarian" characteristics in their subjects (and some did not), it is essential to point out what conclusions can fairly be drawn from them. No association is more plausible to the ordinary person than that between certain ideas he or she finds offensive and "pathological" personality structures on the part of their advocates: during the early 1960s a wide range of otherwise well-informed observers portrayed right-wing activists as "nuts." That assumption, however, was rejected by social scientists: in the words of one summary of the literature, "on neither absolute nor relative grounds can authoritarian persons be characterized empirically as more (or less) pathological" (Kirscht and Dillehay 1967, 53). Chesler and Schmuck emphasized the "normality" of their "superpatriots": "Most of them seemed to be pleasant, considerate, and law-abiding. They were comfortable and happy with their familial relations and very much in touch with the relationships and events in their interpersonal spheres" (Chesler and Schmuck 1969, 183). Rohter also argued that "psychopathic explanations," such as the belief that "right-wing extremism is a phenomenon led and populated by embittered misfits," must be rejected (Rohter 1970, 626). A person with an "authoritarian personality," in other words, is perfectly capable of being a loving spouse and parent, a model worker, and a good citizen.

The actual attempts to find out whether the right-wing activists of the early 1960s were "authoritarian" were inconclusive. The Birchers interviewed by Broyles, Chesler and Schmuck's "superpatriots," Rohter's sample of Oregonians, and the participants in the Freedom Center analyzed by McNall were all unusually likely to exhibit at least some of the attitudes associated with the "authoritarian personality": they were, for example, likely to be "dogmatic," "closeminded," or "extrapunitive."[27] But Schoenberger found that members in his sample of New York Conservatives were no more "authoritarian" than a comparable sample of Republicans, and on some items less so (Schoenberger 1969, 284–85). And in an intensive study of a small sample of letter-writers in Dallas, Alan Elms reached a similar conclusion: his "extreme rightists"—a category including Birchers as well as those who generally believed that Communists had subverted major American institutions—were no more ethnocentric, "dogmatic," or "authoritarian" than contrasting groups of "conservative-moderates" and "liberals."[28]

[27] Broyles 1963, p. 53; and Broyles 1964, pp. 149–50, 165; Chesler and Schmuck 1969, pp. 184–85; Rohter 1969, pp. 229–34; McNall 1975, pp. 157, 160.

[28] Elms 1969. In a subsequent article, Elms made the point that the Birchers he interviewed shared with millions of other Americans both the need to understand a complicated world and the

In view of the supposed linkage between personality structure and various kinds of racial and religious prejudice—a supposition that lay at the very heart of *The Authoritarian Personality*—it is somewhat surprising that none of the researchers who studied the "radical right" tested for it. We have, for example, only tiny bits of evidence in these studies on rightists' attitudes toward Jews.[29] Attitudes toward blacks can be extracted only with the greatest difficulty, partly because no one asked exactly the same questions and partly because at the time these studies were conducted, civil rights had become such a major issue that many social scientists chose to infer attitudes toward blacks from attitudes toward public policy. In some of these studies there was a startling pro-civil-rights response. The Wolfinger group found two-thirds of those attending Schwarz's Bay Area School "opposed to the southern position on desegregation," while McNall found a surprisingly large number of Freedom Centerites supportive of governmental efforts to secure minorities equal access to employment and housing (Wolfinger et al. 1969, 24; McNall 1975, 153). Another kind of response was uncovered by Grupp who found a lack of concern among his sample of Birchers over the issue of civil rights, in spite of repeated pronouncements from national headquarters that the civil rights movement was the vanguard of the ubiquitous Communist conspiracy (Grupp 1969, 106).

There remained, of course, those right-wing activists who were openly unsympathetic to the civil rights cause. From the evidence at hand, however, there is no way of telling why they were so opposed: they may have favored the perpetuation of the existing racial hierarchy (which would be closest to actual racism); they may have favored a hierarchical society organized along nonracial lines; they may have been classical liberals sympathetic to the idea of racial equality but fearful of the extension of state power necessary to implement the civil rights agenda; or they may have seen the movement's tactics as Communist-inspired "agitation." All of these responses were made by the "superpatriots" studied by Chesler and Schmuck.[30]

Another variable sometimes associated with the "authoritarian personality," but more often with individuals in the context of a "mass society," was

hope that they could do so without extensive intellectual effort. Given the conservative political climate of Dallas, which tended to shut out alternative explanations of reality, it was completely "rational"—"functional" in terms of their personality development—for them to join the Society (Elms 1970, pp. 58–59).

[29] Chesler and Schmuck did ask their respondents about Jews and concluded that they showed a tendency to stereotype, but cautioned that "this does not mean necessarily that super-patriots were anti-Semitic" (Chesler and Schmuck 1969, p. 185). In his analysis of Californians who supported the John Birch Society, Lipset found that in general they were more prejudiced against racial minorities than were opponents of the Society but that the differences in attitudes toward Jews were relatively minor (Lipset 1963a, pp. 360–61).

[30] Chesler and Schmuck 1969, pp. 174–75. See also McEvoy's analysis of Goldwater supporters (in chapter 7).

political alienation. One analyst of the literature has summarized the prevailing argument this way:

> The alienated believe that all politicians are corrupt, that there are few important differences between what the established parties and candidates stand for, that politics are for all practical purposes, a case of 'them' trying to put 'this' over on 'us'. Thus, their alienation and negativism lead the discontented to withdraw from politics under normal circumstances; yet these same attributes increase their 'availability to groups with dictatorial ambitions.' Lacking the political restraints implied in cohesive social communities, the alienated are readied for service in mass movements 'bent on transformations of the world.' They form a natural constituency for demagogues and, therefore, may upset the stability of democratic government in the modern era.[31]

It soon became evident to many of those studying political alienation that the concept was multidimensional, including both a sense of powerlessness (or inefficacy) as well as one of distrust (or cynicism). Applying this differentiation to the studies we have been discussing, what do we find? On the distrust dimension the results are unambiguous but, given the belief of many of the respondents that the political system had been subverted, hardly surprising. Of those who addressed this problem, both Koeppen, in her analysis of those attending Schwarz's school in San Mateo, and Rohter, in his analysis of rightists in Oregon, found deep suspicion of major governmental institutions (Koeppen 1969a, 64–72; Rohter 1969, 226–27).

On the dimension of powerlessness, however, the studies differed sharply but—confirming a vast amount of other research—their conclusions divided rather neatly along class lines. In general, those (such as Wolfinger and his associates) who studied groups of a broadly "upper middle class" character found the individuals within them to have a high sense of efficacy.[32] On the other hand, researchers studying groups of a broadly "lower middle class"

---

[31] James D. Wright, *The Dissent of the Governed: Alienation and Democracy in America* (New York: Academic Press, 1976), pp. 1–2. My discussion here follows that of Wright, especially pp. 1–11.

Perhaps the most ambitious attempt to relate the concept of political alienation to the "radical right" of the early 1960s was that of Gilbert Abcarian. He first extracted certain ideological themes from rightist literature—conspiratorial thinking, fundamentalism, hostility to collectivism, and so on—and hypothesized that all of these corresponded to the psychological needs of the politically alienated. Subsequently he confirmed his hypothesis (in his mind at least) by administering a questionnaire to a sample of individuals in the Toledo area and finding that the dimensions of alienation correlated positively with each of his ideological themes. Unlike the studies discussed here, however, Abcarian did not draw his sample from either members of specific right-wing organizations or from right-wing activists generally, so the specific relevance of his conclusions remains doubtful (Abcarian and Stanage 1965; Abcarian 1971).

[32] Wolfinger et al. 1969, pp. 29–31; Koeppen 1969a, pp. 57, 77. In addition, Chesler and Schmuck found that their "superpatriots," who differed only slightly from the population as a whole, were not especially prone to feelings of powerlessness (1969, p. 183).

character (such as the small group in which Chesler and Schmuck participated or McNall's Freedom Center) found that individuals in them had a low sense of efficacy.[33]

Furthermore, the different findings of these researchers affected their emerging models of right-wing political behavior. Broadly speaking, those researchers who found that the individuals they studied were powerless tended to argue that in participating in right-wing organizations, in McNall's words, "the symbolic meaning of the action is more important than specific economic or political goals." McNall was clearer than most in drawing a direct analogy between the Freedom Center and religious institutions.[34] In contrast, the researchers who did not find the individuals they studied subjectively powerless tended to portray the membership of right-wing groups in more narrowly instrumental terms and to argue that joining a right-wing organization was, in Schoenberger's words, primarily "a legitimate means to express political and economic dissatisfactions and desires," not an "outlet for clinical and social-psychological maladjustments."[35] Alone of the researchers discussed here, Grupp raised the obvious possibility that because of the differing needs of different individuals, no one kind of motivation would predominate (Grupp 1969, 109–18).

The Sources of Right-Wing Activism: Socioeconomic Position and the Transmission of Values

Having reviewed these empirical studies of the "radical right" of the early 1960s, and having noted that the evidence points in a number of different directions, can we draw any substantive conclusions at all? Plainly the right-wing activists whom these researchers studied were not all alike. Is it possible then that they fell into two groups? At first glance, it might seem so. We might posit on the one hand a broadly "upper middle class" group, relatively young, consisting of well-integrated individuals who sought to overturn specific public policies and who had "nonauthoritarian" personality structures. The members of the New York Conservative party studied by Schoenberger would be the clearest example of this group. Then we might posit on the other hand a broadly "lower middle class" group, relatively old, consisting of isolated individuals who joined organizations to regain a lost sense of community; pre-

---

[33] Chesler and Schmuck 1963, pp. 24–25; McNall 1975, pp. 141–43. Rohter's sample also felt powerless, though he distinguished between "powerlessness" and "inefficacy" (see Rohter 1969, pp. 227–28).

[34] McNall 1975, pp. 15, 99–107. (Compare Rohter 1969, pp. 227–28; Broyles 1963, p. 55; Chesler and Schmuck 1963, pp. 26–28.)

[35] Schoenberger 1969, p. 298. This is also the implication of Wolfinger et al. 1969 and Koeppen 1969a.

occupied with a purported internal Communist threat, these individuals had clear "authoritarian" (or at least "dogmatic") tendencies. The participants in the Freedom Center studied by McNall would probably be the clearest example of that group, although the discussion group in which Chesler and Schmuck participated and the sample of activists in Oregon analyzed by Rohter would come close.

While it is possible that such a dichotomy is valid in some ultimate sense and that other studies would confirm it, those other studies do not exist. In the evidence we do have, too many bits of data simply do not fit. For example, the participants in the various schools set up by Schwarz, studied first by the Wolfinger group and then by Koeppen alone, appeared to fit the first model— but turned out to be overwhelmingly preoccupied with the "internal Communist threat." The sample of midwestern "superpatriots" studied by Chesler and Schmuck revealed certain "authoritarian" (or at least "dogmatic") tendencies but had no distinctive class or age profile and no particular feelings of alienation. The national sample of members of the John Birch Society studied by Grupp conformed very nicely to the first model—which, if we follow through on the differentiation, means that in some ways Birchers were not "radical rightists" at all!

If it turns out—at least from a reading of the evidence at hand—that the right-wing activists of this era fell into not one, or even two, but many possible categories, were there any sociological or psychological characteristics that held them together? Is it possible that right-wing activists were drawn randomly from the entire white Christian population of the United States? If not, where did they come from? The emphasis of political scientists like Koeppen on "the loyal Republicanism of the radical right" is valid as far as it goes, but it does not go very far: it fails to explain what led these individuals to become "radical rightists" in the first place. Other widely used explanations of the sources of right-wing activism, whether derived from the "authoritarian personality" literature or the many kinds of "status" theories, appear to be insufficient.

Even beyond the particular methodological flaws in individual cases, one must consider the possibility that these social-scientific studies of right-wing activists were as inconclusive as they were because they based their research on irrelevant premises. Let us try therefore to conclude this discussion by constructing an alternative explanation, using scattered insights from the studies reviewed and where necessary introducing new material. We begin with the observation that these right-wingers were Republicans. Though not especially helpful in explaining much else about right-wing activism, at least this conclusion allows us to investigate aspects of the Republican party with which these activists might have affinity.[36] One difference between the two major parties

---

[36] My argument here has been influenced particularly by Howard L. Reiter, "Gerald or Ronald?

that political scientists have noted is that, while the Democratic party is primarily a coalition of disparate groups and its viability is dependent on the accommodation of interests, the Republican party is an association of relatively homogeneous individuals and its viability is dependent on the maintenance of ideological consensus. Given this, one scholar has recently been bold enough to question openly whether much of the conceptual baggage of contemporary American political science—Americans as members of groups, political parties as group coalitions—is not in fact a model of the Democratic party and only of the Democratic party.[37] If she is correct, and an emphasis on groups and coalitions fails to explain Republican organization, then a comparable emphasis might well fail to account for right-wing activism. Insofar as right-wing activists see themselves as individuals and not as members of groups—as nothing more than ordinary "Americans"—then elaborate inquiries as to their age and sex, their place of residence, or their occupational and educational backgrounds may be largely beside the point. Moreover, moving away from a focus on the social origins of these individuals spares us from having to choose between two dubious assumptions: either that right-wingers are "irrationally" projecting their anxieties or that they are "rationally" pursuing narrowly defined economic interests.

What would seem to be a more fruitful approach would be an investigation of those cultural factors that might bring together individuals from different social backgrounds into common cause. If these individuals' location in the social structure is not a particularly useful way of understanding their right-wing proclivities, what about perceived challenges to their values? The obviousness of one point, which has been reiterated throughout this discussion, should not blind us to its potential significance: the right-wing activists of the early 1960s were reacting not only to the specific changes of the 1954–1964 decade but also to more deeply rooted transformations within society. That idea brings us back to Bell's essay, "The Dispossessed," but also requires us to look again at Chesler and Schmuck's study of midwestern "superpatriots." In that study they reached conclusions somewhat similar to Bell's, paying specific attention to the changes in norms that accompanied institutional change in modern America. They noted, for example, "the movement away from individual glorification and reward for individual effort to a priority upon cooperative and collaborative work in teams," and also a new concern for "life goals that may at times be opposed to . . . material achievement and success," a trend reflected in a new emphasis on security and "a diminution of adventurous and risk-taking behavior." The values of the "superpatriots" they studied were quite different, however. "Super-patriot ideology is clear in its con-

Winter Book on the GOP," *Nation* 222 (February 7, 1976): 135–38; and by Jo Freeman, "The Political Culture of the Democratic and Republican Parties," *Political Science Quarterly* 101, 3 (1986): 327–56.

[37] Freeman, "The Political Culture of the Parties," p. 352.

cern for the maximization of individual effort, initiative, and reward'' (Chesler and Schmuck 1969, 178, 180–81, 181–82).

Since the available evidence does not allow us to see these values as springing directly from individuals' socioeconomic position, what other structures might be creating and transmitting them? Alone among the researchers mentioned in this chapter, Rohter suggested one obvious answer: churches and families perpetuating the traditions of religious fundamentalism. Fundamentalism was in his view conducive to ''radical rightism'' for two reasons (the second to be discussed later)—but, first of all, because fundamentalism's own ''values produce an ideological proclivity to the acceptance of rightist political views'' (Rohter 1970, 638).

Those comments of Rohter appeared in 1970, and at first glance it might seem that we are being pulled back to the speculations of Danzig and Bell almost a decade before. That is not quite so; for in the years between, two developments had occurred that gave Rohter's hypothesis greater plausibility. The first was a growing recognition by social scientists that religious preference influenced political behavior independently of other variables. Thus by the late 1960s it was at least admitted as a possibility that religious fundamentalism *could* predispose individuals to right-wing politics, regardless of their socioeconomic position. The second and more important development was the work of sociologists such as Benton Johnson, who were finding that fundamentalist religion *did* predispose individuals to right-wing politics. For Johnson the core of the relationship lay in the fact that fundamentalist Protestantism, unlike the modernist tendency, still adhered to the original Calvinist idea of the calling, what Max Weber had termed ''the Protestant ethic.'' This ''ascetic Protestant idea of the calling,'' Johnson wrote, ''stressed output of effort from the individual toward the physical and social environment and markedly deemphasized the input of gratifications from the environment to the individual''; it ''constrained the believer . . . to produce and to achieve, and to curtail his interest in immediate consumption'' (Johnson 1962, 36–37). All that might help explain the emphasis the ''superpatriots'' placed on ''individual effort, initiative, and reward.''

The second reason that fundamentalism was conducive to ''radical rightism,'' Rohter argued, was that ''the culture milieu of fundamentalism produces and reinforces authoritarian personality traits,''[38] since in common with the original Protestants of the sixteenth and seventeenth centuries the fundamentalists believed that the child was innately sinful and (in the words of an earlier era) his will had to be broken. Rohter undoubtedly stressed ''authoritarianism'' too much, but few right-wing activists came from what would later

[38] Rohter 1970, p. 638. Rohter's analysis here would be strengthened by subsequent work that treated ''authoritarianism'' culturally as a way of understanding the world, rather than psychoanalytically as the result of children's conflicts with their parents (see particularly Gabennesch 1972).

be called "permissive" families. The most relevant data on this question came from the work of Lawrence Schiff, who studied the youthful right-wing activists in the Young Americans for Freedom. Significantly, though Schiff did not find his sample particularly "authoritarian," he did find them conformist and under tremendous parental pressure to work hard and to succeed. He also suggested that the one-third or more of his sample who believed they had "converted" to rightist beliefs while in college had in fact simply returned to their parents' values and directed their rebellious impulses against their peers and professors (Schiff 1964; Schiff 1966).

Far more than the initial definitions of "status politics," "fundamentalism" would seem to be helpful in accounting for the way right-wing activists could be drawn from a wide range of socioeconomic backgrounds.[39] It is of course true that fundamentalism did not characterize all right-wing activists of the era; and no scholar claimed that it did. Nonetheless, fundamentalism was one of the factors most clearly correlated with right-wing political activism in the studies done at the time; and if additional studies had been made of some of the overtly fundamentalist right-wing groups (groups such as Hargis's Christian Crusade) that correlation might have been clearer still.

Seeing a link between fundamentalism and right-wing political behavior is also useful because it points us to the potential constituency for the later manifestations of right-wing activism, particularly in the late 1970s.[40] Johnson had found that the more the lower-class fundamentalists in his sample attended their churches, the more they were pulled in a conservative (Republican) direction; the more the middle-class members attended their modernist churches, the more they were pulled in a liberal (Democratic) direction (see esp. Johnson 1964). Johnson conducted his research in the late 1950s when politics still revolved around the economic issues raised by the New Deal and less affluent men and women still had powerful emotional ties to the Democratic party. What he foresaw would be even more apparent twenty years later when the rise of divisive "cultural" issues such as abortion persuaded right-wing activists to try to reach a constituency far broader than either the proverbially frightened rich or the little old ladies in tennis shoes.

[39] It should be noted that, in spite of the attention they spent trying to find out why some individuals developed right-wing attitudes, almost no scholars investigated why some right-wing individuals became activists. Were all the activists studied "upper middle class," one could relate their activism to such well-known factors as greater information, greater self-confidence, greater leisure time, and so on; but too many of the activists investigated—notably those analyzed by Chesler and Schmuck in their first study, by Rohter, and by McNall—were not "upper middle class" at all. What induced these "lower middle class" individuals to become part of the politically active minority of Americans remains unexplained.

[40] Relevant here is the recent study by Clyde Wilcox, based on 1964 Survey Research Center data on public attitudes toward the Christian Anti-Communist Crusade. He found that no other variable (not even Republican partisanship) correlated as strongly with support as did membership in a fundamentalist denomination (Wilcox, 1987e).

Seven

Hofstadter: The "Radical Right," Fundamentalism, and the Paranoid Style

THE BEST-KNOWN SCHOLAR who tried to trace the relationship of fundamentalist religion to the "radical right" of the late 1950s and early 1960s was unquestionably Richard Hofstadter. Though he had already begun to explore what he saw as "the essentially theological concern that underlies right-wing views of the world" (Hofstadter 1963b, 134), it is in his 1965 book *The Paranoid Style in American Politics and Other Essays* that the relationship is most suggestively detailed. Most of the material in *The Paranoid Style* had originally appeared elsewhere: approximately half of it (the title essay, two essays on "pseudoconservatism," and one on the Goldwater campaign) concentrated on right-wing politics since World War II, but the other half (essays on the imperialist mood of the 1890s, the evolution of the antitrust movement, and the ideology of free-silver advocates) dealt with a much earlier period. What connected the essays, Hofstadter explained in his introduction, was that "all deal with public responses to a critical situation or an enduring dilemma." It was true, he conceded, that these essays "tell more about the milieu of our politics than about its structure. They are more centrally concerned with the symbolic aspect of politics than with the formation of institutions and the distribution of power. They focus on the way large segments of the public respond to civic issues, make them their own, put them to work on national problems, and express their response to these problems in distinctive rhetorical styles" (Hofstadter 1965b, viii).

This emphasis on milieu rather than structure did not "stem from the belief that, of the two, milieu is more important." Instead, Hofstadter felt, an emphasis on milieu was a necessary complement to the older conception of politics as "an arena in which people define their interests as rationally as possible and behave in a way calculated to realize them as fully as possible." To the present generation of historians and social scientists, however, "it has become increasingly clear that people not only seek their interests but also express and even in a measure define themselves in politics; that political life acts as a sounding board for identities, values, fears, and aspirations. In a study of the political milieu these things are brought to the surface" (Hofstadter 1965b, viii, ix).

The first part of the book, subtitled "Studies in the American Right," opened with the best-known essay, "The Paranoid Style in American Politics.'' He was not, Hofstadter cautioned at the outset, using the word ''paranoid'' in a clinical sense: ''I have neither the competence nor the desire to classify any figures of the past or present as certifiable lunatics. In fact, the idea of the paranoid style would have little contemporary relevance or historical value if it were applied only to people with profoundly disturbed minds.'' In both the accepted clinical definition and his own historical definition of paranoia, ''the feeling of persecution is central, and it is indeed systematized in grandiose theories of conspiracy''; but, while the clinical paranoid sees hostile forces ''directed specifically against him,'' the spokesman for ''the paranoid style'' sees himself as an unselfish defender of ''a nation, a culture, a way of life'' threatened by hostile forces (Hofstadter 1965b, 3–4).

''Of course the term 'paranoid style' is pejorative, and it is meant to be,'' Hofstadter freely admitted: ''the paranoid style has a greater affinity for bad causes than good.'' It was true that ''nothing entirely prevents a sound program or a sound issue from being advocated in the paranoid style''; and he hoped to underscore the distinction between ''style,'' which ''has to do with the way in which ideas are believed and advocated,'' and ''the truth or falsity of their content.'' Nonetheless, as his choice of historical illustrations would indicate, ''a distorted style is . . . a possible signal that may alert us to a distorted judgment, just as in art an ugly style is a cue to fundamental defects of taste'' (Hofstadter 1965b, 5, 6).

The essay was filled with a discussion ''of a few leading episodes in our past history in which the style emerged in full and archetypal splendor'': in the 1790s, the New England ministry's fear of the allegedly subversive activities of the secret society, the Bavarian Illuminati; in the 1820s and 1830s the widespread popular fervor against the supposed atrocities perpetrated by the Masonic Order; and throughout the nineteenth and early twentieth centuries persistent attacks on the Roman Catholic Church as the handmaiden of European despotism and the sponsor of a licentious clergy. Hofstadter concluded the essay by surveying contemporary right-wing spokesmen, with their beliefs that there was a ''conspiracy, running over more than a generation, and reaching a climax in Roosevelt's New Deal, to undermine free capitalism,'' that ''top government officialdom has been so infiltrated by communists'' that American policy has in fact been one of official treason; and that ''the country is infused with a network of communist agents . . . so that the whole apparatus of education, religion, the press, and the mass media are engaged in a common effort to paralyze the resistance of loyal Americans'' (Hofstadter 1965b, 10, 25, 26).

From all these examples Hofstadter distilled ''the basic elements in the paranoid style'': the belief not that there are conspiracies in history but that conspiracy is ''*the motive force* in historical events''; the intense conviction that the situation has reached a critical turning point; the apocalyptic sense that the struggle can only end in total victory for one side and total defeat for the other;

the image of "the enemy" as "a kind of amoral superman: sinister, ubiquitous, powerful, cruel, sensual, luxury-loving"; the urge to imitate the enemy's apparently successful tactics in one's own organizations; the "special
significance that attaches to the figure of the renegade from the enemy cause";
and "the curious leap in their argument" from the pedantic recital of facts to
conspiratorial conclusions (Hofstadter 1965b, 29–37).

Hofstadter pointed out that "the paranoid style is an international phenomenon": indeed, "the single case in modern history in which one might say that
the paranoid style has had a consummatory triumph occurred not in the United
States but in Germany." He chose American examples, he explained, because
he was a student of American history; but without pursuing it, he also raised
the possibility that "certain features of our history have given the paranoid
style more scope and force among us than it has had in many other countries
of the western world." From remarks scattered throughout the book, it is possible to draw certain conclusions as to why Hofstadter thought the paranoid
style was so prevalent in America. There is, for example, his observation that
"the paranoid disposition is mobilized into action chiefly by social conflicts
that involve ultimate schemes of values and that bring fundamental fears and
hatreds, rather than negotiable interests, into political action." There is also
his comment that the paranoid style, while "today . . . of particular interest
as it is manifest on the extreme right wing . . . is not a style of mind confined
to the right wing" (Hofstadter 1965b, 38, 6–7, 39, xi). In fact, he explained,
the antimasonic movement was aggressively egalitarian and attacked Masons
not only because of their supposed barbaric rituals but also because of their
disproportionate membership among the affluent and powerful; and, though
he hardly mentioned them at all in his essay, the same "left" orientation characterized the Populists.

What was it then in the American experience that could bring together
"right-wing" and "left-wing" movements into a common "paranoid style"
and that so easily turned public issues into "questions that involve ultimate
schemes of values"? The answer for Hofstadter, on the basis both of comments in *The Paranoid Style* as well as his previous book, *Anti-Intellectualism
in American Life*, would seem to be the pervasive influence upon American
life of evangelical Protestantism, of which twentieth-century fundamentalism
was the most militant remnant.[1] His comparison between free-silver spokes-

[1] See the extended analysis in Hofstadter 1963b, pp. 53–141, for the ways in which "the American mind was shaped in the mold of early modern Protestantism."

Recently two historians of the Revolutionary era have attempted to locate the origins of "the
paranoid style" in various eighteenth-century developments. Gordon S. Wood stresses the way
shared philosophical assumptions—the beliefs, for example, that since specific effects flow from
specific causes, "evil" policies must be the conscious work of "evil" men—gave a strident tone
to political debates on both sides of the Atlantic. James H. Hutson, on the other hand, argues that
"the paranoid style" had its beginnings in the interaction of ideology and experience, which
convinced men that freedom had to be "jealously" guarded against the abuse of political power.
Not until the new national government was fully legitimated and durable political parties offered

man William H. ("Coin") Harvey and contemporary leaders of the "radical right" brings out this point most forcefully. There runs through both, he argued,

> the tendency to secularize a religiously derived view of the world, to deal with political issues in Christian imagery, and to color them with the dark symbology of a certain side of Christian tradition. "Coin" Harvey's expectations of this profane world were based on a faith, stated quite explicitly in his later years, that social issues could be reduced rather simply to a battle between a Good and Evil influence. His almost superstitions Manicheanism, his belief that the Evil influence, if not soon curbed, would bring about a terrible social apocalypse, were not unlike the conceptions prevalent on the extreme right today. (Hofstadter 1965b, xi–xii)

It seems plausible then to say that for Hofstadter the prevalence of "the paranoid style" in American politics was due in large part to the influence of evangelical Protestantism on American culture. If in the past "the paranoid style" had characterized various spokesmen at points across the political spectrum, what now accounted for its affinity with the extreme right, with what Hofstadter had previously called "pseudoconservatism"? In his original essay, "The Pseudo-Conservative Revolt," it will be remembered, he had adapted some of the concepts of *The Authoritarian Personality* for his own purposes and had attempted to explain support for McCarthy primarily in terms of the suppressed rage of the products of upwardly mobile (and thus overconformist) immigrant families. Eight years later when *The New American Right* was reissued as *The Radical Right*, Hofstadter added "A Postscript" in which he indicated some changes in his views; two years after that, he elaborated on those changes in an essay entitled "Pseudo-Conservatism Revisited."

Though often ignored by his subsequent critics, these changes are important. In his 1963 postscript, for example, Hofstadter indicated that he was "disposed to regret" the original essay's "excessive emphasis on the clinical

---

safety-valves for the opposition, he concludes, did "paranoid" concerns shift to nonpolitical institutions such as the Masonic Order and the Catholic Church. Wood, "Conspiracy and the Paranoid Style: Causality and Deceit in the Eighteenth Century," *William and Mary Quarterly*, 3d ser., 39 (July 1982): 401–41; Hutson, "The Origins of 'The Paranoid Style in American Politics': Public Jealousy from the Age of Walpole to the Age of Jackson," in David D. Hall, John M. Murrin, and Thad W. Tate, eds., *Saints and Revolutionaries: Essays on Early American History* (New York: Norton, 1984), pp. 332–72.

Suggestive as the arguments of Wood and Hutson are, however, in my view both historians are wrong to criticize Hofstadter for omitting the eighteenth-century background. I would maintain in contrast that he was essentially correct in tracing "the paranoid style" directly back to the eschatology of the Reformation, as in his deliberate use of the phrase "the apocalypse" to describe the climax of various "paranoid" scenarios. Wood and Hutson would also have difficulty in finding nonreligious explanations for either the significance exemplars of "the paranoid style" attach to "renegades" (i.e., "converts") or for their sexual fantasies about their adversaries (Hofstadter 1965b, pp. 30, 31–32, 34–35).

side of the problem.'' He now believed that ''a good deal more might have been said on purely behavioral and historical grounds to establish the destructive and 'radical' character of pseudo-conservatism'' (Hofstadter 1963a, 84). In addition, he argued in his 1965 revision, he had overstated the role of recent-immigrant groups (and thus of the status concerns of the upwardly mobile) in contributing to the extreme right: their support for McCarthy, he now implied, might well have been a transient phenomenon of the early Cold War years (Hofstadter 1965b, 68). Finally, he indicated both in his 1963 postscript and in his 1965 full-scale revision that he had said much too little about the role of fundamentalism, which ''would now loom very large indeed'' (Hofstadter 1963a, 86).

If the first part of *The Paranoid Style in American Politics and Other Essays* has a central argument it would seem to be this: ''the paranoid style'' of the extreme right wing is due to their fundamentalist worldview, and fundamentalism's affinity for ''the paranoid style'' springs not only from its own belief system (particularly its apocalyptic and dualistic elements) but also from its association with ''status politics.'' It is essential to note, however, that in the decade that had elapsed between his initial essay on ''The Pseudo-Conservative Revolt'' (and for that matter his account of the origins of progressivism in *The Age of Reform*) and his essays in *The Paranoid Style*, Hofstadter had changed his definition of what constituted ''status politics.'' In the original essay, he had tried to distinguish between ''interest politics, the clash of material aims and needs among various groups and blocs,'' and ''status politics,'' which he had rather imprecisely defined as representing ''the clash of various projective rationalizations arising from status aspirations and other personal motives.'' In his 1963 postscript, he still insisted on the distinction but now felt that perhaps ''status politics'' was not quite the right term:

> No doubt social status is one of the things that is at stake in most political behavior, and here the right wing is no exception. But there are other matters involved, which I rather loosely assimilated to this term, that can easily be distinguished from status, strictly defined. The term ''status'' requires supplementation. If we were to speak of ''cultural politics'' we might supply part of what is missing. In our political life there have always been certain types of cultural issues, questions of faith and morals, tone and style, freedom and coercion, which become fighting issues. . . . There are always such issues at work in any body politic, but perhaps they are particularly acute and important in the United States because of our ethnic and religious heterogeneity. (Hofstadter 1963a, 82–83)

Hofstadter, Gusfield, and the Reformulation of ''Status Politics''

Interestingly, in his postscript in *The Radical Right* Hofstadter used the example of the struggle over prohibition, in which ''economic interests played the most marginal role," as an example of "cultural politics" (Hofstadter 1963a, 82–83). That same year the most influential sociological analysis of the prohibition struggle appeared: Joseph Gusfield's *Symbolic Crusade: Status Politics and the American Temperance Movement*. Gusfield gave a new meaning to the concept of "status politics," one that Hofstadter found useful in shaping his own thinking on the subject.[2]

The appeal of Gusfield's book lay first of all in the persuasive way in which he defined "status" and differentiated it from "class." Unlike the contributors to *The Radical Right*, he went directly back to Weber's original formulation. For Gusfield as for Weber a "class" consists of individuals held together by common interests in the control and allocation of goods and services: "they are subject to a similar fate on the market." A "status group," in contrast, consists of individuals who share "a common culture in the form of standards of behavior" and who seek to control the distribution of prestige. Accordingly, "class politics is political conflict over the allocation of material resources," while "status politics is political conflict over the allocation of prestige." Since status is subjective, it is dependent on reinforcement through acts that symbolize attitudes; what those engaged in "status politics" seek therefore is the use of governmental power (or often merely the symbols of legitimacy) to sanctify their subculture and to stigmatize others (Gusfield 1963, 14, 16, 18, 167–72).

Much of Gusfield's analysis was compatible with that of the authors of *The New American Right* and in fact he drew freely on Hofstadter and Lipset. Several differences between his analysis and theirs should be noted, however. First, he was far more emphatic in his rejection of the idea that cultural (or "status") conflicts were somehow subsidiary to, or calculated diversions from, economic ("class") conflicts. Second, he did not accept Hofstadter's earlier suggestion that, since "status politics" represented primarily "projective rationalizations," it was expressive in nature. Instead, he insisted, its objectives were as concrete as those of "class politics": "The crucial idea is that political action can, and often has, influenced the distribution of prestige. Status politics is an effort to control the status of a group by acts which function to raise, lower, or maintain the social status of the acting group vis-à-vis others in the society. Conflicts of status in society are fought out in public arenas as are conflicts of class" (Gusfield 1963, 1–2, 19).

"Drinking (and abstinence)," Gusfield pointed out, "has been one of the major characteristics through which Americans have defined their own cultural commitments"; and the persistent attempt in nineteenth- and early twentieth-century America to limit the consumption of alcohol formed the perfect illustration of his thesis. Though at different periods the temperance movement included Americans from different social backgrounds, in every case they linked their cause to their own subjective sense of status, seeing its prog-

---

[2] See the discussion of Gusfield in Hofstadter 1965b, pp. 87–90.

ress as affirming their sense of respectability. In the half century leading up to the Prohibition Amendment, he argued, the temperance movement narrowed its social concerns to one issue and increasingly regarded drinkers as enemies to be coerced rather than as potentially repentant victims of a social system. Since repeal in 1933, the remnants of the temperance movement have increasingly demanded the restoration of older values, attacking laws and institutions such as New Deal economic legislation and the United Nations, which have nothing to do with drinking but which represent a threatening modernity (Gusfield 1963, 3, 69–110, 149–52, 157–60).

The innovation of Gusfield's approach has to be emphasized, especially in view of the somewhat inconclusive results achieved by those of his fellow sociologists who tried to test the various "status" hypotheses empirically. If one follows Gusfield and conceives of status politics as a struggle between subcultures over the allocation of prestige, then the attempts we have reviewed that tried to measure an individual's social mobility or his or her "status consistency" become irrelevant. For the purpose of developing Gusfield's "status politics" model, what is necessary is to locate the individual in his or her subculture and to determine the nature of the current struggles between adherents of various subcultures. That takes us back to Johnson's empirical investigations into the relationship of religious belief on political behavior and forward to Hofstadter's more general discussion of fundamentalism and right-wing politics.

Hofstadter's discussion of the subject in *The Paranoid Style* was similar to and undoubtedly influenced by Bell's essay on "the dispossessed." Like Bell in defining fundamentalism "in a rather extended way to describe a religious style rather than firm doctrinal commitments," Hofstadter pointed in *The Paranoid Style* to the fundamentalist background of right-wing spokesmen such as Schwarz, Hargis, and (with some qualifications) even Welch. For all of them, Hofstadter remarked, "the Manichean conception of life as a struggle between absolute good and absolute evil and the idea of an irresistible Armageddon have been thinly secularized and transferred to the cold war. The conflict between Christianity and communism is conceived as a war to the death, and Christianity is set forth as the only adequate counterpoise to the communist credo." This adaptation of their apocalyptic and dualistic themes to the ongoing international struggle helped the fundamentalists immeasurably, he added, for their "anti-communist crusade brings lavish outpourings from right-wing foundations and from some of the nation's largest business firms" (Hofstadter 1965b, 72, 74, 81). Moreover, their new emphasis on anticommunism made it possible for these militant Protestants to unite for the first time with like-minded Catholics, "who share a common puritanism and a common mindless militancy on what they imagine to be political issues, which unite them in opposition to what they repetitively call Godless communism" (Hofstadter 1963b, 141).

Hofstadter's attempt to explain the role of "fundamentalism" in determining positions on domestic issues was more nuanced than is usually remembered. He never maintained that all fundamentalists were supporters of the right wing: some, he noted, "interpret their religious commitment as a reason to withdraw from worldly politics," while others "have traditionally been sympathetic to economic reforms." Nevertheless, he argued (and here he revealed his indebtedness to Johnson's research as well as Gusfield's formulation), "the moralistic quality of its economic ideas" could produce a right-wing orientation among lower-middle-class fundamentalists who might otherwise support the policies embodied in the welfare state. As that strain in Protestant thinking which "has always looked to economic life . . . as a vast apparatus of moral discipline, of rewards for virtue and industry, and punishments for vice and indolence" is emphasized by fundamentalist leaders, their supporters may respond in ways directly contrary to their "interests." Following Gusfield, Hofstadter used the example of attitudes toward deficit spending to make his general point. Deficit spending was opposed by many Americans not because it harmed them economically ("as a matter of interest politics, deficit spending might work to their advantage") but because it represented "a shocking repudiation of the moral precepts upon which their lives have been based." This latent economic conservatism among fundamentalists also gave them new and influential allies, for "the impulses of Protestant asceticism can thus be drawn upon to support business self-interest and the beautiful mathematical models of the neo-classical economists" (Hofstadter 1965b, 73, 81, 90, 82).

It might be useful at this point to pause in our consideration of Hofstadter's argument and reflect upon what he was trying to do in these essays. It would be an understatement to say that those behaviorally oriented social scientists who liked to keep their conceptual categories as tight as possible were not particularly enthusiastic about Hofstadter's work.[3] They could fault him for not defining "fundamentalism" in such a way that its influence on economic attitudes could be empirically tested and for not consistently differentiating between the relative significance of fundamentalism in shaping the attitudes of right-wing activists and its significance in shaping the attitudes of the general public. For such critics Hofstadter's discussion of attitudes on deficit spending would seem to prove their point: he moved from the specific influence of fundamentalism on the economic attitudes of its adherents to public

[3] At this point the reader may be interested to know of the intellectual relationship, if any, between Hofstadter's essays in *The Paranoid Style* and the empirical studies we discussed earlier, which appeared both before and after his book. Hofstadter cited the two most important that had already been published: Chesler and Schmuck 1963, and Wolfinger et al. 1969 (which had originally appeared in 1964). He had doubts about the usefulness of the Wolfinger study, however, because "the hostility of a large proportion of members to student interviews" suggested to him that "the Wolfinger group's respondents represent the less extreme members of the movement" (Hofstadter 1965b, pp 76–77n). On the other hand, Hofstadter's later essays in *The Paranoid Style* received much less attention from social scientists, such as the contributors to *The American Right Wing*, than had his earlier essay in *The New American Right*.

opposition to deficit spending without supplying the necessary missing link: that opponents of deficit spending were disproportionately likely to be fundamentalists.

Without denying the validity of such criticisms, it can be said in Hofstadter's defense that he was trying to approach the problem of the sources of right-wing politics historically, revealing the way in which general patterns of political culture intersected with specific social tensions over time. He consistently maintained, for example, that the assumptions of contemporary right-wing spokesmen—that "the vocational life was a moral testing ground" not to be violated by government interference; or that "in the world the national will can be made entirely effective, as against other peoples, at a relatively small price"—represented what was until very recently a broad national consensus (Hofstadter 1965b, 82, 133). He also argued that that consensus in turn reflected certain moral and religious themes central to the Protestantism of the era in which the nation was founded.

Seen in this light, Hofstadter's discussion of the opposition to deficit spending looks somewhat different. The degree to which fundamentalists were disproportionately opposed to deficit spending is an interesting empirical question but not really central to his argument, which is that the same "ascetic Protestant" values that most deeply shaped fundamentalists' views also influenced other Americans to a lesser extent. To a degree to which neither his own insistence on using terms like "pseudoconservatism" nor the charges of his critics ever did full justice, in these essays Hofstadter took right-wing spokesmen at their word: they were indeed the advocates of "fundamental" values from which other segments of the society had departed.

If that was so, then an analysis of fundamentalism was crucial to understanding the contemporary right wing only partly because it helped explain the background of so many right-wing activists. It also helped explain their tactics, which rested on the assumption that a significant portion of the American people wanted to return to an earlier world of laissez-faire domestic policy and the pursuit of "manifest destiny" abroad. Fundamentalism, defined as a broadly reactionary tendency in political culture as well as in formal religion, thus helped create "the milieu" (to return to his argument at the beginning of *The Paranoid Style*) in two ways. First, the older beliefs that it still militantly advocated already defined the world for many Americans. Second, the persisting appeal of those beliefs allowed right-wing activists to continue to communicate with a wide audience on current public issues.

Goldwater and His Supporters: The Hofstadter Thesis Examined

All of this is preparatory to the last of Hofstadter's "Studies in the American Right" in *The Paranoid Style*—his essay on Goldwater. It was perhaps proof of the pervasiveness of the fundamentalist worldview that its leading spokesman in the America of the early 1960s would turn out to be a Jewish convert to Episcopalianism, and Hofstadter had little difficulty placing Senator Barry Goldwater in this framework. From the emphatic statement in the foreword to *The Conscience of a Conservative* that "the challenge is . . . how to apply established truths to the problems of the contemporary world," to the senator's assertion in one of his campaign speeches that "the trouble with the so-called liberal today is that he doesn't understand simplicity. The answers to America's problems are simple," Goldwater stood revealed as the prime advocate of the fundamentalist style.[4]

In spite of the senator's shifts as a candidate in search of a suitable image (see esp. Kessel 1968, 185–217), there was, Hofstadter believed, an underlying consistency in Goldwater's rhetoric, a consistency revealed in the fact that for him "the answers to America's problems" essentially came down to the restoration of older values. That underlying theme united Goldwater's militancy in foreign policy, his critique of the welfare state, and his constant emphasis on crime and immorality. For Goldwater, "domestic demoralization, foreign failures, and the decline in our prestige abroad were together the consequence of the failure of the old virtues and the old moral fiber. In response, he urged a twofold stiffening of the moral backbone: first, 'take the bureaucratic shackles off,' put 'our main reliance on individuals, on hard work, on creativity, investment, and incentive'; then, reassert American power overseas. *Stop the spread of socialism at home and communism abroad*" (italics in original). This was what Gusfield had defined as "status politics" with a vengeance, and Hofstadter implied that Goldwater (or at least his strategists and speechwriters) was fully aware of it. Indeed, seeing the senator's campaign strategy as a self-conscious attempt to replace "interest politics" with "status politics" made sense of some of Goldwater's more inexplicable tactics—such as attacking the TVA in Knoxville—for it indicated that he believed that "appealing separately to a variety of special interests in the course of a campaign and then trying to act as broker among them . . . was an ignoble kind of politics, vastly inferior to a politics that would address itself to realizing the religious and moral values of the public" (Hofstadter 1965b, 118, 121).

For Hofstadter, Goldwater's entire public career branded him a "pseudoconservative." How could anyone call a man a true conservative, he asked, "whose whole political life has been spent urging a sharp break with the past, whose great moment as a party leader was marked by a repudiation of our traditional political ways, whose followers were so notable for their destructive and divisive energies, and whose public reputation was marked not with standpattism or excessive caution but with wayward impulse and recklessness"? (Hofstadter 1965b, 94). And what of his followers? "On the whole,"

---

[4] Barry Goldwater, as quoted in Hofstadter 1965b, pp. 95, 124.

Hofstadter wrote in an article that appeared during the campaign, "the Goldwater delegates seem to shade off from the extremist right of the John Birch Society, the Ku Klux Klan, and the White Citizen's Councils toward a more moderate center where ultraconservatism and general conservatism meet." He also stressed that they "were newcomers who had just entered politics and who had only recently won places for themselves in precincts and counties throughout the country . . . neither poor, rustic, nor uneducated; they hardly seemed to be suffering great deprivation under the welfare state they detest so much." Rather, they were "dedicated enthusiasts and malcontents, who want to do something good for America and for the world." They may "think of themselves as conservatives," he concluded, but "their basic feeling is a hatred of what America has become and a fierce and uncompromising insistence that it be made what they think it once was" (Hofstadter 1964, 10, 11). "Pseudoconservatives" in their hostility toward the present, they were utopian radicals in their goals for the future.

The attitudes and backgrounds of these supporters of Goldwater could be empirically investigated, and in the late 1960s a number of studies appeared that are revealing when matched against Hofstadter's impressionistic portrayal. The first was by the political scientist Aaron Wildavsky, who interviewed delegates to the 1964 convention and found them classifiable into "purists" and "politicians." The "purists," he argued, were distinguished by their "emphasis on internal criteria for decision, on what they believe 'deep down inside'; their rejection of compromise; their lack of orientation toward winning"; and "their stress on the style and purity of decision." While not all Goldwater delegates were "purists," he added, all the "purists" at the convention were Goldwater delegates. The "politicians," on the other hand, were distinguished by a "belief in compromise and bargaining; the sense that public policy is made in small steps rather than big leaps; the concern with conciliating the opposition and broadening public appeal; and the willingness to bend a little to capture public support" (Wildavsky 1965, 395, 394, 396).

Wildavsky wished to emphasize that the orientation toward winning of his "politicians" did not indicate an amoral opportunism; in fact many of them opposed appealing to white resistance to civil rights, even though it might be popular, because of the dangers of increased racial polarization. As this example showed, however, their morality, unlike that of the Goldwater "purists," was concerned with the consequences of their actions rather than the purity of their intentions. The Goldwater "purists," on the other hand, argued that the senator's criticisms of the Supreme Court's desegregation decision and his vote against the 1964 Civil Rights Act would not have a deleterious effect on race relations because he himself was unprejudiced (Wildavsky 1965, 397, 401). The compatibility of Wildavsky's conclusions with Hofstadter's contrast between the pragmatism of most politicians and the moral absolutism of right-wing activists should be obvious. Support for such a distinction could also be found in an empirical study of Goldwater delegates from the

Deep South by Bernard Cosman. Cosman found that nine out of ten of the delegates he interviewed disagreed with the statement that the role of the political party was to reconcile different interests (Cosman 1966, 31–32).

Hofstadter's impressions of the Goldwater delegates were, however, sharply challenged in the next study, though it concentrated on the Goldwater delegates' background rather than on their attitudes. Critically examining Hofstadter's statement that the Goldwater delegates "had just entered politics," Edmond Constantini and Kenneth Craik analyzed the alternative delegate slates in California. They found that the Goldwater delegates—whether measured by participation in county organizations, financial contributions, or the duration of their party activism—were in fact more deeply rooted in the Republican party than were those on the losing Rockefeller slate (Constantini and Craik 1969).

Since the delegates who actually nominated Goldwater were generally regarded as representative of those in the general public who had favored his nomination and in some cases actually worked for him, the Constantini-Craik study was accompanied by James McEvoy's much broader attack on the prevailing image of Goldwater supporters as "outsiders" who had "infiltrated" the Republican party. Using data gathered by the University of Michigan's Survey Research Center, the young sociologist investigated the attitudes and backgrounds of those who supported Goldwater before the convention, those who can be said to have constituted the real Goldwater "movement." In his conclusions about their attitudes, McEvoy confirmed what most commentators already believed—that the initial supporters of Goldwater held extremely conservative views—but the intention behind his study was to refute what he saw as the widespread belief that they (along with other right-wing activists) were "unsocialized political actors lacking either the prerequisites or the stability to be trusted with political power and as representing segments of the society which are, by definition, antidemocratic." On the contrary, he argued, the data revealed these early Goldwater supporters to be disproportionately college-educated, upper-income professionals and businessmen, who showed no tendency toward either "status inconsistency" or fundamentalist religion, and who maintained high levels of political participation and a high sense of political efficacy (McEvoy 1969, 247–58, 266–68, 243, 244, 274, 259–62).

McEvoy's conclusions differed radically, however, from the only other study of prenomination Goldwater supporters in the general public, by Irving Crespi, vice-president of the Gallup organization. Extracting from Gallup polls taken in the spring of 1964 all the pro-Goldwater responses and subjecting them to further analysis, Crespi found that the variable that correlated best with this early pro-Goldwater sentiment was region: the senator was most popular in the South and least so in the East.[5] In comparison, all other variables—

[5] Crespi 1965, p. 531. The most perceptive analysis of the regional aspects of the election itself is Burnham 1968a.

age, sex, religion, occupation, income, education, even partisan identification—were relatively insignificant. The sharpest difference from McEvoy's
profile came in Crespi's assessment of Goldwater support as related to income
and occupation. Whereas McEvoy had found early Goldwater supporters in
his national sample to be largely upper-income professionals and businessmen, Crespi detected only two slight "bulges" in Goldwater support—but
they occurred among farmers and among those earning between $3,000 and
$4,999 a year.[6]

As we conclude this discussion, it might be useful to summarize the points
of agreement and disagreement between Hofstadter, McEvoy, and the others
on the characteristics of the Goldwater supporters, whether delegates or not.
None of the empirical studies challenged Hofstadter's impressionistic account
of their attitudes. McEvoy himself made the point that "in many respects they
are 'extremists' in the statistical sense of deviating strikingly from the society's 'mean' on any number of policy variables." Wildavsky found Goldwater
delegates to be "purists" in their style of politics, and for that matter McEvoy
found that Goldwater supporters in the public ranked high on his personal-
dogmatism scale (McEvoy 1969, 278, 269). There was, however, disagreement over the background of the actual delegates: Hofstadter saw them as
newcomers who had just entered politics; Constantini and Craik showed that
in California at least this was not so; whether it was true for the rest of the
country remains to be determined. Had Hofstadter simply said that 1964 was
their first convention and that the turnover among delegates was extraordinarily high (three-quarters having attended neither the 1956 or the 1960 conventions: Polsby 1966, 100–101), he might have attracted far less criticism.

Though the various analysts disagreed about whether the Goldwater delegates were simply new to their roles as delegates or new to the party organization, they concurred that these individuals had received considerable support and encouragement from the existing party organization, especially at the
state and county levels. That Republican party organization leaders were far
more conservative than rank-and-file Republican voters was a proposition that
had already been advanced, using data gathered from the 1956 convention
(McClosky 1960). The proposition was reinforced by Gallup polls in the early
spring of 1964 that showed that while Goldwater was the preferred choice of
barely more than a fifth of all Republican voters, he received a near-majority
of first-choice votes from county chairmen across the country.[7] Hofstadter had
noted that the party organization in many areas had "gravitated into the hands

---

[6] Crespi 1965, p. 529. Interestingly, the only region where Crespi's findings matched Mc-
Evoy's was the West, where he too found prenomination support for Goldwater correlating with
increasing education, income, and occupational prestige (ibid., p. 530).

[7] George H. Gallup, *The Gallup Poll: Public Opinion, 1935–1971*, 3 vols. (New York: Random House, 1972), 3:1871.

of a leadership that is considerably more conservative than its voters.''[8] From that perspective, then, the problem was, as Wildavsky put it, ''the existence of a political elite, in a position to control a major national party, which holds views widely at variance both with the general voting population and its own followers'' (Wildavsky 1965, 411).

While an emphasis on the conservatism of the party organization helps account for the ease with which Goldwater supporters moved toward their goal, it does not answer the fundamental question: what kind of people were they? On that question we are left with a good many suggestive possibilities but very few clear answers. Hofstadter was clearer about how the Goldwater movement was ''pseudoconservative'' than about why. Having already abandoned his earlier reliance on some of the theories in *The Authoritarian Personality* but unwilling or unable to apply his newer cultural explanations to the Goldwater delegates, he left us with no explanation of their intense hostility to the status quo. McEvoy's conclusion—that Goldwater supporters in general were broadly ''upper middle class''—failed to differentiate them from the moderate Republicans who opposed them on major issues; and in any case it was contradicted by Crespi's findings. The profile of the California delegation drawn by Constantini and Craik is clear enough, and the reader will note its similarity to the profile of the participants in Schwarz's anticommunist schools drawn by Wolfinger and his associates. Clearly in California well-established ''upper middle class'' individuals were heavily represented in right-wing activity; but California may not have been typical of the nation in this regard. It is revealing, for example, that in the adjacent state of Oregon, it was the Freedom Center studied by McNall, staffed by poorly educated people, the very models of ''unsocialized political actors,'' that became the primary state Goldwater headquarters in the 1964 campaign (McNall 1975, 69–70).

Hofstadter and the Paranoid Style in Retrospect

However closely other findings did or did not match Hofstadter's impressions of the Goldwater supporters, his analysis of that particular historical phenomenon was only a small part of his larger interpretation of right-wing politics in America. And it was that larger interpretation, revolving around ''the paranoid style'' and a reformulated definition of ''status politics,'' that captured the attention of scholars in the more than two decades since he wrote the essays in *The Paranoid Style in American Politics*. One kind of reaction has been to reject the very concept of ''the paranoid style,'' a reaction that fell not so much upon Hofstadter (who died in 1970) as upon others, as in the case of a younger

---

[8] Hofstadter 1965b, p. 139. The same observation was also being made by Lipset (1964, pp. 20–21).

historian who used it to explain the emerging sectional crisis in the 1840s and 1850s and was severely criticized for doing so.[9] His description of the growing northern belief in a "slave power conspiracy" as an example of "the paranoid style" was met with the charge (obviously applicable to other events at other times) that he failed to confront the crucial question of whether the rhetoric he analyzed was "irrational and absurd" or whether instead it described a real threat to the interests and the values of those who used it.[10]

Yet if some historians rejected all efforts to "find paranoia throughout our history,"[11] others complained that, by seeing it as the expression primarily of "minority movements," Hofstadter had not applied the concept thoroughly enough. In truth, these historians insisted, "the paranoid style" characterized the major conflicts in American history, and one obvious place to look for it was in the repression of radicals. This argument gained much of its force after disclosures in the mid-1970s revealed that government bureaucrats had persistently engaged in the surveillance and harassment of groups and individuals whose beliefs and life-styles they regarded as "subversive." Given that, it was easy to find examples of "the paranoid style" not only in the marginal right-wing spokesmen with whom Hofstadter was concerned but at the highest levels of the United States Government.[12] At the same time, an even more expansive view of "the paranoid style" was taken by scholars who focused on white Americans' subjugation of Indians and enslavement of Africans. Working from this position Rogin would eventually postulate nothing less than an "American political demonology" and in doing so maintain that "racial conflict placed the paranoid style at the center and origin of American history," not at its periphery (Rogin 1987, 276–77).

[9] David Brion Davis, *The Slave Power Conspiracy and the Paranoid Style* (Baton Rouge: Louisiana State University Press, 1969). Davis and Hofstadter clearly influenced each other. Davis's article—"Some Themes of Counter-Subversion: An Analysis of Anti-Masonic, Anti-Catholic, and Anti-Mormon Literature," *Mississippi Valley Historical Review* 47 (September 1960): 205–24—became the main prop for Hofstadter's argument that the urge to imitate the enemy's tactics was one of the basic elements of "the paranoid style" (Hofstadter 1965b, pp. 33–34). Davis in turn expressed his gratitude to Hofstadter, and his own analysis of "the fear of conspiracy" reveals his intellectual debt to the older historian. See the "Acknowledgements" and "Introduction" to his collection of documents, *The Fear of Conspiracy: Images of Un-American Subversion from the Revolution to the Present* (Ithaca: Cornell University Press, 1971), pp. vii, xiii–xxiv.

[10] William W. Freehling, "Paranoia and American History," *New York Review of Books* 17 (September 23, 1971): 37. Though the parallel apparently eluded him, Freehling's charge that Davis begged the question of whether the threat of slavery was real closely paralleled right-wing complaints that the contributors to *The New American Right* begged the question of whether the threat of subversion was real: see, for example, Russell Kirk's review, in American Academy of Political and Social Science *Annals* 305 (May 1956): 184–85.

[11] Freehling, "Paranoia and American History," p. 36.

[12] Frank J. Donner, *The Age of Surveillance: The Aims and Methods of America's Political Intelligence System* (New York: Knopf, 1980), pp. 10–11, 14–17; and David J. Garrow, *The FBI and Martin Luther King, Jr.* (New York: Norton, 1981), pp. 208–13.

Hofstadter's other major conceptual effort in these essays, his attempt to transmute "status politics" into "cultural politics," also met with criticism. Between the publication of "the Pseudo-Conservative Revolt" and his death a decade and a half later, even as he reformulated it his concept of "status politics" remained controversial. Historians and social scientists who found little conflict that could not be described by earlier "economic" models (whether "class" or "interest group") would of course have no use for "status politics" at all. Meanwhile another group of scholars, primarily historians, attacked it for having too many "economic" overtones, insofar as it implied that what they would come to call "ethnocultural issues" (such as prohibition) "were less real, more derivative, less rational, than were economic issues."[13] On the contrary, they argued, far from being "derivative from more subconscious forces," the conflicts that produced these issues, "ethnic and religious, as well as racial conflicts," were as "fundamental in themselves," as "inherent in man's basic predispositions . . . as irreducible to other factors as those which arise from differences in occupation."[14] Hofstadter, whose attachment to the concept of "status politics" had antagonized one group of scholars, did not move far enough in the direction of a pure "cultural (or ethnocultural) politics" model to satisfy another; and thus on this issue, too, he was attacked from both sides.

The fact that his critics marched off in so many different directions is surely one reason why Hofstadter's essays in *The Paranoid Style in American Politics* still find a receptive audience. There are more substantial reasons as well. Whatever else his guiding concept of "the paranoid style" does or does not explain about our history, it remains one of the more useful ways of understanding certain strains in American culture that crystallized in the American right wing. Also, though Hofstadter was not as precise in his differentiations as Gusfield had been, his increasingly culturally oriented interpretation of "status politics," with a broadly defined "fundamentalism" as the key variable, remains for all its limitations a more fruitful explanation of the "radical right" of the late 1950s and early 1960s than the competing interpretations that concentrated either on "status inconsistency" or social mobility.

Probably the major reason for the continuing appeal of these essays, however, is the course of events in America in the twenty-five years or so since they were written, a course of events that ironically contradicted Hofstadter's assumptions about the future. In a brief reflection on the defeat of Goldwater

[13] Samuel P. Hays, "Political Parties and the Community-Society Continuum," in William N. Chambers and Walter D. Burnham, eds., *The American Party Systems: Stages of Political Development* (New York: Oxford University Press, 1967), p. 158. For a similar observation, see Paul Kleppner, *The Cross of Culture: A Social Analysis of Midwestern Politics, 1850–1900* (New York: Free Press, 1970), p. 18.

[14] Hays, "A Systematic Social History," in George A. Billias and Gerald N. Grob, eds., *American History: Retrospect and Prospect* (New York: Free Press, 1971), 336.

that appeared a few months before *The Paranoid Style*, he made what now appear to be two outstandingly bad predictions. The first was that what he called "the malady so frighteningly displayed at San Francisco has been contained" so that "the Cow Palace convention may come to be seen as the high tide of the radical right." The second was his prediction that, unlike Roosevelt who expended the prestige acquired from his 1936 landslide in the divisive Supreme Court fight, Johnson as a "master of consensual politics will not make the mistakes that so quickly dissolved Roosevelt's coalition in 1937" (Hofstadter 1965a, 66, 70). As we now know, in part because of his policies at home and abroad and in part because of the expectations raised by those policies, Johnson ended his second term in far worse shape than had Roosevelt. With his coalition shattered, he left office against a backdrop of bitter political polarization and a degree of civil disorder unparalleled in recent American history. Out of the collapse of the Johnsonian consensus and the ensuing confrontations, the "radical right," with even clearer fundamentalist overtones, would emerge once again.

Part Three

THE WALLACE CONSTITUENCY

FEW PRESIDENCIES in American history have been as troubled as that of Lyndon Johnson, and almost none (perhaps only Herbert Hoover's) declined so rapidly from overwhelming elite and public support to equally overwhelming repudiation. In 1965 Johnson had been hailed as the master architect of a whole range of public policies, of which the series of civil rights laws and the innovative "war on poverty" were merely the most notable. By 1968 he was perceived, by critics to his left as well as to his right, as a failure, and those same policies as marking the long-overdue end of the whole tradition of welfare-state liberalism going back to the New Deal. In foreign affairs Johnson had portrayed himself (and been portrayed by others) as simply continuing the long-established approach to the nation's Communist adversaries, resisting aggression when necessary but offering promises of peaceful cooperation when possible. By 1968 his foreign policy (as symbolized by his intervention in Vietnam) had become so unpopular as to polarize the country and produce a host of critics who would challenge, for the first time since before World War II, the basic assumptions behind America's activist role in the world.

Elected in his own right as president in 1964, in one of the greatest landslides in American history, by 1968 Johnson had become a political liability, an albatross for the national Democratic party. Faced with the insurgent candidacies of Senators Eugene McCarthy of Minnesota and Robert Kennedy of New York, Johnson announced in March that he would not seek renomination; his personal choice, Vice President Hubert Humphrey, was awarded the nomination in August in the angriest (and bloodiest) national party convention of the recent past; and in the election in November Humphrey received only 43 percent of the popular vote. Humphrey was the victim of what one political scientist called "a negative landslide," for the electorate showed little more enthusiasm for the victorious Republican, former Vice President Richard Nixon, giving him a margin of only about 560,000 more votes, a mere .7 percent of the total (Burnham 1968b, 19).

Although only about 13.5 percent of the vote went to the once-and-future governor of Alabama, George C. Wallace, running on the American Independent ticket, it was he, rather than Humphrey or Nixon, who became the chief object of scholarly attention. This seemingly perverse concentration on a minor-party candidate can be explained in several ways. It may be true, as Rogin suggested at the time, that since "America fell apart in the year and a half before this election" and "only Wallace addressed the mass anxiety . . . interpreters came to see in his movement their own sense of what had gone wrong in this country" (Rogin 1968, 310, 312). An equally plausible explanation of Wallace's popularity as an object of study is simply that so many scholars found themselves well prepared to study him. As a quintessential southerner appealing to regional traditions, he attracted the interest of the large number of historians and political scientists already studying southern politics. As a man whose political career had been built on appeals to white fears of court-ordered desegregation and civil rights laws and of the black insurgency that had brought them about, he aroused the interest of those sociologists and social psychologists who had been investigating the behavioral and institutional components of racial discrimination.

Scholarly interest in Wallace, however, also arose from his connections with the American right wing, connections that reopened some of the questions originally raised by the contributors to *The New American Right* but submerged in the scholarly criticisms that followed their particular interpretation of McCarthyism. Specifically, the Wallace candidacy raised anew the possibility that the right wing (what some scholars still called the ''radical right'') could exist apart from the ideological and organizational context of the Republican party. Similarly, Wallace's rhetoric and the favorable response it received from segments of the electorate raised the question of the degree to which right-wing candidates could draw on the complex legacy of American ''populism.''

On the first question, the fact that the Wallace campaign in 1968 was constructed and staffed by right-wing activists was obvious to journalists and social scientists alike. What further whetted their interest in the campaign was the fact that those activists represented far narrower backgrounds and viewpoints than had Goldwater's supporters four years before, and their commitment to Wallace represented an obvious repudiation of the Republican party. The emergence of this minority-within-a-minority arose out of the relative optimism most of the Goldwater activists still felt about their position as Republicans. They had maintained control of party organizations in key states such as California; and the 1966 gubernatorial victories of Ronald Reagan in that state and of Claude R. Kirk, Jr., in Florida suggested to them that attacks on welfare spending, racial integration, and campus protests could bring victory at the polls (Koeppen 1969b, 81–82; Reinhard 1983, 216–18). While the most likely candidate, Richard Nixon, might not have been their first choice for president in 1968, he was by no means hostile to their aims and programs (Reinhard 1983, 218–19).

This satisfaction with the Republican party on the part of most of the Goldwater activists meant that advocacy of the formation of a third party was confined to those who regarded Nixon and the Republicans as irredeemably under the control of ''liberal'' influences: individuals such as Robert Welch and other leaders of the John Birch Society, increasingly embracing various conspiracy theories; the unyielding segregationists active in the Citizens' Councils; and the Liberty Lobby, with its close ties to both white-supremacist and anti-Semitic propagandists.[1] It was men and women with such affiliations who launched a series of statewide third parties in 1965 and 1966 and ultimately the American Independent party of 1968; and these activists—mostly Birchers, but also members of the Klan and even the paramilitary Minutemen—would sustain the Wallace organization during the campaign.[2]

[1] Epstein and Forster 1967, pp. 41–50; Mintz 1985, pp. 93–96, 131–32. The situation of the John Birch Society deserves special comment. The massive American intervention in Vietnam beginning in 1965 presented Society founder Robert Welch with a problem: because he had already argued that the Communist conspiracy controlled American foreign policy, he now had to account for the obvious effort to halt the Communist-led insurgency in Vietnam. At first he tried to bridge the gap between theory and reality by invoking his "principle of reversal," in which (because of clever Communist manipulation) everything was the opposite of what it seemed. Thus "Communist" antiwar demonstrations urged American withdrawal from Vietnam only to mask the real Communist intention, which was to weaken the United States by involving it ever more deeply in the Vietnamese conflict. When he proposed as the Society's slogan, "Get US out of Vietnam," he was greeted with a storm of criticism from Republican politicians and right-wing spokesmen generally, and after considerable soul-searching, came up with a new slogan, "Let's win the war in Vietnam—and get out!" (Welch's difficulties are described in Epstein and Forster, pp. 121–25; a suggestive social-psychological interpretation, which sees his evolving arguments as an attempt to resolve "cognitive inconsistency," is Bennett 1971.)

In 1966, Welch moved even further down the road of conspiracy theory, when he began to argue that the Communists were merely the agents of a larger "diabolic force," those he called "the INSIDERS." This conspiracy of "the INSIDERS," according to Welch, went back at least to the Society of the Illuminati founded in Bavaria in 1776 and had also been responsible for the French Revolution and both world wars. Welch's resulting isolation on the right wing was one factor in the decline in Society membership in the mid-1960s; and prior to the appearance of the American Independent party the Society seemed even more marginal than before, with perhaps its only notable gains occurring among policemen, whom it aggressively supported against charges of "police brutality." The third party of 1968, however, gave it a new lease on life, and its subsequent influence is revealed by what happened after the assassination attempt on Wallace in 1972. The convention of what was now called the American party gave its presidential nomination to a Society member, California Representative John G. Schmitz, who devoted his campaign to warning of a conspiracy, headed by the Rockefellers, that controlled the governments of both the United States and the Soviet Union, and that—unless he was elected to halt it—would soon achieve its goal of a "one-world socialist system." On Welch and the Illuminati, see Epstein and Forster, pp. 118–19, and Mintz, pp. 20–21, 59–60, 142–43; on the Society and the police, Lipset and Raab 1970, pp. 317–20; on Schmitz in 1972, George Vecsey, "Schmitz Details Theory on Plots," *New York Times*, August 6, 1972, p. 43, and Stephen Lesher, "John Schmitz Is No George Wallace," *New York Times Magazine*, November 5, 1972, pp. 22, 29.

[2] Chester 1969, p. 703; Crass, 1976, p. 109; Lipset and Raab 1970, pp. 352–54. There are only two systematic investigations of 1968 American Independent party (AIP) activists by social scientists. The first compared AIP county chairmen in Texas with their counterparts in the two major parties. On the basis of responses received, the authors concluded that they were poorer, less educated, and more likely to have fundamentalist religious affiliations; were more right-wing in their policy positions than even the Republicans; and were in general more "issue-oriented" (Wrinkle and Elliott 1971).

The second study studied AIP campaign workers in some of the suburbs around Detroit. Although he did not directly compare them with Democratic and Republican activists, the author strongly implied that they (like the Texans discussed above) were less affluent and less educated,

For a brief moment in 1968 these activists held center stage, not because of their influence but because of George Wallace's popular appeal. Since almost all the scholarly studies focused in one way or another on those who responded positively to that appeal, by actually voting for Wallace, planning to vote for him, or expressing a favorable opinion of him, it is useful to investigate the basis of that appeal by briefly exploring Wallace's politics. One might think that, after almost three decades, we would know a great deal about his politics and, in terms of the sheer amount that has been written, we do. Most of this material is fragmented, however, bouncing off one aspect or another, and few analysts have tried to see it as a whole. Even fewer have tried to solve the major riddle of the 1968 Wallace campaign: why did right-wing activists—activists who, in view of their attitudes, can with some justification be called "extreme"—work for the candidacy of a man whose economic positions were those of a New Deal liberal?

Trying to put the different perspectives on Wallace together, one must start with the fact that, unlike either Joseph McCarthy or Barry Goldwater, Wallace had never been a Republican, and also take notice of the fact that on the economic issues that from the 1930s to the 1960s had divided the parties, he was very much a Democrat. It is not so clear, however, that one can go very far beyond those general statements. One of the terms, for example, most frequently applied to Wallace has been "populist," and so journalists have closely scrutinized his record as governor (1963–67, 1971–79, 1983–87) to see if it conforms to "populist" standards.[3] If redistribution can be regarded as the touchstone of economic "populism," then Wallace failed to meet the test: he made no effort as governor either to overhaul the state's highly regressive tax structure or to demand legislation improving working conditions. One problem with such an approach, however, is that, according to a historian who has studied them closely, the Alabama Populist legislators of the 1890s had no consistently "redistributive" record, either.[4] The most that can be said, therefore, is that because of his support for road and school construction, for

---

far more "issue-oriented," and far more right-wing in their policy positions. His most suggestive conclusion is that these campaign activists sorted themselves out into two subgroups, which prefigured later splits within the 1968 organization. The southern-born among them tended to be white-supremacist and concerned about crime—he called them "racial reactionaries"—but relatively moderate on other issues; the native Michiganians—whom he called "ultraconservatives"—were less fixated on race but more likely to take extreme positions (approximating those of the John Birch Society) on all issues (Canfield 1985).

[3] My discussion here is an attempt to synthesize the different views of Frady 1968, pp. 137–38; Sherrill 1968, pp. 292–93; and Crass 1976, pp. 80–81, 206–7.

[4] Sheldon Hackney has pointed out that, for example, most of the Populist state legislators in Montgomery voted against a bill that would have shifted the tax burden from farmers to railroads. Hackney, *Populism and Progressivism in Alabama* (Princeton: Princeton University Press, 1969), pp. 72–73.

clean water, and for public welfare, Wallace was on the moderately progressive side of the economic spectrum.

Interesting though all this may be as an academic exercise, trying to place Wallace on an economic-policy spectrum—whether as heir of the Populists, latter-day New Dealer, or something else—has its limits, because the available evidence suggests that Wallace never saw economics as his primary strength.[5] For all his rhetoric about being the representative of ordinary Americans—of cab drivers and beauticians and steelworkers—he talked very little in 1968 about the economic issues that bothered them.[6] It is true that he gave somewhat more emphasis to those issues in his 1972 primary campaign; but even then, in spite of his charge that ordinary Americans were being squeezed by taxes, he never made it clear whether he advocated tax reduction, tax reform, or both (Carlson 1981, 223). One anecdote about Wallace's response to an earlier tax issue, however, helps unravel the mystery of how the candidacy of a "progressive" Democrat could be supported by the "extreme" right wing. When asked as governor how he could sign into law an increase in the sales tax, Wallace is said to have replied, "I'll just yell 'nigger' and they'll never know or care a goddamn about taxes" (as quoted in Crass 1976, 213). Except at its beginning and its end—and certainly during the time he was a major national figure—Wallace's career was built on exploiting racial fears and hatreds; and that was what, in the minds of an increasing number of scholars, linked him to the right wing.

Shortly before he was sworn in as governor in 1963, Wallace remarked to a group of legislators, "I'm gonna make race the basis of politics in this state, and I'm gonna make it the basis of politics in this country" (as quoted in Frady 1968, 140). His inaugural address is best remembered for its climactic battle cry, "Segregation now! Segregation tomorrow! Segregation forever!" It also contained a remarkably thorough-going defense of racial segregation: "Each race, within its own framework, has the freedom to teach, to instruct, to develop, to ask for and receive deserved help from others of separate racial station . . . but if we amalgamate into the one unit as advocated by the Commu-

[5] Ecological analysis alone suggests that Wallace's support in his home state did not follow the usual economically based divisions, which (as V. O. Key described them in his classic study) pitted the smaller farmers of the predominantly white counties of the northern (and southeastern) parts of Alabama against the planters of the south-central "black belt" and the industrialists of Birmingham and Mobile. In the 1962 election that gave him the governorship, Wallace's support was concentrated in the "black-belt" counties, the traditional centers of opposition to Populist and subsequent progressive candidates. But then, to complicate matters further, in the 1966 and 1970 elections, Wallace's support declined in the "black-belt" counties (because of the reentry of blacks into the electorate) and rose in the rural counties of the north (for reasons that are unclear). (See Key 1949, pp. 36–57; Black and Black 1973a; Black and Black 1973b.)

[6] As Lipset and Raab perceptively observed of Wallace in 1968, "his antielitism . . . provides the shadow of economic radicalism where its substance may be missing" (Lipset and Raab 1970, p. 348).

nist philosopher, then the enrichment of our lives, the freedom for our development is gone forever. We become, therefore, a mongrel unit of one under a single all-powerful government.''[7] In his first year in office Wallace proved as good as his word. He used the state police to block desegregation everywhere he could while he himself "stood at the schoolhouse door" to protest the admission of two black students to the University of Alabama. In at least two sensational cases, he went out of his way to block the punishment of those convicted of violent crimes against blacks (Frady 1968, 148; Sherrill 1968, 268).

By 1964, when he decided to challenge President Johnson in the Democratic primaries, Wallace had already established himself as the carrier of most of the overt racist sentiment in the country. Stressing the supposed evils of the pending civil rights legislation that year, he received a vote far greater than expected in the primaries he entered: in Wisconsin about 34 percent; in Indiana about 30 percent; and in Maryland about 43 percent.[8] Much of that support— and even more notably, of that which he received in 1968—was, like his support in Alabama, attributed to white racism. Wallace himself never tired of pointing out, however, that he never made direct racial appeals in his national campaigns; his key words were always neutral-sounding abstractions: "property rights," "states' rights," "local control," and in 1968, "law and order." As a team of British journalists covering the 1968 campaign observed, what lifted Wallace out of the parochialism of most segregationist politicians and made him a candidate with national appeal was that "he had learned to adapt to northern sensibilities one of the oldest devices in the southern politician's armory. He talked in code" (Chester 1969, 279). "Talking in code," however, presents problems both for the speaker and for the subsequent analyst: neither ever knows how many listeners understand the code and how many take the words at their face value. Thus, as we shall see in subsequent pages, one of the issues facing scholars studying Wallace's support was how much of it came from racial prejudice and how much from responses to the rhetoric itself, either because of opposition to federal power or because of fear of social disorder.

Wallace was entering the 1968 presidential race, he announced at the outset of his campaign, to offer an alternative: "There's not a dime's worth of difference in the way the leaders of both parties think" (as quoted in McEvoy 1971, 109). Nonetheless, it was not for his sustained exposition of alternative policies that Wallace is best remembered, but rather for his specific comments: terse, pointed, and (for some at least) terrifying in their implications. There were the continual denunciations of those arrayed against him and the "ordinary folks" Wallace represented: the "pointy-headed professors," the "Fed-

[7] Wallace's first inaugural, as quoted in Frady 1968, pp. 141–42.
[8] For an overview of Wallace's 1964 campaign, see Carlson 1981, pp. 27–44.

eral judges playing God," the bureaucrats (many of whom had beards), the "sissy-britches," the "intellectual morons," and the "theoreticians" who "don't know how to park a bicycle straight" (as quoted in Chester 1969, 281). Even more notable were his persistent evocations of violent repression: "If any demonstrator lies down in front of my car when I'm President, that'll be the last car he lies down in front of." The "professors . . . who are advocating a victory of the Vietcong Communists should be dragged figuratively by their beards before a Federal grand jury and put in the penitentiary." If we "let the police run this country for a year or two, there wouldn't be any more riots." How to handle antiwar protesters? "I'd take a billy club and I'd drive it two inches into their skulls."[9]

Wallace's rhetoric had an unmistakable flavor about it, and most commentators described the view of the world behind it as "populist."[10] That description, however, immediately raised the issues that sociologists, political scientists, and historians had already been debating in the case of McCarthy. Was Wallace a "populist"? Defined in economic, redistributive terms, the question can only be answered in a complicated way, as we have seen, depending on one's assessment of the original Alabama Populists and Wallace's record as governor, among other variables. What of the noneconomic dimensions of "populism"? If one follows Peter Viereck and Edward Shils and broadly defines populism as those tendencies in American political culture that advocate "government by direct unfettered mass pressure" (Viereck 1956, 31), then it is easy to see Wallace as a populist. His political theory was remarkably straightforward: "There's one thing more powerful than the Constitution, than any constitution, and that's the will of the people. What is a constitution anyway? They're the products of the people, the people are the first source of power, and the people can abolish a constitution if they want to" (as quoted in Frady 1968, 237). As the tensions of the late 1960s arose, Wallace could conjure up a vision of the people in motion that exceeded even Viereck's nightmares: "Hell, all we'd have to do right now is march on the Federal courthouse there in Montgomery, take over the post office and lock up a few of those judges, and by sunset there'd be a revolution from one corner of this nation to the other. We could turn this country right around" (as quoted in Frady 1968, 9).

Another aspect of Wallace's rhetoric is best captured by a different perspective on "populism": Wiebe's description of the original Populists as one manifestation of the ongoing determination of local communities to defend their way of life against alien and distant centers of power. Whatever the validity

[9] George Wallace, as quoted in Chester 1969, p. 283; in Crass 1976, p. 96; in Lipset and Raab 1970, p. 356; and in Crass 1976, p. 115.

[10] Wallace's rhetoric itself, it should be noted, has been the subject of a number of studies by scholars in the field of communications. A recent contribution, which cites the earlier literature, is Hogan 1984.

of Wiebe's model in other contexts, it is hard to think of a better description of Wallace's career, articulating as he did the fears of communities of whites who felt besieged by an unholy trinity of federal officials, cosmopolitan intellectuals, and militant blacks. That connection, between populism and localism, helps explain otherwise contradictory aspects of Wallace's position, especially on "law and order." When just before he became governor he was urged to condemn racially motivated violence as a matter of defending law and order, Wallace is said to have replied, "I've gotten sick and tired of that kinda talk. The folks have already heard too much hollerin about law and order" (as quoted in Frady 1968, 140). But for Wallace (and, one suspects, for a sizable segment of other Americans) the situation had decisively changed by the late 1960s. For these people, to suppress white violence in Alabama was to violate the will of the local community; to suppress ghetto riots and student protest in the nation at large was to uphold it.[11]

These, then, were the lineaments of the campaign that attracted so much attention from social scientists: a third party organized by right-wing activists, a candidate whose career had been built on appeals to racists and opponents of civil rights, and a rhetoric saturated with a certain kind of "populism," concerned less with economic redistribution than with the defense of the community. Each of the turbulent events of 1968—the riots after Martin Luther King, Jr., was shot, the murder of Robert Kennedy, the disorder attending the Democratic convention—increased Wallace's standing in the polls, and between early spring and early fall his potential share of the vote more than doubled, from 9 to 21 percent. His strategy—of sweeping the South and Border states, deadlocking the Electoral College, and throwing the election to the House, where he could extract concessions from Nixon or Humphrey—seemed possible of realization. He was quite specific as to what those concessions would have to be: the abandonment of all civil rights legislation, curbs on the Supreme Court, and the returning to the states of all power over desegregation and reapportionment (Crass 1976, 107).

That scenario never came to pass, both because of the atmosphere of violence, physical as well as rhetorical, that came to surround the Wallace campaign and because the major parties carefully whittled away at the pillars of his strength, the Republicans aiming at southern middle-class conservatives and the Democrats at northern workers. Even with his eventual decline in

[11] In one of the last essays he completed before his death, Hofstadter provided a complementary interpretation of this shift in the perception of violence on the part of so many Americans, including Wallace and his supporters. He pointed out that, traditionally, American violence had been "initiated with a 'conservative' bias . . . , to protect the American, the southern, the white Protestant, or simply the established middle-class way of life and morals." But in the 1960s, "violence has now become, to a degree unprecedented in the United States, the outgrowth of forcible acts by dissidents and radicals who are expressing hostility to middle-class ways and to established power" (Hofstadter 1970, p. 11).

popularity, however, Wallace ran well enough to have an enduring impact. For most politicians and journalists his race revealed the existence of powerful currents of popular anger apart from—and opposed to—the more widely discussed protests in the ghettoes and on the campuses, currents that these professionals would do well to try to master. (Unresolved was the question of whether Wallace himself shaped the election, pulling Nixon and to a lesser extent Humphrey in his direction; or whether he was simply less constrained in riding such currents in the public mood.) For right-wing activists, Wallace's showing was evidence of a national constituency, one that (unlike Goldwater's) cut unto the nonsouthern working class; although still small, it was a base from which to build. For social scientists, to whose work we now turn, the Wallace campaign of 1968 offered an unprecedented opportunity to investigate the impact of right-wing appeals on voting behavior.

Eight

Southern Support for Wallace: The Politics of Place

RUNNING AS THE American Independent candidate for president in 1968, George Wallace received approximately 9.9 million votes or 13.5 percent of the total cast. Those who voted for him shared one common characteristic that, in view of the nature of his appeal, was hardly surprising: they were almost all white. Also, far more than those who cast their ballots for Nixon or Humphrey, the Wallace voters were likely to be southerners. If the South is defined as the eleven states of the former Confederacy, that region's electorate cast only about one-fifth of all the votes for presidential candidates in 1968; but about half of the Wallace votes came from the South.[1] In addition, the two states in which Wallace won absolute majorities (Alabama and Mississippi), the three in which he won pluralities (Arkansas, Georgia, and Louisiana), and the three in which he came in second (North Carolina, South Carolina, Tennessee) were all in the South.

Conversely, if the South contributed disproportionately to Wallace's final vote, so was he in many ways the dominant force in southern presidential politics that year. Overall, he came within half a percentage point (34.3 percent to Nixon's 34.7 percent) of being the preferred choice of southern voters.[2] However marginal his candidacy might have seemed elsewhere, in the South Wallace was a major party candidate. As such he attracted a great deal of attention from social scientists studying southern politics—more, probably, than any comparable figure in the recent past.

[1] Estimates are based on figures in Richard M. Scammon, comp., *America Votes 8: A Handbook of Contemporary American Election Statistics 1968* (Washington: Governmental Affairs Institute, 1970), p. 1. In making this computation, I am following a well-established tradition among historically minded analysts of American politics and defining "the South" as the eleven states of the former Confederacy: Alabama, Arkansas, Florida, Georgia, Louisiana, Mississippi, North Carolina, South Carolina, Tennessee, Texas, and Virginia.

Many political scientists using survey methods, however, follow the Bureau of the Census and include in "the South" the District of Columbia, Kentucky, Maryland, Oklahoma, and West Virginia as well. Under that more inclusive definition about 58 percent of the Wallace vote came from the South, and the region cast about 26 percent of the total vote for president in 1968. Throughout this discussion of the Wallace vote I will continue to define the South in the first (ex-Confederate) sense; where the definitions of the researchers under review clearly differ I shall indicate so.

[2] Estimates from Bartley and Graham 1975, p. 127.

The Wallace Vote in the South: Ecological Analysis

To find out what characterized the Wallace voters, what distinguished them from those supporting other presidential candidates, social scientists had at their disposal two alternative methods of analyzing voting behavior. The best-established was to subject aggregate data to ecological analysis, or in simpler terms, to look at the returns to find out *where* the votes came from, placing the voting patterns in the context of their physical and social environment. "By correlating election returns with indicators of significant social characteristics," one exponent of this method has pointed out, "it is possible to ascertain the interests and predispositions which are present in an area as well as the social divisions which may be reflected in the voting."[3] Alternatively, analysts of voting behavior could utilize individual data, primarily in the form of "sample survey data," which "consist of recorded responses directly obtained from certain individuals selected as constituting a 'representative sample' of the population being studied."[4] This survey method had the great advantage of uncovering the subjective aspects of the individual voter's decision (attitudes, motivations, and so on).

By the 1960s many social scientists had turned toward the survey method and away from reliance on aggregate data and ecological correlation, largely because of their awareness of the "ecological fallacy," the unwarranted assumption that correlations based on aggregate data could "produce reliable descriptions or explanations of the behavior of individuals."[5] Those who insisted on working with aggregate data (either because they preferred to do so or because they had to do so since reliable survey data did not exist before about 1940) now found themselves on the defensive. Later, some of them would try to meet the challenge by devising more accurate techniques involving "ecological regression." Initially at least, however, those working with aggregate data were willing to accept its limitations; and even though they acknowledged that their methods could not "reveal how individuals . . . actually behave or what influences them," they expressed the hope that their findings would continue to be fruitful.[6]

[3] Perry H. Howard, *Political Tendencies in Louisiana*, rev. ed. (Baton Rouge: Louisiana State University Press, 1971), p. xi.

[4] Austin Ranney, "The Utility and Limitations of Aggregate Data in the Study of Electoral Behavior," in Ranney, ed., *Essays on the Behavioral Study of Politics* (Urbana: University of Illinois Press, 1962), p. 91.

[5] Ranney, "Utility and Limitations of Aggregate Data," p. 98. The classic analysis of the "ecological fallacy" is W. S. Robinson, "Ecological Correlations and the Behavior of Individuals," *American Sociological Review* 15 (June 1950): 351–57; for a review of the subsequent controversies see the essays in Mattei Dogan and Stein Rokkan, eds., *Quantitative Ecological Analysis in the Social Sciences* (Cambridge, Mass.: M.I.T. Press, 1969).

[6] Howard, *Political Tendencies in Louisiana*, p. xix. For Howard's own ecological analysis of the 1968 election, see his study of voting behavior in Baton Rouge: Howard 1971.

Its methodological limitations notwithstanding, ecological correlation was still widely used by social scientists studying the southern Wallace vote because, as a method, it was unusually well-suited to research problems that could only be understood in a historical context. "If the research on contemporary behavior and social structure cannot ignore the weight of history," wrote one prominent political sociologist, "it cannot ignore ecological data."[7] Clearly "the weight of history" lay heavily upon the 1968 Wallace campaign and the response it evoked from southern whites. Forty years before, an eminent southern historian had in fact located "the central theme of southern history" in the white population's "common resolve indomitably maintained— that it shall be and remain a white man's country."[8] The idea could be phrased more crudely, as Wallace's Georgia campaign manager did early in 1968, "When you get down to it, there's really going to be only one issue, and you spell it n-i-g-g-e-r."[9] There was more to southern support for Wallace than simple racial prejudice, as we shall see, but to miss his appeal to regional traditions of "white supremacy" is to miss a very large part of his campaign.

Although those regional traditions of "white supremacy" were clearly waning in 1968, they remained powerful enough to produce Wallace's strong showing in the South. *Which* southern whites, social scientists therefore asked, were still so committed to "white supremacy" as to express it by voting for an "extremist" third-party candidate? The answer ecological analysis provided had been suggested some twenty years before by V. O. Key, in his classic book on southern politics. His analysis of southern voting behavior suggested to him that it was those whites in the areas of the greatest black population, the "black belts" of the declining plantation economy, "who have the deepest and most immediate concern about the maintenance of white supremacy." He further concluded that those "black-belt" whites would directly express that concern in their voting, whether continuing their traditional allegiance to the Democratic party or (as in 1948) breaking with it to support a white-supremacist candidate (Key 1949, 5, 317–44). Key's hypothesis was substantially confirmed in a later analysis of southern voting behavior in the years after the Supreme Court's 1954 school-desegregation decision: in almost all state elections, support for the most "militant segregationist" candidates was concentrated in the white population of the "black belts" (Black 1973).

Given the plausibility of Key's hypothesis, it was not surprising that it continued to attract political scientists: two concluded from their study of 1968 voting patterns that "the greater the concentration of blacks in a Congressional district, the greater the propensity of whites in that district to vote for Wal-

    [7] Juan Linz, "Ecological Analysis and Survey Research," in Dogan and Rokkan, eds., *Quantitative Ecological Analysis*, p. 99.
    [8] Ulrich B. Phillips, "The Central Theme in Southern History," *American Historical Review* 34 (October 1928): 31.
    [9] Roy Harris, as quoted in Bartley 1970, pp. 84–85.

lace'' (Schoenberger and Segal 1971). Key's hypothesis could in fact be extended, because the urbanization of the South raised the possibility that it might well be urban whites, especially working-class whites, who now (in Key's phrase) ''would have the deepest and most immediate concern about the maintenance of white supremacy.'' Studies of voting behavior in several southern cities confirmed that the 1968 Wallace vote contained a solid white working-class component,[10] and one suggested that urbanization itself might correlate with the Wallace vote (Wrinkle and Polinard 1973, esp. 319). But the inherent problems of ecological correlation, compounded by the dramatic reentry of blacks into the southern electorate, made it increasingly hazardous to conclude, solely on the basis of aggregate data, how individual southerners voted. Furthermore, such methods raised almost as many questions as they answered: why, for example, should the percentage of the population that was black correlate *positively* with the percentage of the vote cast for Wallace in counties in the Upper South (Arkansas, Florida, North Carolina, Tennessee, Texas, Virginia) but *negatively* in the Lower South (Alabama, Georgia, Louisiana, Mississippi, South Carolina), especially since blacks in the Upper South were more likely to be registered and thus offset their white neighbors' support for Wallace?[11]

By the mid-1970s several researchers had hit upon a solution to some of these problems which, they believed, would combine the strengths of ecological analysis and the survey method. Their procedure was straightforward: first they pulled out of the total survey sample all the pro-Wallace respondents; then they determined the correlation of that preference with the usual variables (age, income, occupation, etc.) *as well as* the percentage of blacks in the counties from which those respondents came. Thus armed with this more sophisticated method, they reexamined Key's hypothesis (or what other scholars were calling the ''contextual effect'') and confirmed it. The most important such confirmation was by Gerald C. Wright, Jr.[12] Utilizing an exceptionally large body of data compiled by the Comparative State Election Project at the University of North Carolina and drawn from respondents in over 300 counties (including from the eleven ex-Confederate states and from some others as well), Wright concluded that ''in 1968 southern white voting for Wallace for President increased with the relative size of the black population.''[13]

[10] On voting patterns in Georgia cities, see Bartley 1970, p. 84; on similar patterns in Louisiana and North Carolina cities, Bartley and Graham 1975, pp. 128–29; on Tennessee, Berenson 1971.

[11] Wasserman and Segal 1973. For registration, see the figures compiled by the Southern Regional Council, in Pat Watters and Reese Cleghorn, *Climbing Jacob's Ladder: The Arrival of Negroes in Southern Politics* (New York: Harcourt, Brace, 1967), pp. 376–77.

[12] Wright 1976; Wright 1977. Another study utilizing a very similar approach, but with a far smaller sample, is Knoke and Kyriazis 1977.

[13] Wright 1977, p. 507. He included in ''the South'' the District of Columbia, Kentucky, Maryland, Oklahoma, and West Virginia.

In reaching this conclusion Wright also clarified the role of subregional political cultures. While other political scientists had been puzzled by the question of why the "contextual effect" seemed strongest in states outside the Lower South, Wright believed he had the answer. In Lower South states like Mississippi, he argued, the political culture was so dominated by racial themes that the presence of high percentages of blacks in a county did little to increase the Wallace vote; while in Upper South states like Tennessee, attitudes were more likely to vary according to the size of the black population. As a result, the "contextual effect" in such states was more likely to produce differences in white voting behavior between counties with high and those with low black populations (Wright 1977, 503).

Finally, Wright's analysis revealed a striking divergence between the rural and urban South. In urban areas, the "contextual effect" worked in *reverse*: the higher the black percentage of a city's population, the *less* likely the whites were to vote for Wallace, and—most surprisingly—the less likely they were to be concerned about the possibility of racial disorder, and the less hawkish they were on the Vietnam War (Wright 1976, 214, 212). He did not suggest why this should be so (probably some other, "cosmopolitan" factors were at work), but his findings clearly convey a division between an urban South and a rural South, within which the variable of black concentration shaped the contours of the 1968 Wallace vote. Wright's work went farther toward establishing the validity of the "contextual effect" (and Key's original hypothesis) than that of any other scholar.

The ecological analysis of the 1968 Wallace vote in the South, then, uncovered a strong racially motivated component, as shown by the positive correlation between the relative size of the black population and the tendency of whites to vote for Wallace. In general, Key's twenty-year-old hypothesis still stood, although at least at the county level it worked somewhat better for the Upper South than for the Lower South and far better for rural areas than for urban ones. Other components of the southern Wallace vote received less attention, but several analyses of aggregate data suggested that it contained a "fundamentalist" component (as shown by its correlation in Atlanta, Houston, Memphis, and Richmond with opposition to the sale of liquor by the drink) and possibly an "anti-establishment" component as well (as shown in Richmond by its association with opposition to bond issues).[14] Do the much-vaunted methods of survey research confirm any of these conclusions? What else do they tell us about those southerners who voted for George Wallace in 1968?

---

[14] For Atlanta, see Bartley 1970, p. 87; for Houston and Memphis, Lubell 1970, p. 145; for Richmond, Lubell 1970, pp. 145, 151–52, and Pettigrew and Riley 1971, pp. 232–34.

The Southern Wallace Supporter as Revealed
in Survey Data: Sociological Profiles

As in the portion of this book that analyzed the right-wing activists of the early 1960s, we shall review the available survey data by beginning with analyses using *sociological* variables: sex and age; income, occupation, and education (the so-called "class variables"); political orientation; religious affiliation; place of residence (urban/rural); and so on. We will then proceed to analyses using *psychological* variables: first, the attitudinal characteristics explored in the "authoritarian personality" literature, such as hostility to democratic procedures, racial and religious prejudice, and so on; and finally the various measures of political alienation such as distrust and feelings of powerlessness.

Although individual researchers conducted smaller-scale surveys, most of the survey data came from two sources, the "standard" sources in the 1960s for analysts of contemporary American electoral behavior. The first was the data collected by George Gallup's American Institute of Public Opinion (AIPO); the second, the data collected by the Survey Research Center (SRC) at the University of Michigan. For our purposes in understanding the Wallace vote, the major interpreters of this data are: for AIPO data, Gallup organization vice president Irving Crespi in an important 1971 article, and Seymour Martin Lipset and Earl Raab in their major work on "right-wing extremism," *The Politics of Unreason*; for SRC data, the Michigan political scientists themselves in their quadrennial analysis of presidential elections for the *American Political Science Review*, James McEvoy in his book on "the contemporary American right," and Jody Carlson in her study of the four Wallace presidential campaigns. It is essential to add one cautionary note: some of the surveys were of those who actually voted for Wallace, but others were of those who chose him as their preferred candidate at various points in the summer and early fall of 1968. Among the latter (as we have seen) were many who later rejected him. In most of the categories we shall be reviewing, the difference between the Wallace supporters of August and the Wallace voters of November is inconsequential; but in some categories it is major, and a failure to acknowledge it can produce serious misunderstandings of what happened in 1968.

Among white southerners Wallace proved somewhat more attractive to men than to women, and this gender-linked difference in response was about the same in the summer as in the final vote in November.[15] The relationship of age to the Wallace vote drew far more comment, for there was in the South, in the conclusion of the SRC team, "a faint negative correlation between age and the Wallace vote" (Converse et al. 1969, 1103). In other words, the younger

[15] Crespi 1971, p. 128; Lipset and Raab 1970, p. 391; Converse et al. 1969, p. 1103.

the voter, the more likely he would vote for Wallace.[16] Why was this so? Lipset and Raab speculated that these young adults were impressionable teen-agers during the confrontations over desegregation and thus were exposed to "opinions which stressed the need to protect the institutions, values, and autonomy of the white South against a threat from outside liberals and the Federal Government" (Lipset and Raab 1970, 371). However, as the political scientists associated with the Survey Research Center pointed out, there was no evidence that younger voters agreed with Wallace's positions any more than older ones; it was simply that, as much of the literature on political socialization would predict, they were not old enough to develop an identification with either major party and thus were freer to express their views with a vote for a third-party candidate (Converse et al. 1969, 1103–4).

Of the "class variables," Lipset and Raab showed, Wallace's southern support divided sharply at the $10,000-a-year income level; below that level he drew the votes of a near-majority of southern whites, above it only about a sixth. Among occupational categories, he received comparable majorities from both southern farmers and southern workers whether skilled or unskilled, and he ran particularly well among southern service workers, "a conglomerate which includes police, domestic servants, and the military." Lipset and Raab also found, however, that families of union members in the South were considerably less likely to vote for Wallace than nonunion families (40 percent to 58 percent).[17]

Wallace ran far less well among nonmanual categories of southerners: his percentage of the vote among white-collar workers was slightly below his regional average of 34 percent and his showing among businessmen and professionals barely half of that (Lipset and Raab 1970, 389). It is noteworthy, however, that, for all the attention social scientists lavished on southern youths and southern blue-collar workers, the political behavior of southern businessmen was far more dramatic. According to AIPO data cited by Lipset and Raab, during the summer and fall almost half of southern businessmen preferred Wallace as their candidate, a figure (46 percent) far closer to the levels of support among southern farmers (53 percent) than among southern professionals (26 percent). By the election, however, they had abandoned him in such numbers that along with southern professionals they ranked lowest in Wallace support (18 percent) (Lipset and Raab 1970, 389). No other group of voters in the United States (in any region, occupation, or other category) abandoned the Wallace candidacy as massively as did southern businessmen. Since we also know that southern defections from Wallace rose, however slightly, with levels of income, it is not hard to connect these trends to the Republican

[16] Crespi, however, detected a slight bulge of support among respondents in their thirties (Crespi 1971, p. 128).

[17] Lipset and Raab 1970, pp. 388–89; Lipset and Raab 1969, p. 26; also Crespi 1971, p. 121.

counteroffensive. Among these affluent right-wingers, as Lipset and Raab noted, "it would seem that the efforts of the southern conservative Republicans (headed by Strom Thurmond) to convince them that a vote for Wallace would help Humphrey were effective."[18]

Within educational categories, in the South (as elsewhere) the Wallace vote correlated negatively with the level of education received: thus college graduates were less likely to prefer Wallace (during the campaign or on Election Day) than were high school graduates, who in turn were less supportive than those with only a grade-school education (Lipset and Raab 1970, 389). Crespi, who measured this variable while controlling for the others, found education to be a particularly significant correlate of the Wallace vote, in the South as elsewhere, even when income was controlled. His finding that southern college graduates at every income level were far less likely to support Wallace than either of the less-educated categories led him to conclude that education was a better predictor of support for Wallace than income by itself (Crespi 1971, 124, 126).

Attempts to identify the political orientation of Wallace voters through their subjective party identifications produced conflicting results. Although there was general agreement that Wallace ran very poorly among self-identified Republicans, researchers using AIPO data found that Wallace did best among those white southerners who considered themselves Independents (Lipset and Raab 1970, 388; Crespi 1971, 120, 121, 125); but other researchers using SRC data found that Wallace ran best among southern Democrats and that it was Nixon who was the preferred choice of southern Independents.[19] More important than the relative proportions of Independents and Democrats among those who initially supported him, however, was Wallace's ability to hold on to those Democrats who did. The data compiled by Lipset and Raab showed significant defection rates among southern Republicans and Independents but none among southern Democrats (Lipset and Raab 1970, 388). This meant that the attempt of the Humphrey campaign to persuade voters to abandon Wallace and return to their partisan "home," whatever its success elsewhere, had practically no impact in the South.[20]

The use of party identification as a measure of political orientation is not without its problems, for, as two critics of this approach have pointed out,

[18] Lipset and Raab 1969, p. 29. On Thurmond's crucial role, see Chester 1969, pp. 433–50, 457–66.

[19] E. M. Schreiber, " 'Where the Ducks Are': Southern Strategy vs. Fourth Party," *Public Opinion Quarterly* 35 (Summer 1971): 164; Paul A. Beck, "Partisan Dealignment in the South," *American Political Science Review* 71 (June 1977): 484. It is difficult to account for the different results: the slightly different definitions of "the South" (Crespi included respondents from Kentucky, Oklahoma, and Tennessee in his sample "South"; Beck did not) hardly seem to explain it (Crespi 1971, p. 117; Beck, "Partisan Dealignment," p. 477).

[20] For confirmation of this point, see Lehnen's study of Florida and North Carolina voters: Lehnen 1970.

"identification often lags behind behavior" and "people may continue to think of themselves as belonging to a church long after they have stopped attending it." Instead, they suggested, one might better measure political orientation by the candidates the voter actually supported.[21] Using this method and looking at the immediately preceding presidential election, Lipset and Raab found that the 1968 Wallace voter in the South was most likely not to have voted at all in 1964; but if he did vote he was more likely to have voted for Goldwater than for Johnson.[22]

It seemed probable to many observers that the contours of the southern Wallace vote would be shaped by the unique religious environment of the region, "the most church-oriented part of the country" and "also the region most noted for fundamentalist, pietistic Protestantism" (Cleghorn 1968, 26). The religious overtones of the Wallace campaign in the South were hard to miss: the cars bearing two bumper stickers, "God Give Us A Leader" and "Wallace 1968," for example, or the campaign literature portraying Wallace as part of "God's plan" for America (Cleghorn 1968, 27; Bartley 1970, 86). Though the survey data indicated that the Wallace supporters were less likely to attend church than were others in the sample, they were indeed more likely to be affiliated with "pietistic" denominations such as the Methodists and the Baptists or with the smaller "neofundamentalist" sects.[23] Only one researcher tried to measure the actual impact of fundamentalist attitudes (toward Biblical authority, for example, or toward drinking) on candidate preference: the sociologist Anthony M. Orum. In his analysis of a sample of Atlanta residents, Orum discovered two significant correlations. First, the widely noted affinity of fundamentalists for Wallace was not simply an artifact of their church affiliations. *Within* each denomination, those with fundamentalist attitudes were the more likely to have voted for Wallace. And second, the fundamentalist-Wallace connection could not be explained away (as Lipset and Raab tried to do) by pointing to the lower educational levels of the fundamentalists; at all levels of education, the correlation between fundamentalist attitudes and vot-

---

[21] Everett Carll Ladd, Jr., and Charles D. Hadley, "Party Definition and Party Differentiation," *Public Opinion Quarterly* 37 (Spring 1973): 21–34 (quotation at p. 22).

[22] Lipset and Raab 1970, p. 389. The additional fact that two-thirds of the 1964 southern Goldwater voters went for Nixon four years later (Lipset and Raab 1969, p. 26) warrants reconsideration of the often-expressed view that Goldwater and Wallace appealed to largely the same constituency: Lubell, for example, stated that "in the South, Goldwater swept 235 counties which had never voted Republican for President. Wallace won 221 of them" (Lubell 1970, p. 46). Even those using ecological correlation, however, were unable to substantiate that view, one finding the correlation between the Goldwater vote and the Wallace vote in Georgia to be relatively insignificant and two others finding the correlation in Tennessee to be in fact negative. Bartley 1970, p. 87; Lee S. Greene and Jack E. Holmes, "Tennessee: A Politics of Peaceful Change," in William C. Havard, ed., *The Changing Politics of the South* (Baton Rouge: Louisiana State University Press, 1972), p. 185.

[23] McEvoy 1971, pp. 130–31; Carlson 1981, p. 89; Lipset and Raab 1970, p. 387.

ing for Wallace held. These correlations, Orum concluded, showed that "Wallace appealed to a very definite and clear segment of the religious community" and that fundamentalism had an independent impact on the Wallace vote (Orum 1970, 686; Lipset and Raab 1970, 392). Finally, for another characteristic frequently associated with fundamentalist beliefs, all the analysts using survey data confirmed the conclusions of those who relied on ecological analysis: southern Wallace supporters were far more likely to live in rural areas or in small towns than were Nixon or Humphrey supporters.[24]

The Southern Wallace Supporter as Revealed in Survey Data: Psychological Profiles

Since analysts of the southern Wallace vote did not investigate the impact of the other sociological variables mentioned earlier in this book, such as those connected to mobility and "status inconsistency," we will turn now to the analyses using psychological variables, which in some ways give a much sharper picture of the southern Wallace voter. The first thing that must be said about the Wallace supporters taken as a whole (i.e., nonsouthern as well as southern) is that they had the clearest issue-orientation of any of the candidate-preference groups in the 1968 campaign.[25] On this point the data compiled by the Survey Research Center is especially revealing. On economic issues, Wallace supporters were relatively liberal.[26] But on the three issues that the SRC analysts considered the major ones in 1968—the war in Vietnam, civil rights, and urban disorder (including both ghetto riots and antiwar demonstrations)— these supporters clustered at the right-wing end of the spectrum, favoring the most hawkish, the most segregationist, and the most repressive policy preferences on those respective issues.[27]

To what extent did the segregationist and repressive policy preferences of the Wallace supporters reflect deeper patterns of intolerance? Reviewing the

[24] Lipset and Raab 1970, pp. 389–90; Converse et al. 1969, p. 1101; McEvoy 1971, p. 117.

[25] See the review of the election studies dealing with this question in Daniel A. Mazmanian, *Third Parties in Presidential Elections* (Washington: Brookings Institution, 1974), pp. 15–19.

[26] Converse et al. 1969, p. 1100; Carlson 1981, pp. 90–91. Although they concurred that Wallace supporters occupied a "middle" position on economic issues, Lipset and Raab, on the basis of their analysis of AIPO data, found them closer to the Nixon supporters on these measures than did those using SRC data; southerners in general—whether backing Wallace, Nixon, or Humphrey—were less economically liberal than nonsoutherners (Lipset and Raab 1970, p. 402).

[27] Converse et al. 1969, p. 1097. Both McEvoy 1971 (p. 138) and Carlson 1981 (pp. 91–92) pointed out interesting contradictions in attitudes. Wallace supporters may have been the most belligerent in their policy preferences on the war, but (by a small margin) they were the least enthusiastic about the initial commitment in Vietnam. Humphrey supporters, on the other hand, were the most supportive of the initial commitment but by 1968 the most willing to de-escalate the conflict.

responses to the civil rights index devised by the SRC (which measured attitudes on specific civil rights legislation as well as racial segregation in general), McEvoy found that southern Wallace supporters were overwhelmingly
opposed to civil rights policies, three-quarters of them clustering at the "hostile" end of the scale. They were, moreover, far more likely to have negative
attitudes toward black people in general than were either Nixon or Humphrey
supporters.[28] Furthermore, they were somewhat more likely than the other
candidate-preference groups to have negative attitudes toward both Catholics
and Jews (McEvoy 1971, 132–33). Finally, when southern respondents were
asked "Which groups are responsible for trouble in the country?," Wallace
supporters were most likely to name Communists, the Federal Government,
blacks, hippies, students, and clergymen (in that order), least likely to name
the police or the Ku Klux Klan.[29]

By far the most significant difference between Wallace supporters and the
other southerners in this poll was that almost four-fifths of them named the
Federal Government as "responsible for the trouble in the country"; in fact,
the Federal Government ran only ten points behind "the Communists" as the
chief culprit in their minds (Lipset and Raab 1970, 399). However else we
interpret it, that opinion certainly indicates a high degree of political alienation; and the alienation of Wallace supporters was a question to which Mc-
Evoy devoted considerable attention. Using a national sample, he found that
of the three candidate-preference groups in 1968, Wallace supporters were the
most likely to score low on SRC scales measuring the legitimacy of government and the legitimacy of political institutions. McEvoy speculated that this

[28] McEvoy 1971, pp. 131–34, 158–59. The same conclusion was reached by Lipset and Raab
in their review of AIPO data (1970, p. 403). The most striking evidence on the role of racial
prejudice in the southern Wallace vote came from a small-scale study of residents of Memphis.
Like the others, these researchers found that Wallace support ran highest in the manual-worker
and less-educated categories. But they were also struck by the degree of support Wallace received
from "the upper-class, businessmen, white-collar, higher-income groups, as well as those who
have received postgraduate education." On the other hand, when they measured racial attitudes
(toward school desegregation, open housing, and integration in general) they found that it was
those attitudes that correlated best with the Wallace vote, even when all other variables were
controlled. In other words, "irrespective of one's education, income, class identification, and
type of job, the more deeply he was for segregation, the more likely it was that he would vote for
Wallace" (Wie and Mahood 1971, quotation at p. 542).

In contrast, a later study using 1972 survey data for the entire nation concluded that "in the
South attitudes toward Wallace were not influenced by racial beliefs," because "white southerners have been socialized into a set of racial beliefs that are independent of their political positions." However, the author's research design—correlating respondents' answers to "Do you
believe blacks come from a less able race?" with their ratings of Wallace on a scalometer—is so
different from those we are surveying here that it is hard to use his findings for comparative
purposes (Wasserman 1979; quotation at p. 247).

[29] Lipset and Raab 1970, p. 399. Southern Wallace supporters were slightly more likely to
name Jews than supporters of the other two candidates, but only 9 percent did so (as opposed to
8 percent of Humphrey supporters and 7 percent of Nixon supporters).

alienation, insofar as it was shared by southern Wallace supporters, reflected the identification of the Federal Government with the enforcement of civil rights and the political process with the acceptance of black demands (McEvoy 1971, 118–19, 144, 161–62). His speculations were confirmed by a study of 1968 campaign activists in five southern communities, which found that the Wallace activists were the most alienated of the three groups "largely because national policy on the race question had run counter to their preferences for more than a decade" (St. Angelo and Dobson 1975, 55).

This manifest *political* alienation, however, was not linked to any unusual degree of *personal* alienation. Carefully distinguishing between the two in her analysis of the responses of a national sample, Carlson found that those who preferred Wallace were not much different than those preferring the other candidates in their feelings of either personal distrust or personal powerlessness. It was specifically in the area of political distrust and political powerlessness that the Wallace supporters were strikingly high.[30] Similarly, McEvoy found that when Wallace supporters were tested on standard indexes of general "authoritarianism," they were not significantly different from other candidate-preference groups. But when he devised his own "political vengeance" index (asking respondents to agree/disagree with statements such as "Sometimes I have felt that the best thing for our country might be the death of some of our political leaders"), the Wallace supporters scored very high: "At every educational level, Wallace supporters were *at least* twice as likely, and sometimes three or four times as likely, as the other candidate-preference groups to score at the extreme high end of the Political Vengeance Index. These people were very angry indeed with the government, and the recurring themes of violence in Wallace's campaign must have met with the approval of 30 to 50 percent of his supporters" (McEvoy 1971, 136–38, 140, 162).

The Southern Wallace Voter: A Composite Profile

Having surveyed all the published evidence about which southerners voted for George Wallace in 1968 and what broader attitudes might have led them to make that presidential choice, we can briefly summarize the findings. The typical southern Wallace voter, so the cumulative survey data tells us, was probably a young man, more certainly someone who worked either as a manual worker or as a farmer and who had received relatively little formal educa-

---

[30] Carlson 1981, pp. 111–20. She rejected the possibility that Wallace's supporters were alienated because they were already marginal participants (ibid., pp. 99–102). The marginal-participation hypothesis had been raised by McEvoy; but on the basis of his data he had been unable to determine what the effect of their low education, weak party identification, and rural residence—all variables associated with "marginal" political participation—was on the Wallace supporters' feelings of powerlessness (McEvoy 1971, pp. 111, 124).

tion. Whether he considered himself a Democrat or an Independent is a matter of dispute but he was not a Republican; in any case, in 1964 he had either voted for Goldwater or did not vote at all. In both his individual religious beliefs and his denominational affiliation he was probably a fundamentalist Protestant. He was more likely than not to live in a rural area or small town.

We have also seen the degree to which "the weight of history" so impressed the social scientists analyzing the southern Wallace vote that many of them preferred to use methods involving ecological correlation. The conclusions of those using those methods were that the typical Wallace voter lived not only in a rural area but in one containing sizable concentrations of black people. That suggested a racial motivation behind the Wallace vote, a suggestion confirmed by the overwhelming evidence accumulated by survey research on southern Wallace voters' attitudes. In turn racism was probably, as McEvoy speculated, the primary source of their profound political alienation and specifically of their distrust of government and their support for political violence.

It may well be that attitudes themselves rather than background characteristics were the best predictors of southern Wallace support. Certainly that was the conclusion of one small but suggestive survey of Memphis residents which found that a preference for Wallace correlated with opposition to desegregation even when income, occupation, and education were controlled (Wie and Mahood 1971). McEvoy, too, concluded from his far larger survey sample that "in the South, the strongest predictor of support for Wallace is . . . direct opposition to civil rights for Negroes" (McEvoy 1971, 144). On another attitudinal dimension, Orum found that religious fundamentalism independently correlated with Wallace support, which would account for certain patterns of behavior (such as voting against the sale of liquor by the drink) that racism could not. But the two attitudes may have been more closely connected than was commonly thought. Samuel Lubell, for example, came away from interview with Wallace voters in Richmond convinced that "they shared an ingrained, almost religious prejudice that the races ought to be kept separate. . . . One remark was repeated, as if from a Sunday school lesson, 'God didn't intend for whites and blacks to mix' " (Lubell 1970, 148).

Whether measured separately or taken together, racism and fundamentalism were part of the traditional political culture of the South, and it is hardly surprising that so many southerners responded warmly to what Lipset and Raab called the "preservatist" tone of the Wallace campaign: "for law and order, against government intervention in social problems," perhaps above all, "against the acceleration of change" (Lipset and Raab 1970, 340). Nor should we be surprised that those from the region's small towns and rural areas disproportionately supported George Wallace's crusade, since (in the words of one analyst of his campaign in Georgia) the candidate himself "spoke the idiom of the countryside. He combined racism and a (white) common-man campaign style with a general defense of rural-southern-small-town values. The Wallace campaign substantially rested on the assumption that folk customs and traditional modes of behavior were of more importance than laws, constitutional processes, and intellectual theories.''[31] If that assumption had a special resonance in the South, so too did Wallace's determination to defend traditional values against alien forces (most notably, the Federal Government) seeking to subvert them. As so often in the past the "plain people" of the South were once again being summoned to join in what W. J. Cash almost three decades before had called the ''"ritualistic assertion of the South's continuing identity, its will to remain unchanged and defy the ways of the Yankee and the world in favor of that one which had so long been its own.''[32]

[31] Bartley 1970, p. 85. Relevant to this broader interpretation of southern Wallace support is a study conducted in the fall of 1971 by Harold G. Grasmick. From his survey of a sample of North Carolinians, Grasmick concluded that a "traditionalist" value-orientation (including attitudes such as a belief in male dominance and tight kinship networks, a commitment to the local community, a fatalistic attitude toward life, and a suspicion of novelty) sharply differentiated Wallace supporters from other southerners even when racial attitudes were controlled. The implication he drew was that the southern Wallace movement was as much a reaction to the post–World War II industrialization and urbanization of the South as it was to racial protest and federal intervention (Grasmick 1974).

[32] Wilbur J. Cash, *The Mind of the South* (New York: Knopf, 1941), p. 337.

Nine _____

Nonsouthern Support for Wallace: The Politics of Protest?

BECAUSE OF ITS ROOTS in the South's traditional political culture and because it was so clearly part of a larger regional disaffection from the national Democratic party, the southern Wallace vote was relatively easy to comprehend. The Wallace vote outside the South, however—and half of his total came from outside the states of the old Confederacy—was both more startling and harder to explain. It was also a subject of far greater controversy among social scientists. Part of the problem they faced was the inadequacy of the data with which they had to work. Since there were practically no ecological analyses of aggregate data for the country outside the South in 1968, almost all the evidence they analyzed took the form of survey data.[1] However, since George Wallace received only about 8 percent of the vote outside the South, with a survey sample drawn from that 8 percent the risk of statistical insignificance

[1] One exception to this statement might be the study of Pennsylvania by Walter Dean Burnham and John D. Sprague, which touched upon the Wallace vote (Burnham and Sprague 1970).

This lack of analyses of aggregate data from outside the South leaves us particularly disadvantaged in explaining certain anomalies in the Wallace vote, especially in the West. Wallace ran best, as we have seen, in the states of the former Confederacy and adjacent Oklahoma, Kentucky, Maryland, and Delaware. But his best "nonsouthern" states turned out to be Nevada (13.2 percent), Idaho (12.8 percent), and Alaska (12.1 percent). In contrast he did slightly less well in the next, more "predictable" group of states, states with large concentrations of urban blacks and working-class whites such as Ohio (11.8 percent), Indiana (11.4 percent), and Missouri (11.4 percent). In Idaho, at least, "his greatest strength was in rural areas" and "he received his highest percent in an isolated area of small mines and farms located more than 100 miles from the nearest city of 5000 or more people." Herbert S. Duncombe and Boyd A. Martin, "The 1968 Election in Idaho," *Western Political Quarterly* 22 (September 1969): 497.

We can only speculate as to the basis for this pattern of western Wallace support. One study, which did not deal with political preferences, is nevertheless highly suggestive on its cultural context. Respondents in a Nevada town were given a series of attitudinal measures based on Frederick Jackson Turner's famous characterization of the "frontier personality"; the researchers conducting the study then correlated the results with the respondent's support for "reactive violence." The results "appear to emphasize the view that capable, praiseworthy individuals, much like the respondents themselves, are threatened by both 'outlaws' and unreasonable government controls and as a consequence they must own guns, stand ready to defend home and family, and support the use of force by public authorities against their outgroup enemies"—all major themes in the Wallace campaign. James Shields and Leonard Weinberg, "Reactive Violence and the American Frontier: A Contemporary Evaluation," *Western Political Quarterly* 29 (March 1976): 86–101 (quotation at p. 99).

or outright error was inevitably magnified when the sample was further broken down for analysis.

The Nonsouthern Wallace Supporter as Revealed in Survey Data

Turning to the survey data on Wallace support outside the South, we must first of all dispose of a substantive problem. We have already shown that southerners disproportionately supported the Wallace candidacy and suggested that their support was due in large part to Wallace's "southernness." As we shall shortly see, his nonsouthern supporters shared many of the same background characteristics and attitudes as his southern supporters. From all of this it is plausible to conclude that, even though we have left the geographical boundaries of the South, we are still talking about the same people, that (in other words) the nonsouthern Wallace vote was primarily the vote of transplanted southerners. Data from the Survey Research Center does indicate that whites who were raised in the South had a more favorable opinion of Wallace and were more likely to vote for him, whether they now lived in the South or not, than were whites who had been raised outside the South (Converse et al. 1969, 1103; Lipset and Raab 1970, 391). Nevertheless, it must be emphasized that there were not many of these "transplanted southerners" among Wallace voters, either in absolute or relative terms: at least 85 percent of "transplanted white southerners" did *not* vote for Wallace in 1968, and almost 90 percent of the nonsoutherners who did support Wallace came from outside the South (Lipset and Raab 1970, 391; McEvoy 1971, 115–16).

The nonsouthern Wallace supporter (including those who actually voted for him) was likely to be male,[2] and likely to be young.[3] He probably earned

[2] Lipset and Raab 1970, p. 386. Unlike the southern case, however, the male preference for Wallace did not hold in every category: within some of the very lowest income categories (family incomes of between $3,000 and $4,999 in the East and West); and among western manual workers, women were more likely to support Wallace than were men (Crespi 1971, p. 128).

[3] How much younger is difficult to say given the different age categories used by the various analysts. Lipset and Raab, for example, meticulously divided voters in their twenties into "21-to-25" and "26-to-29" categories but then lumped all the rest into two: "30-to-49" and "50-and-over." Crespi also began by using consistent categories ("21-to-29" and "30-to-39") but then lumped those in their forties and fifties into "40-to-59" and ended with a "60 and over" category.

As Crespi also pointed out, the correlation between preference for Wallace and youth varied significantly by region. Only in the East did the correlation strictly hold, with those in their twenties more supportive of Wallace than those in their thirties, who in turn were more supportive than those in their forties, and so on. In the Midwest, in contrast, those in their forties were *more* supportive than those in their thirties; and in the West (as in the South) those in their thirties were *more* supportive than those in their twenties. Even allowing for the usual margin of error, Crespi's

between $3,000 and $6,999 a year.[4] But, as in the South, a relatively low educational level was a more powerful predictor of Wallace support than low income (Lipset and Raab 1970, 385; Crespi 1971, 124). Occupationally, Wallace support outside the South was unusually concentrated among skilled and unskilled workers. Nonsouthern businessmen and service workers never found him attractive, and nonsouthern farmers, who initially had found him almost as attractive as did workers, abandoned him almost totally on Election Day (Lipset and Raab 1970, 384–85).

This concentration of the nonsouthern Wallace vote among skilled and unskilled workers attracted considerable attention from scholars, because it raised the question of the role of unions in structuring that vote. Initially, union families outside the South had been more likely than nonunion families by 25 percent to 17 percent to consider supporting Wallace (Lipset and Raab 1970, 385; Crespi 1971, 128). This surprising pattern was explored only by McEvoy who suggested an intriguing explanation; in his analysis of a national sample, he found that Wallace supporters were both more likely to consider themselves "working class" and to express feelings of class solidarity than were even the Humphrey supporters (McEvoy 1971, 129). Although by the time of the election the unions had succeeded in bringing down their members' Wallace vote to the nonunion average (Lipset and Raab 1970, 385), the initial appeal of Wallace to the rank-and-file seemed, for many observers, further evidence for the persistence of a combined race and class consciousness that had long troubled union leaders.

The political orientation of the nonsouthern Wallace voters was similar to that of their southern counterparts in that they were likely, at least according to AIPO data, to consider themselves Independents. In contrast to the South, however, those identifying themselves as Republicans were as likely (or slightly more likely) to vote for Wallace as were self-identified Democrats (Lipset and Raab 1970, 384). Using the alternative measure of a voter's political orientation, the candidates supported in a previous election, Lipset and Raab found that the nonsouthern Wallace voters were slightly more likely to have supported Goldwater than Johnson in 1964 but, as in the South, even more likely not to have voted at all (Lipset and Raab 1970, 384).

Unlike the variables we have so far discussed, the relationship of religion to the nonsouthern Wallace vote reveals a unique pattern. It is true that, as in the South, Baptists led all other Protestant denominations in voting for Wallace, with 16 percent voting for him (Lipset and Raab 1970, 385). Nonetheless, the second highest religious group in voting for Wallace outside the South

---

analysis should give pause to anyone trying to turn the modest correlation of youth with Wallace support into a major thesis (Crespi 1971, p. 128).

[4] The percentage differences in Wallace support by income level as revealed in AIPO data are clearer for the West than for either the Midwest or the East and were more obvious to Lipset and Raab than to Crespi (Lipset and Raab 1970, p. 385; Crespi 1971, p. 128).

was Roman Catholic (8 percent), and his vote was so low in Protestant denominations other than the Baptists that it is possible to say that outside the South Catholics were more likely than Protestants to vote for Wallace (Lipset and Raab 1970, 387). Jews, largely resident outside the South, gave virtually no support to Wallace (Lipset and Raab 1970, 387).

Finally, while there was a correlation for the South (revealed both through ecological analysis and survey methods) between living in a small town or in a rural area and voting for Wallace, no such correlation existed for the non-South as a whole. In the Midwest his early support was already disproportionately urban, and everywhere outside the South his rural support fell off dramatically between the summer and the election (Crespi 1971, 118; Lipset and Raab 1970, 385–86).

Only a few social scientists attempted to analyze the nonsouthern Wallace supporters in terms of the "status inconsistency" model that had earlier been suggested as a general explanation of right-wing behavior. Of those who did, only one found a correlation, and that among a small sample of activists in one city (Eitzen 1970). Others working with national samples found no significant correlations, and concluded, like Carlson, that "theories of status politics were simply useless in explaining any aspect of the Wallace voting in 1968" (Crespi 1971, 126; McEvoy 1971, 127–28; Carlson 1981, 109).

The attitudes of the nonsouthern Wallace supporters on specific issues apparently resembled those of the southerners; but unfortunately the researchers involved—in this case Lipset and Raab, as well as McEvoy and Carlson—seldom differentiated the attitudes of Wallace supporters on the basis of region. The evidence we do have indicates similar patterns of attitudes: moderately liberal on economic issues, opposed to civil rights, negatively predisposed toward blacks, deeply hostile to the Federal Government, and scoring high on McEvoy's "political vengeance" index.[5] In one interesting variation, nonsouthern Wallace supporters were much more likely than their southern counterparts to single out "Jews and college professors" as among those groups most "responsible for trouble in the country" (Lipset and Raab 1970, 399).

We have then a profile of the Wallace supporter outside the South; but because of the absence of complementary ecological analysis, because of ambiguities in the survey data, and because of the data that we do not have, it must of necessity be less conclusive than our southern profile. The typical nonsouth-

---

[5] Lipset and Raab 1970, pp. 399, 402–5; McEvoy 1971, pp. 120, 131. Two differences are worth noting. Though, as in the South, the Wallace supporters stood between the conservative Nixon supporters and the liberal Humphrey supporters in their position on economic issues, they were closer to the Nixon backers in their views than they were in the South (Lipset and Raab 1970, p. 402). And in their attitudes on civil rights, Wallace supporters outside the South were more likely to place themselves in a "neutral" position; only a small (as opposed to an overwhelming) majority clustered at the "hostile" end of the scale (McEvoy 1971, p. 131).

ern Wallace voter was a male, slightly more likely to be in his twenties, and most likely an unskilled worker and with an education that stopped at the twelfth grade. He was most likely to consider himself an Independent and in 1964 not to have voted at all. If he was a Protestant, he was most likely to be a Baptist. We have no evidence to indicate the degree to which he was more (or less) hawkish or repressive in his attitudes than his southern counterpart, although McEvoy believed that urban disorder rather than civil rights policies was the most salient issue to those nonsoutherners who had supported Wallace in the summer and early fall (McEvoy 1971, 144–45). Looking at his other attitudes, we can say that like the southerners the nonsouthern Wallace supporter was opposed to civil rights policies and likely to have negative attitudes toward black people (though in both cases to a lesser degree), and he would name approximately the same groups as the southerners as being "responsible for the trouble in the country," putting the Federal Government second only to "the Communists."

Wallace Support and the Working Class: An Explanation

Although the profile of the nonsouthern Wallace voter, as it emerged from the first wave of research, resembles that of the southerner in many ways, there were enough differences and enough unanswered questions to persuade some social scientists to undertake further investigations. Two differences already established were that those who actually voted for Wallace in the East, the Midwest, and the West were far more likely to live in large cities than in rural areas and that both among preelection supporters and among actual voters Roman Catholics were a higher proportion than in the South. These urban and/or Catholic voters constitute groups far removed from the rural fundamentalist milieu of the latter region. Why then were so many of their attitudes similar to those of the southerners? The most important work attempting to answer this question came from the research team of Thomas F. Pettigrew, Robert T. Riley, and Reeve D. Vanneman, who analyzed precinct-level aggregate data from the 1968 election and conducted their own voter surveys at various points between 1968 and 1970 in several northern cities, primarily Boston, Cleveland, and Gary.

The profile of the Wallace voter in these cities, as drawn by Pettigrew and the others, confirmed much of the material we have already presented. The major difference between their sample and the others we have considered so far is that, at least in Gary, the Wallace vote disproportionately came from those earning between $7,500 and $10,000 a year, a somewhat higher income level than in the data we have reviewed.[6] This profile presented a problem, for

[6] Pettigrew 1971, p. 240. The only new variable they introduced was that of geographical

the background characteristics of Wallace voters did not match their attitudes: "We had a picture of solid, fairly comfortable, fairly well-educated persons displaying psychological characteristics—political alienation, fear, distrust, racial bias—that generally are found most intensely among the worst-educated and most poverty-stricken segments of the population" (Pettigrew 1972, 49). Why was this so?

One particular response on their questionnaire gave them a clue: Wallace voters were by far the most likely of the three candidate-preference groups to agree with the statement that "the condition of the average man is getting worse" (Pettigrew 1971, 247). To follow the implications of that correlation they decided to use the well-known concept of "relative deprivation" as refined by the British sociologist W. G. Runciman.[7] Under Runciman's formulation, feelings of relative deprivation could come from an individual's comparison of his own fortune with that of others in his group, or with individuals in other groups, or with both. Applying his categories to the problem they were investigating, Pettigrew and his associates found that, even when all other variables were controlled, the Wallace voters came disproportionately from the ranks of the "fraternally deprived": those voters felt deprived not as individuals but as a group, as "white workers" who were not making gains comparable to those made by other groups. Which other groups? Blacks, obviously, but also white-collar workers and in particular professionals: their "resentment of the gains of professionals was consistently greater than resentment over the gains of black Americans." Further—this was the second major finding—the feelings of fraternal deprivation underlying such resentments were a better predictor of Wallace support than racial attitudes. Thus, they concluded, "the Wallace appeal had a strong economic as well as a racist flavor" (Vanneman and Pettigrew 1972, 471–74).

Pettigrew and the others should not be misunderstood: while they regarded it as an "oversimplification to view the Wallace movement in merely racial terms without fully considering class factors"[8]—that, after all, was the main

---

mobility: the Wallace vote in all three cities was more likely to have come from precincts that were unstable, whose "residents had lived somewhere else five years earlier" (ibid., p. 237).

[7] Though the general idea behind it goes back at least to Tocqueville, the concept first gained wide attention with the publication of Samuel A. Stouffer et al., *The American Soldier*, 2 vols. (Princeton: Princeton University Press, 1949). The reformulation is in W. G. Runciman, *Relative Deprivation and Social Justice: A Study of Attitudes to Social Inequality in Twentieth-Century England* (London: Routledge and Kegan Paul, 1966). For a critical review of the many sociological studies using "relative deprivation" (arguing that the concept is imprecise and lacks empirical confirmation), see Gurney and Tierney 1982. Curiously, however, they do not refer to the Pettigrew studies at all.

[8] Pettigrew 1971, p. 92. Pettigrew and his associates persistently referred to "class factors" in their articles and specifically pointed out that the Wallace voters were quite accurate in their perception of the greater income gains made by white-collar workers and professionals (Vanneman and Pettigrew 1972, p. 470). I should think that would exempt them from the charge that

point of their argument—they had no intention of minimizing the racism of the Wallace voters. They emphasized "fraternal deprivation" to the extent that they did *not* because it could best explain their respondents' racism but because it could best explain their vote. The "doubly deprived," for example—those who saw themselves falling behind as individuals and as members of the working class—were as likely as the fraternally deprived to reveal "contact racism," such as opposition to someone in their family bringing a black person home or to a black family moving next door; but they were far less likely to reveal "competitive racism," far less likely to believe that there was a conspiracy behind the ghetto riots or that elected officials paid too much attention to black demands than were the fraternally deprived (Vanneman and Pettigrew 1972, 476–81). It was a particular kind of racism, then, one more closely associated with a sense of group deprivation, that predisposed an individual to vote for Wallace. The bitter irony, the Pettigrew research team concluded, was that the Wallace voters "understandably deduce from all the publicity about the progress in civil rights in the past decade that Negroes, in contrast with themselves, are in fact 'making it big.' Yet the hard truth is that most Negroes . . . are not 'making it'—indeed, do not as a group approach the position of the Wallace supporters who see themselves threatened" (Pettigrew 1971, 251).

The studies by Pettigrew, Riley, and Vanneman, which subordinate the racist component in the nonsouthern Wallace vote to deeper feelings of "relative deprivation," offer us a somewhat different perspective from other analyses. Similar in his background and attitudes to his southern counterpart, the Wallace voter outside the South was quite possibly even more of a protest voter. He protested not, as did the southerners, against challenges to regional traditions but against his own position in the social structure. He voted for the man who attacked those who were—unfairly, as he saw it—getting ahead of him, a group including (but by no means confined to) black people. It is surely significant in this regard that, according to data cited by Lipset and Raab, nonsouthern Wallace supporters were likely to call their candidate a "radical" rather than use his own preferred designation of "conservative" (Lipset and Raab 1970, 364).

That Wallace possessed a "class" appeal for many of his nonsouthern working-class supporters, which was not identical with racism, raises the possibility that another candidate, with a different approach to the same resentments, might have won their loyalty. And that brings us to the great unanswerable question of the politics of 1968: what if Robert Kennedy had lived? The Kennedy literature, adulatory though it largely is, nonetheless contains so

---

social scientists using relative deprivation models seek to have it both ways, that "by arguing that injustice is in the eye of the beholder" they can "simultaneously justify protest movements and avoid condemning societal institutions" (Gurney and Tierney 1982, p. 44).

many references to the senator's appeal to Wallace voters that the possibility that many of them would have voted for him cannot be easily dismissed. The general argument of Kennedy partisans begins with the observation that in a number of states—but especially Indiana—Kennedy's primary victories were based on his sweep of working-class precincts.[9] Second, they argue, many of the white workers who had voted for Kennedy in the spring supported Wallace in the fall.[10] Third, they conclude, these workers voted for Kennedy in spite of his passionate commitment to racial equality; and they offer as evidence incidents such as the following interchange with a television correspondent at a rally in Gary:

> "Well, what do you think of Kennedy?"
>
> "We like Kennedy very much."
>
> "Why do you like him?"
>
> "He's a good man. We like what his brother did. Besides, he makes sense. We like what he says."
>
> "You know how he feels about Negroes?"
>
> "Yeah."
>
> "But I understand you're not terribly crazy about Negroes?"
>
> "Naw, don't like Negroes. Nobody around here likes Negroes."
>
> "Here's a man who stands for helping the Negro, and you say you don't like them. How can you vote for him?"
>
> "I don't know. Just like him."[11]

Two reasons were commonly offered for this apparent pattern of Kennedy-Wallace support. First, on the issue that concerned the nonsouthern Wallace voters the most, urban disorder, "all of these people felt that Kennedy would really do what he thought was right for the black people but, at the same time, would not tolerate lawlessness or violence. The Kennedy toughness came through on that. They were willing to gamble."[12] Beyond that, working-class whites "felt government had forgotten them: they too were among the unrepresented," but they believed that Kennedy would respond to their concerns.[13] It is almost impossible to evaluate the validity of these claims retrospectively; but it is at least suggestive that in 1972, according to one Election Day poll, Senator George McGovern, a far less appealing figure than Kennedy and widely portrayed as the candidate of antiwar protesters and the "counter-

---

[9] Jack Newfield, *Robert Kennedy: A Memoir* (New York: Dutton, 1969), pp. 253–54, 264.

[10] Newfield, *Robert Kennedy*, p. 83.

[11] Charles Quinn, interview, in Jean Stein and George Plimpton, eds., *American Journey: The Times of Robert Kennedy* (New York: Harcourt, Brace, Jovanovich, 1970), p. 247.

[12] Quinn, interview, in Stein and Plimpton, *American Journey*, p. 248.

[13] Arthur M. Schlesinger, Jr., *Robert Kennedy and His Times* (Boston: Houghton Mifflin, 1978), pp. 880–81.

culture,'' received the votes of almost as many of the 1968 nonsouthern Wallace voters as did President Nixon.[14]

The Background: The Discovery of "Middle America"

At the time most of the studies we have been considering appeared, the general impression was that the white working class had become politically conservative, part of a ''middle America'' that rejected the demands of the black, student, and antiwar insurgents of the late 1960s. Though never precisely defined, ''middle America'' was an aggregate which at its widest included all those whites who were neither affluent nor poor: its center appeared to lie somewhere between the upper ranks of blue-collar workers and the lower ranks of white-collar workers and the self-employed. An appeal to the various anxieties of this vast assemblage of people had of course been a major part of the Wallace campaign of 1968; but for many journalists the political significance of those anxieties received decisive confirmation in the municipal elections in the spring of 1969. In Los Angeles voters reelected right-wing maverick Sam Yorty after an inflammatory campaign against a moderate black opponent; in Minneapolis policeman Charles Stenvig running as an independent defeated the candidate of the dominant Democratic-Farmer-Labor party; and in the New York City mayoral primaries Republican voters rejected the liberal incumbent John Lindsay and Democrats chose their most conservative candidate. Though local factors affected the outcome in each case, what impressed most observers was the common pattern: in each case the victorious candidate stressed his firmness in repressing campus unrest and street crime; and in each case, against opposition from both nonwhites and the upper middle class, his margin of victory appeared to come from working-class and lower-middle class precincts.

With the contours of the Wallace vote the year before still in their minds and the results of the spring municipal elections even fresher, journalists spent a great part of 1969 and early 1970 studying these ''middle Americans.''[15] The people they interviewed saw ''a terrible unfairness in their lives, and an increasing lack of personal control over what happens to them'';[16] in the absence of a candidate who was responsive to their needs (Robert Kennedy was

[14] CBS News poll, cited in Theodore H. White, *The Making of the President, 1972* (New York: Atheneum, 1973), p. 344. In contrast, virtually the entire 1968 Wallace vote in the South appears to have gone to Nixon in 1972 (Bartley and Graham 1975, pp. 173–74).

[15] The journalistic literature on this subject is voluminous but see especially Pete Hamill, ''The Revolt of the White Lower Middle Class,'' *New York* 2 (April 14, 1969): 27–30; Peter Schrag, ''The Forgotten American,'' *Harper's* 239 (August 1969): 27–34; ''The Troubled American: A Special Report on the White Majority,'' *Newsweek* 74 (October 6, 1969): 29–73; and Michael Lerner, ''Respectable Bigotry,'' *American Scholar* 38 (Autumn 1969): 606–16.

[16] Hamill, ''Revolt of the White Lower Middle Class,'' p. 30.

frequently invoked) they would turn to the negative appeals of a Sam Yorty or even of a George Wallace. So stated, the argument paralleled the more sophisticated social-scientific analysis of Pettigrew and Riley which emphasized feelings of "relative deprivation." Obviously many blue-collar workers *felt* deprived; but analysts continued to disagree on their objective economic situation, some arguing that they were indeed falling behind, others that they had made solid gains both absolutely and relative to other groups in the population.[17]

Perhaps the sources of this working-class anger were as much cultural as economic or, as one observer put it, "as much because their lives have been mocked for so long as because their taxes have been high."[18] Those engaged in the mockery of what journalists were calling "traditional American values" resided chiefly on college campuses, and it may have been the various symbolic gestures associated with campus protests—the obscene language, the use of drugs, the flag-burnings, and so on—that as much as the sporadic violence set so many "middle Americans" against the students. The anger that student protest could provoke was unforgettably symbolized on May 8, 1970, in New York City. A week before, President Nixon had announced that American forces were invading Cambodia in order to destroy enemy sanctuaries; four days before, protesting students had been shot by National Guardsmen on the Kent State campus in Ohio; the escalation of the war and the shootings together precipitated the most massive student protest in American history. Now, on May 8, an otherwise peaceful group of antiwar demonstrators in the Wall Street area was savagely attacked by construction workers who then forced their way into a nearby college and assaulted the students. The attack was less the spontaneous expression of working-class anger than it first appeared,[19] but to many analysts it represented, in the words of one well-known political scientists, only "the top of an iceberg of hard feelings" on the part of workers.[20]

Certainly the Nixon administration lost no time in offering its support to the construction workers. Following the attack Vice President Spiro Agnew let it be known that he regarded "that wave of revulsion that shook these construc-

[17] Compare, for example, Brendan Sexton, " 'Middle-Class' Workers and the New Politics," *Dissent* 16 (May–June 1969): 231–37, and Gus Tyler, "White Workers/Blue Mood," *Dissent* 19 (Winter 1972): 190–96, with Herman P. Miller, "A Profile of the Blue-Collar American," and Sar A. Levitan and Robert Taggart III, "The Blue-Collar Worker Weathers the 'Ordeal of Change,' " in Levitan, ed., *Blue-Collar Workers: A Symposium on Middle America* (New York: McGraw-Hill, 1971), pp. 47–75, 359–84.

[18] Dennis Hale, review of *A Populist Manifesto*, by Jack Newfield and Jeff Greenfield, *Commonweal* 96 (August 11, 1972): 434.

[19] See particularly the investigation of Fred J. Cook, "Hard-Hats: The Rampaging Partisans," *Nation* 210 (June 15, 1970): 712–19.

[20] Milton J. Rosenberg, Sidney Verba, and Philip E. Converse, *Vietnam and the Silent Majority: The Dove's Guide* (New York: Harper and Row, 1970), p. 72. The author of the phrase appears to have been Converse ("Acknowledgements," p. vii).

tion workers when they saw the flag of the United States defiled" as "understandable,"[21] and three weeks later President Nixon invited the leaders of the union to the White House. "We can't get the unions on the economic issues," one administration strategist remarked, "but maybe we can get them on the war."[22] The attitudes of union members on the war at this point—or for that matter those of the working class generally—are difficult to uncover,[23] but the administration was clever enough to connect the war with the disorder associated with antiwar protest. In a class-oriented rhetoric similar to Wallace's, spokesmen such as Agnew continually linked the disorder to a privileged elite, perceiving that many "middle Americans," as one sociologist put it, saw and resented "the protesters and the militants as sons and daughters of the well-to-do, who have attended elite colleges and are supported financially by their parents through all their radical activities."[24]

Nonsouthern Wallace Support and Racial Attitudes: A Reconsideration

This then was the political context in which the analyses of the 1968 Wallace vote appeared. Not only was Wallace running for governor in 1970 and look-

---

[21] Spiro Agnew, as quoted in Howard L. Reiter, "The Making of a Household Word," *Ripon Forum* 7 (March 1971): 18.

[22] As quoted in Elizabeth Drew, "The White House Hard Hats," *Atlantic* 226 (October 1970): 57.

[23] Much of the evidence compiled at the time suggested that blue-collar workers were among the more dovish groups in the electorate. An ecological analysis of referenda on the war in several cities, for example, found that working-class precincts were more likely to vote against the war than were middle-class precincts (Harlan Hahn, "Correlation of Public Sentiments About War: Local Referenda on the Vietnam Issue," *American Political Science Review* 64 [December 1970]: 1186–98). Gallup surveys taken three weeks after the Cambodian invasion and during the student strike showed "manual workers" more likely to favor immediate withdrawal than any other occupational group, and more likely to believe the war a mistake than either professionals or businessmen (*Gallup Opinion Index* 61 [July 1970]: 4, 5).

On the other hand, a subsequent review of all the changes in public opinion on the war offered some support to the 1970 perception of "middle American" backing for the war. After 1968, the authors concluded, "the well-educated and well-off members of society . . . joined the least advantaged members . . . in substantial opposition to the war," while "more modestly situated citizens remained more hawkish (and more supportive)." This group (which under their definition would seem to include many workers) remained more supportive, they continued, because "unlike the lowest status members of society, they did not have a negativism towards government born of a long history of poor treatment and privations, but their skepticism was not developed as finely as their better educated brethren, and their patriotism associated opposition to the war with disloyalty and other characteristics perceived as undesirable." William M. Lunch and Peter W. Sperlich, "American Public Opinion and the War in Vietnam," *Western Political Quarterly* 32 (March 1979): 40–41.

[24] Andrew J. Greeley, "The War and White Ethnic Groups: Turning Off 'The People,' " *New Republic* 162 (June 27, 1970): 15.

ing toward another presidential race in 1972, but in its rhetoric and actions, the Nixon administration gave every indication of trying to win Wallace's 1968 constituency away from him. Furthermore, by 1970 there was an emerging consensus on the part of politicians, journalists, and social scientists alike on two propositions about the Wallace following: on the issues that mattered to them and to which their candidate spoke (the war, civil rights, and social disorder), Wallace voters were far "to the right" of most other Americans; and those voters were disproportionately working class and/or lower middle class. Consequently Republicans gloated and Democrats worried over the possibility of building a "new majority" of voters on those issues, while the more impartially civic-minded expressed concern over the susceptibility of these segments of the population to "right-wing extremism."

A few social scientists, however, dissented from this emerging consensus, although it is significant that none of them seems to have disagreed with its portrayal of the *southern* Wallace voter as primarily racist in motivation and working class in background. For those who doubted that such a description fit the nonsouthern Wallace voter there were two possible lines of criticism. The easier of the two was to accept as proven the working-class base of Wallace support outside the South and then try to show that the anxieties that underlay its apparent racism could be addressed in a more enlightened manner. This was certainly the approach taken by the Kennedy partisans as well as by a number of independent journalists; and to some extent it was supported by the research of Pettigrew and his associates which stressed Wallace's appeal to those with feelings of "relative deprivation."

The more ambitious option was to argue that, in one way or another, working-class support for Wallace had been exaggerated. Some analysts argued this position by rearranging and reanalyzing the data on presidential voting preference in 1968.[25] But the most convincing challenge to the prevailing interpre-

---

[25] The most notable case of this rearranging of the data can be found in the work of the sociologist Richard F. Hamilton (Hamilton 1972, esp. pp. 460–67; and Hamilton 1975, pp. 147–82).

By creating a "manual worker" category, and including within it not only all kinds of blue-collar workers but farmers as well, Hamilton was able to argue that there was no significant difference between the proportion of the nonsouthern Wallace vote that came from "manual workers" and that which came from "nonmanuals," including professionals, businessmen and white-collar workers. (See Hamilton 1972, pp. 460–61, 504; Hamilton 1975, pp. 160–61, 164–65. Compare the conclusions in Converse 1969, p. 1102; McEvoy 1971, p. 115; Crespi 1971, p. 122; and Lipset and Raab 1970, p. 387.)

By breaking down responses to the SRC questions on civil rights item by item (education, employment, housing, and so on), he was also able to argue that these nonsouthern Wallace voters were not as generally opposed to civil rights as most observers had thought. McEvoy, who aggregated those responses, concluded that indeed they were (Hamilton 1972, pp. 463–66; McEvoy 1971, pp. 132–33, 158–59).

Furthermore, some of Hamilton's conclusions resulted not only from different analysis but from different evidence. He implied, for example, that outside the South "nonmanual" Wallace voters were more hostile to civil rights than the "manual" Wallace voters were. But Lipset and Raab found that when nonsouthern respondents were asked specifically whether the pace of black prog-

tation was devised by J. Michael Ross, Vanneman, and Pettigrew, who argued that voting preference, in the rapidly changing political context of the 1960s, was not the only, or even the most useful, way of evaluating either attitudes toward Wallace or toward civil rights for blacks. They constructed an alternative method, relying on the scalometer ratings developed by the Gallup organization for use in their AIPO surveys, in which the respondent was asked to place a candidate in one of ten boxes, from +5 ("someone . . . you like very much") to −5 ("someone . . . you dislike very much").[26] The data collected during a six-year period (from 1964 to 1970) had, they believed, the advantage of revealing Wallace support over time, unrelated to the particular circumstances of the 1968 presidential election.

What the data revealed was that the individuals outside the South who gave Wallace a highly favorable rating on the scalometer had profiles quite different from those of the Wallace supporters as commonly described. To be sure, income and education were correlated with attitudes toward Wallace in the usual ways, but gender predicted attitudes so well that it made many other correlations spurious: women simply did not like George Wallace. Even more significant were their findings that, as measured by the scalometer ratings, those nonsoutherners who did find Wallace attractive were more likely to be middle class, Republican, and Protestant, and less likely to live in large cities, than the Wallace voters studied by Lipset and Raab (Ross 1976, 74–80).

Equally striking were their conclusions about the correlation of attitudes with ratings of Wallace. Contrary to what might have been assumed, there was no significant correlation between those ratings and answers to the question, "Would you vote for a well-qualified Negro for President if your party nominated one?" Among nonsoutherners at various educational levels, Wallace's ratings (as McEvoy had also implied) correlated far better with attitudes toward repression or urban disorder than with attitudes toward civil rights (Ross 1976, 80–82). Like McEvoy, too, Ross and the others suggested that part of Wallace's appeal lay in his call for victory in Vietnam.

Returning to a discussion of attitudes and actual voting behavior in their conclusion, Ross, Vanneman, and Pettigrew found that, among those who felt "the Johnson administration is pushing racial integration too fast," it was Nixon not Wallace who was the chief beneficiary on Election Day 1968. Believing that "the role of antiblack attitudes on the selection of Wallace, while applicable to the South, has been exaggerated in the North," they stressed

---

ress should be accelerated, "manuals" clearly emerged as the more hostile category (Hamilton 1972, pp. 464–65; Lipset and Raab 1970, p. 403).

[26] Ross 1976, p. 71. For a parallel effort by two political scientists using what they called a "feeling thermometer," see the work of Herbert F. Weisberg and Jerrold G. Rusk, "Dimensions of Candidate Evaluation," *American Political Science Review* 64 (December 1970): 1167–85; and Weisberg and Rusk, "Perceptions of Presidential Candidates: Implications for Electoral Change," *Midwest Journal of Political Science* 16 (August 1972): 388–410.

other factors that led voters to respond favorably to him. One, obvious in view of their earlier work, was his "class" appeal to feelings of "relative deprivation"; another, his simplistic solutions, which were "most likely to be accepted by the less sophisticated segments of the population"; a third, his "aggressive attacks against a large number of targets," which "provided a socially acceptable outlet for the psychological tensions among males (particularly the under-30 cohort) that the political situation in the 1960s generated" (Ross 1976, 83, 85, 86).

In view of the way the conclusions of this article differ from almost all the others we have discussed, what are we to make of it? In the first place, it is obvious to even the most casual reader that Ross, Vanneman, and Pettigrew had more than a limited academic purpose in writing it. As committed supporters of racial integration, they expressed concern at the very outset that Wallace's various electoral successes had been "interpreted as demonstrating that white racial antagonism is increasing" and that "unless elected officials alter their pro-civil rights policies . . . serious repercussions will follow." The result of those interpretations was that "both parties have come to feel they must oppose the type of civil rights programs that characterized the 1960s" (Ross 1976, 69, 90); and so the authors set out to challenge the interpretations that had made such regression possible.

Insofar as Ross, Vanneman, and Pettigrew arrayed their conclusions against the prevailing view, to some extent they were able to do so by setting up the proverbial "straw man." In fact, none of the other social scientists had ever argued that each and every Wallace supporter was a racial bigot. Lipset and Raab, for example, had noted that almost half of all Wallace supporters, including the southerners, did *not* believe that "Negro progress was too fast."[27] The evidence that these academic dissenters introduced made relatively small changes in the actual patterns of data. But the strikingly different emphasis of their studies was in itself a contribution to the debate, challenging the oversimplified images of Wallace supporters that had emerged among journalists and even among some scholars. In particular they helped redirect attention toward racist and repressive attitudes among the more affluent, better-educated middle class which had loomed so large in the early 1960s as the source of right-wing political activity and which was already producing right-wing leaders with an appeal far greater than George Wallace's.

[27] Lipset and Raab 1970, p. 402. On the other hand, 44 percent of Wallace supporters *did* think "Negro progress was too fast," as opposed to 24 percent of Humphrey supporters and 22 percent of Nixon supporters (ibid., p. 401).

Ten

Wallace in Context: Reaction, Realignment, and a Society in Crisis

IN THE EARLY 1970s most social scientists analyzing George Wallace's support spent their efforts examining survey data in order to locate his principal constituency, and most of them located that constituency in the white working class. These findings raised a larger issue: many of those who stressed Wallace's working-class support also explained it as another example of a political "extremism" that found its followers among those who, because of their lack of education or their isolation, were not integrated into broader national norms. But was that assumption necessarily correct? Or were the better-integrated segments of society—and perhaps the norms themselves—conducive to "extremism," at least under certain conditions?

The first scholar to raise that question as far as Wallace support was concerned was Rogin, who had already established himself as the major critic of earlier attempts to explain support for McCarthy as a legacy of Populism. When he subsequently moved on to analyze Wallace's support, Rogin sketched out an extraordinarily bold and suggestive explanation of right-wing political behavior which he would then apply to comparable developments in his adopted state of California. Unlike the other researchers studying the subject, however, Rogin was less interested in Wallace's 1968 support than in his earlier showing in the 1964 primaries.

In 1964, it will be remembered, Wallace had received about 34 percent of the vote in Wisconsin, about 30 percent in Indiana, and about 43 percent in Maryland. At the time Lipset, like most observers, had attributed this surprising strength to the growing tendency of "normally Democratic white working-class areas" to vote "most heavily against civil rights," whether against fair-housing referenda or for candidates like Wallace (Lipset 1964, 22). In two articles—one on the Wallace vote in the Wisconsin primary, one covering Indiana and briefly touching on Maryland—Rogin expressed his disagreement with those conclusions. It was true enough, he wrote, that in the 1964 primaries "the Wallace vote was first and foremost an anti-Negro vote" (Rogin 1969, 40), but that vote was not, as Lipset had implied, uniformly a working-class vote. On the contrary: in Wisconsin, the data revealed that, while Wallace did indeed run well in working-class precincts, "the center of racist strength was not in working-class areas, but in the wealthy upper-middle-class suburbs of Milwaukee" (Rogin 1966, 100).

For Rogin to argue that Wallace found a significant proportion of his support in the upper middle class was to challenge a widely held assumption among social scientists that (as he phrased it) workers were "culturally deprived, prone to the use or acceptance of violence, less committed to the democratic rules of the game," and thus more likely to act on their racially prejudiced attitudes. This assumption, most notably articulated by Lipset, maintained that workers were liberal on economic issues but not on civil rights and civil liberties. On those increasingly salient issues "social scientists place greater trust in the economically more conservative urban middle class" (Rogin 1966, 99).

Upper-middle-class support for Wallace in Wisconsin, however, suggested to Rogin an alternative conclusion, one that would become central to his evolving interpretation of right-wing behavior. Unlike workers who "live a more concrete, present-oriented existence" and need a direct threat to which to respond, he argued, the "members of the middle class are more likely to be frightened by distant and abstract threats," including "the potential presence of Negroes." Those who sought to create homogeneous communities in the suburbs were terrified by this "potential presence," however remote in actuality, and "they perceive a threat both to property values and life-styles. In voting for Wallace these suburbanites could express their general resentment against outside interference in their lives—from government as well as Negroes. They could include a vote for Wallace in their generally conservative politics" (Rogin 1966, 107, 106).

Later, critics would question Rogin's methodology and object that there was no *direct* evidence that these middle-class Republicans had "crossed over" to vote for Wallace because of his racial stance.[1] Nevertheless, the concept of middle-class racism would become central to Rogin's subsequent analysis, and not only because of the increasing visibility of the black population in the late 1960s. Middle-class racism also illustrated the dangers inherent in the middle-class capacity for abstraction, so that what for some social scientists might indicate superior skills in ordering a complex social reality would become for Rogin an almost limitless inclination for hysterical reaction.

Rogin confined his analysis of the 1968 Wallace vote to a very brief comment written shortly after the election. As one might expect from his previous

[1] Rogin's chief methodological problem stemmed from basing his analysis on Wallace's percentage of the Democratic primary vote. Doing so, as Raymond Wolfinger and Fred Greenstein pointed out, "inflates the score attained by middle-class districts. The more Republican the district, the fewer the number of Democrats voting in the Democratic primary and hence the greater the proportion of the total Democratic vote contributed by Republicans crossing over" (Wolfinger and Greenstein 1968, pp. 758–59). M. Margaret Conway made a similar point in her examination of the Wallace vote in the 1964 primaries. While confirming Rogin's conclusions as to the extent of middle-class support for Wallace in Wisconsin, she cautioned that it could have come from a general "economic and political conservatism not connected with civil rights." In the two later primaries, in contrast, Wallace was more openly identified as an antiblack candidate and his support was thus more overtly racist (Conway 1968).

work, he was impressed—more, probably, than he should have been—by various Election Day polls that purported to show Wallace doing better in the upper-middle-class suburbs than in working-class precincts. Most of all, however, he emphasized the way in which the fixation of the various campaign commentators on Wallace, and on the violence, racism, and alienation associated with him, had led them to ignore the fundamental fact that "America fell apart in the year and a half before the election" and the Wallace movement was merely "the major symptom of the disease." He was aware, too, that, when the votes had been counted, something else happened: "Wallace, having focused the significance of the election around himself, had saved the two-party system. The meaning of the election came to reside in the flight from Wallace. . . . It was not just that Wallace made the other candidates look attractive; it was more as if Wallace had absorbed the poison in the body politic, and his weakness could then reassure us that things were not as bad as we thought" (Rogin 1968, 311, 312).

There are only two references to California in this brief essay but they foreshadow Rogin's next book. At one point he indicated that Wallace's poor showing in southern California, "the traditional center of right-wing strength," showed that "where a major party organized the grievances of a potential Wallace constituency" it could cut into his appeal. At another, he warned against the tendency to associate antiblack, antistudent, anti-intellectual rhetoric exclusively with Wallace supporters: "In California assaults on the colleges have come not from Wallaceite masses but from political leaders and those who actually administer places of learning" (Rogin 1968, 311, 312). Rogin wrote those lines as a faculty member at the University of California at Berkeley, where he would watch the mounting spiral of tension between the state and the students reach its bloody climax in the spring of 1969. It is impossible to understand the essay that culminates his next book—*Political Change in California*, coauthored with historian John L. Shover—without remembering that context. The book is in fact dedicated to the campus "victims of law and order" of 1969, the three students who died after Governor Ronald Reagan sent in the National Guard.

Rogin's Southern California: Right-Wing Politics Without Wallace

On one level, Rogin's analysis of political developments in twentieth-century California in this book, especially in the second chapter, parallels the analysis in his earlier state studies in *The Intellectuals and McCarthy*. We are again in familiar territory: as in Wisconsin and North Dakota, so in California, progressivism diverged from its Republican roots and foreshadowed the Democratic coalition of the New Deal era; as in those two midwestern states, the progressive coalition was created by a politician of rare skill, in this case Hiram Johnson; and as in the two midwestern states the progressive coalition was economically based, though in California not on farmers but on urban workers (Rogin, 1970a). Again, as in the two midwestern states, one essentially conservative group—in this case, the inhabitants of the eight counties of southern California, largely Protestants of British stock—temporarily joined the progressive coalition, in this case under the economic duress of the 1930s (Rogin 1970b, 160–65, 211–12n). Even as primary elections and referendum campaigns revealed southern Californians' distinctive right-wing orientation during this period,[2] the memory of the Depression was able to mute regional cleavages in the party vote in general elections through the 1950s. Then in 1958 right-wing activists from southern California took over the state Republican organization, succeeded in nominating their candidates, and "reoriented the party vote" (Rogin 1970b, 175). By the presidential election of 1964 and the gubernatorial election of 1966, the old regional split of the pre-Depression era had again become the major cleavage in California politics.

A distinction between tolerant, liberal northern Californians and moralistic, conservative southern Californians had long been part of the state's political folklore; and at the time Rogin's essay appeared the distinction had already been empirically confirmed for recent elections (Wolfinger and Greenstein 1969). Rogin, however, wanted to know *why* southern Californians were predisposed to right-wing attitudes. He rejected two possible answers at the outset: if, according to his scales, the influence of party could be ruled out (that is, if southern Californians were not disproportionately right-wing simply because they were more Republican), so could the influence of "tangible class and ethnic interests," which, no matter how they were defined, could not explain the southern affinity for right-wing politics. Instead, he asserted, it was necessary to leave mainstream political science's emphasis on "interests" and turn to anthropology's concern with "cultural symbols." Voters may not possess "worked-out political ideologies" but they do "respond to concrete political symbols." The problem, he went on, is to "explain what the symbols

[2] To demonstrate the continuity of the right-wing southern California political tradition, Rogin selected a number of key elections to investigate: "The present analysis was made from two antisubversive referenda, one in 1952, the other (the 'Francis Amendment') in 1962; the 1958 'right-to-work' referendum; the 1964 anti-fair-housing referendum (Proposition 14); the 1966 anti-obscenity referendum (Proposition 16); the Goldwater vote in the 1964 Republican presidential primary; and the 1966 Republican gubernatorial primary support for Ronald Reagan." "Analysis of electoral patterns in these contests revealed a general right-wing belief syndrome," he concluded: in other words, counties that disproportionately supported the antisubversive referendum in 1952, which won, also disproportionately supported the "right-to-work" referendum in 1958, which lost. Even though right-wingers tended to be Republicans, the "right-wing constituency" that clustered around primary candidates and ballot proposals "bore little relation to the normal party vote." Bay Area counties might vote Republican but they "consistently opposed the right-wing causes" mentioned above (Rogin 1970b, pp. 168–170).

of right-wing politics mean, and why they have found a home in southern California.'' What is it about ''Communists, saloons, Negroes, and pornography'' that as ''right-wing symbols . . . makes them so powerful south of the Tehachapis?'' (Rogin 1970b, 174, 180, 182–83, 184).

''A full answer to these questions,'' Rogin admitted, ''would require anthropological field work beyond the scope of this study''; what he hoped to achieve in this essay was the construction of ''a tentative theoretical orientation'' (Rogin 1970b, 184). In that effort, he drew upon diverse sources: traditional political theory, literary appraisals of life in southern California, even psychoanalysis. He began by drawing on Louis Hartz's insights in his comparative study *The Founding of New Societies*, in which Hartz worked out the implications of the fact that the American colonies had been settled at a particular point in the evolution of European political culture (Hartz 1964). What was an emerging ''Lockean-liberal'' ideology in the present culture became, in the American ''fragment culture,'' the only ideological tradition. ''Suppose,'' Rogin suggested, ''we look at southern California as a distended fragment of the American fragment, magnifying certain aspects of liberal, bourgeois culture'' (Rogin 1970b, 185).

Ever since the collapse of the railroad boom in 1886, the history of southern California had been a continual ''cycle of optimism, restlessness, longing, and dissatisfaction,'' a cycle that only exaggerated tendencies within the larger ''egalitarian, capitalist society.'' As Tocqueville was the first to point out, the egalitarian revolution that America symbolized had emancipated individuals from their traditional bonds, but in doing so it had also destroyed the ties that had provided life with meaning, and made them lonely. ''Seeking protection against their loneliness, men tried to immerse themselves totally in the world around them'' in two ways: ''through frenetic activity to control, dominate, and incorporate nature'' and ''through immersion in the crowd.'' In southern California the drive ''to control, dominate, and incorporate nature'' was unobstructed; the result was not only ''a technology . . . emancipated from any humanly comprehensible purposes'' but a general refusal of the southern Californian to admit that ''the world has an existence independent of his will and desire.''[3]

In the face of this synthetic environment, it was not surprising that ''southern Californians assert the values of home and family all the more strongly.'' The irony, however, was that ''family life has internalized the values of . . . public life,'' so that, while in theory the family ''is a refuge from the competitive, anonymous outside world,'' in fact family love is ''a tool in the fashion-

---

[3] Rogin 1970b, pp. 187, 189–90, 194, 195. In these comments Rogin was foreshadowing a major theme of his next book, an extended analysis of the ways equally ''lonely'' Americans of the early nineteenth century attempted to ''incorporate nature'' by subjugating the ''children of nature,'' the American Indians (see Rogin 1975).

ing of the child" to make him the success his parents hoped to be but were not (Rogin 1970b, 196, 197).

At the profoundest level, therefore, life in southern California is unreal. But it is also the logical consequence of the American dream. Since "southerners have no place to turn but to their dream: to give up the dream would be to give up everything"—they deflect their frustrations onto those who seem to threaten it. Here again, as "a distended fragment," they could only exaggerate the tendencies within the larger "Lockean-liberal" culture for, as Hartz had noted, "alien ideas are peculiarly threatening in a fragment universe since they challenge the organizing principles of the symbolic world and its very definition of reality." The targets of southern Californians' frustration thus included the two major presences in the 1960s that made "the southern California way of life seem anything less than inescapable": the dissident youths who would not be "mastered and incorporated," and angry blacks who would not be "incorporated or assimilated" (Rogin 1970b, 188, 189, 198, 199).

This search for scapegoats fit into a larger pattern of "hallucinatory politics" in southern California. The small-town, individualistic values constantly invoked by the region's right-wing spokesmen had as inauthentic a relationship to the real environment as did so much of the region's architecture: "Right-wingers attack government in an area that lives off the aerospace industry and has always depended on government water and land. Southern Californians demand a return to moral standards while engaging in orgies of credit buying, expense-account living, and cutthroat office politics. They assert frontier individualism in a world dominated by giant bureaucratic corporations and complex technology." Rogin concluded his discussion by noting that the right-wing tradition in southern California is rooted not "in an experienced past and present" but in "fantasies." Thus the logical political consummation of those fantasies was not even Goldwater, "the actual cowboy" who "has too many real ties to the past," but "an image on a screen, whose acts are dissociated from his being . . . Ronald Reagan, the man who plays cowboys" (Rogin 1970b, 189, 192, 200–201).

Several themes connect this interpretation of the right-wing politics of southern California to Rogin's earlier investigations of the sources of Wallace's support. In both cases, he emphasized the ways in which a perception of "distant and abstract threats," as well as more concrete class and racial conflicts, could predispose voters to support right-wing candidates; and in the case of southern California he suggested that the salience of those perceived threats was determined in large part by the social and cultural environment, so much so that it had given rise to a larger pattern of "hallucinatory politics." Further, it was the success of right-wing Republicans in exploiting these perceived threats that showed that "where a major party organized the grievances of a potential Wallace constituency" it could cut into his support. He suspected, too, that Reagan, as the latest and most successful product of that regional right-wing tradition, might be an attractive candidate at the national level to the "alienated working-class and petit-bourgeois elements" to which Wallace had appealed (Rogin 1968, 311).

A Second Look at Rogin's Southern California

Like many other social scientists in the late 1960s, Rogin sensed that the political landscape was undergoing an upheaval, with old alignments collapsing and new ones emerging under the pressures of racial conflict, cultural rebellion, and a protracted and divisive war. The Wallace movement and the right-wing ascendancy in California were indications of that upheaval. In contrast, the era of Joseph McCarthy now seemed one of tremendous partisan stability: McCarthy had arisen within a distinctive Republican context and had a largely Republican following. Further, he could not have led a right-wing mass movement because Communism, however much it aroused traditionally conservative elites, did not engage the attention of many ordinary Americans. Blacks, Rogin now argued, were far more potent as right-wing symbols. "For workers, like other urban residents, race has a reality that the Communist issue lacked" (Rogin 1966, 106). For middle-class suburbanites in Wisconsin and in southern California (though apparently not in northern California),[4] blacks were also powerful negative symbols, for reasons Rogin had already laid out. Because of these divergent sources of support, he would not rule out the possibility that "white racism may culminate in a mass anti-Negro political movement" (Rogin 1969, 45).

In spite of these continuities with his analysis of Wallace support, however, Rogin's essay on southern California is different from anything he had written before: more speculative, more impassioned, and more ambitious. Especially when compared to most social science literature, it is a dazzling performance. Yet the essay's undeniable brilliance does not eliminate the fundamental question: given Rogin's intention of constructing an alternative explanation of right-wing behavior, how well did he succeed in his objective? How valid is his explanation of the sources of right-wing behavior, either in southern California or in the nation as a whole?

One answer to that question came shortly after the book appeared, in the 1970 election.[5] A good deal of the urgent tone that underlies Rogin's essay comes from the book's major focus on "critical elections," those elections in which large numbers of voters shift their votes from one party to the other and

---

[4] Note for example the striking contrasts in the vote on the anti-fair-housing Proposition 14 in 1964, between two economically equivalent upper-income communities equally proximate to black ghettoes. In southern California, San Marino went four-to-one for it; in northern California, Pacific Heights split almost evenly (Wolfinger and Greenstein 1968, p. 762).

[5] Much of what follows in the next two paragraphs is indebted to the perceptive critique of Rogin's essay by Francis Carney (Carney 1971).

retain their new allegiance for decades thereafter. Rogin believed that "right-wing political appeals in southern California produced a critical realignment starting in the 1960s" and that the election of 1966 which sent Reagan to Sacramento with a million-vote plurality was one such election in that broader realignment (Rogin and Shover 1970, xv). In 1970, however, although Reagan was reelected to a second term, the Democrats regained control of the legislature and in two of the most visible contests, right-wingers were defeated, incumbent Republican George Murphy losing to Democrat John Tunney in the U.S. Senate race and, most remarkably, right-wing hero Max Rafferty losing to a black challenger, Wilson Riles, in the nonpartisan race for Superintendent of Public Instruction.

At a number of key points the 1970 results cast considerable doubt on the predictive power of Rogin's analysis. If the right-wing forces suffered setbacks in California that year, it was not for lack of effort. Tunney, in particular, had at various points in the campaign been accused of tolerating street crime, campus violence, and drug use; in one of their final political spots, the Murphy strategists portrayed the choice for the Senate as "between Anarchy or Law and Order. Senator George Murphy has supported every law-and-order bill. Representative John Tunney has not. It's that simple."[6] Now, according to Rogin, these themes would not only have a peculiar appeal to anxiety-ridden southern Californians but because of "the realignment in the 1960s" would determine the outcome. In fact, while Tunney did do better in northern California than in the southern part of the state, he did not need those northern votes at all: he would have been elected if *only* the eight southern California counties had voted. In the gubernatorial race, for reasons Rogin's hypothesis cannot explain, Reagan's vote between 1966 and 1970 *declined* far more sharply in the southern California counties than in all but one of the supposedly liberal Bay Area counties, thus narrowing the regional spread that according to Rogin was supposed to increase.[7] Indeed, two political scientists analyzing the election found that ideology played less of a role in the gubernatorial contest, where right-winger Reagan won, than in the race for Superintendent of Public Instruction, where right-winger Rafferty lost.[8] Whatever else may be said about the course of California politics in the last two decades,

[6] As quoted in Totton J. Anderson and Charles G. Bell, "The 1970 Election in California," *Western Political Quarterly* 24 (June 1971): 268.

[7] Thus between 1966 and 1970 Reagan's vote fell off about 7 percentage points in Los Angeles County, about 6 percentage points in Riverside and San Bernardino counties, about 5 in Orange County, 4 in Imperial, 3 in San Diego and Santa Barbara, and 2 in Ventura. Conversely, in the Bay Area counties, it fell off 6 percentage points in Alameda County but less than 2 percentage points in Contra Costa, less than 1 percentage point in Marin—and it actually increased, however slightly, in San Francisco and San Mateo counties. Statistics are from Richard Scammon, comp., *America Votes 7: A Handbook of Contemporary American Election Statistics 1966* (Washington: Governmental Affairs Institute, 1968), p. 45, and *America Votes 9: . . . 1970* (Washington: Governmental Affairs Institute, 1972), p. 43.

[8] Anderson and Bell, "The 1970 Election in California," p. 263.

the critical realignment producing a right-wing ascendancy that Rogin predicted does not seem to have occurred.

Even aside from its apparent lack of predictive power, his analysis contains a number of methodological and conceptual flaws that weaken his conclusions. The particular quantitative ecological methods he used in this essay differed only slightly from those employed in *The Intellectuals and McCarthy*; yet, for the early 1970s, especially when compared with the work on the southern Wallace vote we have discussed, his methods seem remarkably primitive. Although in his analysis of California he at least gave evidence of correlating elections with some demographic variables (instead of with each other, as in the first book), he once again relied primarily on county-level returns without either acknowledging or trying to overcome the limitations of such data.

In his essay on southern California, Rogin portrayed the region's inhabitants en masse as projecting the anxieties induced by an ultimately unbearable environment onto blacks, hippies, and Communists; but even in his first electoral triumph Reagan was opposed by sizable numbers of southern Californians. What distinguished those who voted for him, those who in Rogin's view had succumbed to the "hallucinatory politics" of the region? Since Rogin was not particularly clear on this point, we can only guess whom (other than those who were neither black nor Hispanic) he was talking about. One possibility is that he was really writing about the susceptibility of *middle-class* voters to right-wing political symbols ("middle-class" as defined by most social scientists in terms of particular income, occupational, and educational levels); but that is dubious because Rogin practically never used the term "middle class" to describe the voters of southern California. More probably, he was arguing along different lines, trying to make the point that the symbols that drew southern Californians' hostility were so potent they obliterated the class alignments of the New Deal era.

Although overemphasized by journalists intent on describing a conservative "middle America," the possibility that at least some segments of the white working class were, in the late 1960s, drifting rightward politically in response to social and cultural crisis must be taken seriously. In the specific case of southern California, one analysis of survey data at the time clearly suggested deep working-class anger over black and student protest and offered some support for the idea that the working class there was committed to traditional American (bourgeois?) beliefs in the value of hard work and the openness of the class structure.[9] We also have ecological analyses of the 1969 Los Angeles mayoral election indicating that incumbent Sam Yorty, who in many ways resembled Wallace more than did Reagan, ran equally well in white, non-

[9] H. Edward Ransford, "Blue-Collar Anger: Reactions to Student and Black Protest," *American Sociological Review* 37 (April 1972): 333–46.

Jewish precincts regardless of income level.[10] These analyses, appearing after Rogin's essay, tend to confirm his description of southern California working-class voting; neither offers an explanation. But, even before his essay appeared, two political scientists had independently of each other suggested that home ownership might help explain right-wing political behavior within the working class. One argued that home ownership had been a key variable in predicting Wallace support in the 1964 primaries;[11] the other pointed out that home ownership had always been more widespread in southern California than in the Bay Area.[12] All of this is to suggest that Rogin could have substantiated a good part of his thesis about a southern California "consensus" had he been willing either to utilize aggregate data below the county level or to undertake survey research.

Ultimately, in order to explain southern California political behavior, Rogin drew upon an older tradition of sociological analysis and emphasized the role of social mobility and demographic and economic expansion in creating the politics of the region. By the time he wrote his essay, however, it was becoming clear that there was no simple relationship between right-wing politics and such mobility and growth. Rather the evidence now suggested that neither new arrivals to California nor those moving around within the state were disproportionately right-wing and that there was no clear correlation between areas of population growth and areas of right-wing activity (Wolfinger and Greenstein 1969, 77–80). Rogin therefore was forced to argue that the connection between the two lay in the fact that in southern California "mobility and restlessness are *cultural* experiences" (Rogin 1970b, 208n; italics added).

Consciously aware of what he was doing or not, in his essay on southern

---

[10] "Yorty became mayor of Los Angeles, capitalizing on the subversive issue, anti-intellectualism, and a know-nothing political style. In the 1960s he easily incorporated racist resentments into his appeal" (Rogin 1970b, p. 212n).

The first major analysis of the 1969 mayoral contest in Los Angeles argued that the vote for Thomas Bradley (Yorty's opponent) correlated negatively with income and educational levels, implying that the working class opposed Yorty. Challenged by others, the authors subsequently reanalyzed their data and discovered that they had failed to control for race. Upon reanalysis they found only the slightest positive correlation of Bradley support with income and education, suggesting that among whites there was little difference in support for Yorty. Their critics found a higher positive correlation but suggested that was because of Jewish opposition to Yorty; with religion controlled, white working-class and upper-middle-class precincts showed little difference. The debate can be followed in Harlan Hahn and Timothy Almy, "Ethnic Politics and Racial Issues: Voting in Los Angeles," *Western Political Quarterly* 24 (December 1971): 719–30; Alan C. Acock and Robert M. Halley, "Ethnic Politics and Racial Issues Reconsidered," *WPQ* 28 (December 1975): 737–38; Hahn, David Klingman, and Harry Pachon, "Cleavages, Coalitions, and the Black Candidate: The Los Angeles Mayoralty Elections of 1969 and 1973," *WPQ* 29 (December 1976): 507–20; Halley, Acock, and Thomas H. Greene, "Ethnicity and Social Class: Voting in the 1973 Los Angeles Municipal Election," ibid., pp. 521–30.

[11] Edward Schneier, "The Scar of Wallace," *Nation* 207 (November 4, 1968): 455.

[12] James Q. Wilson, "A Guide to Reagan Country: The Political Culture of Southern California," *Commentary* 43 (May 1967): 38, 40.

California Rogin blended his own commitment to the left-wing politics of the late 1960s with insights drawn from a quite different tradition, that of the European conservatives of the nineteenth century who deplored the rise of a "mass society" in the aftermath of the French and Industrial revolutions. Abstracted from his specific discussion, Rogin's argument about American society appears to be much the same: cut loose from the bonds of tradition, Americans are a nation of individualists run amok; knowing no limits they pursue the unattainable and, like Melville's Captain Ahab, end by destroying their environment and themselves.

In contrast to this general trend of the society, which southern California only exaggerated, Rogin praised "the organic character" of cities like San Francisco in which "urban actors emerged with their special crafts, limited by the city's past, its ethnic diversity, its architecture, even its natural surroundings." In such cities, he noted approvingly, "partial identification insulated residents from universal goals" (Rogin 1970b, 191). Readers of *The Intellectuals and McCarthy* will appreciate the irony here: having in that book berated other scholars for portraying mass movements of ostensibly rootless individuals as threats to a humane social order (Rogin 1967, 16–26, 271–82), Rogin was now making a very similar indictment of unobstructed bourgeois liberalism.

Putting his analysis of political behavior in Southern California in perspective, what is the significance of Rogin's contribution? Any accurate assessment must acknowledge its weaknesses as well as its strengths. Rogin's tendency to overgeneralize makes it difficult to confirm or disprove his theories with empirical data, and when those theories could be tested, they were not always confirmed. His failure to distinguish between different groups within Southern California fatally weakened his attempts to predict statewide political trends. But granting all this, Rogin must still be credited with a brilliantly evocative description of American right-wing ideology and a sharp assessment of its probable sources; at least part of his analysis has been confirmed by subsequent research. He retrieved some of the more valuable insights of "mass society" theory. And finally, his work reminded other social scientists of the shared values and symbols that transcended the usually defined boundaries of class and that would make it possible for "working-class" Americans to become enthusiastic participants in right-wing coalitions.

Burnham: Wallace, Hitler, and the Comparative Dimension

Whatever their ideological persuasion, those who employed "mass society" concepts inevitably conjured up the historical phenomenon most frequently and most vividly linked to "mass society" theory in recent times—the Third Reich, with the attendant horrors of the Holocaust and World War II. Rogin did relatively little to develop the analogy between Germany in the early 1930s and America in the late 1960s, though he did remark, in his comment on the 1968 election, that "Wallace began, in September, with 22 percent of the popular vote; Hitler, catapulted to the center of German politics by the 1930 election, had won 18 percent''; and like Hitler, Wallace "could easily do better next time" (Rogin 1968, 310, 312). Had he decided to pursue that analogy, he would have had, first of all, to confront the fact that, for all its difficulties, America in the late 1960s was simply not Germany in the early 1930s. Here the democratic political system was long-established and overwhelmingly accepted; there was no major economic crisis; the frustrations of Vietnam were nowhere equivalent to the German defeat and humiliation of 1918–19—to take only the most obvious differences. Still, there were enough disturbing parallels—including not only broader evidence for youthful alienation and middle-class fear of disorder but specific charges by military and political leaders (including Wallace) that the armed forces had been "denied" victory in Vietnam—to suggest that a careful comparative analysis might have some utility.[13]

As it had evolved, "mass society" theory had tended to emphasize the importance of groups that integrated individuals into the social order. As Rogin described this emphasis, "groups direct the attention of their members away from the political satisfaction of deep-seated psychological grievances and toward bread-and-butter goals. In a meaningful psychological sense, groups control their members and make them rational" (Rogin 1967, 19). The most obvious institutions that might exercise such control were churches, political parties, and trade unions. If one chose to investigate the parallels between the American elections of the late 1960s and the German elections of the early 1930s and between those who supported Wallace and those who supported Hitler while holding to this "mass-society" model, one would first want to know what the impact of party identification and of union membership was on voting behavior. In the German case, it is generally agreed, the unions and the Social Democratic party to which they were closely linked remained the most durable bastions of opposition to the Nazi movement. In the American case, the obvious parallel would be the conjoined institutions of the unions, especially the mass-production unions in the old CIO, and the Democratic party.

The AIPO survey data as discussed by Lipset and Raab confirm what one holding this general perspective might expect: Democrats, in both the South and the non-South, were less likely to vote for Wallace than Independents,

---

[13] Theodore Draper, "The Specter of Weimar," *Social Research* 39 (Summer 1972): 326–27. The "Weimar analogy" would return a decade later, with decadence and inflation replacing disorder, but the delegitimization of institutions remaining, as key variables. See, as examples, Robert Alan Cook, "American Weimar," *Worldview* 23 (July 1980), 11–14; and Kevin P. Phillips, *Post-Conservative America: People, Politics, and Ideology in a Time of Crisis* (New York: Random House, 1982), pp. 155–64.

who by definition lacked strong party identification. Similarly, in the South union members were less likely to vote for Wallace than nonunion members; while there was no difference outside the South in the actual vote, union members were far more likely to have abandoned Wallace for Humphrey during the summer and early fall than nonunionized workers. Young adults, less integrated into either their party or their union, were also more likely to vote for Wallace than their elders. Unquestionably the Lipset-Raab analysis offers the strongest support for the "mass-society" interpretation of the 1968 election: to a considerable degree they found that the Democratic party and the unions did indeed "direct the attention of their members . . . toward bread-and-butter goals."

On the other hand, as we have seen, not all the data support the Lipset-Raab analysis. Some in fact contradict it. First, there is the SRC finding that southern Democrats were more likely to vote for Wallace than southern Independents. That can perhaps be explained away by the argument that within the traditional political culture of the region Wallace was considered the real Democrat. But the relative weakness of American union leadership is more difficult to explain. While in Weimar Germany the most unionized segments of the working class were least likely to vote for the Nazis,[14] in the nonsouthern United States the intense pro-Humphrey pressure on the part of union leaders succeeded only in bringing the Wallace vote of their membership down to that cast by nonunion workers. Those findings leave one with two alternatives. Perhaps parties and unions in general do not inhibit voters' "extremist" tendencies, in which case the "mass-society" model had best be scrapped. Or—and this is the alternative we shall be pursuing here—some more precise distinctions are needed. Perhaps *some* parties and *some* unions in *some* places, more in Germany than in the United States, are capable of curbing "extremist" tendencies: the question then becomes why. Why should AFL-CIO members and registered Democrats be *relatively* more susceptible to Wallace's appeal than their ostensible counterparts in Germany a generation before were to Hitler's?

The most plausible answer to that question—and in many ways the most interesting effort to put the Wallace vote in a broader historical context—came from the political scientist Walter Dean Burnham. At the outset it must be emphasized that, while Burnham drew the Wallace-Hitler analogy more sharply than any other analyst, he never argued that Wallace was another Hitler or that "German history will be repeated in any recognizable form in the United States" (Burnham 1972, 3). Rather, he was interested in exploring the parallels between the Wallace movement in the American context and the Nazi movement in the German context. Certainly he saw similarities. The Wallace

---

[14] Thomas Childers, *The Nazi Voter: The Social Foundations of Fascism in Germany, 1919–1933* (Chapel Hill: University of North California Press, 1983), pp. 110, 185–87, 253–57.

movement, he wrote at one point, ''should be identified for what it is: a cryp-tofascist or neofascist movement dedicated to the preservation of the petit-bourgeois 'little man' against the personalized conspirators—symbols for many of the large social forces at work—who are threatening both his material interests and his 'way of life.' ''[15]

Burnham's conceptual framework paralleled that of Rogin's essay on south-ern California, for he based much of his interpretation on the insights of Louis Hartz, particularly the conclusion that ''the overwhelming majority of Amer-icans have accepted bourgeois individualism and its Lockean-liberal political variant as their consensual value system.'' The existing literature on ''fascist and extreme right-wing movements,'' Burnham went on to explain, ''empha-sizes their close links with the radicalization of an anxiety-ridden middle class which is threatened with loss of either social values or social status, or both.'' Since ''the middle-class individualist value system'' dominates almost all so-cial strata in the United States, however, there might be ''neither a lower nor an upper limit, granted sufficiently disruptive social conditions, to the poten-tial appeal of a fascist movement in the United States'' (Burnham 1970, 176, 189, 190).

Given the dominance of these ''middle-class'' values, it was hardly likely that blue-collar workers would oppose an American fascism. ''Where work-ing-class people are not absorbed in political socialism and the discrete *Welt-anschauung* which goes with it, they will tend politically to behave like the European lower middle classes. That is, they will tend like their European *petit-bourgeois* counterparts to support left-liberal parties in relatively tranquil periods. But they will also tend to be exceptionally receptive to extremist movements of the 'radical center' when the pressure of crisis grows severe.'' This was particularly the case in the United States, Burnham continued, where ''the view of the world which the 'American common man' has is the antith-

---

[15] Burnham 1970, p. 189. Burnham's identification of ''fascism'' with the anxieties of the petite bourgeoisie or lower middle class certainly reflected the conventional view as of 1969, but such an identification—especially in the German case—has been sharply challenged by more recent research. On the basis of his ecological analysis of electoral data from Germany's major cities, Richard Hamilton concluded (1) that the conventional view that Nazi support came dispro-portionately from the lower middle class had no empirical basis, and (2) that in fact the Nazis ran best in upper-middle and upper-class districts (Hamilton, *Who Voted for Hitler?* [Princeton: Princeton University Press, 1982]). In his study (*The Nazi Voter*), Childers reached very similar conclusions, although in a more modulated fashion.

In another way, however, Burnham's analysis is actually strengthened by these findings. Ac-cording to Hamilton, previous scholars had been misled by the assumption of a close association of class and voting in the Weimar era which in fact did not exist. It was not therefore those from a particular social stratum (e.g., the ''lower middle class'') who abandoned the traditional con-servative and liberal parties to vote for the Nazis but all those voters (including a significant minority of working-class voters) adhering to a ''bourgeois'' ideology who did so (Hamilton, *Who Voted For Hitler?*, pp. 87–91, 119–23, 263–64, 451–52). It is precisely the dominance of that ''bourgeois'' ideology in the United States that was Burnham's starting point.

esis of that provided by Marxism. . . . [It] is not of the sort which suggests
that the individual as an individual has much control over his social or political
destiny. Still less does it suggest even the possibility that disciplined collective
action with others in the same class position could achieve sweeping and ben-
eficial social change through political action."[16]

American workers, in other words, were vulnerable "to capture under crisis
pressure by a reflexive and authoritarian mass movement" precisely because
they were so deeply imbued with prevailing middle-class values. That the
leadership of the American labor movement accepted those values, and those
of the capitalist institutions to which they were connected, is well-known,
which is probably why Burnham felt no need to discuss it. A labor movement
still largely operating on the "business-unionism" formula laid down by Samuel Gompers eighty years before had difficulty insulating its members against
an extremist movement such as Wallace's. It could also be argued—although
Burnham did not—that many union members' receptivity to Wallace came
directly from their self-interest in maintaining their particular unions as institutions protecting the privileges of *white* workers.[17]

What about the effectiveness of the Democratic party in insulating its adherents against extremism? Here Burnham was bothered by what he saw as
crucial omissions in the political science literature. Students of political socialization had emphasized that, in their individual life-cycles, voters became
relatively more fixed in their party identification and thus more "immune" to
the appeals of other parties, including extremist ones; their data however was
not only primarily American but drawn from the politically stable years of the
1940s and 1950s. At the same time, students of comparative party ideology
and structure differentiated between kinds of parties, some of which, like the
two major parties in the United States, were "voluntary, limited-liability associations" while others, especially in Continental Europe, were "political
churches with comprehensive world views." Burnham called the latter "confessional" parties, in which "the individual adherent may gain knowledge

---

[16] Burnham 1972, pp. 16–17. Relevant here is the work of the sociologist Donald I. Warren
which began to appear in the mid-1970s. From the interviews he and his associates conducted, as
well as data from a national sample, Warren concluded that many contemporary political phenomena—including the support given the presidential candidacy of George Wallace—could be traced
to the anger and alienation expressed by what he called "middle American radicals." Although
they were preponderantly blue-collar workers, these individuals did not so much represent a specific social stratum as share a common perception that they were squeezed between the rich and
the poor and that their concerns were being ignored by existing institutions, whether churches,
unions, or governments. Alienated and angry though they were, however, Warren stressed that,
unlike the college-educated "leftists" in his sample, these "middle American radicals" saw their
problems as caused not by defects in institutional structure but rather by character defects of
individuals, whether the "laziness" of the poor, the "arrogance" of educators, or the "deceit-
fulness" of politicians (Warren 1974; Warren 1976).

[17] For speculation along these lines, see Wasserman 1979, pp. 252–53.

through right belief about the world as to what his right conduct in it should be'' (Burnham 1972, 1, 2, 3). The most obvious example of European ''confessional'' parties were the Marxist groupings, the Socialists and Communists, but in some situations conditions of persecution could produce other ''confessional'' parties, the most relevant case here being the Catholic Center party in Germany. To what extent, Burnham wanted to know, did the ''political immunization'' as conceived by one group of political scientists depend upon the ''political confessionalism'' as conceived by the second? To answer that, the German experience might be relevant. At the same time, how meaningful were the American data on ''political immunization,'' since the United States had not in the twentieth century faced a crisis comparable to that of Europe? Here the appearance of the Wallace movement in the context of the turbulent late 1960s might be relevant.

Briefly summarized, what Burnham found was this: a longitudinal analysis of aggregate data from various electoral units in Germany revealed that, as expected, the members of the ''confessional parties,'' whether Marxist or Catholic, were relatively ''immune'' to the Nazi ''contagion.'' Those who voted for the Nazis, on the other hand, came disproportionately from the same areas that had supported the older nonconfessional (middle-class Protestant) parties which had played a major role in parliamentary politics before World War I. ''The issue, then, is not one of time [as some of the theorists of political socialization seemed to think] but of comparative political sociology. . . . When crisis comes, the crucial differentiation lies not in the *length of exposure* before the crisis, but in the relative *intensity of political commitment* to traditional patterns'' (Burnham 1972, 4–15).

Burnham suspected, however, that parties in the United States, particularly the heterogeneous Democrats, were unable to inculcate the ''intensity of political commitment'' necessary to ''immunize'' their supporters against extremism. What impressed him about the Wallace insurgency in 1968 was not its erosion under the attacks of labor leaders and politicians but rather ''the sheer size and penetrative power of the movement even at the end of the campaign.'' In fact, ''nearly one-quarter of the American voting population—and nearly one-fifth of the non-southern voting population—gave a Wallace vote serious consideration.'' Even that may have understated Wallace's potential because his poor showing outside the South—and thus his overall percentage—could have been due to a ''wasted-vote'' syndrome. ''If the United States had the kind of proportional representation which ruled the elections of Weimar Germany,'' he speculated, ''might not Wallace's share of the *non-southern* vote have equalled or exceeded Hitler's 18.3 percent in the 'breakthrough' election of 1930?'' (Burnham 1972, 20).

Like Rogin, therefore, Burnham was arguing that right-wing politics—in this case the Wallace movement—was the logical outcome of a ''liberal,'' bourgeois society in crisis. Since in the United States those bourgeois values

were shared even by those who under definitions might be considered working-class, they too would be susceptible to its appeal. This interpretation forms
only part of Burnham's broader analysis, however: we have yet to consider
his general explanation of why the Wallace movement appeared in the first
place.

Burnham: Wallace and the Crisis of the American
   Political System

Like Rogin and many other political scientists since Key had first formulated
the concept,[18] Burnham was interested in "critical elections" and the realignments they constituted. There had been three such realignments since the creation of the existing two-party system, each characterized by two or more
critical elections in a short period, in which old majorities dissolved and new
ones were created, followed by a generation of party stability: one in the mid-
1850s, which produced the Republican party and made it competitive in all
the states outside the South; one in the mid-1890s which gave it clear majority
status in the nation; and one in the late 1920s and early 1930s in which the
Republicans lost that majority status to the Democrats. In each case of realignment the appearance of third parties—the Free Soil party in the first case, the
Populists in the second, the LaFollette Progressives in the third—had preceded
the critical-election sequence, storm signals for the impending hurricane.
Given the atmosphere of crisis that accompanied the election of 1968 and its
aftermath, it was not unreasonable to see the American Independent party as
another such harbinger.[19]

Where Burnham diverged from other theorists of "critical elections"—and
what would seem to be his chief contribution—was his attempt to explain *why*
they occurred. Again he turned to the idea that "the overwhelming majority
of Americans have accepted bourgeois individualism." This dominance of
"Lockean-liberal" values not only affected individual behavior, he argued,
but had profound institutional consequences. On the one hand, "the socioeconomic system had developed and transformed itself from the beginning with
an energy and thrust unparalleled in modern history." On the other, the political system remained "dispersive and fragmented" and "dedicated to the defeat . . . of any attempt to generate domestic sovereignty." Over time, therefore,

[18] V. O. Key, "A Theory of Critical Elections," *Journal of Politics* 17 (February 1955): 3–18.
[19] See in general Burnham 1970, pp. 11–70, especially pp. 27–30. For the argument that the
American Independent party played no such role, see John F. Freie, "Minor Parties in Realigning
Eras," *American Politics Quarterly* 10 (January 1982): 47–63.

the socioeconomic system develops but the institutions of electoral politics and policy formation remain essentially unchanged. Moreover, they do not have much capacity to adjust incrementally to demand arising from socioeconomic dislocations. Dysfunctions centrally related to this process become more and more visible, until finally entire classes, regions, or other major sectors of the population are directly injured or come to see themselves as threatened by immediate danger. Then the triggering event occurs, critical realignment follows, and the universe of policy and of electoral coalitions is broadly redefined. (Burnham 1970, 176, 181)

Looking back, it was easy to discern the "socioeconomic dislocations" that the political system could not handle: in the 1850s slavery in the context of American expansionism, in the 1890s the strains of rapid industrialization, and after 1929 the catastrophe of the Depression. What comparable dislocations in the very recent past might make the elections of the late 1960s part of a realignment? Burnham pointed both to "the massive but uneven spread of material affluence" and to "one of the great population transfers of modern times," in which "large parts of the southern rural proletariat—particularly the black proletariat"—moved "from the countryside into the central cities" (Burnham 1970, 137–38). Whether or not those two developments quite explain a larger realignment, they were certainly essential in explaining the specifics of the Wallace movement, in terms both of proximity to an expanding black ghetto and of feelings of "relative deprivation" on the part of the blue-collar workers.

Another development that Burnham mentioned, however, may be the most illuminating: "the tendency of the social structure to be transformed under the pressure of the postwar technological explosion from the classic capitalist stratification pattern—owners, middle classes, working classes, farmers—into a pattern made up of those who can be classified in David Apter's terms as technologically competent, technologically obsolescent, and technologically superfluous." The first category, "the technologically competent," consisted of "a professional-managerial-technical elite . . . closely connected with the universities and research centers," many of whom "have been drawn—both out of ideology and interest—to the Federal Government's domestic social activism during the past decade."[20] Defining this group on the basis of its command of technology means placing the notably illiberal engineers at its center[21]—perhaps "mass intelligentsia" would be a better term. Nevertheless, his assumption that those in this broad category were "more politically cos-

[20] Burnham 1970, pp. 137, 139. Burnham borrowed this classification from the introductory essay in David Apter, ed., *Ideology and Discontent* (New York: Free Press, 1964), especially pp. 33–34.

[21] In one survey of college students cited by Lipset and Raab, engineering majors were far more supportive of the Wallace candidacy than any comparable group of students (Lipset and Raab 1970, p. 369).

mopolitan and socially permissive than . . . the society as a whole'' can be empirically substantiated, and the growing liberal attitudes and Democratic identification among professionals have been confirmed by subsequent survey data.[22]

Burnham was also perceptive in concluding that those in the third category, ''the technologically superfluous . . . , the people, white and black, who tend to be in the hard-core poverty areas'' formed ''clients and natural political allies'' of ''the new technological cosmopolitan elite.'' He offered as evidence the composition of John Lindsay's winning coalition in the New York mayoral race: having lost the Republican primary he ran on a third-party ticket and was able to forge an alliance between upper-income professionals in Manhattan and the black and Puerto Rican poor throughout the city (Burnham 1970, 139, 159–65).

In between the highly educated and the poor were the journalists' ''middle Americans,'' or what Burnham called ''an aggregation of Apter's 'technologically obsolescent' mixed no doubt with other elements.'' It was this group that constituted the major potential for realignment and from which Wallace drew the great bulk of his support. Like the previous third parties that had preceded realignments, the Wallace movement represented a counteroffensive ''by groups who felt they were outsiders against an elite whom they frequently viewed in conspiratorial terms.'' Unlike earlier insurgencies—but responding to the recent changes in the American social structure Burnham had outlined— the Wallace movement was ''rightist'' in orientation, attacking not only blacks but the Federal Government, intellectuals, and urban-cosmopolitan attitudes in general (Burnham 1970, 139, 29, 145).

As Burnham drew it the circle was now complete, American society in a trap from which it could not escape. The dominance of ''Lockean-liberal values'' had helped produce an autonomous socioeconomic system largely unconstrained by a ''dispersive and fragmented'' political system: hence the periodic crises and subsequent realignments resulting from massive but unforeseen change. On the other hand, the very pervasiveness of those values precluded any real alternative from gaining popular support. Those victimized by current social transformations were in fact ''the chief carriers and defenders of the old American middle-class dream and its associated values'' (Burnham 1970, 139), which is why they responded favorably to right-wing ''preservatist'' candidates.

Given this general interpretation of the present political situation, it was not hard for Burnham to conjure up frightening scenarios for the future. Should realignment come, it would be organized around cleavages that would mobi-

[22] Burnham 1970, p. 139. For confirmation see especially the data in Everett Carll Ladd, Jr., and Charles D. Hadley, *Transformations of the American Party System: Political Coalitions from the New Deal to the 1970s*, 2d ed. (New York: Norton, 1978), pp. 185–91, 211–31, 239–49, 284–91.

lize "black against white, peripheral regions against the center, parochials against cosmopolitans, blue-collar whites against both blacks and affluent liberals, the American great middle, with its strong attachment to the values of the traditional American political formula, against urban cosmopolitans, intellectuals, and students who have largely left that old credo behind." Whether the Republicans attempted "to absorb the Wallace following, and with it its militarism and racism" or the Wallace movement continued to grow, penetrating "the lower and lower-middle strata of the population until it reached perhaps a quarter or more of the total electorate" was less important than the polarization such cleavages would bring. "A political realignment organized around these terms would have as large a civil-war potential . . . as any critical realignment in our history" (Burnham 1970, 169, 170).

The similarities with Rogin's analysis of California politics should be obvious; but unlike Rogin—and this is perhaps the most important difference in their analyses—Burnham was not so much prophesying doom as constructing a model. Rogin was predicting on the basis of his analysis that the right wing *would* dominate the politics of the nation's largest state; Burnham, in contrast, was saying that *if* a realignment was occurring *then* the Wallace movement was a good indicator of the kinds of cleavages around which that realignment would be organized. But he was not at all sure that such a realignment was occurring. First, he argued, for a critical realignment to occur "the mere existence of explosive volatility in the electorate or of accumulating strain in the socioeconomic system" is insufficient; there must be "a detonator . . . some triggering event of scope and brutal force." The "accumulating social disaster in our metropolitan areas" constituted too gradual a process: "as long as most of the 'great middle' can exercise their Lockean prerogative of evading the confrontation by flight into remote suburbs there is little reason to suppose that they will feel under enough pressure to realign" (Burnham 1970, 170, 172).

Second, and equally important in the long run, the possibility of any realignment was negated by another major phenomenon of contemporary American politics, what Burnham called "disaggregation." A whole series of indicators—including the growth in the number of voters who split their tickets since the 1950s as well as the sharp rise in the number of self-styled Independents since the mid-1960s—suggested that "political parties are progressively losing their hold upon the electorate." Furthermore, "this continuing progression toward electoral disaggregation presupposes the disappearance at some point of system capacity for critical realignment" (Burnham 1970, 130, 191); if voters were losing their identification with parties in general, in other words, it was hard imagining them decisively abandoning one for the other, as opposed to choosing between individual candidates, and still harder to see parties as effective instruments of government. Whatever else may be said, the Nazis created a durable party; it was unclear whether George Wallace could do so.

Compelling as Burnham's model was, it left out the possibility that the increasingly erratic performance of the American economy would shape subsequent elections. As late as 1969 he could still describe Americans as "bathed in the warm glow of diffused affluence, vexed in spirit but enriched economically by our imperial military and space commitments" (Burnham 1970, 133), unaware that the quarter-century of American economic preeminence that had made such hopeful generalizations possible was just about to end. That same year a recession began; and, in part because of the Nixon administration's initial adherence to traditional Republican policies of fiscal and monetary restraint, voters began blaming the Republicans for it. As a consequence, the Republican attempt to forge a new majority based on "social issues" was met by the Democrats' effort to refurbish their old majority based on economic issues; and the Republican strategy to run against hippies was checked by the Democrats' determination to run, yet again, against Herbert Hoover.

Amidst such cross-currents in the 1970 midterm election, it was not easy to detect where, if anywhere, realignment had occurred. The most likely places to look were in the Senate races, especially in New York and Tennessee. In New York, the new Senator James Buckley was the first Conservative Party candidate to be elected to statewide office. Although the circumstances attending his election were unusual (he won with only 39 percent, in a three-way race), it is certainly suggestive that at the county level the Buckley vote appeared to correlate better with the Wallace vote of two years before than with the normal Republican vote in the past few elections (Feigert 1972, 272; Gargan 1975, 172–73). In Tennessee the three-term incumbent Democrat Albert Gore was defeated by Republican William Brock in a campaign directly appealing to the Wallace constituency. In a last-minute media blitz, for example, the Brock campaign stressed Gore's support for school busing to achieve racial integration and for gun registration and his opposition to the reimposition of school prayer and to the Supreme Court nominations of Clement Haynsworth and G. Harrold Carswell (Bartley and Graham 1975, 157–59). Elsewhere, as we have already seen in the case of California, the 1970 results either revealed continuing Democratic strength or were too ambiguous to lend much support to realignment models.

Still, as a model Burnham's theory had much to commend it. A realignment might not have occurred in the elections of 1968 and 1970, he could point out, but that did not rule out the possibility of its occurrences in the future. Indeed, insofar as his model indicated that "a decisive triumph of the political right is more likely than not to emerge in the near future," because of electoral disaggregation among other factors such a triumph "would most probably be a somewhat vague and ambiguous affair. It might very well emerge gradually" (Burnham 1970, 192). The fragmentary evidence we have just reviewed from New York and Tennessee would seem to confirm his hypothesis that, if a realignment were to occur, the Wallace voters would play a major role in it.

Even more important for our purposes, Burnham's model suggests the potential breadth of a right-wing appeal to the threatened "Lockean-liberal" values of the "great middle" of the American electorate. At the very least his analysis challenges the utility of trying to single out which of the narrowly defined categories of voters ("skilled blue-collar workers," "white-collar workers," etc.) would be most susceptible to such an appeal. It would be far easier to list those who would be least susceptible: nonwhites, obviously, but also portions of the "mass intelligentsia." In this connection it is worth reminding ourselves that in 1968 one of the best predictors of *not* voting for Wallace was having a college degree. In fact Crespi concluded his analysis by offering the observation that the structuring of Wallace support that year did not involve "traditional class conflicts so much as conflicts between educational strata" (Crespi 1971, 132). One would make the case that the elites Wallace so vociferously attacked in 1968 were defined not by their financial assets but by their academic credentials: "all those over-educated ivory-tower folks with pointed heads looking down their noses at us," as Wallace put it at one point in the campaign (as quoted in Lipset and Raab 1970, 350). It is also important to note that, for Burnham's realignment scenario to occur, a right-wing appeal need not persuade everyone or even a majority of those in the "great middle" in order to be successful. All that would be necessary would be for such a right-wing appeal to produce enough additional votes which, when combined with the normal party vote, would produce a durable majority.

Burnham's attempt to place Wallace in context is perhaps the most broadly useful of any explanatory model discussed so far. It not only helps us understand right-wing political behavior within the American electorate in the late 1960s, but provides a framework within which we can more easily comprehend the maneuverings of elite political strategists. To return to the events of 1968, it is highly likely that right-wing activists, whether or not they were actually involved in the Wallace movement, were drawing conclusions that paralleled Burnham's. First of all, far more than Joseph McCarthy or the right-wing efforts of the early 1960s, the Wallace campaign clearly revealed the existence of right-wing attitudes—on race, on repression, on the war—outside the Republican party which could be translated into votes. Some of the Goldwater strategists of 1964 had also detected such attitudes and attempted to mobilize them, but they were hobbled by their candidate's insistence on defending traditional right-wing economic positions. Wallace's genius was not so much that he sounded like an old-fashioned Populist on economic issues— a point most commentators misinterpreted—as that he did not talk about economic issues much at all. More than anyone else, Wallace was the first to build his campaign around what pundits were coming to call "social issues," and his relative success in reaching a largely Democratic, or more precisely, a non-Republican audience by doing so was the second lesson right-wing activists learned from 1968.

The old Democratic majority had become so fractured that, so long as a right-wing candidate did not actually attack the New Deal, enough of its segments could be pulled away to constitute a realignment. This was the implication of Burnham's model; it would also become, as we shall see, the goal of right-wing activists in the 1970s. But it could not be achieved—this was the third lesson of 1968, reinforced by the bitter memories of 1964—by candidates who scared the voters, which both Wallace and Goldwater did. In addition to all those who saw both men as "extremists," each alienated key segments of a potential right-wing constituency, Goldwater appearing too doctrinaire and aloof to many Wallace supporters and Wallace appearing too plebeian and disreputable to many of Goldwater's. Furthermore, both in their own individual ways were old-style candidates; neither adapted well to the medium of television. What was needed therefore—and what right-wing activists would spend the early 1970s trying to find—were attractive candidates who could deliver their right-wing appeals in soothing, carefully modulated tones. And where better to look than to southern California where, as Rogin had shrewdly observed, political careers had been built out of images on the screen?

Part Four

THE ''NEW RIGHT''

THE 1970s, IT HAS BEEN OBSERVED, began on August 9, 1974, the day Richard Nixon left the White House, and ended on January 20, 1981, the day Ronald Reagan entered it.[1] Whatever else might be said about that observation, for the purposes of understanding right-wing politics its implicit relegation of the Nixon years to "the 1960s" is a helpful one. The issues and tensions of those years, which the right wing had tried to exploit, were those of the previous decade. Most obviously, Nixon's career as president was determined by *the* event of the 1960s—the war in Vietnam. His triumphant reelection in 1972 came to a considerable degree from his apparent ability to transcend the divisions created by the war; but the revelations of 1973 made it clear that, from the time he became president, he had seen the opposition to the war as so threatening as to justify an extraordinary abuse of power. Congressional and public reaction to those revelations eventually forced him to resign. With Congress increasingly opposed to further involvement, and without Nixon's personal support, the pro-American regimes in South Vietnam and Cambodia collapsed within nine months of his resignation.

George Wallace, too, had profited from the divisions of the 1960s, most notably those over desegregation. Running for the Democratic presidential nomination in 1972, he had been able to win primaries in states as diverse as Florida, Michigan, and Maryland in large part because of his adamant stand against court-ordered busing.[2] Yet 1972 would turn out to be Wallace's last stand as a national figure, and only partly because a would-be assassin's bullets left him physically disabled. "Busing" was losing its drawing power as an issue: when Wallace again tried for the presidency in 1976, he found that except in racially polarized Boston the busing issue served him poorly; and that was a major reason why his campaign collapsed.

By mid-decade both the containment of Communism in Vietnam and the elimination of racial segregation at home were increasingly regarded as the

---

[1] Charles Krauthammer, "The Mea Culpa Generation," *New Republic* 184 (February 21, 1981): 17.

[2] The crucial role of the busing issue in Wallace's 1972 primary victories is strongly suggested in the newspaper polls taken at the time. See, for example, for Florida the Knight Newspapers poll as analyzed in Carlson 1981, pp. 157–72; and the Daniel Yankelovich poll for the *New York Times* as reported in Jack Rosenthal, "Times Survey Finds Nixon Is Florida's Hidden Victor," *New York Times*, March 17, 1972, pp. 1, 30. For Michigan, see the Market Opinion Research–*Detroit News* poll in Robert L. Pisor, "Michigan Protest Vote Strong," *Washington Post*, May 18, 1972, pp. A1, A11; and the Yankelovich–*New York Times* poll in Rosenthal, "Times Study Finds Doubt About War," *New York Times*, May 18, 1972, p. 30. For Maryland, see the Peter Hart–*Washington Post* poll in Haynes Johnson, "Nixon the Real Winner in Maryland," *Washington Post*, May 18, 1972, pp. A1, A11.

overcommitments of "the 1960s." The country was becoming very quiet, so much so that, while the fear of street crime remained, the sharper edge of the "law-and-order" issue—as reflected in widespread public opposition to riots and demonstrations—was now missing. Yet, even without a divisive war, black militancy, or palpable evidence of social unrest to exploit, the American right wing persisted. Not only did it persist but it expanded throughout the 1970s, so that by 1980 it had in all probability more participants, greater financial resources, tighter organization, and greater access to political power than at any point since World War II.

One of the major premises of this book has been that the forms the American right wing has taken over time cannot be understood without considering the pattern of events within which particular public perceptions have developed. This is particularly true for the phenomenon that would come to be called the "new right." The analyses of survey data and studies of activists that social scientists undertook make little sense without some consideration of the events that made "the 1970s" a crucial period for right-wing activity.

What events, then, help account for the development of the "new right"? A survey of the journalistic, as well as the scholarly, literature on America in the late 1970s allows us to reach some tentative conclusions. Certainly at one level the "new right" was a response to the women's movement that emerged in the 1970s, to the issues it raised, and to the policies it advocated. As one feminist commentator noted, "If there is anything genuinely 'new' about the current right wing in the United States, it is its tendency to locate sexual, reproductive, and family issues at the center of its political program—not as manipulative rhetoric only, but as the substantive core of a politics geared . . . to mobilizing a nationwide mass following" (Petchesky 1981, 207). The women's movement, along with the collateral movement for "gay liberation" and the broader phenomenon of the "sexual revolution," did in fact challenge traditional definitions of sexuality and the family and as such played a crucial role in mobilizing right-wing activists at the local level.

To perceive the "new right" as a reaction in this way, however, is to grasp much of the truth but not quite all of it. As we shall also see, the women's movement, the gay movement, and the "sexual revolution" all unfolded in an era of economic stagnation at home and the decline of American power in the world.[3] That context helps explain the organizational successes of the "new right" at the national level, in raising funds, in forming alliances with other conservative groups, and in gaining access to key business and political elites. It also helps account for aspects of the "new right's" ideology, since what would make the "new right" a major force in American politics was the

---

[3] My thinking about the relationship between opposition to the sexual-liberation movements of the 1970s and the general perception of political and economic crisis has been particularly stimulated by Walter Dean Burnham's essays (Burnham 1982, pp. 251–320).

way it used its antifeminist, antigay, and antisexual arguments to explain the larger societal crisis.

The demands of women and gay men for equal civil rights and economic opportunities were controversial enough, as the struggle over the proposed Equal Rights Amendment (ERA) and local antidiscrimination ordinances would prove. The impact of the "sexual revolution" on the two movements would, however, have even more socially divisive consequences because both incorporated a radical affirmation of human sexuality. Male exponents of gay liberation were straightforward and enthusiastic advocates of the "sexual revolution," one of them writing that "the new gay culture represents an affirmation of sexual play and experimentation that goes far beyond the repressive norms most people in this society including many homosexuals have internalized," and even arguing that in the current "search to reconcile unlimited sexual freedom and the emotional security of committed relationships" one could find evidence of "the 'homosexualization' of modern society."[4] The women's movement's response to the "sexual revolution," however, was more ambivalent: feminists divided among themselves, for example, over whether what they saw as pornography's degradation of women was a greater danger than the restrictions on freedom of expression which censorship would entail. Nonetheless, an affirmation of women's sexuality ran through both sides of the feminist debate over pornography and was even more notable in the feminist defense of abortion. Without an implicit acceptance of women as sexual beings, the proabortion argument could easily be turned aside by appeals to abstinence. Thus feminists' defense of abortion ultimately entailed a defense of the sexually active woman, the single adolescent as well as the married adult.[5]

The interaction of these two movements with the ongoing "sexual revolution" would have created problems for them in the best of times, but the 1970s were not the best of times. After 1973–74 the most obvious problem confronting Americans was the faltering performance of the economy; and it was the economic situation, as much as any other single factor, that defeated the next two occupants of the White House, the Republican Gerald Ford and the Democrat Jimmy Carter. Contrary to what might have been predicted by the dominant economic models, inflation continued to increase in spite of persistent unemployment. Clearly one factor in the growing dislocation was the steep

[4] Dennis Altman, *The Homosexualization of America, The Americanization of the Homosexual* (New York: St. Martin's, 1982), pp. xi, 172.

[5] It should be said that feminists have not always been clear on this crucial point; two who have been—and whose thinking has shaped my argument here—are Ellen Willis and Rosalind Pollack Petcheskey. See especially Willis's essay, "Abortion: Is a Woman a Person?" in *Beginning to See the Light: Pieces of a Decade* (New York: Knopf, 1981), pp. 205–11; and in general Petcheskey's book, *Abortion and Woman's Choice: The State, Sexuality, and Reproductive Freedom* (New York: Longman, 1984).

rise in the price of oil brought about by the actions of the Organization of Petroleum Exporting Countries; but, while malevolent-looking sheikhs continued to serve as targets for popular wrath, more sober commentators began to notice other, apparently unrelated weaknesses in the American economy. Arab machinations could not, for example, explain why the United States was becoming less competitive in world markets or why for the first time in the twentieth century America was becoming a net importer of manufactured goods.

The economic crisis of the mid-1970s broke upon a society still committed to the use of government power to rectify the problems arising out of economic growth. In the Nixon years the poor and racial minorities may not have been the favored objects of public policy they once had been, but the trend toward increasing regulation showed no signs of abating. In fact, by one estimate Nixon as president oversaw the creation of more regulatory agencies than even Franklin Roosevelt;[6] and much of this "new regulation" dealt not with specific industries but with problems affecting the private sector as a whole: environmental pollution, health hazards in the workplace, defective products, and sexual discrimination. Perceiving that even more challenges to management's prerogatives would follow the Democratic congressional landslide of 1974, business leaders decided to revamp their lobbying techniques and coordinate their efforts through organizations such as the Business Roundtable; and when revisions in the campaign-finance laws permitted them to do so, they quickly created corporate political action committees.[7] Equally important in the long run, corporations increased their support for research institutes and individual intellectuals rediscovering the virtues of the "free market" and eager to reshape Americans' thinking about economic policy.[8]

As a result of this business mobilization and the apparent irrelevance of the older economic wisdom, by the end of the 1970s a remarkably broad consensus had emerged not only as to what was wrong with the economy but as to what should be done about it. Since the direction of this consensus ran unmistakably in a laissez-faire capitalist direction, it directly or indirectly challenged many of the policy assumptions of the preceding four decades. In this emerging view both the failure of the private sector to compete effectively in world markets and the continuing rise in prices came from the same sources: union wage demands that drove up prices and reduced sales; government regulations

[6] Alfred A. Marcus, *Promises and Performance: Choosing and Implementing an Environmental Policy* (Westport, Conn.: Greenwood, 1980), p. xi.

[7] For the business mobilization of the mid-1970s, see Michael Useem, *The Inner Circle: Large Corporations and the Rise of Business Political Activity in the U.S. and U.K.* (New York: Oxford University Press, 1984), pp. 160–71; and Thomas Byrne Edsall, *The Politics of Inequality* (New York: Norton, 1984), pp. 107–40.

[8] For the growing support given "free market"–oriented research, see Saloma 1984, pp. 7–37; and Blumenthal 1986, pp. 32–86.

that increased costs, narrowed profit margins and hampered efficiency; welfare programs that demoralized the recipients and fueled government deficits; and a tax structure that reduced the incentives for investment. The message conveyed by spokesmen for this view was double-edged. To entrepreneurs and to those who identified with them, the message was liberating, a call for greater freedom. For others the call was clearly for greater discipline: more work for less pay, fewer government supports, less spending and more saving. For the advocates of this renascent laissez-faire ideology, the broadly defined enemy was hedonism,[9] a hedonism that for many of them was symbolized by the affirmation of sexuality being developed by feminists and gay men. Not only had sexuality long been suspect as a disruptive social force everywhere in the Western world, but in America the prevalence of what Weber had called "the Protestant ethic" meant that sexuality was inextricably associated with leisure; and leisure by definition was the antithesis of work.

Here then we have our first clue to the emergence of the "new right" in the latter half of the 1970s. As we shall see, local right-wing activists would oppose the specific policy objectives of the women's and gay movements, doing battle over the Equal Rights Amendment and legalized abortion and antidiscrimination ordinances; and in their opposition many of those who entered the lists against those adversaries never went beyond the issues at hand. To grasp the "new right" in its totality, however (its organizers and financial backers and resident intellectuals as well as those grass-roots activists), it is essential to remember the economic context of those conflicts, the general perception of stagnation and decline and the renascence of laissez-faire ideology. It is true enough that the antihedonistic and antisexual implications of that ideology were often left unspoken so that most Americans may not have even been aware of them; and it is also true that a sizable number of young professionals and managers saw nothing inconsistent between sexual adventure and promising careers in the corporate structure. Nonetheless, for crucial segments of the population—whether evangelical Protestants, aspiring Republican politi-

[9] This is of course precisely the term Daniel Bell used at the outset of his influential book, *The Cultural Contradictions of Capitalism* (New York: Basic Books, 1976), to describe what he had already seen as "the prevailing value" in American society at the beginning of the 1970s. To place the trends I have been describing within Bell's framework, the conservative spokesmen of the latter part of the decade agreed with him that the society was breaking down because of "the disjunction between the kind of organization and the norms demanded in the economic realm, and the norms of self-realization that are now central in the culture." They departed, however, from his pessimistic view that such "contradictions" were inherent in capitalism itself, and they had far more faith that massive doses of "that old-time religion" (in every sense of the phrase) could restore what Bell had called "the traditional bourgeois value system," with its emphasis on work, sobriety, frugality, and sexual restraint (quotations from ibid., pp. xi, 15, 55). For an account of the conservative revival of the 1970s, notable because it both describes and endorses this conviction that the authority of older values could be restored, see Burton Yale Pines, *Back to Basics: The Traditionalist Movement That Is Sweeping Grass-Roots America* (New York: Morrow, 1982).

cians, or influential business leaders—the connections between capitalism and "morality" were very real; and it was the mission of the spokesmen for the "new right" to convince them that the restoration of one was dependent on the preservation of the other.

The relationship between the United States and the rest of the world in the years after Nixon's departure also became increasingly traumatic for Americans, a second factor that helped to create a favorable environment for the antifeminist and antigay arguments of the "new right." The initial impact of the Vietnam experience had suggested a somewhat different outcome. The bitterness and frustration arising from the war had left most of the public suspicious of further entanglements, suspicions reflected not only in the new willingness of Congress to impose restraints on the traditionally interventionist executive branch but in the executive formulation of foreign policy itself. Henry Kissinger, who remained as Secretary of State under Gerald Ford, advocated a continuation of Nixon's ambitious effort to maintain world stability at relatively low cost, through trade agreements and arms-control negotiations (what was called "détente") with the Soviet Union and the delegation of defense responsibilities to regional powers such as Japan, Iran, and South Africa. Then the Carter administration took office maintaining that the bipolar conflict between the United States and the Soviet Union was increasingly irrelevant in a world confronted by global energy and environmental crises, economic rivalries between the capitalist powers, and the gap between an impoverished and underdeveloped "South" and a prosperous industrial "North"—all problems that required cooperation in the creation of a new world order.

A significant number of politicians and national-security bureaucrats had, however, never accepted Kissinger's assumptions about the possibility of détente and had never rejected the older, "Cold War," bipolar model of international conflict. Organizing into such groups as the Committee on the Present Danger and well represented in both parties, they emphasized what they saw as a threatening Soviet military buildup and Soviet "adventurism" in the Third World. As early as the 1976 presidential campaign, they began to have a decisive effect on American politics and foreign policy, forcing Ford and Kissinger to abandon their defense of détente; for the next four years they attacked Carter. As the winds of revolutionary change spread across the globe in the late 1970s and governments created by or identified with the United States succumbed to revolutions and were replaced by anti-American regimes—as in Ethiopia, Nicaragua, and Iran—those criticizing American "weakness" and calling for the use of force to defend American interests grew in number and in stature; and the public became increasingly receptive to their arguments. As early as 1976 advocates of an increase in defense spending once again began to outnumber its opponents; those who believed it was important that the United States should remain the world's leading military

power began to outnumber those who did not; and the percentage of those
willing to use military force to defend American interests accelerated.[10]

The assumptions underlying a forceful assertion of American power in the
''new Cold War'' had far-reaching implications for the women's movement
and the gay movement. Just as their affirmation of sexuality represented ''hedonism'' to spokesmen for the emerging capitalist ideology, so, for many of
those calling for a demonstration of American ''will,'' the broader challenge
to gender roles which underlay both movements represented a dangerous
''feminization'' of American society. The ''new right'' was particularly enthusiastic about expounding the ways this ''feminization'' would lead inevitably to the decline of American power in the world and ultimate Communist
victory. To adopt one of their favorite images, at a time when Americans
needed a new John Wayne to defend them against the encroaching barbarians,
the country was being turned over to women opposed to the traditional mas-
culine role and to gay men who had rejected it.[11] The appeal of this argument
did not necessarily depend on the accuracy of specific charges. Take, for example, the statement from a retired military officer incorporated into the best-
known right-wing campaign tract of 1980, Jerry Falwell's *Listen America!*:
''The top command structure of our military forces, the Pentagon is . . . under
the complete control of avid supporters of the women's liberation movement.'' As a description of empirical reality, the statement is controvertible.
As a metaphor for American ''weakness,'' however, it is undeniably compelling; and it fits in perfectly with Falwell's larger lament that America lacked
''male leadership,'' that the nation suffered from a ''tremendous vacuum of
godly men.''[12]

This then was the historical context in which the ''new right'' took shape;
the ''new right'' itself remains to be investigated. Its development occurred in
several stages, and at each stage scholarly analysis was dominated by particular questions. At first there were simply groups of activists defending what
they saw as the ''traditional family,'' most obviously against the challenges of
the women's and gay movements, but also against educational changes such as
the institution of sex education courses, the use of contemporary fiction in
literature courses, and the reintroduction of theories of evolution into the science curriculum. Many social scientists focused directly on these activists,
most notably in the case of the opponents of the Equal Rights Amendment and

[10] Potomac Associates poll, as analyzed in ''Concern for National Security Rising in U.S., Poll
Finds,'' *New York Times*, September 4, 1976, p. 6; for a review of relevant survey data for the
entire decade, see Bruce M. Russett, '' 'Don't Tread on Me': Public Opinion and Foreign Policy
in the Eighties,'' *Political Science Quarterly* 96 (Fall 1981): 381–400.

[11] On John Wayne as right-wing symbol see Crawford 1980, pp. 78–80, and Stephen B. Oates,
''Ghost Riders in the Sky,'' *Colorado Quarterly* 23 (Summer 1974): 67–75.

[12] Jerry Falwell, *Listen America!* (Garden City, N.Y.: Doubleday, 1980), pp. 158–59, 16–17.
The statement, according to Falwell, is from retired Brigadier General Andrew J. Gatsis.

of abortion. Some of these scholars were also interested in developing a theory that could explain their activism and they turned to various revised models of "status politics" for such a theory, whether they called it "cultural politics," "symbolic politics," or "the politics of lifestyle concern."

In the second stage, these "profamily" activists were linked to each other, and to networks of financial contributors, research institutes, and political candidates as well, by organizers such as Richard Viguerie, Howard Phillips, and Paul Weyrich. Though arguably this was the defining stage of the "new right," and therefore a precondition for everything that followed, this second stage attracted relatively little attention from social scientists, with two exceptions: those interested in the "new right's" ties to corporate leaders and—paradoxically—those studying the "new right's" self-consciously "populist" rhetoric.

In the third stage, men like Viguerie, Phillips, and Weyrich helped create organizations that sought to transform evangelical and fundamentalist Protestants into a major political force in support of the "new right" agenda: Jerry Falwell's Moral Majority would become the best-known of these organizations. In this third stage social scientists tended to concentrate on exploring the potential of organizations such as the Moral Majority, and to ask how many evangelicals and fundamentalists it could mobilize and why at that particular point in our history so many of them seemed available for mobilization.

The final stage, at least for our purposes here, was the 1980 election, by which point the "new right" was fully developed. With its network of political action committees, research institutes, and mobilization organizations such as the Moral Majority, it quickly took credit for the election of Ronald Reagan and many other Republican candidates. Social scientists, however, questioned whether the "new right" played quite the role it claimed and much of the media assumed it had. Such scholars attempted to uncover not only the factors behind the Republicans' victory but the degree to which the issues the "new right" stressed played a significant role in the outcome.

Eleven

Studies of "Profamily" Activists: "Status Politics" Revised and Revisited

EVEN BEFORE the strategists and spokesmen for the "new right" began making ideological connections between "morality" and capitalist growth, and between masculinity and the survival of the "Free World," signs of significant right-wing mobilization at the local grass-roots level appeared in the emergence of a variety of protest movements that had as their common denominator the defense of the "traditional family." The model of the family which they affirmed has been succinctly defined by two historians as one in which the father was "head and provider," the mother "nurturer and manager," and the children "replicas of the older generation" (Mathews and Mathews 1982, 14). In one way these protests were certainly reactions to the women's movement and, to a lesser degree, the gay movement. But these protests also expressed a positive desire to transmit traditional values to the younger generation. Not only were those values being challenged directly by feminists and gay activists but the ability to transmit them was being eroded by structural changes in American public education.[1] The most salient of those changes were the consolidation of school systems and the increasing dominance of such systems by administrators whose point of reference was their professional peers throughout the country rather than the community in which they served.

Given that situation it is not surprising that the mobilization of many "profamily" activists occurred before the mid-1970s (in the 1960s, in fact) over the efforts of school administrators to revise and expand the curriculum in a number of sensitive areas. One source of continuing controversy, which seems to have peaked in the late 1960s, was over the institution of courses in sex education. Those courses were neither as "value free" as their proponents claimed nor as "permissive" as their opponents feared; rather, as two political scientists observed, the controversy over sex education arrayed those who believed sexual impulses were to be *controlled* within a rationally determined

---

[1] It is primarily for this reason that I am not calling the often closely related protests discussed in this chapter "countermovements," a term currently enjoying popularity among sociologists to describe "conscious, collective, organized attempt[s] to resist or to reverse social change" (Mottl 1980, p. 620). But a "countermovement" has to have a "movement" to "counter," and "movements to teach a creationist theory of human origins or to prohibit sex education are not countermovements because the opponents are not social movements but professions" (Lo 1982, p. 119).

moral framework against those who believed such impulses were to be *denied* in accordance with traditional religious precepts.[2] A second area of dispute was over literature courses, less in this case because of dramatic curricular changes than because fiction itself—the material to be used in such courses, even as abridged and anthologized—had over the course of the past century moved far away from Victorian standards of propriety.[3] By far the longest-running dispute, however, occurred in the field of biology, specifically over the incorporation of the evolutionary theories of Charles Darwin.[4] Contrary to a widespread impression, the notorious Scopes trial of 1925 was in fact a victory for those fundamentalist Protestants who opposed the teaching of Darwinism, so much so that in the 1940s one survey showed that less than half of the biology teachers in the United States taught anything at all about evolution. In the context of rising concern over American science education in the late 1950s and 1960s, however, teams of scientists drafted revisions of curricula that were then incorporated into textbooks and Darwinist theory reappeared. The fundamentalists remained in opposition but changed their tactics and they now demanded "equal time" in the classroom for what they called "scientific creationism."

The politics of these controversies was very similar. Procedurally, the parents felt excluded from policy decisions and used the elected school boards to overrule the professional educators; substantively, the parents saw the new curricula and the accompanying textbooks as imposing alien values on their children and demanded their elimination. Ideologically, too, there were marked resemblances in the arguments of parents opposing sex education, modern literature, and Darwinian theory. One of the repeated concerns of those opponents of an expanded literature curriculum, for example, was the appearance of "obscene" words or allusions to sexual activity, fears that also were reflected in the opposition to sex education. Similarly, while it might seem hard to include opponents of Darwinian theory among "profamily" activists, what appeared to bother many of them was evolutionary theory's implicit challenge to traditional, absolutist religious and moral codes. "If man is an evolved animal," wrote one, "then the morals of the barnyard and the jungle are more natural . . . than the artificially imposed restrictions of premarital chastity and marital fidelity. Instead of monogamy, why not promiscuity and polygamy?"[5]

---

[2] Hottois and Milner 1975, pp 3–5. See also Richardson and Cranston 1981.

[3] For a survey of these disputes, see Edward B. Jenkinson, *Censorship in the Classroom: The Mind Benders* (Carbondale: Southern Illinois University Press, 1979).

[4] My analysis of the controversy over the teaching of "evolution" follows that in Dorothy Nelkin, *The Creation Controversy: Science or Scripture in the Schools* (New York: Norton, 1982).

[5] From a publication of the Institute for Creation Research, as quoted in Nelkin, *The Creation Controversy*, p. 168.

Beginning with the John Birch Society's initiative in leading the opposition to sex education in various cities, right-wing organizers entered these disputes[6] and came away convinced that success could be achieved by attacking remote interest groups and bureaucracies staffed by cosmopolitans. In many ways their attacks paralleled those made by George Wallace in his campaigns for the presidency, except that they focused on sexuality, the family, and the socialization of the young—topics that would loom steadily larger in right-wing discourse as the 1970s progressed. Finally, many of the opponents of these curricular changes believed they could trace the sources of the changes they opposed to a specific network of influential men and women who, significantly, were not "Communists" but something else, something they called "humanists," advocates of a "humanist religion."[7]

Profiles of "Profamily" Activists and Their Context

A determination to control the values imparted to one's children and the perceived threat from the educational bureaucracy accounted for the opposition to sex education, "modern" textbooks, and the teaching of "evolution" that we have just described; and those taking such positions constituted an important part of the emerging right-wing "profamily" constellation. Those individuals were not, however, systematically studied by social scientists. Rather, scholars concentrated on those who arose in opposition to the resurgent women's movement, which directly challenged the "traditional family." Whether it is true, as one distinguished historian has asserted, that "the equality of women and the institution of the family have long been at odds with each other" because "the historical family has depended for its existence and character on women's subordination," that was certainly the perception of the women's movement.[8] Determined to assert the rights of women to be individuals, feminists believed "that a call to the common welfare, whether it be to the well-being of children, or to the future of the family, or to the stability of society, has all too often abridged women's freedom of action."[9] Those who saw such goals as outweighing an individual woman's "self-fulfillment" were not long in responding.

The most dramatic evidence for this came in the unexpected defeat of a proposed amendment to the United States Constitution: "Equality of rights

[6] Mary Breasted, *Oh! Sex Education!* (New York: Praeger, 1970), pp. 10–12, 199–207; Clabaugh 1974, pp. 17–31, 49–56.

[7] As quoted in Breasted, *Oh! Sex Education!*, p. 58

[8] Carl N. Degler, *At Odds: Women and the Family in America from the Revolution to the Present* (New York: Oxford University Press, 1980), p. vi.

[9] Sheila M. Rothman, *Woman's Proper Place: A History of Changing Ideals and Practices, 1870 to the Present* (New York: Basic Books, 1978), p. 290.

under the law shall not be denied or abridged by the United States or by any state on account of sex.'' The defeat was a surprise because although the ideal of an equal rights amendment had been circulating for half a century, the end of opposition by organized labor (which had feared the removal of legislation protecting women at work) and the dynamism of a resurgent women's movement had made congressional passage possible for the first time in the spring of 1972. Furthermore, the overwhelming support the amendment received in Congress suggested its political popularity, a popularity also indicated by the rapidity of its ratification by state legislatures. Hawaii, for example, ratified the amendment within hours after its passage; five other states did so within two days; by the first anniversary of its passage, thirty had done so.

In the spring of 1973, the proposed Equal Rights Amendment thus lacked the votes of only eight state legislatures for its final adoption. Contrary to the optimistic assumptions of its supporters, however, only five of those eight states ever materialized. And so in June 1982 the amendment died, the legislatures of fifteen states still refusing to ratify it. In retrospect what had happened is fairly clear. As one political scientist studying its defeat noted, legislators typically seek to avoid ''controversial'' issues and in this case initial passage was due largely to the absence of opposition. When opposition emerged, state legislators first tried to avoid the issue and then, when pressed, simply voted it down (Boles 1979, 104–9, 120–21, 132–34, 183–84). That opposition included a broad array of right-wing groups, including many of those already surveyed in this book—the John Birch Society, the Christian Crusade, the Young Americans for Freedom, and the American Independent party, among others (Boles 1979, 66–71, 200–202)—but the must notable organizations fighting the ERA were those composed primarily of women and guided by Phyllis Schlafly.

Wife of an Alton, Illinois, lawyer and mother of six, Schlafly was also the possessor of a master's degree in political science and a law degree, the author of six books, an activist in right-wing politics for a quarter of a century, a prominent figure in the Illinois Republican party and twice an unsuccessful candidate for Congress. She had also been involved in militant anticommunist activities in the late 1950s and early 1960s, such as the organization founded by her sister-in-law, the Cardinal Mindzenty Foundation. The John Birch Society's founder Robert Welch is reported to have claimed at one point that Schlafly ''was one of our most loyal members'' but she has consistently denied any connection with the Society, and her biographer could find no evidence to corroborate Welch's statement (Felsenthal 1981, xviii). Schlafly first achieved national attention with her 1964 critique of the moderate Republicans' domination of presidential conventions, *A Choice Not an Echo*; thereafter, she spent most of her intellectual effort chronicling what she saw as trends toward unilateral disarmament running through the Kennedy, Johnson, Nixon, and Ford administrations. In the course of all these activities, she built up a network of intensely loyal conservative women, subscribers to her *Phyllis Schlafly Report* and, after 1975, members of her Eagle Forum. It may well be that it was they who first drew her attention to the ERA—while she was still concentrating on national-security issues—and then persuaded her to assume the leadership in the fight against it.[10]

Mobilizing her far-flung network of women (calling themselves Stop ERA) at crucial points in the ratification process, Schlafly made two basic arguments against the Equal Rights Amendment. Most clearly summarized in her tract *The Power of the Positive Woman*, these two arguments neatly tied together the changing concerns of the American right wing and met the needs of several different constituencies, all of which feared a change in the status quo. Her first argument was that American women had already achieved equality and did not need further government "interference" to do so. In her view the ERA was simply unnecessary ("ERA does not give women *any* rights, privileges, benefits, or opportunities that they do not now have"), and the "American free-enterprise system" already afforded women the opportunity to compete on equal terms with men. More important, "the gender-free, rigid, absolute equality of treatment" mandated by the ERA would actually hurt women, by denying the wife's right to be supported by her husband, by abolishing protective labor legislation for women, and by subjecting all women to the military draft. And she emphasized the way implementation of the amendment would increase the size of government bureaucracy and expand federal power at the expense of the states and private associations.[11]

If that argument appealed to older right-wing concerns, such as those expressed in the Goldwater movement, her second argument was more attuned to the right-wing sentiments crystallizing in the 1970s which stressed the necessity of women's subordination within the traditional family. From this point of view the problem with the ERA was that it was the consequence of a feminist ideology that challenged the order of creation. Schlafly did not oppose women choosing careers, but in her view they could not have both a career and a family. The unalterable fact from which women's other roles sprang was that only women could bear children: "Those who think it unfair that women have babies, whereas men cannot, will have to take up their complaint with God." Similarly, feminists' anger at power relationships within the family ignored the natural prerequisites for human organization: "Every successful country and company has one 'chief executive officer'. . . . If marriage is to be a successful institution it must likewise have an ultimate decision-maker, and that is the husband." And since, in Schlafly's view, the proposed amendment was based on the perverse assumption that gender roles

[10] This is suggested in Felsenthal 1981, pp. 239–40, 269–70.

[11] Phyllis Schlafly, *The Power of the Positive Woman* (New Rochelle, N.Y.: Arlington House, 1977), pp. 138, 30–31; 68–79, 112–18, 96–103; 118–33.

were interchangeable, its ratification would not only weaken the institution of the family, but challenge the values behind it and sanction such social evils as homosexuality and abortion.[12]

ERA supporters expended their efforts in the state legislatures and in the national media refuting each one of Schlafly's arguments; their efforts were unsuccessful in part because they simply could not comprehend the basis of her appeal. She succeeded in mobilizing thousands of women not because they made careful calculations of the amendment's actual impact—in one study, 85 percent of anti-ERA activists believed it would require unisex toilets (cited in Conover and Gray 1983, 85)—but because, as two historians subsequently noted, they had in common "subjective experiences," certain "patterns of behavior and shared ways of talking about self and community," which accepted traditional gender roles and which made the ERA seem "unnatural." Moreover, they suggested, those who saw the amendment as violating "natural" distinctions in principle could easily foresee all kinds of "unnatural" consequences flowing from it: "women-who-want-to-be-men" in the armed forces, "men-who-refuse-to-be-men" enjoying legalized homosexual relationships, and "women-who-refuse-to-be-mothers" having access to legal abortion (Mathews and Mathews 1982, 13, 14).

However popular the ERA was in the cosmopolitan centers on the East and West Coasts, in the nonratifying states traditional gender roles were still deeply embedded in the political culture, and it was Schlafly's appeal to such fears that carried the day.[13] Schlafly's agitation was followed by a steady weakening of the Republican leadership's support for the amendment: at the 1976 convention, the platform committee deleted the party's long-standing commitment to the ERA and only the personal intervention of President and Mrs. Ford reversed the decision; in 1978 a majority of House Republicans voted against extending the ratification deadline; and at the 1980 convention the party's formal commitment to the Equal Rights Amendment was finally ended.[14]

Perhaps because like other cosmopolitans they had assumed that ratification was a foregone conclusion, few social scientists studied the organized opposition to the Equal Rights Amendment. Such data as we have come from

[12] Schlafly, *The Power of the Positive Woman*, pp. 38–39; 12; 50; 88–96. The connection between the ERA and abortion made by Schlafly and her allies proved politically significant. One study of public opinion suggests that, especially in the nonratifying states, it was largely white women against abortion who moved from support to opposition during the fight over the amendment (Bolce 1986). For the feminist contribution to the linkage, see Mansbridge 1986, pp. 122–28.

[13] For evidence supporting these observations, see Miller and Linker 1974; Boles 1979, pp. 15–21, 184–89; Wohlenberg 1980; Carver 1982; Nice 1986.

[14] The importance of this Republican shift in ultimately defeating the amendment is developed in Gilbert Y. Steiner, *Constitutional Inequality: The Political Fortunes of the Equal Rights Amendment* (Washington, D.C.: Brookings Institution, 1985), pp. 23–24, 33–35.

small, nonrandom samples from two southern states: Texas, where Kent Tedin and his associates interviewed some of the women attending a rescission hearing of the legislature; and North Carolina, where Theodore Arrington and Patricia Kyle interviewed some of those men and women who had publicly spoken or written either for or against ratification.[15] The data confirm what even a moderately well-informed observer of the debate might expect: in both states activists supporting the ERA were "liberals," opponents "conservatives." In Texas ERA opponents were like Schlafly clearly right-wing, women who, in the words of the researchers, "believe in a domestic Communist conspiracy, feel big government in the United States is a menace, and are very preoccupied with the state of morality."[16]

In their background characteristics the ERA opponents resembled the right-wing activists studied in the early 1960s: disproportionately Republican, middle- to upper-middle class, and better educated than average, though in this case not as well-educated as the pro-ERA activists.[17] On an issue such as the ERA, both teams of researchers considered it important to note that the women actively opposing it were largely housewives while the women activists supporting it tended to be employed fulltime. Finally, both research teams found a significant religious correlation with opposition to the ERA: in both states opponents were heavily fundamentalist, in Texas more so than the state's population as a whole. Indeed, Tedin suggested that intense religious commitment might have been the prime motivation behind these individuals' opposition to the amendment (Tedin 1978, 404).

A reaction to the assumptions and achievements of the women's movement even more impassioned than to the proposed ERA came in the aftermath of the Supreme Court's 1973 abortion decision.[18] Probably more than any other single goal, "abortion on demand" symbolized feminists' commitment to the freedom of individual women, including what one sympathetic commentator called their "freedom to choose *not* to become mothers—or even wives." That kind of freedom might be in the best interests of women, she continued, "but it was not necessarily in the best interests of husbands or of society in general. Even its most passionate supporters recognized that a proabortion

---

[15] Brady and Tedin 1976; Tedin et al. 1977; Tedin 1978; Arrington and Kyle 1978. Two studies that are relevant but not strictly comparable to those above are an analysis of those leading the fight for and against an equal rights amendment to the Massachusetts Constitution (Mueller and Dimieri 1982) and an in-depth exploration of the ideologies of a handful of activists in the mid-Atlantic area (Deutchman and Prince-Embury 1982).

[16] Brady and Tedin 1976, p. 574. The six women interviewed by Deutchman and Prince-Embury had right-wing political views almost identical to the Texans studied by Tedin and his associates (Deutchman and Prince-Embury 1982, pp. 46–47).

[17] In her analysis of the ratification debates in Georgia, Illinois, and Texas, Boles came across some *lower-middle-class* housewives active in the opposition to the amendment, though they appear to have been in a minority (Boles 1979, pp. 83, 95).

[18] *Roe v. Wade*, 410 U.S. 113 (1973); *Doe v. Bolton*, 410 U.S. 179 (1973).

policy did entail benefits to some at costs to others."[19] To many others, however, those costs—the destruction of potential human life, the diminution of
male authority, the implicit acceptance of sexual freedom—were simply unacceptable.

Historians are generally agreed that restrictions on legal abortion were in-
stituted in the last third of the nineteenth century at the instigation of a medical
profession that wished to expand its claims to legitimacy, was concerned over
women's health, and feared that too many women of "superior stock" were
not reproducing.[20] By 1900 they had succeeded in their objective—to prohibit
abortion except to save the life of the mother—in almost every state and territory of the Union; and there matters quietly rested for the first half of the
twentieth century, largely because the definition of "saving the life of the
mother" was left up to the individual physician.[21] During this period, however,
a large and articulate segment of the public came to endorse those restrictions on
abortion, often on the basis of their religious convictions. Many such individuals
paid little attention to the efforts of the late 1960s—again led in many cases by
physicians—to "reform" the laws to permit abortions if the mother's broadly
defined "health" was endangered, if the pregnancy were the result of rape or
incest, or if the baby would be born deformed. As a result of their isolation, these
opponents of abortion were stunned by the Supreme Court's 1973 decision,
which seemed to them to grant feminist demands for an unqualified right to abortion. They regarded it, as one perceptive analyst has put it, as a "frighteningly
radical departure from traditional views" (Luker 1984, 141).

Those traditional views were most consistently articulated by the Roman
Catholic Church, whose historic opposition to abortion and whose institutional
strength enabled it to take the initiative in leading the efforts to overturn the
Court's decision. The exact financial role of the Church in supporting the antiabortion movement at various points is disputed;[22] but analysts concur that
its role as facilitator—providing activists with a supportive environment in
which to hold meetings, develop wider communication networks, recruit new
members, and maintain morale—has been of immeasurable importance.[23] The
ideological influence of the church hierarchy is more difficult to assess. At the
time the antiabortion movement was being organized in the 1970s, the hier-

---

[19] Rothman, *Woman's Proper Place*, pp. 245, 246.

[20] This summation of the history of abortion is based primarily on James C. Mohr, *Abortion in
America: The Origins and Evolution of National Policy, 1800–1900* (New York: Oxford University Press, 1978), but also on Luker 1984 and Rubin 1982.

[21] Four states (Louisiana, Massachusetts, New Jersey, and Pennsylvania) refused to incorporate
even this "life-saving" exemption into their abortion statutes (Tatalovich and Daynes 1981, p.
24).

[22] Compare the observations on the Church's financial role in Tatalovich and Daynes 1981, pp.
155, 167; Rubin 1982, p. 89; Paige 1983, pp. 58–63; and Luker 1984, pp. 222–23.

[23] The clearest statement of this is Granberg and Denney 1982, p. 42; see also Paige 1983, p.
58; and Luker 1984, p. 223.

archy's position on other major issues, especially foreign and economic policy, was steadily moving in a progressive direction. For many in the hierarchy, and unquestionably for some antiabortion activists, a determination to protect the "unborn" was part of a broader commitment to the exploited and powerless throughout the world. And, as we shall see, "prolife" activists as a whole by no means took a uniformly conservative position on public issues. Yet it would be erroneous to assume from this that the activists in the movement simply reflected the emerging ideology of the hierarchy. In fact one author has persuasively argued that "there are really two different conceptual frameworks within the right-to-life movement": the hierarchy's, which "ties opposition to abortion to other liberal peace and social justice issues"; and the activists', which "ties opposition to abortion to beliefs about the sanctity of the traditional family" (Neitz 1981, 265). It was this "profamily" framework that made the antiabortion movement a suitable instrument for right-wing organizers.

Social scientists have conducted three major studies of "prolife" activists, each comparing them with their "prochoice" counterparts: Marilyn Falik's 1973 interviews with fifty top officers of the New York organizations most active in the abortion controversy; Kristen Luker's interview with 212 California "activists" defined as those investing several hours a week in their cause, in the late 1970s; and Donald Granberg's analysis of questionnaires from a sample of 900 members of the National Right to Life Committee (NRLC) and the National Abortion Rights Action League (NARAL). All three studies found the activists to be predominantly female, and overwhelmingly Catholic. But since many Catholics dissented from the hierarchy's position to support the legality of abortion, these "prolife" activists must have been a special kind of Catholic, and so they were. Approximately 90 percent told Luker that religion played an "important" or "very important" part in their lives; 50 percent attended church every week with an additional 13 percent attending *more* than once a week.[24]

The antiabortion activists studied by Falik, Luker, and Granberg were also (with modifications according to the sample) "middle class." All three researchers agreed that "prolife" activists were less educated than "prochoice" activists, including in their ranks more individuals with a high school education or less. But compared to the general public, they were, as Granberg put it, "overeducated": 56 percent of Falik's sample, 60 percent of Luker's sample, and 58 percent of Granberg's NRLC sample had completed college. As for income levels Falik found no significant difference between "prolife" and "prochoice" activists in New York in 1973; and Granberg found only a slight difference in his sample of NRLC and NARAL members in 1980. Luker at-

[24] Falik 1983, pp. 125, 213; Luker 1984, pp. 194, 196–97; Granberg 1981, pp. 158, 160. The profile of the activists in New York who created a statewide Right to Life party also reveals a preponderance of devout Catholic women (Spitzer 1987, pp. 84–86).

tracted more attention by emphasizing income differentials, finding that in California the average "prolife" activist had a family income of $30,000 while her "prochoice" counterpart had a family income of $50,000. She did add, however, that the differential was determined in part by the "prolife" activists' decisions to raise children and not to enter the work force; and given their level of education, their husbands' occupations (small businessman or white-collar worker), and their family income, Luker's California activists would also seem to deserve "middle-class" designation.[25]

What then led these middle-class Catholic women to involve themselves so deeply in the antiabortion movement? At one level, as Luker pointed out, their opposition came from their deeply held conviction that life is a gift of God, that life begins at conception, and that the fetus is a person. But she and Falik also emphasized that this opposition came out of a broader worldview that affirmed the authority of the nuclear family and traditional gender roles for men and women. In both studies and in Granberg's as well, the great majority of women who were "prolife" activists were married and full-time mothers and homemakers. Respondents in all three samples opposed the Equal Rights Amendment, Falik's New Yorkers seeing it, like abortion, as derogating traditional roles, while Luker's Californians were more ambivalent. Both Falik and Luker noted that "prolife" activists were opposed to publicly funded day-care centers on the grounds that they constituted unwarranted government interference with parental authority and the integrity of the family.[26]

The activists interviewed by Falik and Luker also believed that, because sex was sacred and reproduction its ordained consequence, they should not use contraception themselves; and they did not, preferring "natural" methods of birth control. In contrast, in Granberg's larger and perhaps less "committed" sample of NRLC members, almost half the women had used oral contraceptives. Of those researchers who asked the relevant question both Luker and Granberg found their sample opposing premarital sexual relations and Granberg found his almost unanimously opposing homosexual relations as well. Luker implied that "prolife" activists' emphasis on the procreative purpose of sex as well as their concern with preserving parental authority led them to oppose both the dissemination of contraceptives to minors and sex education

[25] Falik 1983, pp. 189–91; Luker 1984, pp. 194–95; Granberg 1981, pp. 158–59; Granberg and Denney 1982, p. 41. In contrast only 39 percent of the Right to Life party activists had completed college (Spitzer 1987, p. 85).

[26] Falik 1983, pp. 31–33, 123, 190, 122, 177–79; Luker 1984, pp 146–47, 174–75, 159–62, 195, 205, 173; Granberg 1981, p. 162; Granberg and Denney 1982, p. 41. Especially in view of the opposition to day-care centers expressed by the antiabortion activists in Falik's and Luker's samples, one wonders about the significance of Granberg's finding that NRLC members overwhelmingly supported the idea of "a married woman earning money" even "if she has a husband capable of supporting her." Asking his sample about the idea of "a mother with young children earning money" would seem to be the more relevant question (Granberg and Denney 1982, p. 43; for her observations on this kind of response, Luker 1984, pp. 160–61).

in the schools. Asking slightly different questions, Granberg found a majority of NRLC members favoring sex education if parental involvement was guaranteed. For many "prolife" activists the very means that feminists saw as fundamental prerequisites for women's autonomy—access to contraception and abortion—were simply further incentives to human selfishness. The separation of sexual pleasure from procreation marked a further cultural decline into materialism and hedonism, and the emphasis on a woman's right to terminate her pregnancy at the expense of the fetus's right to life sundered all women from their traditional—and socially essential—nurturant roles.[27]

While the moral traditionalism and sexual conservatism of the "prolife" activists is clear, on other issues their opinions were by no means as stereotypically right-wing as some of their feminist adversaries charged. The most relevant study here is Granberg's, which compared his NRLC sample not only with their NARAL counterparts but also with the general public. On a number of questions he found a surprisingly "liberal" response: on those relating to controversial speakers and publications, for example, NRLC members were significantly more supportive of freedom of expression than was the public as a whole, though not as much as the militantly civil-libertarian NARAL members. A clear majority opposed capital punishment, a proportion at almost the same level as the NARAL sample and twice as high as the general public.[28]

Yet, at the same time, when Granberg compiled his sample in 1980 those in the NRLC were more likely to consider themselves Republicans and "conservatives" than the public as a whole or than the disproportionately "liberal," Democratic NARAL. Having always believed that abortion was wrong, these activists "sought out an organized political group that shared their values" and became active participants in the "prolife" movement. Attending meetings, joining demonstrations, and pressuring legislators, they developed deep commitment to their cause, a commitment simply not matched during the 1970s by their "prochoice" opponents. The survey data on the difference in intensity between the two groups of activists is striking: Granberg found that

[27] Falik 1983, pp. 110–13; Luker 1984, pp. 163–67, 171–72, 173–74, 186–87; Granberg 1981, pp. 161–62. The attitudes of Luker's sample of California "prolife" activists on these matters match those of the "prolife" activists in a small North Dakota city studied by Faye Ginsburg (Ginsburg 1984). It should be emphasized in this connection that it is their beliefs about gender roles and women's sexuality that warrants calling these individuals "traditionalist." As Michael Cavanaugh has persuasively demonstrated, neither opposition to abortion nor the extension of concepts of human rights to the fetus are "traditional" in any meaningful historical sense (Cavanaugh 1986).

[28] Granberg and Denney 1982, p. 44. On the other hand, Falik's findings tend to reinforce the image of antiabortion activists as "conservative." On selected economic issues, for example, she found that only 16 percent of her sample (but 88 percent of her "prochoice" activists) supported proposals for a guaranteed annual income, and only 32 percent (but 72 percent of the "prochoice" activists) believed that conservation of natural resources was more important than economic growth (Falik 1983, p. 182).

84 percent of his NRLC sample, but only 47 percent of his NARAL sample, would refuse to support a candidate *solely* because of his/her position on abortion.[29] Whatever their attitudes on other public questions, then, the intensity with which these "prolife" activists approached the question of abortion— their tendency to become "single-issue" voters—meant that they would be remarkably easy to mobilize on behalf of "prolife" candidates. Given the growing identification during the 1970s of feminism with liberalism and both with the Democratic party, that mobilization would almost certainly occur under right-wing auspices.

By 1980 these intensely committed opponents of abortion had made abortion a national issue and in the process intimidated scores of politicians. One result was the decision of Congress and most state legislatures to cut off the public funding of abortions for poor women. On the other hand, state legislative attempts to impose new restrictions on abortion were overturned by the Supreme Court. Most important of all, Congress proved unwilling to pass any of the proposed constitutional amendments overruling the Court's 1973 decision. In contrast, those opposing the demands of the newly emerged "gay liberation movement" had more initial successes, partly because they, like the opponents of the ERA, could achieve their objectives by simply maintaining the status quo.

The "gay liberation movement" they opposed was, like the women's movement, a product of the 1960s and differed from the earlier "homophile" organizations both in its militancy and in its mass mobilization. As one sympathetic spokesman phrased it, they "considered it more strategic to bring pride and power to homosexuals than to try to edify heterosexuals."[30] Under pressure from gay organizations a growing number of legislatures repealed their broadly defined antisodomy laws: municipal officials felt compelled to limit police harassment of gay men; and, in a number of cities, municipal antidiscrimination ordinances were broadened to prohibit consideration of sexual orientation in employment and housing.

Opposition to these gay demands soon arose. The Equal Rights Amendment and legal abortion may have implicitly threatened traditional gender roles, but gay activists did so openly, raising the most fundamental questions about what it meant to be a "man" or a "woman." In doing so they met an even more impassioned response than had the women's movement. Perhaps the most intense—certainly the best-publicized—conflict over homosexual rights took place in Florida in the spring of 1977. At the beginning of the year, the Dade County commissioners were considering an ordinance, one of a number being

[29] Granberg and Denney 1982, pp. 44, 42; Luker 1984, pp. 218–19; Granberg 1981, p. 163.

[30] Toby Marotta, *The Politics of Homosexuality* (Boston: Houghton Mifflin, 1981), p. 94; the historical background is covered in John D'Emilio, *Sexual Politics, Sexual Communities: The Making of a Homosexual Minority in the United States, 1940–1970* (Chicago: University of Chicago Press, 1983).

advocated at the time, that would prohibit discrimination in employment, housing, and public accommodations on the basis of sexual orientation. Anita Bryant, former beauty queen, successful pop singer, and current Miami resident, found out about the proposed ordinance from her Baptist minister; and, as she subsequently put it, "because of my love for Almighty God, because of my love for His Word, because of my love for my country, because of my love for my children" decided to lead the opposition to the ordinance.[31] When the referendum was held in early June, 69 percent of those voting agreed with her and repealed the ordinance.

Bryant soon faded from view, but others of like mind were inspired by her example to block further antidiscrimination efforts. Within a year ordinances similar to that in Dade County had been repealed in referenda in cities as dissimilar as St. Paul, Wichita, and Eugene (Oregon). Congressional efforts to amend federal civil rights laws to forbid discrimination on the basis of sexual orientation died in committee. And some of those who, like Bryant, feared the legitimation of homosexuality decided to take the offensive. Before passing from the scene Bryant had persuaded the legislature of her native state of Oklahoma to pass a law permitting the dismissal of schoolteachers either for "public homosexual activity" or for advocacy of homosexual rights. In California, State Senator John Briggs collected enough signatures to place an almost identical proposal on the ballot for November 1978. But in California, at least, a concern for freedom of speech outweighed the fear of homosexuals and a formidable coalition successfully opposed it. In the end, the "Briggs initiative" lost, 58 to 42 percent.

While Bryant herself warned voters that "homosexuals can't reproduce so they must recruit" and were thus inherently unfit for teaching positions,[32] some of Bryant's allies expressed concern less about possible sexual solicitation than about "role-modeling homosexuals, the ones who aren't openly recruiting, but who don't stay in the closet." In their view antidiscrimination ordinances would encourage "the homosexual who is blatant in his profession of his preference and who gives the impression to young people that this lifestyle is not odd or to be avoided, but just an alternative."[33] Like the opponents of the ERA, many of whom seemed less interested in the specific legal consequences of the amendment than in what was perceived as its derogation of traditional sex roles, much of the opposition to antidiscrimination ordinances, such as that in Dade County, appeared motivated by wider fears about the ensuing "legitimation" of homosexuality.

[31] Anita Bryant, *The Anita Bryant Story: The Survival of Our Nation's Families and the Threat of Militant Homosexuality* (Old Tappan, N.J.: Revell, 1977), p. 13.

[32] Bryant, *The Anita Bryant Story*, pp. 62, 89–90, 116–19.

[33] Mike Thompson, as quoted in Morton Kondrake, "Anita Bryant Is Mad About Gays," *New Republic* 176 (May 7, 1977): 14.

From "Status Politics" to "The Politics of Life-Style Concern"

As the 1970s drew to a close, a variety of movements were championing values associated with what they perceived as the "traditional family," with the father as head and provider, the mother as nurturer and manager, and the children as replicas of the older generation. This traditional form was, so its emergent defenders believed, under attack from a number of quarters and directly threatened by current policies and proposals: the Equal Rights Amendment, and even more the ideology behind it, challenged the father's dominance; legal abortion challenged the mother's nurturant role; and sex education, "modern" textbooks, and homosexuals in positions of authority all challenged the assurance of the continuity of values across generations. Both because of the traditionalism that lay at their foundation and because liberal intellectuals and Democratic politicians were largely on the other side, these movements were right-wing either in inception, as with the opposition to the ERA, or in potential, as with the antiabortion movement.

As they tried to analyze these various movements, no concept proved more popular among social scientists than that battered relic of the 1950s, "status politics." To be more accurate, one should say the concept they would use was "status politics" as reformulated by the sociologist Joseph Gusfield in his 1962 study of the temperance movement, *Symbolic Crusade*,[34] for while Gusfield relied in part on the concept as developed by the contributors to *The New American Right*, he went beyond them and in doing so had made two important contributions. First, he was far more precise in his definition than Hofstadter and Lipset had been, returning directly to Weber, in defining "status politics" as the conflict over the allocation of prestige and "class politics" as the conflict over the allocation of goods and resources.[35] Second, he rejected both the idea, implicit in much of Lipset's work, that these cultural conflicts were subsidiary to, or diversions from, "real" economic conflicts, and the idea, explicit in Hofstadter's, that these conflicts represented unconscious "projective rationalizations" (Gusfield 1963, 19, 23, 175–76, 178–80).

---

[34] Gusfield 1963. The other application by sociologists of the concept of "status"—their definition of "status" far more broadly, as the ranking on various stratification hierarchies (income, occupation, education, race, religion, etc.) and their attempt to measure inconsistencies between those "statuses"—had by the 1970s run into severe theoretical and methodological criticisms. Consequently, that application of the concept of "status" played only a minor role in the research we are about to survey. The major exception comes from the work of Louis A. Zurcher, Jr., and his associates in their studies of participants in local antipornography movements, who raised the possibility that those participants might in various ways have "inconsistent statuses": see Zurcher 1976, pp. 18–23, 266–72; Wilson and Zurcher 1976; Bland and Wallis 1977; and Wilson and Zurcher 1977.

[35] Compare Gusfield 1963, pp. 13–15, with Max Weber, *Economy and Society*, ed. Guenter Roth and Claus Wittich (New York: Bedminister Press, 1968), pp. 302, 305, 926–27, 935.

Rather, he insisted, the conflicts over prestige were as "real" as those over resources and the objectives of those engaged in them as concrete and programmatic as the aims in "class politics."

This revised concept of "status politics" was first applied to the emerging conflicts of the 1970s by Louis Zurcher and his associates in their studies of grass-roots opposition to pornography.[36] To put these studies in context, it is important to remember that the data they gathered was from the mid-1960s, a period both in which films and mass-circulation magazines were less explicit than they would become (in the researchers' words, *Playboy* was still "in its pre-pubic-hair era": Zurcher and Kirkpatrick 1976, 256) and in which pornography was opposed almost exclusively on the basis of traditionalist conservatism rather than egalitarian feminism. Investigating "decency" movements in two small cities, Zurcher and his colleagues found that these antipornography groups, like the temperance groups studied by Gusfield, represented "moral crusades" in which "members of a status group could strive to preserve, defend, or enhance the dominance and prestige of their style of life against threats from individuals or groups whose life style differed from theirs." In this specific case, Zurcher and the others emphasized, the threat to "status" did not come from within the local communities, where these opponents of pornography were well established and in no sense marginal. Rather, "the challenges to the prestige of their life style" came from outside: from the mass media, which "reminded them that the 'now generation' or the 'counterculture' was becoming more widespread, more forceful, more prestigeful"; from "more than a few reputable legislators, theologians, doctors, entertainers, and educators" who "were seen to be contributing to the legitimacy of life styles different from, even opposed to, that of 'right-thinking' and 'solid' Americans," and, most disconcerting of all, from "the Supreme Court, that most revered guardian of 'basic values,' which was eroding support for their life style" and its " 'no prayer in the schools' and 'freedom for pornography' decisions."[37]

The centrality of Gusfield's model in these researchers' argument is further apparent in their emphasis on the degree to which the fervor of these antipornography crusaders stemmed from more than revulsion at specific materials. Though they agreed, for example, that pornography had socially harmful effects, there was no consensus among them as to what actually constituted pornography, and two-thirds indicated they had never read a pornographic book.

---

[36] The most important of these for our purposes is Zurcher et al. 1971, in most respects an anticipation of the main arguments that would appear five years later in Zurcher and Kirkpatrick 1976. For a somewhat similar study, see Rodgers 1975.

[37] Zurcher et al. 1971, pp. 218, 222. Significantly, on the usual measures of alienation, the opponents of pornography were less likely to be distrustful, less likely to feel powerless, than those among their neighbors who were willing to tolerate the presence of "adult" bookstores and theaters. On this point, see Zurcher et al. 1973, pp. 81–83.

Nor were the proverbial "smut peddlers" their only targets: when asked who disagreed with their antipornography efforts, most of them cited not those who directly profited from pornography but "radicals," "young people," "college students," "hippies," and "university professors"—all of whom, as Zurcher pointed out, were "modernists" representing threatening "social change and alternative styles of life." The "symbolic" aspect of the crusade was also borne out afterward, when in spite of the fact that they had achieved very little (in one community the number of adult theaters actually increased, and in the other the temporarily closed adult bookstore reopened with two new branches), the participants felt they had accomplished something. Said one, "Maybe the bookstore will stay open, but the decent people in this town have gone on record about how they feel, and what they can do if they want to, and everybody knows it" (Zurcher et al. 1971, 224, 231).

In their attempt to use Gusfield's model in their own research, Zurcher and his colleagues ran into criticism, primarily because in the minds of many sociologists "status politics" was inextricably associated with Lipset's use of the concept. It may fairly be said that for Lipset "the defense of the traditional moral position is merely the 'baggage' " for the defense of "the social position of those who subscribe to it" (Hottois and Milner 1975, 15); but Zurcher and his colleagues implied that the antipornography crusaders they studied were primarily "fighting to defend their lifestyle—that system of values, customs, and habits with which they had been accustomed and to which they had become committed" (Zurcher et al. 1973, 70). So, in reply to the first set of critics they pointed out that for them "status" meant far more than simply the location of individuals' positions in a social hierarchy (Wilson and Zurcher 1977, 431; Zurcher and Kirkpatrick 1976, 271). Several years later, another team of critics offered religious and educational socialization as an alternative to the "status politics" model, failing to notice that Zurcher and his colleagues were less interested in accounting for the origins of the *attitudes* of their antipornography crusaders, which might indeed have been religious and educational, than in the factors motivating them to *participate* in a social movement (Wood and Hughes 1984).

The next study of the emerging defenders of the "traditional family," by Ann Page and Donald Clelland, looked at the particularly bitter textbook controversy in Kanawha County, West Virginia, in 1974–75, which had resulted in mass meetings, pickets, work stoppages, beatings, and firebombings before the school board finally agreed to abandon the disputed books. In formulating their conclusions, the authors tried to avoid the problems that had confronted Zurcher and his colleagues: they stated that, in their opinion, the potential usefulness of the concept of "status politics" had been damaged by several faulty assumptions on the part of those who had hitherto applied it. Many of those assumptions—that "status politics" was somehow "irrational," that it tended toward merely "symbolic" victories, and so on—we have already surveyed. But Page and Clelland pointed out one problem for the first time and in doing so further refined and reformulated the concept. Previous application of "status politics," they noted, had been marred by a confusion as to whether it arose from conflicts over prestige or from conflicts over lifestyle. While what Weber had called "status groups" are "engaged in constant claims for social honor [i.e., prestige], they are not neatly ordered in any hierarchy because there can be no full consensus across groups concerning the basis for such a hierarchy." Given the absence of such a hierarchy, "status politics is not in essence the attempt to defend against declining prestige but the attempt to defend a way of life." Page and Clelland therefore coined a new term—the "politics of life style concern"—which conveyed the solid core of the "status politics" concept without the unnecessary and unwarranted associations that the latter term had incurred. They then concluded their theoretical discussion with the statement that "we believe that the politics of life style concern is the master concept which should be applied to all struggles involving noneconomic belief systems . . . for the simple reason that humans are symbolic animals who organize the world in symbolic terms" (Page and Clelland 1978, 265, 266, 267).

Since "a style of life can be maintained or propagated only to the extent that its adherents exercise some control over the means of socialization," educational controversies such as the Kanawha County dispute over which textbooks should be used in the public schools could best be understood as examples of this "politics of life style concern." Pitting "cultural modernists" against "cultural fundamentalists," such conflicts typically cut across economic and educational lines. In no sense did the West Virginia dispute array the working class or the countryside against middle-class urbanites: there were, for example, no significant differences in income level between areas of high and low protest activity, and only slight educational differences were revealed in letters to local newspapers written by activists on either side. In addition, the specific objections to the textbooks' contents, such as alleged disrespect for traditional religious concepts and for authority, and supposed advocacy of moral relativism, "can be viewed as objections to an ideology of secular humanism as a substitute for a preferred authoritarian theocentrism." As such they represented "statements of concern about the destruction of a style of life." There was little evidence that the protest represented "a sublimated response to status frustration stemming from a slippage in a hierarchical social order." Rather, "the central concern of status group members is the viability of their way of life," in this case "a life style and world view which are under threat from a variety of sources—the educational system, the mass media, the churches—fundamentally from every socialization agency beyond their immediate control."[38]

[38] Page and Clelland 1978, pp. 267, 272–73, 274, 275, 276, 279. Page and Clelland did note

By the early 1980s other social scientists were applying what was now, after Page and Clelland, called "the politics of lifestyle concern" to the groups they were studying. In one case, Louise Lorentzen found that those supporting an evangelical candidate for the U.S. Senate nominations at the 1978 Virginia Democratic convention were linked together as evangelicals, regardless of their formal denominational affiliation, and had entered politics because of their concern over "the pervasiveness of liberal influences that come to bear on the family," including the prohibition of school prayer and the proposed Equal Rights Amendment. For them, Lorentzen concluded, "life style" was centered on their churches and especially on their families, so that when they spoke of "the necessity of preserving the moral climate of America" they were in fact talking about "preserving a life style" centered on church and family against these threatening "secular" influences. Finally, in perhaps the clearest indication of the "symbolic" aspect of these individuals' policies, she noted that almost six times as many supported their preferred candidate because he would bring a countervailing "Christian influence" to bear as supported him because he would advocate specific legislative policies.[39]

In the evolving applications of the concept of "status politics" since Gusfield, two developments are particularly notable: first, the growing emphasis on "lifestyles" or "worldviews" as its basis; and second, the deemphasis on its purely "symbolic" aspects. As summarized by Lorentzen, under this new interpretation "life style concern is the *motivating factor*, and preservation and protection of a life style are the *goals* of noneconomic political movements. As such these goals are instrumental in nature. The *tactics* employed to reach the goal of life style protection may be either *instrumental*, oriented directly at protecting or defending a life style, or *symbolic*, representing the

---

that the leadership of the protesters largely consisted of "lay" ministers in fundamentalist congregations, who had less formal education than those who led the pro-textbook faction (ibid., p. 271). A study of a very similar conflict, in "Mountain Gap," Virginia, gave more emphasis to this pattern of clerical leadership and reached somewhat different conclusions. Finding relatively little community concern over the textbook issue, the researchers concluded that the controversy was largely the product of the anxieties of local ministers. In terms quite compatible with the traditional "status politics" interpretation, they argued that, while "historically fundamentalist ministers in the rural South have exercised tight control over the right to define what constitutes proper community morality," they now found that authority challenged by school systems "staffed and controlled by individuals subscribing to cosmopolitan value orientations and beliefs" (Cummings 1977; quotations at pp. 8, 16).

[39] Lorentzen 1980, pp. 150, 151, 152–53. In another study, Matthew Moen adapted the Page-Clelland model to his own analysis of attitudes toward school prayer within the general public. Surveying a sample of Oklahoma City residents, he found that support for the reinstitution of prayer in the public schools not surprisingly correlated both with religious traditionalism and with the perceived threat to those values, but after subjecting the data to regression analysis, more with the latter than with the former. That correlation confirmed his hypothesis that "prayer is better understood as a status politics issue than as a public policy issue grounded in belief over religion" (Moen 1984; quotation at p. 1070).

many instances and circumstances that call for action but are not directly connected to the goal'' (Lorentzen 1980, 147).

At the same time, however, the role of conflicts over prestige in such a politics was still unresolved. Of major importance in Gusfield's interpretation, the association of prestige with a position in a social hierarchy created problems for Zurcher and his colleagues when they tried to adapt Gusfield's model. Page and Clelland then eliminated prestige as a factor in their "politics of lifestyle concern" on the grounds that there was no agreement on the basis for such a hierarchy. Rightly insisting on the importance of "lifestyles" as sources of conflict independent of social position, they may have gone too far in disregarding conflicts over prestige.

It is of course true, as Page and Clelland pointed out, that the existence of conflict over lifestyle showed that there was no agreement on the basis for such a hierarchy; but that assessment overlooks the possibility that participants on both sides of the conflict ultimately sought to win or to maintain societal support for one particular prestige hierarchy—their own. It is almost impossible to account for the passion of the groups emerging in the 1970s that claimed to defend the "traditional family" without noticing the degree to which they felt that their particular prestige hierarchy—the one in which they had invested—was scorned by educational elites, by government policymakers, and most of all by feminist and gay activists. Furthermore, the centralization of the mass media in the cosmopolitan centers on the East and West Coasts made it particularly likely to pick up the voices of these advocates of "cultural modernism." As a result, to an extent perhaps unrecognized by Page and Clelland, traditionalists everywhere felt besieged, confronted every time they turned on their television sets by what they saw as a new prestige hierarchy sponsored by the media. In sum, on this question one is inclined to agree not with Page and Clelland but with Lorentzen when she writes that "particular life styles are accorded varying degrees of prestige" and "status is indeed defined by society's valuation of a particular life style" (Lorentzen 1980, 146).

Applying "Status Politics" to Both Sides in a Conflict

At least the issue of prestige as a factor in "status politics" or the "politics of lifestyle concern" was addressed in these studies; another, possibly more important, issue was not even raised. Several years before, two sociologists had criticized Hofstadter and Lipset for using "status politics" pejoratively, "as a conceptual vehicle for explaining reactionary political behavior" that they abhorred (Brandmeyer and Denisoff 1969, 9). They did not, however, pursue the theoretical argument suggested by their comment, that not only Hofstadter and Lipset but also Gusfield and those following him tended to apply the concept of "status politics" in a curiously one-sided manner—to the side defending traditional values ("status," lifestyle," etc.) which, feeling itself threatened, attempted to use government to legitimate those values. Was this in fact usually the case, with only one side engaged in "status politics"? Or would it not be likely that those advocating new values and unorthodox "lifestyles" were also engaged in "status politics," equally interested in using government to sanctify their subculture and to stigmatize others?

These two issues—whether concern for prestige could be totally discounted as a factor in "status politics," and whether the concept could be applied to innovators as well as traditionalists—would seem to have particular relevance to the movements of the 1970s aiming at "liberation" (female and/or homosexual), and to the opposition they engendered. For here, even more than in the area of educational policy studied by Page and Clelland, were conflicts over prestige in Weber's original sense of "social honor": admitted homosexuals "dishonored" for centuries and now demanding acceptance; or housewives feeling "dishonored" by the sudden approbation given self-conscious women professionals. And here, too, as Gusfield would have predicted, both sides turned to government to sanctify their subculture, whether through the retention of antisodomy laws or the passage of antidiscrimination ordinances, the restoration of restrictions on abortion or the ratification of the Equal Rights Amendment.

With the exception of a short journalistic piece by Gusfield himself (placing the 1978 Briggs initiative in California within this general framework),[40] no social scientists analyzed the conflict over homosexual rights. Of the major studies of the conflicts triggered by the women's movement, Luker's analysis of abortion activists easily lends itself to a reformulated "status politics" interpretation, although she did not openly use it in her analysis. Nevertheless, it is hard to miss the components of this model in her book: the abortion controversy as representing a struggle between different worldviews and lifestyles; the perception that the "prestige" of motherhood or a career was linked, positively or negatively, to the availability of abortion (even her opinion that antiabortion activists might settle for a relatively ineffective constitutional amendment because they wanted to make "a moral statement").[41]

If Luker did not directly apply the revised "status politics" model—what was now called "the politics of lifestyle concern"—to her discussion of con-

[40] Gusfield 1978. In terms of Gusfield's own work, two points may be made about this article. First, nowhere did he use the term "status politics," referring only to those "moral issues in American politics . . . that reflect the importance of government as a ceremonial and symbolizing agent." Second, racial conflicts, which in 1963 he had put on the "status politics" side, now fifteen years later he linked to "class politics" (compare his discussion in *Symbolic Crusade*, pp. 22, 172–73, with his 1978 article, p. 635).

[41] Luker 1984, pp. 158–215, 234. For an interpretation of the conflict over abortion that does see it as an example of "status politics," see Markson 1985.

flicts over the family, the political scientist Pamela Johnston Conover did, both in a brief theoretical article and in her book, coauthored with Virginia Gray, *Feminism and the New Right: Conflict Over the American Family*. She began her article by reviewing the extant sociological explanations for "right-wing extremism" and concluded that it was the "symbolic politics" model following Gusfield that seemed best to explain the emergence of right-wing groups concerned with "family" issues (Conover 1983, 634).

To confirm her hypotheses, Conover drew on data gathered from delegates to one of the three regional White House Conferences on Families held in 1980, this one in Minneapolis and representing the states of the Mississippi Valley. Dividing the delegates into "New Rightists" (who opposed both the ERA and abortion) and "nonrightists" (who favored the ERA whether or not they supported abortion), Conover tested various explanations of right-wing behavior. Although her "New Rightists" did tend to score higher on scales measuring "authoritarianism," the usual measures of status, status inconsistency, feelings of powerlessness, and actual political involvement revealed no significant differences between the two groups.[42] The strongest differences between her "New Rightists" and Her "nonrightists" came on "measures of symbolic conflict": not only in their self-designation as conservatives but in their commitment to the "old morality," their support for traditional gender roles, and their preference for "traditional economic arrangements" (i.e., men in the labor force, women in the home). Her "New Rightists' " political activity, Conover concluded, "represents a way of combating more than just specific issues like abortion and ERA; it is a way of fighting the deeper lifestyle changes these issues appear to symbolize" (Conover 1983, 640–41, 646; Conover and Gray 1983, 102–4).

The right-wing emphasis on the ERA and abortion issues served other "symbolic" purposes as well: "it is an attempt to re-establish the right as the group that defines public morality," a position right-wingers believed had been usurped by their adversaries in the women's movement. Conover and Gray showed the degree to which right-wing mobilization was a direct response to feminists organization when they investigated factors correlating with the emergence of right-wing "profamily" organizations at the state level. Correlations between the number of such groups and what might be termed

---

[42] Conover 1983, pp. 642–43. In fact Conover and Gray found their "New Rightists" to have had somewhat *more* political experience than their "nonrightists," which may have reflected the fact that many feminist activists chose not to participate in the conference. (Conover and Gray 1983, p. 115). Nonetheless, the possibility that right-wing women activists typically have greater political experience than their opponents deserves further investigation, especially since a number of observers have noted their greater effectiveness as lobbyists in legislative and bureaucratic contexts. For this point in connection with the opposition to the ERA, see Mansbridge 1986, pp. 159–63; and for a comparable study of right-wing women and feminists at a textbook-adoption hearing in Texas, see Freeman 1983.

"objective" threats to the "traditional family"—the availability of legal abortion, the rate of divorce, and the percentage of women in the labor force, for example—were virtually nonexistent; only with the rate of abortion was there any positive correlation at all. But the correlation with the number of feminist groups was much stronger—in fact, the highest of all correlations—indicating to the researchers that the "profamily" right was primarily "a defensive mobilization effort" against the feminist movement, "a countermovement engaged in a symbolic protest over the American family" (Conover and Gray 1983, 89, 174–84, 185).

Unlike the other researchers whose work we have reviewed, Conover closely studied both sides in the conflict over family-related issues and placed that conflict within a specific theoretical framework. In the book coauthored with Gray she also discussed the way both feminists and their right-wing adversaries consciously used symbols—"equality," "woman's right," "the family," "human life"—for purposes of mobilization (Conover and Gray 1983, 35–49, 61–63, 89–90). In spite of her attempt at balance and conceptual rigor, however, Conover's application of her "symbolic politics" model reflects that one-sided quality that has already been noted. She has indicated elsewhere that she regards her concept as applicable to both sides, but one could conclude from her book that feminist goals were primarily instrumental, the symbols being used only to rouse supporters, while for antifeminists the goals themselves were symbolic.[43] That may in fact be the case—there may be something about right-wing politics that predisposes its participants toward "symbolic" goals—but Conover does not provide the necessary evidence. A brief, final look at the conflict over the ERA suggests that on both the "symbolic" and "instrumental" dimensions the differences between the two sides are less than clear-cut.

In the beginning much of the active support for the Equal Rights Amendment was, indeed, "instrumental": women worked for its ratification because they saw it as a major weapon against discrimination in the workplace and elsewhere. But as one historian has shrewdly commented, the amendment would also have "elevated a new definition of womanhood to a national norm," one in which "women had to find fulfillment in their own accomplishments, not in their husband's or children's." That was surely a "symbolic" goal, analogous to earlier efforts to "enshrine temperance as a national norm."[44] Then, as the drive for ratification stalled, the amendment was increasingly seen as a referendum on feminism itself, so that by the end of the 1970s journalists were observing that for many in the women's movement the significance of the ERA "may lie less in what it would do if passed than in its

[43] Pamela Johnston Conover, letter to author, February 6, 1984; but compare the parallel sections in Conover and Gray 1983 on the role of issues in mobilization, pp. 61–63, 89–90.
[44] Rothman, *Woman's Proper Place*, p. 260.

symbolic value: its defeat would signal that women do not have enough political clout to earn the response of elected politicians."[45]

Whatever the limitations of individual studies, by the late 1970s many social scientists were persuaded of the utility of some kind of framework that would encompass those conflicts, essentially noneconomic in nature, that pit "lifestyles" or worldviews against each other. Their primary disagreement was over what to call such a framework. "Symbolic politics," the term Conover favored, is open to the criticism that it ignores the "instrumental" component in such conflicts, a component that other researchers were increasingly emphasizing. "Status politics" has, as Zurcher and his colleagues found out, too many confusing associations to be acceptable. The "politics of lifestyle concern" is clearer but the term lacks elegance; and, especially for those outside the field, "lifestyle" may be too freighted with associations of hot tubs and white wine to bear the weight of matters of ultimate concern. "Cultural politics" is another possibility, except that the definition of "culture" has varied so widely over time, from that of nineteenth-century literary critics to that of modern anthropologists, that no scholarly consensus seems likely as to what "culture" would actually include. The issue of terminology therefore remains unresolved.

"Status Politics" and the Religious Basis of "Profamily" Activism

However social scientists chose to describe it, the proliferation of right-wing groups that claimed to defend the values associated with the "traditional family" was certainly one of the major developments of the 1970s. The transformation of these "profamily" activists into the base of what would come to be called the "new right" was made possible, first of all, because to a remarkable degree the worldviews of these groups and individuals already converged.[46] To take only the most notable examples, the antiabortion activists whom Luker interviewed opposed sex education, Schlafly spoke out against homosexual rights, Bryant rejected the ERA because of the role of lesbians in the women's movement, and right-wing fundamentalist ministers easily alternated between attacking "evolution" and attacking "gay liberation." In most if not all cases the views of these "profamily" activists had specifically religious origins: that was true of the "creationists," of the textbook protesters in West Virginia, of the anti-ERA women in Texas interviewed by Tedin, of Luker's "prolife" activists in California, and of Anita Bryant herself. The profiles of

[45] Linda Charlton, "Sisterhood, Powerful but Not Omnipotent," *New York Times*, July 17, 1977, sec. 4, p. 10.

[46] One of the first observers to note this convergence was the journalist Andrew Kopkind: see his "America's New Right," *New Times* 9 (September 30, 1977): 21–23.

the right-wing delegates to the White House Conference studied by Conover and Gray further suggested that the religious foundation of their "profamily" activism came not only from their specific denominational affiliations but from their religiosity, as measured by their high level of church attendance (Conover and Gray 1983, 190).

The discovery of the common religious factor behind the various manifestations of "profamily" activism forced further modifications of the revised "status politics" model, whether it was called "symbolic politics," "cultural politics," or "the politics of lifestyle concern." Students of conflicts such as that over the Equal Rights Amendment had tended to see the "status" at issue as linked directly to women's roles: "Whose definition of the appropriate role for women shall prevail in our society?" (Scott 1985, 500). In this view the ERA arrayed feminists and more generally women in the work force, who saw their status enhanced by new roles and opportunities, against the opponents of the ERA and abortion and housewives generally, who saw their status demeaned by such an expansion of options.[47] The problem with this model was that survey data did not reveal the expected cleavage: contrary to a widespread impression, with all other factors controlled housewives were no more opposed to the ERA than were women in the work force.[48]

If it was not their "status" as housewives that determined these women's opposition to the ERA, could it be the content and "status" of their religiously derived worldview, a possibility that captures some of the other meanings of "the politics of lifestyle concern"? The sociologist Jerome Himmelstein has forcefully argued on the basis of survey data that it is their religiosity and not their dependent economic position that distinguishes female opponents of the ERA and abortion from their supporters, and that this holds true for the general public as well as for activists (Himmelstein 1986). Like Conover and Gray he found that antifeminists are likely to be frequent church attenders, and he plausibly suggested that this greater degree of involvement not only makes their mobilization possible—the antiabortion movement being the obvious case—but that it predisposes them to a view of the world that emphasizes both the need to protect the family and women's special responsibility for that task.[49] This view, Himmelstein added, is culturally transmitted through the religious

[47] Scott 1985, pp. 499–505; and especially the work of Susan E. Marshall (Marshall 1984; Marshall 1985; Marshall and Orum 1986).

[48] Sandra K. Gill, "Attitudes Toward the ERA," *Sociological Perspectives* 28 (October 1985): 458.

[49] Suzanne Staggenborg has extended Himmelstein's argument in her analysis of the way activists on both sides of the abortion controversy were recruited. Suspecting that the sum of individual motivations was insufficient to explain the dynamics of a social movement, she found that individuals who shared lifestyle characteristics were predisposed to participate in certain institutions (churches, in the case of those opposed to abortion); those institutions in turn made them available for actual recruitment by movement activists and also sustained their commitment through the creation of shared meanings (Staggenborg 1987).

networks in which these women participate; they may hold it quite independently of their actual personal situation. They see women's dependence on
men as part of the order of creation and not necessarily as reflecting their own
lives. As one researcher remarked with astonishment after interviewing some
anti-ERA demonstrators, "I had no idea that the basis for their action was a
literal belief in the Pauline passages from the Bible stipulating that women
must be subject to men" (Mansbridge 1986, 175–76).

The women opposing the ERA and abortion, even more than the parents
protesting sex education, "modern" textbooks, or Darwinian theory in the
schools, had reason to feel that their religiously derived worldviews were under assault. In the disputes over educational policy, what the right-wing protesters called "secular humanism" may, as their critics charged, have been a
catch-all phrase designed to cover whatever they did not like. But in the conflicts over women's roles their adversaries were indisputably "secular." In
Texas, for example, a majority of the ERA's active supporters were unaffiliated with any denomination.[50] In the case of activists supporting abortion, of
the group interviewed by Luker 80 percent never attended church and 63 percent claimed to have no religion at all; in the NARAL sample compiled by
Granberg, agnostics and atheists were heavily overrepresented and only 20
percent considered religion important in their lives (Luker 1984, 196; Granberg 1981, 160). It would not be long before such differences would be exploited by right-wing political strategists and religious leaders; by 1980, to a
degree unmatched in American history since the Jeffersonian era, and perhaps
not even then, conservative forces could identify themselves with religion and
because of the secularity of so many of their adversaries do so with credibility.[51]

The complementarity of worldviews and the underlying religious basis of
those views made possible a convergence on the part of these "profamily"
individuals and groups. For the "new right" to exist these "profamily" activists would have to be linked to a larger network. To understand that organizational network, however, we have to move beyond the studies we have reviewed and look at the organizers who made the "new right" a national force.

---

[50] Tedin 1978, pp. 60–61. Comparable findings are reported in Mueller and Dimieri 1982, p.
665; and Deutchman and Prince-Embury 1982, pp. 43–44.

[51] In this connection it is worth noting that by the early 1980s religiosity, measured both denominationally and doctrinally, clearly differentiated financial contributors to the Republican
party and to conservative PACs from those who gave to the Democratic party and to liberal PACs
(Guth and Green 1986).

Twelve

The Creation of the "New Right": Organizers, Ideologues, and the Search for a Constituency

THE CONSERVATIVE revival of the late 1970s took many forms. One judicious British scholar has singled out four as especially significant: the growing influence of disenchanted, once-liberal intellectuals criticizing public policy from a "neoconservative" perspective; the rise of "new right" political organizers who created networks linking financial contributors, research institutes, local activists, and candidates for office; the mobilization of evangelical and fundamentalist voters by conservative ministers; and the organizational strengthening of the Republican party between 1976 and 1980 (Peele 1984, 1–18). Of these four developments, the one that seems to have attracted most attention was the creation of the "new right" infrastructure and the parallel religious developments to which it was closely related. What then was the "new right"—or, more precisely, what was "new" about it? Few questions about recent American politics have produced so many incompatible answers or so much confusion.

Many assumptions about the "new right," however glibly reiterated by commentators, prove under closer scrutiny to be either unwarranted or subject to careful qualifications. It is certainly true that the spirit of George Wallace's presidential campaigns and their perception of the constituency he was able to attract deeply influenced the "new right's" rhetoric and strategy; but it would be a mistake to conclude from this that the "new right" represented the large-scale entry into politics of predominantly lower-middle-class or working-class individuals hitherto unconnected to the Republican party or right-wing organizations. Certainly most of the men and women at the leadership level had connections of long standing, going back to the early days of the Young Americans for Freedom and the Goldwater campaign of 1964. Nor is the socioeconomic profile of the various "new right" activists that distinctive. Both the activists opposing the Equal Rights Amendment and those joining the Moral Majority, for example, turn out to be, like their predecessors in the John Birch Society and the New York Conservative party, securely upper-middle-class. And while some of the "profamily" activists at the local level may have been lower-middle-class, they too (as the reader of Part Two of this book will recall) had counterparts in the right-wing organizations of the early 1960s.

Looking at the "new right" primarily as an instrument of mobilization, however, can give us a clearer picture of its significance. Though led by veterans of earlier right-wing campaigns and taking positions on a wide variety of policy questions, as a matter of building mass support the "new right" nevertheless placed what Rosalind Pollack Petcheskey described as "sexual, reproductive, and family issues at the center of its program."[1] While many of its activists have worked in the Republican party, and while the overwhelming majority of its beneficiaries have been Republican candidates, the "new right" developed largely outside the Republican organization and has consistently seen itself in broadly ideological rather than narrowly partisan terms. That ideology has itself been distinctive and not, as some analysts have argued, simply part of the broader conservative revival that dominated American political life in the late 1970s.[2] Far more emphatically than either the neoconservative intellectuals or most Republican politicians, "new right" spokesmen have insisted that the survival of American capitalism and the maintenance of American power in the world are dependent upon the restoration of "traditional morality." And far more than the other conservatives, they have consciously utilized a rhetoric that seems to be "populist," though this "populism" turns out to be far more complicated than is often assumed.

The Formation of a "New Right" Organizational Network

[1] Petcheskey 1981, p. 207. My essential agreement with Petcheskey's argument should be clear from my organization of the material. Nevertheless, I should emphasize that "new right" strategists were too shrewd not to perceive the usefulness of non-"family-related" issues in establishing their credibility, issues that might not produce intense adherents to their cause but were of concern to broader segments of the public. Insofar as 1978 marked the point at which the "new right" established itself as a major force in American political life, it was largely because of its opposition to the treaties transferring sovereignty over the Panama Canal to Panama by the year 2000. Having almost succeeded in defeating the treaties in the Senate in the spring, "new right" strategists were generally credited with defeating several protreaty senators in the fall. See George D. Moffett III, *The Limits of Victory: The Ratification of the Panama Canal Treaties* (Ithaca, N.Y.: Cornell University Press, 1985), especially pp. 169–79.

[2] This is my chief quarrel with Rebecca E. Klatch's *Women of the New Right* (Klatch 1987). As a thoroughgoing exploration of the different worldviews of those she calls "social conservatives" and "laissez-faire conservatives," and as a sensitive examination of the factors that led some women to become one or the other kind of activist, her book deserves commendation. As my ensuing analysis should make clear, however, I believe she confuses the general conservative mobilization of the era with the "new right" in particular; and the way she constructs her sample—including women from the Libertarian party, for instance—exaggerates the importance of the "laissez-faire" contingent in what most observers have defined as the "new right." Her analysis also assumes the incompatibility of the two views at the outset and thereby, it seems to me, misses the historically important development, the way "new right" organizers, spokesmen, and politicians have tried to bring "social conservatives" and "laissez-faire conservatives" together behind a positive program and not (as she implies) simply exploit their parallel antipathies to "Communism," "big government," and the feminist agenda.

Just as the previous great wave of right-wing organization-building had occurred during the closing years of the Eisenhower administration, so the "new
right" took shape during the administration of Gerald Ford. In both cases it
was less the challenge of Democratic "liberalism" that provoked the right
wing to organize than its disillusionment with Republican "moderation." Just
as in the earlier period, however, social scientists who studied right-wing politics tended to concentrate on the grass-roots activists, leaving examination of
the political entrepreneurs who had created the right-wing organizations and
their various connections—whether to the Republican party, to the business
community, or to the national-security establishment—largely to journalists.
This narrowness of focus, it should be added, was especially notable in view
of the growing popularity among sociologists of what was called the "resource-mobilization perspective," which, as two of them put it, asks not
"Why do these people want social change so badly and believe that it is possible?" but "How can these people organize, pool resources, and wield them
effectively?"[3] The fact remains that, whatever its attractiveness to other scholars studying other social movements, the resource-mobilization perspective,
with its attendant concern with organizational networks, was seldom used by
those studying the "new right."[4]

Because the organization of the "new right" did not attract the attention of
social scientists—and that attention, as reflected in the scholarly studies they
produce, is the focus of this book—we will only sketch its most significant
aspects. As to why the "new right" was organized at the time it was and took
the shape it did, two developments seem the most plausible explanations. The
first was the right-wing disillusionment with the Republican party in the mid-
1970s. For those who had seen the party as the most promising vehicle for the
conservative cause, the years after 1972 had been disastrous: the Watergate
revelations and Nixon's resignation had taken place against the onset of the
greatest economic slump since the 1930s; and in the Democratic landslide that
followed, right-wing Republicans had suffered disproportionately heavy
losses.[5] Nor from their perspective were Gerald Ford's first few months in
office especially promising: they were alarmed by his willingness to accept
massive federal deficits, bitterly opposed to his offer of limited amnesty for
Vietnam War resisters, and most of all appalled by his selection of Nelson
Rockefeller as Vice President.[6]

[3] Bruce Fireman and William Gamson, "Utilitarian Logic in the Resource Mobilization Perspective," in Mayer N. Zald and John D. McCarthy, eds., *The Dynamics of Social Movements:
Resource Mobilization, Social Control, and Tactics* (Cambridge, Mass.: Winthrop, 1977), p. 9

[4] The exceptions to this generalization are Liebman 1983; Miller 1985; and Staggenborg 1987.

[5] James L. Sundquist, "Hardly a Two-Party System," *Nation* 219 (December 7, 1974): 583;
Walter Dean Burnham, "American Politics in the 1970s: Beyond Party?" in William N. Cham-
bers and Burnham, eds., *The American Party Systems: Stages of Development*, 2d ed. (New York:
Oxford University Press, 1975), p. 356.

[6] Christopher Lydon, "G.O.P. Right Wing Seems to Rule Out Support for Ford in 1976 Campaign," *New York Times*, February 10, 1975, p. 18; Jules Witcover, *Marathon: The Pursuit of*

These activists were complaining about their lack of influence at the same time, ironically enough, that journalists were talking about "a continuing gradual realignment of the two major parties . . . that is making Republican officeholders more consistently conservative across the country,"[7] and party moderates were so concerned that Ford was moving to the right that some threatened to run as independents."[8] Thus, it may have been less their lack of influence in the party that bothered these right-wing activists than the fact that the Republican party itself had so dramatically shrunk both in elected officials and in self-identified voters. On the other hand, they were aware that significantly more Americans considered themselves "conservatives" than considered themselves Republicans; so it was not hard for them to conclude that it was the Republican connection that was the source of their misfortunes. A little-known fund-raiser and direct-mail operator named Richard Viguerie summed up this point of view when he observed, "I know the marketing field, and you just can't market Republican anymore. It means depression, recession, runaway inflation, big business, multinational corporations, Watergate, and Nixon. It's easier to sell an Edsel or Typhoid Mary. Independent and American—those are words which will sell. Don't kid yourself, that's the way we're moving. All the Republican party needs is a decent burial. In ten years, there won't be a dozen people in the country calling themselves Republicans" (as quoted in Crass 1976, 241–42).

Ten years later, of course, the Republican party was doing very well for itself and Viguerie had become one of the most successful political entrepreneurs in the country.[9] Since 1965 he had been operating a direct-mail operation, established initially with lists obtained from contacts in the Young Americans for Freedom and the Goldwater organization. But the success of his operation was made possible by the second political development of the mid-1970s, the steady transformation in the ways in which elections were won or lost in America (Peele 1984, 55–65). The first change, which was already becoming a truism among journalists and political scientists in the mid-1970s, was that partisanship was losing its hold over the electorate: voters were in-

the Presidency, 1972–1976 (New York: Viking Press, 1977), p. 46; Reinhard 1983, pp. 228–30; Ernest R. Furgurson, *Hard Right: The Rise of Jesse Helms* (New York: Norton, 1986), pp. 109–15.

[7] David S. Broder, "Parties Shifting from Old Alignments," *Washington Post*, October 27, 1974, p. A1.

[8] Broder, "Parties Shifting from Old Alignments," A12; James M. Naughton, "Party Moderates Bid Ford Soften Conservative Tone," *New York Times*, September 4, 1975, p. 1; Charles Mohr, "Senator Mathias Is Exploring Possibility of 3rd Political Party," *New York Times*, November 25, 1975, p. 35.

[9] My profile of Viguerie is drawn primarily from the autobiographical material in his *The New Right: We're Ready to Lead* (Falls Church, Va.: Viguerie, 1981), pp. 27–40; and from Nick Kotz, "King Midas of 'The New Right,' " *Atlantic* 242 (November 1978): 52–61; Crawford 1980, pp. 42–77; and Young 1982, pp. 83–95.

creasingly voting for attractive candidates, or voting on the basis of issues without regard to party—or not voting at all.

The second change was more specific, stemming from revisions in the financing of campaigns both by legislation passed by Congress as a response to the Watergate scandals and by subsequent court interpretations of that legislation. As a result of those revisions, on the eve of the 1976 election no individual could give more than a thousand dollars at any stage (primary or general election) of a campaign for federal office. With the role of wealthy contributors thus reduced, candidates were now forced to rely on smaller contributors, and there were few better ways of reaching them than through direct mail. These revisions, moreover, had less of an impact on individual contributions to political action committees: the new rules permitted donations of up to five thousand dollars per committee at both the primary and general-election stages. "Independent" political action committees, those not connected to a candidate, had no effective spending limits at all. As Viguerie realized, the way was now open for an expansion of political action committees going well beyond their usual "interest-group" orientation to encompass contributors along purely ideological lines. Such committees might well help conservatives more than liberals, and not only because there was more money on that side of the political fence.[10] It seems to have been the case that many potential right-wing contributors living in rural areas in the South and West were far more isolated than their liberal counterparts: they were, as one activist put it, "very, very frustrated. They don't have an outlet for their political feelings";[11] and they were more than ready to respond to Viguerie's solicitations.[12]

Viguerie's major accomplishment along these lines was the creation of the National Conservative Political Action Committee, chaired by former YAF member and Young Republican activist John T. (Terry) Dolan, in 1975. But at the same time, he was helping Howard Phillips, another YAF graduate who had been active in the Massachusetts Republican party and was Nixon's selection to dismantle the antipoverty program in his second term.[13] Viguerie's mailing lists enabled Phillips to organize the Conservative Caucus, which would coordinate locally based groups—notably the "profamily" groups we

[10] Viguerie, *The New Right*, p. 23.

[11] Paul Dietrich, president of the Fund for a Conservative Majority, as quoted in Elizabeth Drew, *Politics and Money: The New Road to Corruption* (New York: Macmillan, 1983), p. 132. For a comparison of contributors to conservative PACs with those contributing to liberal PACs as well as with those contributing to both major parties, see Green and Guth 1984.

[12] Viguerie, *The New Right*, pp. 91, 93. Given their enormous overhead costs, it remains to be seen how effective direct-mail operations such as Viguerie's have been in actually channeling money to right-wing candidates; for the argument that corporate PACs have in fact been the major backers of such candidates, see Burris 1987a, p. 39.

[13] On Howard Phillips, see McIntyre 1979, pp. 71–80; Crawford 1980, pp. 38–40, 270–71; Young 1982, pp. 107–16.

have discussed but also those opposed to gun control or to school busing—to construct a national lobbying group to pressure Congress. It was thus Phillips who brought the organizational network Viguerie was developing down to the local level, by making contact with those engaged in the defense of the "traditional family,"[14] a role that, in view of his own attitudes, was not surprising. As Phillips remarked at one point: "I was taught there is good and evil; homosexuality is wrong; abortion is wrong; strong families are important. The primary responsibility of man is to provide. The responsibility of the wife is to help the husband; her role is the transmission of values" (as quoted in Young 1982, 109).

Many of what would later come to be listed as the distinctive characteristics of the "new right," such as the skillful adaptation to new political technology and changes in campaign financing, and the welding of "profamily" movements into a national network, can thus be seen in Viguerie's and Phillips's activities in 1975. Less clear was their long-range political strategy. Initially, their alienation from the Republican party led these right-wing activists to contemplate a third party, and throughout the spring and summer of 1975 they sought out possible candidates.[15] One of them was George Wallace, whose campaign debts from 1972 Viguerie had helped reduce and about whom Phillips was particularly enthusiastic. Another was Ronald Reagan: indeed for many of these activists the dream ticket for 1976 was Ronald Reagan and George Wallace.[16]

At the time most observers would probably have agreed with Lipset and Raab that Reagan and Wallace appealed to "sharply diverse constituencies," with the Wallace supporters poorer and therefore more liberal on economic issues than those backing the Californian;[17] but the interconnected fates of Wallace and Reagan in 1976 challenged the conventional wisdom. In the Democratic primaries, Wallace proved far more vulnerable, particularly to another candidate who was also a southerner and an "outsider," than had been assumed; what Jimmy Carter knew, one of his aides commented, was "the one

[14] Davis 1980, p. 24; Frances Fitzgerald, "The Triumphs of the New Right," *New York Review of Books* 28 (November 19, 1981): 21; Paige 1982, p. 139.

[15] R. W. Apple, "Study of 3rd Party is Approved by Conservatives," *New York Times*, February 17, 1975, p. 1; Christopher Lydon, "Conservative Challenge to Ford Is Forming in New Hampshire," *New York Times*, March 13, 1975, p. 30; "Conservatives Move to Get Third Party on Ballots for 1976," *New York Times*, June 11, 1975, p. 46.

[16] R. Drummond Ayres, "Wallace Is Close to GOP-Oriented Group," *New York Times*, June 22, 1975, p. 24; Dick Behn, "Swinging with Reagan and Wallace: An Odyssey," *Ripon Forum* 11 (May 5, 1975): 1–2.

[17] Seymour Martin Lipset and Earl Raab, *The Politics of Unreason: Right-Wing Extremism in America, 1790–1977*, 2d ed. (Chicago: University of Chicago Press, 1978), p. 530. Those conclusions, however, were based on survey data from the first primaries of 1976; but since Reagan and Wallace were both still listed as candidates, we do not know from the data they present whether—or how many—supporters of the one would have gone to the other.

thing that the rest of the country didn't know, that George Wallace was through and Jimmy could beat him.''[18] Carter's victories over Wallace in Florida and North Carolina proved his point and ended Wallace's career as a national figure.[19] The very close Republican contest between Reagan and President Ford, on the other hand, indicated, among other things, that Reagan's appeal extended far beyond affluent right-wing Republicans. In fact, one poll taken late in the primary campaign indicated that Reagan was running better against Ford among Democrats than among Republicans.[20] Journalists and political scientists assumed that these pro-Reagan Democrats were primarily the Wallace supporters of 1968 and 1972, and where permitted to do so by state law (as in Indiana and Texas) were now voting in the Republican primary for the former California governor.[21] These "crossovers" seemed to suggest that Reagan and Wallace constituencies were not as divergent as had been assumed and gave increased plausibility to the conviction that economic conservatives could be brought together in an antiliberal coalition with those opposed to changes in public education or to the agendas of the feminist and gay movements. The 1976 campaign had two lessons for "new right" strategists: Wallace's demise meant that any significant right-wing effort to launch a third party was futile; and Reagan's strong showing suggested that in the future their energies would be most effectively spent in taking over the Republican party.

It is important to emphasize once again that most of these individuals we have been discussing had at earlier points in their careers been Republican activists; in that sense it is quite accurate to say that "the seeds of the contemporary new right were sown in the Goldwater campaign."[22] What they called their "movement" may have had a higher claim on their loyalty than did the existing Republican organization (Reinhard 1983, 245; Blumenthal 1986, 318). But in the long run, far from leading them into permanent opposition, that allegiance simply reinforced their determination to make the party the vehicle of their cause. Especially after 1976 they saw their mission as purifying the party, eliminating the need of the dominant conservative faction to

[18] Landon Butler, as quoted in Witcover, *Marathon*, p. 116.

[19] For the specific factors in Wallace's 1976 defeat, compare Carlson 1981, pp. 210–14, with Oldendick and Bennett 1978, pp. 480–82.

[20] CBS News–*New York Times* poll, cited in R. W. Apple, "Regionalism and the G.O.P. Race," *New York Times*, May 28, 1976, p. A13.

[21] John Herbers, "Crossover Voting Makes Primaries More General," *New York Times*, May 16, 1976, sec. 4, p. 2; Witcover, *Marathon*, pp. 419–20; Gerald M. Pomper, "The Nominating Contests and Conventions," in Pomper et al., *The Election of 1976: Reports and Interpretations* (New York: McKay, 1977), pp. 19, 22–23.

[22] Paul M. Weyrich, "Blue Collar or Blue Blood? The New Right Compared with the Old Right," in Robert W. Whitaker, ed., *The New Right Papers* (New York: St. Martin's, 1982), p. 51. For a strong statement of the continuity between the individuals and organizations involved in the Goldwater campaign and those in the "new right," see Saloma 1984, pp. 3–4, 39–40, 140–46.

placate what one of them called the party's "liberal minority."[23] For these men it followed that this "liberal minority" had to be eliminated, their seats taken ultimately by conservative Republicans but, if necessary, by Democrats in the interim.

The stronghold of liberal Republicans, as of liberal politicians generally in the 1970s, had been the Senate; and a look at the 1978 elections, the first that the "new right" entered as a coherent force, showed the effectiveness of its strategy. In New Jersey four-term incumbent Clifford Case lost the Republican primary to a right-wing opponent; in Massachusetts Senator Edward Brooke survived right-wing attacks only to lose in the fall; and in Illinois "new right" leaders actually endorsed Charles Percy's Democratic opponent—though their efforts to defeat Percy would not succeed until 1984 (Crawford 1980, 279–84). On the positive side, in 1978 the "new right" added to its initial base of seven senators by helping elect Gordon Humphrey in New Hampshire, Roger Jepsen in Iowa, and William Armstrong in Colorado.[24] In all three races Dolan's NCPAC played an important role in attacking the Democratic incumbents these men replaced; and Viguerie was personally elated by journalistic reports claiming that the "new right" political action committee outscored comparable liberal or labor groups.[25]

The Ideology: Libertarianism, Traditionalism, "Populism"

Defeating moderate to liberal Republicans and electing conservative ones were simply aspects of the "new right" leaders' larger strategic goal, of turning the Republican party into the truly conservative majority party they had long envisioned. Their larger challenge was how to retain the traditionally upper-middle/upper-class "economically conservative" base of the Republican party while at the same time encouraging the lower-middle/working-class "culturally conservative" constituency variously identified with George Wallace or with the "profamily" movements to enter the party and support its candidates. To see how they met that challenge there is no better place to start than to look at the "new right's" chief ideologue—the man who transformed

[23] William A. Rusher, *The Making of the New Majority Party* (New York: Sheed and Ward, 1975), p. xxiii.

[24] My account of the "new right" in the 1978 elections is drawn from McIntyre 1979, pp. 137–43; Crawford 1980, pp. 273–77; Paige 1983, pp. 190–91. Since some older spokesmen such as Barry Goldwater and John Tower were increasingly seen as unreliable on the issues pressed by "profamily" activists, the seven senators who could fairly be called "new right" before 1978 were Jesse Helms of North Carolina and James McClure of Idaho, both elected in 1972; Jake Garn of Utah and Paul Laxalt of Nevada, both elected in 1974; and Orrin Hatch of Utah, Harrison Schmitt of New Mexico, and Malcolm Wallop of Wyoming, all elected in 1976.

[25] Viguerie, *The New Right*, p. 71; McIntyre 1979, pp. 33–34.

the triumvirate of Viguerie, Phillips, and Dolan into a quartet of "new right leaders"—Paul Weyrich.[26]

Like Viguerie and Phillips an example of upward social mobility, and like Viguerie and Dolan the product of a conservative Catholic background, Weyrich first worked as a journalist before joining the staff of a United States senator.[27] His Washington experience gave him first-hand knowledge about politics and policy but also soured him on the leadership of the Republican party, whom he later described as "effete gentlemen of the northeastern establishment who play games with other effete gentlemen who call themselves Democrats."[28] His developing friendship with millionaire brewer Joseph Coors was even more significant, for it was from Coors, a long-time contributor to right-wing organizations including the John Birch Society, that Weyrich received crucial financial support for whatever projects he best believed would serve the conservative cause. One such project—in which Viguerie, not surprisingly, also played a prominent role—was the creation in 1975 of another political action committee, the Committee for the Survival of a Free Congress, which soon became notable for its attention to detail and the precision of its operation.

More than those associated with Viguerie, however, Weyrich's innovations had a clear ideological thrust. Impressed by the fact that right-wingers had no major research institute from which to enunciate positions and influence policymakers in the nation's capital, Weyrich persuaded Coors to help fund the Heritage Foundation.[29] By the end of the 1970s the foundation had become a major fixture of the Washington scene; by that point, as one journalist noted, "hardly a week goes by without some major newspaper or magazine publishing a story or an op-ed piece based on a Heritage report."[30] Attributing much of the lack of influence of earlier generations of right-wing leaders to their lack of coordination, by the late 1970s Weyrich had also organized three different "Coalitions for America," discussion groups that met regularly to plan strategy and draw up legislation: the Kingston Group concentrating on economic

[26] The designation of the four of them as the leaders of the "new right" is widely accepted (see, for example, Davis 1980, p. 21; Young 1982, p. 88).

[27] On Weyrich, see McIntyre 1979, pp. 67–71; Crawford 1980, pp. 10–18; and Young 1982, pp. 123–31.

[28] Weyrich, as quoted in Richard John Neuhaus, "The Right to Fight," *Commonweal* 108 (October 9, 1981): 559.

[29] Although Coors's role in initially backing the Heritage Foundation was crucial, his overall contribution has been exceeded by that of Mellon heir Richard M. Scaife, who between 1973 and 1981 donated 3.8 million dollars to the foundation (for Scaife's role in funding conservative causes generally, see Karen Rothmyer, "Citizen Scaife," *Columbia Journalism Review* 20 [July–August 1981]: 41–50). Unlike almost all other research institutes, the Heritage Foundation has also been funded through small contributions (twenty dollars and under) solicited through direct mail (Morton Kondracke, "Politics: The Heritage Model," *New Republic* 183 [December 20, 1980]: 12).

[30] Kondracke, "Politics: The Heritage Model," p. 13.

issues and general political strategy; the Library Court Group on "family" issues; and the Stanton Group on national-security issues. Insofar as the leaders of the "new right" did in fact "meet continually . . . to discuss tactics and strategy of the 'movement' as a whole"(Crawford 1980, 40), Paul Weyrich was largely responsible.

The ideological impetus for all this activism came from Weyrich's Catholicism, as traditionalist as it is intense. "It is basic to my philosophy that God's truth ought to be manifest politically," he has written. "Collectivism, which is what the left is ultimately advocating in a thousand guises, is an error."[31] So too—from a traditionalist Catholic standpoint such as his—was libertarianism. "*Laissez-faire* is not enough. There has to be some higher value in society. There can be no such thing as an entirely free market. The market has to be responsive to social responsibility."[32] Elsewhere he has indicated his opposition to the premise that "if the free market leaves some people destitute—so be it" and believes instead in "the obligation to the less fortunate which welfare represents."[33] But he has not always been clear as to how this obligation is to be met.

To better grasp the implications of Weyrich's conviction that "God's truth ought to be manifest politically" and of his critique of laissez-faire, one must remember that his primary concern has been the defense of the "traditional family." He is thus highly critical of efforts to broaden antidiscrimination status to include sexual orientation and thus protect homosexuals. When "we're talking about homosexuality," Weyrich said in one interview, "we're talking of course about one of the gravest sins condemned in the Scriptures, a sin which is described and condemned more explicitly than most others. So we are not talking about someone's creed, someone's race, someone's private beliefs. We're talking about the question of morality which, of course, affects society as a whole. To elevate that sin to the level of a civil right and thereby legitimize this kind of life-style, I think sets a dangerous precedent" (as quoted

[31] Weyrich, "Blue Color or Blue Blood?" p. 62.

[32] Weyrich, as quoted in Neuhaus, "The Right to Fight," p. 559. He made similar comments in "The Cultural Right's Hot New Agenda," *Washington Post*, May 4, 1986, p. C1. Insofar as Weyrich maintains that the free market, without an underlying consensus maintaining "traditional values," "will lead only to conspicuous consumption, greed based on wealth gained through speculation rather than production, and narrow politics based on short-term self-interest" (ibid., p. C4), his argument is similar to Daniel Bell's that, "when the Protestant ethic was sundered from bourgeois society, only the hedonism remained, and the capitalist system lost its transcendental ethic" (*The Cultural Contradictions of Capitalism* [New York: Basic Books, 1976], p. 21). Bell, however, added that "the greatest single engine in the destruction of the Protestant ethic was the invention of the installment plan," which inevitably led to "the creation of new wants and new means of gratifying those wants" (ibid). It is not so clear how far Weyrich or the other spokesmen for the "new right" would follow Bell on this point, and efforts to turn them into latent critics of capitalism seem to me to be wide of the mark. Rather than discard the free market, Weyrich and the others want to restore capitalism's "transcendental ethic."

[33] Weyrich, as quoted in E. J. Dionne, "A Conservative Call for Compassion," *New York Times*, November 30, 1987, p. B12.

in Young 1982, 128–29). For Weyrich, then, "government should support certain moral truths" including the propositions that homosexuality and abortion are evils.[34] At the same time, however, his allies and backers on the "new right" are well-known for their hostility to government intervention: what unites them, Viguerie has claimed, "is a desire for less government and more freedom for every American."[35] Not surprisingly many of those studying the "new right" have been perplexed by the insistence of so many of its leaders that the government actively intervene in the sexual realm while (Weyrich notwithstanding) allowing the economy to run itself.

One way of interpreting these attempts to encompass both economic libertarianism and moral traditionalism in one ideology is to note the very different implications such a synthesis has for men and for women. Insofar as the emerging "new right" ideology "combines a defense of men in the market and women in the home," its economic-libertarian component can be seen as designed primarily for men, its moral-traditionalist component primarily for women. Like many Americans before them, "new right" spokesmen affirm the idea of different roles for the sexes; for them the "traditional family" is "the embodiment of self-sacrificing women and self-made men living together with proper, complementary roles for each, self-reliant and hostile to interventions by the state" (Hunter, 1981, 129, 133). So their attack on government intervention stems from both components. Like the right-wing spokesmen of previous generations they charge the welfare state with weakening men's ability to compete in the marketplace. They would also add, however, that insofar as government has made abortions legal, contraceptives more available, divorces easier, and (at least in implication) jobs more accessible, it has weakened women's willingness to commit themselves as mothers and homemakers.

Another perspective more directly confronts the issue of power relationships implied in the evolving "new right" ideology. What ideologues like Weyrich advocate, Petcheskey has written, is "the idea of *privatization*" which, as far as women are concerned, implies the restoration of "heterosexual patriarchy" giving men unchallenged control over their wives and children (Petchesky 1981, 222, 232). Her use of "patriarchy" here is precise:[36] Weyrich, for example, opposes the women's movement because its goals contradict what he calls "the Biblically ordained nature of the family, with the father as head of the household and the mother subject to his ultimate authority."[37]

"New right" strategists like Weyrich perceive, in Petcheskey's view, that

[34] Weyrich, "Blue Collar or Blue Blood?" p. 53; Weyrich as interviewed in Neuhaus, "The Right to Fight," pp. 556, 559.

[35] Viguerie, *The New Right*, p. 98.

[36] One of the earliest feminist analyses of the "new right" distinguished between "patriarchy" as "a specific organization of the family and society" and as "a transhistorical system of male domination," and identified the "new right" with the former (Gordon and Hunter 1977).

[37] Weyrich, as quoted in Leslie Bennetts, "Conservatives Join on Social Conerns," *New York Times*, July 30, 1980, p. B6.

the threat to male authority can only be removed through the retrenchment of government (Petchesky 1981, 232). If government at all levels had less power and male-dominated families more, there would be fewer publicly subsidized abortions, fewer publicly funded day-care centers, fewer interventions in domestic-abuse causes, fewer courses in sex education, fewer adoptions of "modern" textbooks, and fewer efforts to prohibit discrimination against women or gay men. The minimal right of a woman to have an abortion (and, for that matter, anyone's right to obtain pornographic materials) might appear to be unaffected by such retrenchment, except that both rights had been established largely through Supreme Court decisions overturning restrictive state laws; in those areas the retrenchment advocated by the "new right" means curbing the power of the *federal* courts and thus restoring the prerogatives of the *state* legislatures. In any case, their perception of government threatening traditional morality furthered the assimilation of the "profamily" movements in the broader "new right" network, which already included those who saw government as hostile to economic freedom.[38]

Perhaps the best single example of the ways the various strains of the "new right's" ideology could come together in a concrete policy proposal was the proposed "Family Protection Act," drafted by one of Weyrich's associates Connaught (Connie) Marshner, introduced in Congress in the fall of 1979, and because of the controversy it engendered never enacted.[39] The sections that drew the least attention were Titles II (Welfare) and IV (Taxation), both of which would have revised the laws to provide greater financial support for families with aged parents or married couples with children. But Title I (Education) proposed, to take only the major points, to withhold federal funds from states that did not allow public prayer in the schools (thus directly confronting the 1962 Supreme Court decision that had angered right-wing activists for a decade and a half), and further denied federal courts jurisdiction over the question. The bill also would have denied funds to any school that required teachers to belong to a union and to any state that did not permit parental and community review of textbooks. Further, the bill would have denied federal funds to any state that used educational materials that "tend to denigrate, diminish, or deny the role differences between the sexes" as they have been "historically understood in the United States," a provision generally perceived as aimed against women's studies courses in particular and feminists in general. Local schools would have been given the authority to segregate athletic facilities on the basis of sex, thus severely limiting the scope of the National Education Act of 1972 and, in the view of many, denying women students equal access to athletic participation.

[38] Paige 1983, pp. 135–36. For the "new right's" attempt to gain control of the antiabortion movement, and in doing so outflank the NRLC, see ibid., pp. 146–53.

[39] A summary of the bill's provisions may be found in "The Pro-Family Movement," *Conservative Digest* 6 (May–June 1980): 30.

Title III (First Amendment Guarantees) would deny the right of federal agencies to regulate church-owned facilities, thus conceivably exempting them from affirmative-action requirements, desegregation guidelines, or even the requirements of the National Labor Relations Act. Title V (Domestic Relations) would prohibit the Federal Government from changing state statutes on child abuse or spouse abuse, or from instituting child-abuse programs without a state's consent. Any federally supported organization would be required to notify the parents of an unmarried minor before she received contraceptives or abortion. The Legal Services Corporation would be prohibited from using federal funds in litigation involving abortion, divorce, homosexuality, or—interestingly—school desegregation. Finally, in two provisions aimed directly at advocates of gay rights, federal funds would be denied "any organization that presents homosexuality as an acceptable alternative life-style"; and discrimination against declared homosexuals could not be considered an "unlawful employment practice."

As one reviews the development of the "new right" one cannot but help notice the recurrence of certain clearly articulated perceptions of the social and historical context in which the "new right" was moving. Rather than consciously defending the status quo, its leaders, as Weyrich put it, saw themselves as "radicals working to overturn the present power structure in this country" (as quoted in Saloma 1984, 49). They, the activists behind them, and the constituencies they hoped to mobilize were all part of what Weyrich called "a middle-class revolt" against an "elitist upper class" (as quoted in Crawford 1980, 166). This self-image of the "new right"—as a movement of insurgent masses against an entrenched elite—was interpreted by some commentators to mean that it had its primary roots not in traditional conservatism at all but in American "populism." The most notable exponent of this view was Alan Crawford in his book, *Thunder on the Right: The "New Right" and the Politics of Resentment*.

Writing as a self-identified conservative, and very much influenced by his friend Peter Viereck's essay on the McCarthyites twenty-five years before, Crawford portrayed the "new right" in very similar terms.[40] Like Viereck, Crawford saw the movement he was analyzing as based on resentment: the new right tries "to fuel the hostility of lower-middle-class Americans against those above them and below them on the economic ladder." Like Viereck's McCarthyite coalition, Crawford's "new right" reflected sectional as well as eco-

---

[40] Crawford 1980, p. xiii–xv. Those with a longer historical perspective will note a certain irony here. Having worked for both the Young Americans for Freedom and Senator James Buckley, Crawford admired the Buckley brothers and called them genuine conservatives. He also deplored the career of Joseph McCarthy; yet it was William F. Buckley, Jr.'s, defense of McCarthy that persuaded a number of observers in the 1950s (including Viereck) that Buckley was "unconservative" and "anticonservative"—precisely the charges Crawford leveled against the "new right."

nomic antagonisms: it was "an organized attempt to revenge the resentments of the South and West against the settled and cosmopolitan East." And like Viereck, Crawford saw his right-wingers as profoundly "unconservative": "new right" "leaders and the organizations they represent seek radical social and political change."[41]

Perhaps more important, both writers argued that the right wing's ideological roots lay in the American radical democratic tradition. Crawford's "new right," like Viereck's "McCarthyite" coalition, was "neopopulist. . . . a natural outgrowth of antiaristocratic and anticonservative impulses that have been present in American politics throughout our history." To account for the "new right's" origins, Crawford traced its lineage all the way back to Andrew Jackson and continued through Bryan, LaFollette, Huey Long, Father Coughlin— and, of course, Joe McCarthy. With that "populist" heritage, he argued, it was not surprising that the "new right" showed such enthusiasm for tax-cutting initiatives or referenda on gay rights, because it too believed that "more and more issues should be decided by 'the people' through the ballot box rather than by their elected representatives or by intentionally unrepresentative institutions such as the courts."[42]

Suggestive as he is on aspects of the "new right's" rhetoric and tactics, Crawford's larger argument is problematic. His indebtedness to Viereck's analysis renders his thesis vulnerable to many of the same criticism Rogin had originally leveled against Viereck. In his 1967 book Rogin had pointed out that "populist" rhetoric, far from being the exclusive property of progressives and radicals, had been effectively exploited by conservative forces ever since the early nineteenth century. In his view subsequent conservative identification with "the people" had a least two consequences, both of considerable relevance to the "new right." First, as self-styled champions of a homogeneous "people," conservatives could attack those advocating protection for particular races or classes as "undemocratic" advocates of "special privilege," as creators of "un-American" hierarchies, as "aristocrats"—or, in current usage, as "elitists." Second, conservatives could opportunistically use appeals to "the people" not to champion the deprived but to protect specific interests: when "government action poses a threat to the power of locally entrenched elites" they then call "for decision-making by the people in the locality" (Rogin 1967, 49–51).

At the very least, Rogin's comments should direct us to look more closely at what specific interests are being served by the "new right's" appeals to "the people" and their attacks on "elites." Beyond that, they force us to examine the "populist" credentials of the "new right" on economic issues. Pursuing this line of inquiry one finds, for example, that the leaders of the

---

[41] Crawford 1980, p. 5 (cf. Viereck 1955, p. 103); p. 82; p. 5 (cf. Viereck 1955, p. 111).

[42] Crawford 1980, p. 290 (cf. Viereck 1956, p. 208); p. 312.

"new right" have been as staunchly antiunion as any of their right-wing predecessors.[43] One of Viguerie's major clients, and one of the major organizations in the "new right" network (even though it went back to 1955) was the National Right to Work Committee. Working with the NRWC, Viguerie and other "new right" leaders in 1977–78 succeeded in defeating a whole range of labor-backed measures in Congress, including expediting hearings before the National Labor Relations Board and making voter registration easier.[44]

But does its antiunionism mean that the "new right" opposes bigness per se, whether on the labor or management side, thus revealing what some analysts term an "entrepreneurial" or (in the Marxist sense) a "petit-bourgeois" perspective?[45] Though much has been made of it, this supposed hostility to big business on the part of the "new right" reduces itself not to fears about its unwarranted market power or its corruption of the political process, fears that had animated so many of the earlier "populists," but to complaints about its "permissiveness." Railing against corporate advertisements in salacious magazines, sales to Communist countries, or contributions to the campaigns of incumbent Democrats—three of the commonest complaints made by "new right" spokesmen[46]—hardly adds up to a formidable indictment of the giant corporation as an institution. Cynical observers find it easy to explain this tepidity, and point to the sources of funding for both the politicians the "new right" supports and the research institutes it utilizes. And indeed the burgeoning scholarly literature on this question has rather decisively concluded that, far from being primarily dependent on family-controlled firms, the last bastions of independent entrepreneurs, the "new right" has enjoyed the consistent support of some of the largest, most "managerial" corporations in America.[47] Rather than being supported by firms that are somehow peripheral to the economy, the "new right" has in fact been one of the major beneficiaries of the political mobilization of the business community in the 1970s.

On the other hand, "new right" organizers and spokesmen have invested too much energy into establishing their "populism" for us to dismiss it as a ruse; and what makes their claim to the tradition more credible than it might otherwise be is that it is no longer so clear that "populism" in America has been primarily economic. In the past twenty years, as we noted in the case of interpretations of support for McCarthy, historians have tended to underscore the localist, defensive, "cultural" aspects of the American "populist" tradi-

[43] See, in general, McIntyre 1979, pp. 84–91; Crawford 1980, pp. 28–29, 107–8, 250–54; Saloma 1984, pp. 76-78.

[44] Viguerie, *The New Right*, p. 15.

[45] See, for example, Ehrenhalt 1978, pp. 2025–26; Gordon and Hunter 1977, pp. 15–16.

[46] Viguerie, *The New Right*, pp. 107–8; Crawford 1980, pp. 213–17.

[47] The most significant research on this question has been done by Dan Clawson and his associates: Clawson 1985; Clawson 1986a; Clawson 1986b. Also relevant are Jenkins and Shumate 1985; and Burris 1987a, Burris 1987b.

tion. In the case of the Jacksonians, for example, one scholar has noted that "majority rule did not imply popular use of the machinery of state so much as control of society by the predominant customs and mores without interference from the state."[48] As for the Populists, some historians would even account for their protest in the 1890s by connecting their economic concerns to a broader defense of "community" and a commitment to "protecting the integrity of local institutions."[49]

It should be obvious that insofar as the "populist" tradition can be said to represent the defense of the local community against outside interference, the "new right" has a tenable claim to that tradition, especially so when one shifts from economic issues to what Petcheskey described as "sexual, reproductive, and family issues." The "new right's" defense of "community," like its defense of the "family," implies a shift of power away from a Federal Government under the influence of cultural cosmopolitans to the sites of "traditional" values. The "new right" advocates "getting government off the backs of the people" because, in the words of one of its theorists, only then can the government's "abetting of social disintegration" be halted and "the healthy forces of survival and reconstruction natural to normal individuals and real communities have scope for their work."[50] To call the "new right" "populist," therefore, is not necessarily inaccurate as long as one remembers two things: its "populism" is cultural rather than economic; and a cultural "populism" that attacks cosmopolitans rather than corporations has, as the example of Wallace would suggest, more affinity with the right wing than with the left.

The purpose of this summation has been to highlight two aspects of the "new right" that must be grasped before a deeper understanding—even of those subjects social scientists have investigated—can begin. The first is its ideology, or more precisely its ideological emphasis, for the "new right's" attempt to weld moral traditionalism to economic libertarianism was not new.[51] What was new was the emphasis its strategists gave traditionalist positions as part of their overall political strategy, an emphasis nowhere as prevalent in earlier periods of right-wing activity, not even in the Goldwater campaign. Whatever may be said about the coherence of this libertarian-traditionalist synthesis as an abstract proposition,[52] it has certainly proved its

[48] David Montgomery, *Beyond Equality: Labor and the Radical Republicans, 1862–1872* (New York: Knopf, 1967), p. 49.

[49] Alan Brinkley, *Voices of Protest: Huey Long, Father Coughlin, and the Great Depression* (New York: Knopf, 1982), p. 164.

[50] Clyde N. Wilson, "Citizens or Subjects?" in Whitaker, ed., *The New Right Papers*, p. 125.

[51] This point was frequently made in the 1980s; but see especially Himmelstein 1983.

[52] As the Reagan years drew to a close Weyrich expressed concern that the traditionalist component of "new right" ideology and policy was being undercut by the libertarian component and suggested that the "new right" be renamed "cultural conservatives" (Weyrich, "The Cultural Right's Hot New Agenda"; Wayne King and Warren Weaver, Jr., "Briefings: Conservatives

functional effectiveness, allowing "new right" organizers to tap both the financial resources of wealthy individuals and corporate PACs and the religiously inspired zeal of "profamily" activists at the local level.

The second aspect of the "new right" worthy of reemphasis is its organization. As our references to the National Conservative Political Action Committee, the Conservative Caucus, the Committee for the Survival of a Free Congress, and the Heritage Foundation, all created within the space of a few years, would suggest, it is hard to find other instances in recent American history in which so many organizations have been created so quickly by so few individuals. The irony, as the journalist Sidney Blumenthal has perceptively pointed out, is that conservatives in general—and the "new right" in particular—deliberately created a "counterestablishment" to challenge a far less cohesive "liberal establishment." "They imitated something they imagined, but what they created was not imaginary" (Blumenthal 1986, 5). That "counterestablishment," which included both "neoconservative" and "new right" spokesmen, came out of the conservative revival of the late 1970s, was connected to the Republican electoral successes in 1978 and 1980, and even more decisively shaped the policies that followed. Even after, while many of the issues that concerned the public in the late 1970s eventually lost their salience, the organizational network remained.

In the short run, the most significant result of the ideological synthesis and organizational networks these "new right" leaders developed was to allow them to reach out to sources of right-wing strength of untold potential. It is important to remember that as late as 1979 the "new right" network consisted largely of activists of one kind or another; it had not yet developed a way of reaching large numbers of citizens of like-minded views whose collective forces might be brought to bear on public policy or electoral outcomes across the country. The solution for Viguerie, Phillips, and Weyrich was to bring right-wing evangelical ministers into their network and through them to mobilize a constituency of millions.

Astir," *New York Times*, February 7, 1987, p. 8; Dionne, "A Conservative Call for Compassion," p. B12). The degree to which Weyrich's concerns were shared by any of the other leaders—not to mention the financial contributors—remained to be seen.

Thirteen

Locating the Moral Majority: The Religious Factor

FROM THE STANDPOINT of social scientists analyzing right-wing political behavior—and arguably from the perspective of the history of American politics itself—the most important tactical decision that the leaders of the "new right" made was to form an alliance with like-minded evangelical ministers. Whatever the historic meanings of "evangelical," the apparent resurgence of that combination of theological orthodoxy, a personal conversion experience, and missionary zeal which characterizes contemporary evangelicalism became the most talked-about feature of American religious life as the 1970s drew to a close.[1] In the early 1980s a significant number of social scientists, including not only those studying religion but those studying voting behavior as well, would examine various aspects of this evangelical resurgence and explore its political implications. With relatively few exceptions, however, they would focus on the characteristics of the evangelicals who were being mobilized rather than on the process of mobilization itself; they looked at the followers rather than at the leaders. Here is another case where the studies of particular developments within the American right wing tended to minimize the importance of the prominent individuals and organizational networks that made it possible. To place the work of these social scientists in sharper perspective, therefore, it is necessary first to survey both the evangelical resurgence itself and the way "new right" organizers were able to capitalize on it.

The "New Right" and the Evangelical Renaissance

Before either social scientists or journalists turned their attention to it, the evangelical resurgence had been forecast in an influential book of 1972. Looking at figures for the 1960s, the author of *Why Conservative Churches are Growing* pointed to membership declines in the "mainline" denominations (the Episcopalians, the United Church of Christ, the Methodists, the Presbyterians, the Lutherans) and the concurrent growth in those religious bodies that, at least by "mainline" standards, were neither "reasonable" nor "rele-

[1] See for example the cover stories in the two leading national news magazines: Kenneth L. Woodward et al., "Born Again! The Year of the Evangelicals," *Newsweek* 88 (October 25, 1976): 68ff.; "Back to That Oldtime Religion," *Time* 110 (December 6, 1977): 52–58. A good review is Quebedeaux 1978.

vant'' (the Southern Baptists, the Assemblies of God, the Churches of God, the Holiness and Pentecostal groups, the Mormons, the Seventh-Day Adventists, and so on). The evidence suggested to him that religious groups prospered not because they were ''reasonable'' or ''relevant'' but because they were ''strong'' and ''strict,'' demanding a high level of commitment, willing to impose discipline on their members, and unashamed to try to convert others. At the same time, and for many of the same reasons, such religious groups tended to believe they had exclusive possession of the truth, and their members tended to be conformist in their behavior and ''fanatical'' in their communication with outsiders.[2] What made the analysis so compelling was that its author, Dean Kelley, was an official in the ''mainline'' National Council of Churches.

Commentators soon expanded on Kelley's findings by stressing the appeal of ''strong'' churches to men and women looking for secure moral foundations in an era of social and cultural turmoil. But critical scholars pointed out that these ''strong'' churches grew less because of their success in converting ''outsiders'' looking for a demanding faith than through their ability to retain their existing members and to teach their members' children.[3] Moreover, when placed in a broader historical context it was not at all clear that mainline decline and conservative growth in the 1960s had been greater than in earlier decades.[4] Finally, as Kelley himself admitted, there was no inextricable connection between ''conservatism,'' however defined, and what he defined as ''strong'' churches.[5] In spite of these criticisms and qualifications, however, the idea soon took hold among journalists as well as church leaders that theologically conservative churches—largely though not exclusively evangelical—possessed a dynamism unavailable to the more respectable mainline denominations and that for American Protestantism they were quite possibly the wave of the future.

The next question to arise was the extent to which these theologically conservative churches were politically conservative as well. The answer, of course, depends on the population being studied. Basing one's observations

---

[2] Dean M. Kelley, *Why Conservative Churches Are Growing: A Study in Sociology of Religion* (New York: Harper and Row, 1972), pp. 1–11, 20–32, 56–59, 78–81.

[3] See especially the work of Reginald W. Bibby: Bibby and Merlin Brinkerhoff, ''The Circulation of the Saints: A Study of People Who Join Conservative Churches,'' *Journal for the Scientific Study of Religion* 12 (September 1973): 273–83; Bibby, ''Why Conservative Churches *Really* Are Growing,'' *JSSR* 17 (June 1978): 129–38. For confirmation of the view that religious switching is ''a complex, multifaceted phenomenon'' that ''cannot be reduced to a simple, unitary pattern,'' see Wade Clark Roof and Christopher Kirk Hadaway, ''Denominational Sustaining in the Seventies: Going Beyond Stark and Glock,'' *JSSR* 18 (December 1979): 363–79.

[4] This point has been cogently made by William R. Hutchison, in ''Past Imperfect: History and the Prospect of Liberalism,'' *Christian Century* 103 (January 1–8, 1986): 11–15.

[5] Dean M. Kelley, ''Why Conservative Churches Are Still Growing,'' *Journal for the Scientific Study of Religion* 17 (June 1978): 167.

on statements from a sample of church leaders—either clerics or activist lay-people—can produce one conclusion; basing them on a survey of the inarticulate majority of church members can produce quite another; and without a representative sample of either population one can draw no definitive conclusions at all. Such problems must be taken into account when considering the discussion of the political implications of "the evangelical renaissance" of the 1970s. Those arguing for political diversity among evangelicals could point first of all to the most prominent evangelical layman in the country in the late 1970s, President Jimmy Carter. Though Carter's politics remain difficult to classify, he was certainly not a "conservative" as the word was used at the time; on church-state issues, notably prayer in the public schools and tax credits for private schools, he consistently took an advanced, "liberal," separationist position.[6] There was also, to take a second example, the increasing activism of evangelical moderates led by Senator Mark Hatfield, and through him the commanding figure of Billy Graham, on issues of world peace and nuclear disarmament.[7] There was even a small articulate evangelical left wing, such as the group associated with the magazine *Sojourners*, working out a "radical Christian" critique of American capitalism and American power in the world.[8]

On the other hand, there was even more evidence—at least at the leadership/activist level—pointing to a politically conservative outcome. At the beginning of the decade, a number of dissenting evangelical scholars, such as the historian Richard V. Pierard, were already complaining that "the ties linking evangelical Christianity to political conservatism are so numerous and so persuasive that it is possible to say the two are 'yoked together.' " As evidence, they pointed to various evangelical leaders' assertions that "the free-enterprise system is divinely ordained," their unqualified conclusion that "this country is a Christian nation," and their automatic linkage of "God's purposes to American military endeavors" (Pierard 1970, 18–19, 80, 107, 153).

As the 1970s progressed, many of the institutional results of evangelical growth simply accentuated that conservative thrust. There was, for example, the dramatic expansion of religious broadcasting: by the end of the decade 300 radio stations, 36 television stations, and three networks were occupied in full-time religious broadcasting, and a proliferation of TV preachers was engaged

[6] See the analysis in Ronald B. Flowers, "President Jimmy Carter, Evangelicalism, Church-State Relations, and Civil Religion," *Journal of Church and State* 25 (Winter 1982): 113–32.

[7] On the emerging evangelical concern with peace and disarmament in the late 1970s and early 1980s, see especially the reports of Kenneth A. Briggs in the *New York Times*, notably "Evangelicals Adding Powerful New Voice to Movement in Churches for Arms Control," *New York Times*, February 18, 1979, p. 26; "Evangelicals Embracing Hatfield Stand on Arms," *New York Times*, April 1, 1982, city ed., p. B10; "Graham Blends Preaching with Appeal for Peace," *New York Times*, April 25, 1982, p. 28.

[8] For the diversity of political attitudes among evangelical leaders, see (in addition to Quebedeaux 1978) Jorstad 1981 and Fowler 1982.

in what would come to be called the "electronic ministry."[9] All this was
largely an evangelical phenomenon and, as the two closest students of this
development noted, the political message of most of these preachers, insofar
as they had a political message at all, was fully consonant with the ideology
of the "new right": "the United States was created by God to fight the Anti-
Christ" of "Communism"; and "the traditional concept of the male-dominated nuclear family is sacrosanct."[10] The 1970s also witnessed the growth of
private "Christian" schools, usually under evangelical auspices. The parents
who by the end of the decade were sending 1.5 million children to these
schools may have been motivated less by fears of racial integration than critics
assumed, but their decision to escape the public school system was in many
cases a protest against sex education, Darwinism, and "modern" textbooks.[11]
And, as we have already noted, a good part of the energy directed against the
Equal Rights Amendment and the inclusion of gay men and lesbians in antidiscrimination ordinances had religious origins.

Carter's own politics notwithstanding, the emergence of evangelicals as a
political force thus appeared to have heavy conservative overtones. One early
indication of what this might entail was the attempt in the early 1970s by Bill
Bright, leader of the Campus Crusade for Christ, and Representative John
Conlan (Republican of Arizona) to organize each congressional district to
elect right-wing evangelicals to office.[12] Working out of the Christian Freedom
Foundation, Bright and Conlan turned to a right-wing evangelical publishing
house to prepare their educational materials, received financial pledges of support from Amway executives among others,[13] created a group of clergymen to
disseminate their materials, and opened a "Christian Embassy" in Washington to influence legislators and government officials. But the ambitious Bright-
Conlan plan was aborted in early 1976 first when it was exposed in *Sojourners*
and again when Billy Graham expressed concern over the politicization of the
Campus Crusade he had helped found. Bright subsequently concentrated on
more narrowly evangelistic efforts, but not before influencing other ministers
of similar views and bequeathing to them certain tactics such as a "Christian"
index of voting on legislation affecting, in Conlan's words, "individual free-

---

[9] Figures as given in Hadden and Swann 1981, pp. 7–8.

[10] Hadden and Swann 1981, pp. 97–98. For an analysis of the electronic ministry that places it
in the context both of mass communications and of American revivalism, see Frankl 1987.

[11] My interpretation here is based on the findings summarized in Virginia Davis Nordin and
William Lloyd Turner, "More Than Segregation Academies: The Growing Protestant Fundamentalist Schools," *Phi Delta Kappan* 61 (February 1980): 391–94.

[12] What follows is based on Jim Wallis and Wes Michaelson, "The Plan to Save America,"
Sojourners 5 (April 1976): 4–12; and on Kenneth L. Woodward, "Politics from the Pulpit,"
Newsweek 88 (September 6, 1976): 49ff.

[13] For the special role of Amway executives—president Richard DeVos and board chairman
Jay Van Andel—in underwriting organizations promoting the identification of "free enterprise"
and Christianity, see Paige 1983, pp. 158–59; Saloma 1984, pp. 53–55.

dom, free competitive enterprise, and constitutional government based on God's laws.''[14]

So it was not surprising that, as they became aware that right-wing evangelical ministers were creating their own networks, Viguerie, Phillips, Weyrich, and other "new right" leaders sought them out to form a common alliance.[15] To a certain extent the structuring of this developing coalition can, as one political scientist has argued, be interpreted in terms of the bargaining framework typical of interest-group politics (Lienesch 1982, 409–10). The organizers of Christian schools, for example, were worried about losing their tax exemptions because of their largely white enrollments, and the religious broadcasters were concerned over possible government regulation. Both realized that the lobbying skills that the "new right" had developed—especially at the local level—would prove helpful to their interests; and in return the ministers could greatly expand the mass base available for right-wing mobilization, hitherto limited to activists in the "profamily" movements we have reviewed. It is also important, however, to note the common ideology— deeply religious and deeply conservative—that the "new right" leaders shared with the clergymen. It was, after all, Paul Weyrich and not some Baptist preacher who described the conflict over "the traditional family" as "really the most significant battle of the age-old conflict between good and evil, between the forces of God and forces against God, that we have seen in our country.''[16]

One political organization created by right-wing organizers and like-minded evangelicals was Christian Voice, conceived in 1978 and officially launched at the beginning of 1979 after a year of discussions between Gary Jarmin, legislative director for the American Conservative Union and two ministers active in the antihomosexual campaign in California, Robert Grant and Richard Zone.[17] Founded to combat "the unmistakable signs of moral decay . . . all around us: sexual promiscuity and perversion, pornography, legalized abortion, the disparaging of marriage, family, and the role of motherhood," this organization aimed to "clearly focus public attention on the basic moral

[14] John Conlan, as quoted in Woodward, "Politics from the Pulpit," p. 49.

[15] The recent work of several social scientists cautions us against emphasizing the "new right's" evangelical connection to the exclusion of its ties with other conservative religious groups. One such, many of whose leaders had long been active in the "old right" (notably the John Birch Society), which is now working with the "new right" on specific issues, is the Church of Jesus Christ of Latter-Day Saints, commonly known as the Mormons. On the Mormon role in the emerging right-wing coalition, see especially Richardson 1984 and Shupe and Heinerman 1985.

[16] Weyrich, as quoted in "The Pro-Family Movement," *Conservative Digest* 6 (May–June 1980): 15.

[17] This paragraph is based on Young 1982, pp. 101–6; Zwier 1982, pp. 20–22; and Guth 1983a, pp. 31–32.

implications of each issue" before Congress.[18] At first glance Christian Voice appeared to be adopting a method well known to Washington pressure groups, the rating system or "report card" for each legislator, in which selected roll-call votes were listed and evaluated. Christian Voice itself, the tax-exempt, "educational" organization officially headed by Grant, would compile these votes and publicize them; then, on the basis of those votes its political action committee, the Christian Voice Moral Government Fund headed by Jarmin, would decide which congressmen to support or oppose.

Where Christian Voice differed from other pressure groups—and where the influence of the earlier Bright-Conlan effort is clearest—was that the congressmen were evaluated not on their "probusiness" or "prolabor" sympathies, not even on their "conservatism" or "liberalism" per se, but on their "morality." "Morality" under Christian Voice's definition included not only such legitimately "moral" issues as abortion but such right-wing staples as recognition of Taiwan as the seat of the legitimate government of China, opposition to sanctions against the white-dominated government of Rhodesia, support for a balanced budget, and opposition to the creation of a Department of Education.[19] As soon as they began appearing, these "morality ratings" attracted widespread criticism, not only because of their eccentric selection of issues but because, as *Newsweek* tersely put it, "four ordained clergymen in Congress received among the lowest marks—while Richard Kelly, one of the Abscam bribery defendants, was given a perfect, 100 percent rating."[20]

A religious network that held out far more potential for the "new right's" long-range expansion was organized by Robert Billings and Edward McAteer.[21] Billings, a college president and former public school principal outraged at what he saw as the "red tape" and "humanist" philosophy imposed by federal bureaucrats, had been traveling around the country urging equally angry "conservative Christians" to start religious schools. Then in 1976 he met McAteer, the former southeastern sales manger for Colgate-Palmolive, who in his travels had established contacts with churches throughout the region and was now serving as national field director for the Christian Freedom Foundation. The seminars he had started in order to get ministers involved in politics so impressed Howard Phillips that he persuaded him to become field director for the Conservative Caucus; and so it was primarily through McAteer and Billings that by the end of the 1970s Viguerie, Weyrich, Phillips, and the

[18] Christian Voice statement of purpose, as quoted in Young 1982, p. 101.

[19] John Herbers, "Ultraconservative Evangelists a Surging New Force in Politics," *New York Times*, August 17, 1980, p. 52.

[20] Allan J. Mayer et al., "A Tide of Born-Again Politics," *Newsweek* 96 (September 15, 1980): 36.

[21] What follows is based on Dudley Clendinen, " 'Christian New Right's' Rush to Power," *New York Times*, August 18, 1980, city ed., p. B7; Young 1982, pp. 117–22; Zwier 1982, pp. 18–20; and Guth 1983a, pp. 32–33.

others established ties with right-wing ministers throughout the country. By 1979 these men had created a new network, including two new organizations which along with the preexisting Christian Voice would become the institutional basis of what was now called the "new *Christian* right." One was the Religious Roundtable, to serve as a coordinating agency and to sponsor seminars and training sessions to reach out to the broadest possible range of ministers: McAteer would serve as president and James Robison as vice president. The other, a mass-membership organization, was to be called "the Moral Majority." The name was suggested by Weyrich and the first director was Billings, but one of those attending McAteer's seminars had been a Baptist minister from Virginia named Jerry Falwell.

Falwell and the Creation of the Moral Majority

Although the "new Christian right" included more than just the Moral Majority and although the Moral Majority was not created by Falwell alone, it was he who soon established himself in the public mind as the central figure in the Moral Majority and, indeed, in the broader "new Christian right." To a certain extent Falwell's prominence could be dismissed as the result of his skillful manipulation of the often credulous mass media; but there are good sociological reasons for believing that his prominence rested on more solid foundations than media attention. For some time sociologists had been paying increasing attention to the role of "resources" in expediting political mobilization of any kind, and one such "resource" was preexisting networks that could be incorporated by mobilizing groups.[22] This perspective helps reveal the great asset of the Moral Majority, which it possessed to a degree comparable groups could not match: its ability to bring in right-wing clergymen who had *already* come together on behalf of common objectives—whether building new churches, developing Bible colleges, or protecting Christian schools from government interference.[23]

[22] The best-known expositions of this perspective are McCarthy and Zald 1977 and Tilly 1978; for a review of the literature see Jenkins 1983.

[23] For an analysis of the Moral Majority from this perspective, see Liebman 1983. One sociologist has gone further, arguing that the appearance of the "new Christian right" in the late 1970s was almost totally the result of mobilization and did not stem from heightened "lifestyle concerns" (Miller 1985). But the research design from which he drew that conclusion—a content analysis of selected items in evangelical periodicals from 1955 to 1980—is itself problematic (Bruce 1987). And beyond that, resource-mobilization theorists in general tend to assume that in any particular case there is always a level of discontent sufficient to form the basis of a movement (McCarthy and Zald 1977, pp. 1215–16), which is why they focus on the degree to which a specific organization has enough resources to draw on that discontent (as in Liebman 1983). One of the reasons resource-mobilization theory has not been more widely used to explain the rise of the "new Christian right," therefore, may be that so much of the evidence suggests that the *level* of discontent among conservative evangelicals and fundamentalists itself rose in the 1970s.

For the Moral Majority's organizational success, Falwell deserves much of the credit. In fact one of the reasons he had caught the attention of the leaders of the "new right" in the first place was that he had already established himself as an empire-builder.[24] Like them he had created a network of institutions, radiating out of his Baptist church in Lynchburg to include the church-affiliated Liberty Baptist College (now Liberty University); the broadcast of his Sunday morning services as "The Old-Time Gospel Hour" on 373 stations across the country; and a fund-raising operation which brought in about 35 million dollars in 1979. Falwell also attracted the political entrepreneurs of the "new right" because of the convergence of his political views with theirs. In the mid-1970s, like many other evangelicals, he overcame his earlier inhibitions on political action; and he became particularly involved in two of the emerging right-wing campaigns of the end of the decade: the attempt to restore "old-fashioned patriotism" and the resistance to homosexual demands for acceptance.[25] By the time he wrote the two major statements of his views—his 1980 campaign tract *Listen, America!* and his conclusion to a book written by two faculty members at Liberty Baptist College, *The Fundamentalist Phenomenon*—he was already very much part of the "new right's" organizational and ideological network.

The first part of *Listen, America!* is a fairly standard right-wing critique of public policy, but Falwell's argument went beyond the usual denunciations of political, economic, and military failures as he asked why these misfortunes had now descended on the American people. "The strength of America has been in her righteousness, in her walk with God," he maintained. "Now we see national sins that are permeating our nation, and we find that our citizens are without remorse, without regret or repentance, and we are not far from judgment of God upon this great nation of ours. With our erosion from the historical faith of our fathers, we are seeing our erosion in our stability as a nation. We have already shown that we are economically, politically, and militarily sick because our country is morally sick."

Then, in the second part of his book, Falwell turned to an extended discussion of America's "moral sickness," with not only analyses of some fairly recognizable symptoms but, far more controversially, with indictments of the women's movement, efforts to secure legal abortion, the proposed Equal Rights Amendment, and homosexuals' demands for civil rights. All these developments, in Falwell's mind, arose from a common source, the control of the institutions shaping our culture by those he called "humanists" who "believe that man is his own god and that moral values are relative, that ethics are

---

[24] Unless otherwise noted, material in this paragraph is drawn from Fitzgerald 1981. Her description of Falwell's early life and career matches that in Jerry Strober and Ruth Tomczak, *Jerry Falwell: Aflame for God* (Nashville: Nelson, 1979).

[25] See, for example, his statements at the time, as quoted in Fitzgerald 1981, p. 116; and in Jere Real, "What Jerry Falwell *Really* Wants," *Inquiry* 4 (August 3–August 24, 1981): 17.

situational.'' He charged that these ''secular humanists'' were susceptible to a ''naturalistic'' outlook that ''projects man as an animal concerned only with fulfilling the desires of the moment'' and in which ''sexual immorality is just another function like eating and drinking.''[26]

Falwell's attribution of economic and military decline to moral decay followed a logic established by generations of Protestant preachers, the legacy of the seventeenth-century Puritans. In laying the ultimate blame on an entity called ''secular humanism,'' however, he was articulating sentiments that, while not unknown in the evangelical community, had been voiced mainly by local activists fighting sex education and the teaching of ''evolution'' in the schools. And in formally confronting ''secular humanism,'' Falwell and other like-minded ministers, as one historian has put it, ''revitalized fundamentalist conspiracy theory.'' The relativistic and naturalistic currents of modern thought subsumed under ''secular humanism'' could far more plausibly be used to explain social change than ''the old monocausal Communist-conspiracy accounts'' with their ''implausible scenarios of Russian agents infiltrating American schools, government, reform movements, and mainline churches'' (Marsden 1983, 158–59).

It was far more effective, therefore, for Falwell to use ''secular humanism'' to describe so many of the movers and shakers of contemporary culture, ranging from *Playboy* publisher Hugh Hefner to prominent feminists such as Betty Friedan and Gloria Steinem. All of these figures—along with the homosexual activists who since they ''cannot reproduce themselves . . . must recruit''— were in his view part of a ''vicious assault upon the American family,'' steadily undermining ''the fundamental building block and basic unit of our society.'' To rally the overwhelming majority of Americans who believe in a traditional morality based on Scripture against this ''vocal minority of ungodly men and women'' who have brought America ''to the brink of death,'' Falwell came together with other like-minded ministers to establish the Moral Majority organization in 1979.[27]

In fact Falwell and the others established *three* Moral Majority organizations: a Moral Majority Foundation to serve as an educational group; a Moral Majority Political Action Committee; and what most observers took to be *the* organization, the Moral Majority Inc., designed primarily as a pressure group and including not only the national organization but a network of autonomous chapters in each state (Fitzgerald 1981, 124). Here is how Falwell described it:

Our goal is to exert a significant influence on the spiritual and moral direction of our nation by: (a) mobilizing the grass roots of moral Americans in one clear and effective voice; (b) informing the moral majority what is going on behind their backs in

[26] Jerry Falwell, *Listen, America!* (Garden City, N.Y.: Doubleday, 1980), pp. 119–20, 206.
[27] Falwell, *Listen America!*, pp. 124, 153; 185, 121; xi, 258–59.

Washington and in state legislatures across the country; (c) lobbying intensely in
Congress to defeat left-wing, social-welfare bills that will further erode our precious
freedom; (d) pushing for positive legislation such as that to establish the Family
Protection Agency, which will ensure a strong enduring America; and (e) helping
the moral majority in local communities to fight pornography, homosexuality, the
advocacy of immorality in school textbooks, and other issues facing each and every
one of us. (Falwell, *Listen, America*, p. 258)

This general statement of purpose ignored a number of crucial questions.
Was, for example, the Moral Majority primarily a religious or a political organization? Certainly in his statements Falwell insistently emphasized the latter. "Moral Majority is a political organization and is not based on theological
considerations," he wrote, and comprises Americans from a wide variety of
religious backgrounds who were united in their determination to remove the
"moral cancers that are causing our society to rot from within."[28] In the minds
of many, however, the Moral Majority never came close to achieving this
ecumenical goal. Some found Falwell's disclaimers of sectarianism uncon-
vincing and singled out overtly Christian references in Moral Majority literature.[29] Others noted that within the Moral Majority those occupying leadership
positions were almost all Baptist ministers, like Falwell typically "independent" or unaffiliated Baptists (Liebman 1983, 61).

What specific policies would the Moral Majority recommend to eliminate
the "moral cancers" to which Falwell referred? On this question he was ambiguous, perhaps deliberately so. He wrote, for example, that the Moral Majority opposes any attempt to legalize homosexual relationships or in any way
grant " 'special rights' for homosexuals who have chosen a perverted lifestyle," yet at the same time is "committed to guaranteeing the civil rights of
homosexuals." Similarly, while the Moral Majority is opposed to pornography, "we do not advocate censorship"; and Falwell himself was particularly
attracted to the alternative tactic of boycotting the media and their sponsors.
Again, while the Moral Majority believes "the ERA is the wrong vehicle to
obtain equal rights for women" because of "the ambiguous and simplistic
language of the amendment," it also supports legislation to ensure that "every
American woman will earn as much money and enjoy the same opportunities
for advancement as her male counterpart in the same vocation."[30] At least on
the basis of Falwell's description, one can only conclude that, while the Moral

[28] Falwell, "Future-Word: An Agenda for the Eighties," in Ed Dobson and Ed Hindson, *The
Fundamentalist Phenomenon: The Resurgence of Conservative Christianity* (Garden City, N.Y.:
Doubleday, 1981), p. 188. See also "An Interview with the Lone Ranger of American Funda-
mentalism," *Christianity Today* 25 (September 4, 1981): 24, 26; "Penthouse Interview: Jerry
Falwell," *Penthouse* 12 (March 1981): 156.

[29] William R. Goodman and James J. H. Price, *Jerry Falwell: An Unauthorized Profile* (Lynchburg, Va.: Paris and Associates, 1981), pp. 45–47.

[30] Falwell, "Future-Word," p. 189, 192, 190.

Majority may have been formed to eradicate what he termed "moral cancers," the specific means to achieve that eradication remained remarkably imprecise.

If the Moral Majority was a political organization, did it actually support candidates? Falwell wrote both that "we do not endorse political candidates" and, only ten lines later, that the organization supported candidates because of their "commitment . . . to the principles that we espouse" as well as their competency for the office.[31] Inconsistent on their face, these statements can be reconciled in a number of ways. One can note the structural and financial autonomy of the state Moral Majority chapters and point out that, in 1980 at least, it was the state chapters, and not the national organization, that actually endorsed candidates (Fitzgerald 1981, 124, 126). That hypothesis leaves us nonetheless wondering about the purpose of the *national* political action committee. A more plausible explanation underscores the importance of "the principles that we espouse," which desirable candidates would support. In at least one interview that was the position Falwell took regarding his own attitude toward Ronald Reagan: "Someone asked me during the last campaign [1980] if I was endorsing candidate Reagan. I said, 'No, I'm not. I am voting for him because the platform on which he is campaigning is very near the platform that I believe in.' I did not endorse or publicly promote his candidacy because I want to be able, while he is in office, to criticize him when I think he is wrong."[32]

As the political campaign began in earnest in the fall of 1980, the Moral Majority was approximately a year old. At that point the organization, with chapters in almost all of the fifty states, claimed 400,000 members and in its first year had drawn in $1.5 million in contributions. The Moral Majority Political Action Committee had raised $200,000 in less than five months, and Falwell—so one journalist reported—was planning to create similar PACs at the state level, each with a starting fund of $100,000.[33] By the beginning of the 1980 campaign, Falwell asserted that the Moral Majority had already registered 3 million new voters. It was quite an achievement for someone who only a year before had little recognition outside fundamentalist circles; and it was not surprising that, as the national media began running articles on what *Newsweek* called "a tide of born-again politics,"[34] Falwell as "the most visible example of the politicized broadcast evangelists"[35] received the bulk of the publicity.

[31] Falwell, "Future-Word," p. 191.

[32] *Christianity Today* interview with Falwell, p. 26.

[33] Statistics in Dudley Clendinen, "Rev. Falwell Inspires Evangelical Vote," *New York Times*, August 20, 1980, city ed., p. B22. Other observers have noted, however, that in most states chapters were on paper only; only eighteen states had truly viable chapters (Guth 1983a, p. 33).

[34] Mayer et al., "A Tide of Born-Again Politics," pp. 28ff.

[35] Clendinen, "Falwell Inspires Evangelical Vote," p. B22.

The Moral Majority's Constituency: An Examination of the Evidence

During 1980 right-wing religious organizations such as the Moral Majority attracted increasing attention not only from journalists but from social scientists as well. In the aftermath of the 1980 election in fact, two major anthologies appeared that dealt with various aspects of the emergence of this "new Christian right." On the whole, however, researchers devoted relatively little attention to the factors that led individuals to join organizations such as the Moral Majority; in this respect, the contrast with studies of the "profamily" activists reviewed earlier is striking. Instead, perhaps because the claims made by Falwell and by the media presented such a challenge, the major effort of social scientists was directed toward estimating the size of the constituency of the Moral Majority and evaluating its political impact.

Social scientists did find that there was a positive correlation between regular viewing of religious programs on television and support both for the Moral Majority and for the positions it took on various issues; moreover, such regular viewers were more likely to vote than nonviewers.[36] To that extent the "electronic ministry" had indeed become an agency of mobilization, and Falwell's assumptions about his own importance were supported. But how many of these people were there? Precisely whom could Falwell legitimately claim to represent? Since, in his case, the most obvious base for mobilization constituted those who watched "The Old-Time Gospel Hour," the easiest approach for researchers was to assess the size and nature of his viewing audience. By the summer of 1980, when Falwell had established himself both as a media figure and as a presence in the Republican party, he claimed that 25 million people watched his program and some of his spokesmen went further, claiming an audience of 50 million (Hadden and Swann 1981, 47). Two researchers, Jeffrey K. Hadden and Charles E. Swann, decided to investigate those claims in their book *Prime-Time Preachers*. In so doing they found that—according to Arbitron, one of the two major organizations measuring TV viewing—the weekly viewing audience for "The Old-Time Gospel Hour" was slightly under 1.5 million; and those figures closely accorded with those of the other major organization in the field, A. C. Nielsen (Hadden and Swann 1981, 51, 54).

These dramatically lower figures for Falwell's audience were only part of the definition of claims about the influence of the "electronic ministry" that these initial scholarly investigations revealed. At the same time that Falwell was making his claims, for example, the media was accepting, without much examination, the statement of the director of the National Religious Broadcasters that the total viewing audience for the "electronic ministry" was 130 million.[37] Hadden and Swann, however, cited the Arbitron figures to show that in 1980 the combined audience was approximately 20.5 million. By way of comparison, they also noted that this figure was slightly lower than the average weekly audience for either "M*A*S*H" or "The Muppet Show" (Hadden and Swann 1981, 50, 53). A subsequent study, conducted by the Annenberg School of Communications of the University of Pennsylvania and utilizing Gallup data, suggested an even smaller regular audience, of about 13.3 million or about 6 percent of all television viewers.[38]

The second fact that these investigations by social scientists revealed was that, contrary to the claims of the ministers involved, the audience was not growing in size; indeed, there was some indication that by 1980 the size of the combined audience for all religious programs on television was declining and that the period of growth had occurred earlier, between 1970 and 1975, long before the media discovered the "electronic ministry."[39] Third, Hadden and Swann refuted Falwell's claim that he had reached a truly national audience; in fact the viewing audience for "The Old-Time Gospel Hour," and for that matter for all the television preachers except Robert Schuller, was disproportionately southern (Hadden and Swann 1981, 59–61). Finally, other researchers found that the audience for religious programs in general was disproportionately elderly (two-thirds to three-quarters aged fifty or over), disproportionately female, and according to one study, less affluent and less educated than those who did not watch such programs.[40]

These conclusions might seem to establish the narrowness of the audience for "The Old-Time Gospel Hour." But in 1985 the Nielsen organization con-

---

[37] William Martin, "The Birth of a Media Myth," *Atlantic* 247 (June 1981): 7.

[38] Peter Kerr, "Study Assesses Effects from TV Evangelism," *New York Times*, April 17, 1984, p. 20. For an analysis of the study by one of its sponsors, see Fore, "Religion and Television," pp. 710–13; for criticism see Hadden and Frankl 1987 and Frankl and Hadden 1987.

[39] Martin, "The Birth of a Media Myth," p. 11; Hadden and Swann 1981, pp. 55–56.

[40] Hadden and Swann 1981, pp. 61, 62; Martin, "The Birth of a Media Myth," p. 11; Kerr, "Study Assesses Effects from TV Evangelism," p. 20. One disagreement among social scientists studying the electronic ministry was over the relationship between TV viewing and church attendance. Hadden and Swann speculated that the age profile of the audience might come from the fact that "elderly people fail to find a meaningful experience in their local congregations" and turn to the television ministry as an alternative (Hadden and Swann 1981, pp. 63, 67). But the Pennsylvania study was quite positive in maintaining that viewers of religious programs were mostly people who already attended church and who saw their viewing as complementary to their more traditional religious activities (Kerr, "Study Assesses Effects from TV Evangelism," p. 20). The two conclusions are, of course, not necessarily incompatible. Joseph B. Tamney and Stephen D. Johnson found in their study of television viewing in "Middletown" that, for the elderly who watched religious programs, as Hadden and Swann had suggested, religious programs were their major religious involvement; for those in younger age groups who watched such programs, however, regular viewing was simply part of a variety of religious activities (Tamney and Johnson 1984b, p. 311).

ducted another study which included (as earlier ones had not) cable viewers; and the resulting figures were significantly higher. The new data indicated that 21 million households (which, depending on one's computation, translates into between 29.5 and 50.5 million individuals) watched at least some religious programming every week; and Falwell himself reached 5.6 million households (or between 7.8 and 13.4 million individuals) each week, far fewer than he had claimed but far more than Hadden and Swann had given him.[41] These new figures convinced Hadden that he had underestimated the audience for the television preachers.[42] Even before the results of the 1985 Nielsen study were released, however, he was warning other scholars not to base their conclusions about the impact of "new Christian right" leaders on estimates of their television audience at any one point. What made men like Falwell significant in the long run, he insisted, was their "unique access to mass media" and the size of "their potential constituency."[43]

What then was that "potential constituency"? At the broadest level, it was certainly true that on some issues the position taken by the Moral Majority enjoyed wide public support.[44] Indeed, several researchers found that about 30 percent of the adult population agreed with enough issue-positions of the Moral Majority to be counted potential "supporters" or "proponents."[45] Such potential "support" correlated strongly with southern residence, increased age, low education and low income, and regular attendance at church; in addition, women were more likely to be potential "supporters" than men.[46]

[41] Data from "Presidential Prospects," *Christian Century* 102 (November 20, 1985): 1057–58; and from "Power, Glory, and Politics," *Time* 127 (February 17, 1986): 63, 67; my computation of individuals per household follows that of Fore in "Religion and Television," p. 711. For sober reflections on the methodological difficulties in actually measuring "regular viewing" of "religious programs," which produced all the scholarly confusion, see especially Hoover 1987.

[42] Hadden, as quoted in "Presidential Prospects," p. 1058; and in "Power, Glory, and Politics," p. 64. He and Swann had noted in their book that the Arbitron sample tended to exclude cable viewers; but they believed that such potential undercounting was balanced by various methods of overcounting such as Arbitron's counting someone watching five programs five times (Hadden and Swann 1981, pp. 53–54).

[43] Jeffrey K. Hadden, "Televangelism and the Mobilization of a New Christian Right Family Policy," in William V. D'Antonio and Joan Aldous, eds., *Families and Religions: Conflict and Change in Modern Society* (Beverly Hills: Sage, 1983), p. 261. See also Hadden 1984, especially pp. 161–65; and Hadden 1987.

[44] This point has been made most emphatically by John H. Simpson, in Simpson 1984. It should be noted of Simpson's work (especially Simpson 1983), however, that he tends to construct his scales so as to maximize public support for the Moral Majority position. By so doing he is able to reach the remarkable figure of 72 percent of the adult population as either "supporters" or "fellow-travelers" of the Moral Majority (ibid., pp. 188–92).

[45] Simpson 1983, p. 191; Yinger and Cutler 1984, pp. 80–81.

[46] Yinger and Cutler 1984, pp. 82–85; Simpson 1983, pp. 192–96. Since all these estimates are additive, with many of those who agree with the Moral Majority on one or two issues disagreeing on others, the profiles of Moral Majority "supporters" within the general public vary

The close similarity between this demographic profile of potential "supporters" of the Moral Majority and that of the actual audience for religious broadcasters is striking, but there is no way of knowing, from the survey data used, how many of these people were in fact in that audience.

There was, of course, another more obvious way of locating this "potential constituency." Researchers who studied the question found relatively minor differences between Protestants and Catholics in their degree of support for the Moral Majority's positions (Yinger and Cutler 1984, 85; Simpson 1983, 193), but, in at least the Dallas–Fort Worth area and the state of Ohio the Moral Majority itself held very little attraction for Catholics, perhaps because of the anti-Catholic sentiments of some of its local activists.[47] If those findings are at all representative, it is doubtful that Falwell and the Moral Majority or any comparable minister and organization with such a self-consciously "Protestant" background could effectively mobilize even those Catholics who agreed with their positions on many issues. Subtracting the Catholics, with whom then are we left? The answer surely is the Protestant "evangelicals," whose participation in public life in the 1970s represented a development far exceeding in importance the particular organizational network created by Jerry Falwell.

It is essential at this point to emphasize that the "evangelicals" who were now, as the 1980 election approached, becoming the object of scholarly investigations were not quite the same group as the "fundamentalists," whose assumed affinity with right-wing politics had been the subject of much speculation in the early 1960s (most notably by Hofstadter), and who, in at least one study, seemed particularly susceptible to George Wallace's appeal in 1968.[48] Strictly speaking, "evangelical" and "fundamentalist" refer to entirely different aspects of religious life. The former emphasizes the centrality of a personal conversion experience, being "born again," making "a decision for

---

from issue to issue. For confirmation of this point, see the analysis of the responses of a sample of Nebraska residents by Moore and Whitt 1986.

[47] Shupe and Stacey 1983, p. 41; Wilcox 1987a, pp. 49–50. In Nebraska, on the other hand, Catholic support was only slightly less than that of all Protestants, both groups giving only about one-third as much support as fundamentalist Protestants (Moore and Whitt 1986, pp. 429–30).

[48] It should be noted that a number of social scientists did uncover a correlation between "fundamentalism" and support for the Moral Majority, whether among members of "fundamentalist" denominations in the Dallas–Fort Worth area or in the state of Nebraska, or among self-designated "fundamentalists" in the Southern Baptist clergy (Shupe and Stacey 1983, pp. 58–61; Moore and Whitt 1986, pp. 429–30; Guth 1983b, p. 120). Shupe and Stacey classified Nazarenes, Pentecostals, Seventh-Day Adventists, and Baptists not affiliated with the Southern Baptist Convention as belonging to "fundamentalist denominations," but placed the Churches of Christ and the Southern Baptists in another, "conservative" category without explaining the basis for their classification (Shupe and Stacey 1983, p. 25). In a subsequent article, they also found that these "fundamentalists" in their Dallas–Fort Worth sample were the most sympathetic to the right-wing religious critique of public education, opposing sex education, favoring prayer and the teaching of "creationism," and so on (Stacey and Shupe 1984).

Christ''; the latter, adherence to certain ''fundamental'' theological tenets. Thus in theory a person can be one without being the other. It is not at all clear, however many non-''evangelical'' ''fundamentalists'' there actually are because, as the two historians who have most closely studied the subject have pointed out, both contemporary ''fundamentalism'' and ''evangelicalism'' have the same origins in the divisions among American Protestants in the early twentieth century.[49] Both tend to support Biblical inerrancy and some form of premillennialism which stresses the irremediable nature of the world's ills, seizes upon evidence of social and cultural decline, and foresees the imminent return of Christ.

Some of those who specialize in the study of American religion—historians and sociologists as well as journalists—approach the definitional problem in a different way. For them, ''fundamentalists,'' along with ''charismatics'' (those whose religious experience includes ''speaking in tongues'' and divine healing) and those they call the ''neoevangelicals,'' are each a subgroup within the larger ''evangelical'' community (see, e.g., Quebedeaux 1978, 6–9). For them the ''fundamentalists'' are the most intransigent group, the least willing to compromise, and the most likely to perceive threats everywhere, from Rome as well as from Moscow. From the ''fundamentalists'' have come men like Rev. Carl McIntire and his dissident American Council of Christian Churches, and through him political activists such as Fred C. Schwarz, Billy James Hargis, and others who drew Hofstadter's attention in the early 1960s. The ''neoevangelicals'' in contrast are the more ecumenical faction, more willing to ally with nonevangelical Protestants, with Catholics, and with Jews; and they had formed the National Association of Evangelicals, founded *Christianity Today*, and supported the efforts of Billy Graham.[50]

Whether the differences between ''fundamentalists'' and ''neoevangelicals'' are only differences in what one well-known religious historian has called ''attitudes, style, conduct, and manners''[51] or something more substantial, most of the social scientists who studied these individuals in the late

[49] The two historians are Ernest R. Sandeen and George R. Marsden, and their most important works are: Sandeen, *The Roots of Fundamentalism: British and American Millenarianism, 1800–1930* (Chicago: University of Chicago Press, 1970), and ''Fundamentalism and American Identity,'' in American Academy of Political and Social Science *Annals* 387 (January 1970): 56–65; and Marsden, *Fundamentalism and American Culture: The Shaping of Twentieth-Century Evangelicalism, 1870–1925* (New York: Oxford University Press, 1980).

[50] For the connection of Schwarz and Hargis with McIntire, see Clabaugh 1974, pp. 17–31, 49–56. Detailed accounts of the origins and early development of both the American Council of Christian Churches and the National Association of Evangelicals can be found in Louis Gasper, *The Fundamentalist Movement* (The Hague: Mouton, 1963); and in Joel A. Carpenter, ''A Shelter in a Time of Storm: Fundamentalist Institutions and the Rise of Evangelical Protestantism, 1929–1942,'' *Church History* 49 (January 1980): 62–75.

[51] Marty 1976, p. 94; my discussion of the lack of clear distinctions between ''fundamentalists'' and ''evangelicals'' is deeply indebted to his analysis (pp. 80–105).

1970s and early 1980s ignored them: the population described as "fundamentalist" in one study appears as "evangelical" in another.[52] Before condemning these scholars for intellectual sloppiness it should be remembered that Falwell himself contributed to blurring the distinction. On the one hand he considered himself a fundamentalist;[53] but on the other he seems to have seen his mission as reaching all segments of an "evangelical" community embracing about a fifth of the adult population.[54]

The most important question confronting social scientists and journalists watching Falwell's activities was, to what extent could he succeed? To what extent were evangelicals politically conservative and thus available for mobilization by groups such as the Moral Majority? In the early 1960s the sociologist Benton Johnson had forcefully argued the case for conservatism, on the basis of his studies of ministers and their congregations in Oregon and Florida (Johnson 1962; 1964; 1966; 1967). As far as clerical attitudes were concerned, subsequent studies conducted in the next decade and a half confirmed Johnson's findings: indeed, as one moved from the controversies of the early 1960s to those of the mid-1970s—from civil rights through the war in Vietnam to abortion and homosexuality—the political divergence between theologically conservative and theologically liberal ministers steadily increased.[55]

Johnson's conclusions about the laity proved far more controversial. He had also argued that ministers helped shape the political views of the members of their congregations, especially those who regularly attended church, and that therefore members of "evangelical"/"fundamentalist" churches were being led in a politically conservative direction. That argument was soon challenged (Anderson 1966; Johnson and White 1967; Summers 1970), so much so that by the early 1970s the prevailing assumption was quite different: "orthodox laity seem to be no more or no less liberal in their social and political views than

[52] The major exception to this generalization is Clyde Wilcox who, in his study of Moral Majority members in Ohio, did separate "fundamentalists" from "evangelicals." He found relatively little difference in their background characteristics or in their generally conservative-Republican political orientation. The "fundamentalists" were, however, even more conservative than the "evangelicals," although less likely either to vote or to participate in organizations other than the Moral Majority (Wilcox 1986a; Wilcox 1987c).

[53] Falwell, "Future-Word," p. 219.

[54] Hunter 1983, pp. 49, 141; E. J. Dionne, "Poll Finds Evangelicals Aren't United Voting Bloc," *New York Times*, September 7, 1980, nat. ed., p. 34.

[55] The most relevant studies are Jeffrey K. Hadden, *The Gathering Storm in the Churches* (Garden City, N.Y.: Doubleday, 1969), especially pp. 73–83; Harold E. Quinley, "The Protestant Clergy and the War in Vietnam," *Public Opinion Quarterly* 34 (Spring 1970): 43–52; Jack O. Balswick, "Theology and Political Attitudes Among Clergymen," *Sociological Quarterly* 11 (Summer 1970): 397–404; Vincent Jeffries and Clarence E. Tygart, "The Influence of Theology, Denomination, and Values upon the Position of Clergy on Social Issues," *Journal for the Scientific Study of Religion* 13 (September 1974): 309–24; Theodore C. Wagenaar and Patricia E. Bartos, "Orthodoxy and Attitudes of Clergymen Toward Homosexuality and Abortion," *Review of Religious Research* 18 (Winter 1977): 114–25.

laity who have rejected orthodox doctrine.''[56] Even measures of "religiosity," including assent to the denominational creed, high levels of church attendance, high incidence of devotional practices, and so on, one detailed review of the literature found, did not correlate with political conservatism (Wuthnow 1973, 117–32). All these conclusions, however, preceded the 1970s' debate over issues involving women, sexuality, and the family.

A corollary of the assumption that theological conservatives were political conservatives is that evangelicals have traditionally been Republicans. Over the years this answer has been embellished by various hypotheses to explain the assumed relationship, including the influence of wealthy contributors, the affinity of the individualistic premises of evangelical moral teaching with entrepreneurial capitalism, the historic connection between the suspect Catholics and the Democrats, and more recently the identification of liberal politics with religious "modernism" or even "secular humanism."

The problem is that while from a long-range perspective that answer contains a good deal of truth, as a guide to evangelical voting behavior in the recent past it is somewhat misleading. Consider, for example, the reference made by an otherwise careful scholar to evangelical "support of the Goldwater Presidential campaign" in 1964 (Hunter 1983, 44). He must have been thinking of prominent clergymen because, even when we factor out the blacks among them (about a quarter of the total), evangelical *voters* supported Lyndon Johnson in the same overwhelming numbers as their nonevangelical countrymen.[57] For that matter, as Lipset and Raab pointed out in their analysis of the 1980 election, from 1932 through 1964 in all but one case—when they decisively rejected the Catholic Kennedy—white evangelical voters cast their votes for Democratic candidates in proportions comparable to the electorate as a whole. The supposedly traditional conservative politics of white evangelical voters did not in fact manifest itself at the presidential level until 1968, when they began to give about 10 percent less of their vote to the Democratic candidate than did the electorate as a whole. Interestingly, the gap remained approximately the same in 1976, when only about 40 percent voted for Jimmy Carter, who claimed to be one of their own.[58] On the eve of the 1980 cam-

[56] Hadden, *The Gathering Storm in the Churches*, p. 98.

[57] The electoral data in this paragraph comes from Lipset and Raab 1981, p. 27; for roughly similar estimates, based on an ecological analysis of selected counties, see Albert Menendez, *Religion at the Polls* (Philadelphia: Westminster, 1977), pp. 197, 217.

[58] The question of the 1976 white evangelical vote for Carter remains in dispute. In the discussion here I am using the figures given by Lipset and Raab 1981, although they do not indicate the source of their data. Other analysts have given Carter a larger share of the white evangelical vote, even a majority, in 1976; but their conclusions have problems of their own. Some of those who gave Carter a higher proportion of these voters claimed to do so on the basis of CBS News–*New York Times* polls: see, for example, Menendez, "Religion at the Polls, 1980," *Church and State* 33 (December 1980): 16; and Burnham 1981, p. 130. But according to those responsible for conducting the CBS–*New York Times* polls, "evangelical voters" were not categorized as such

paign, 43 percent of evangelicals considered themselves Democrats, about 30 percent Republicans, and about 27 percent Independents—figures not substantially different from those in other religious categories (Hunter 1983, 56).

At first glance this appears to complicate matters. Why, we might ask, would Falwell and the other leaders of the "new Christian right" invest so much effort in trying to reach a disproportionately lower-income constituency with so many Democrats?[59] The answer lies in the connections between evangelical religious beliefs and "conservative" attitudes on certain "cultural" questions, connections overlooked in much of the initial research on religious-political correlations. In the Roosevelt years Democratic politicians did not speak out on cultural issues, much less challenge those who took a conservative position on them; in the 1950s and early 1960s, being a cultural conservative was still not inconsistent with being a Democrat. The situation was very different in the 1970s, as Democratic politicians increasingly moved in a culturally liberal direction; in such an environment those of whatever religious background who were caught between their cultural conservatism and their Democratic allegiance presented a tempting target for the opposition. Falwell appears not to have used the term "realignment," favored both by Republican politicians and "new right" strategies, but surely he thought in the same terms.

Lipset and Raab have summarized the situation this way: "the traditionalism of the evangelicals does not impinge upon their political orientation except when some aspects of modernity radically threaten their status and security" (Lipset and Raab 1981, 27). To that concise formulation, we might add two emendations. First, the response of evangelical voters to threats to their "status" should be seen in the same framework as that developed earlier in the 1970s: "status politics" not as an attempt to defend declining prestige but as an attempt to defend a way of life, a "politics of lifestyle concern."[60] Second, to have any explanatory power, "aspects of modernity" must refer to more than the rising incidence of street crime, sleazy movies, and teenage pregnancy in the 1970s, developments that distressed even Americans who were not evangelicals. What appears to have distinguished the evangelical re-

---

in the 1976 exit polls; and so such claims are invalid (Barbara Farah, telephone conversation with author, October 28, 1986).

The National Election Survey conducted by the Center for Political Studies at the University of Michigan found a significantly higher percentage of white evangelicals voting for Carter than did Lipset and Raab; but their data was drawn from voters *recalling their 1976 vote* in exit polls taken the day of the *1980* election. For the relevant CPS data, see Smidt 1983, pp. 45–47.

[59] The demographic data are presented in Hunter 1983, pp. 49–60. Another study using alternative definitions of "evangelical" reached generally similar conclusions (Rothenberg and Newport 1984, pp. 27–32).

[60] The formulation is that of Page and Clelland 1978, p. 266. Various studies have found no correlation between support for the Moral Majority and either "status inconsistency" or "status anxiety" stemming from declining prestige (Harper and Leicht 1984; Simpson 1985a).

action to these developments was the way they connected them to the wider culture of "modernity."

Curiously, in the search for "aspects of modernity" that might cause evangelicals to abandon their traditional political allegiance, many analysts have ignored the impact of the contemporary social movement that most clearly challenges the evangelicals' "way of life," the women's movement.[61] For while its constituency may be predominantly female, "the mind and voice of evangelicalism remains male" (Pohli 1983, 544). The first kind of evidence that antifeminism is deeply embedded in the evangelical community comes from studies of its most prominent spokesmen. The difference, for example, in the way evangelical leaders responded to the earlier civil rights movement and to the women's movement is striking: in case after individual case the same leaders who had condemned all forms of racial discrimination and subordination as "un-Christian" and "sinful" opposed all but the most modest feminist demands as threatening the "traditional family."[62] The reason for the difference is not difficult to find. Literally construed, the Bible offers powerful support to the idea of the oneness of humankind. As a result, those who in the late nineteenth and early twentieth centuries tried to cite Scripture on behalf of racial subordination had to resort to fanciful and convoluted interpretations of the curse a drunken Noah laid upon his son Ham. Such religious spokesmen were not without influence, especially in the South; but it would be a grave mistake to assume that such racial doctrines were integral to a Bible-centered Protestantism. The Bible, however, does affirm the subordination of women, nowhere more emphatically than in the epistles of Paul: "Neither was the man created for the woman; but the woman for the man" (1 Cor. 11:9) and "Wives, submit yourselves unto your husbands . . . for the husband is the head of the wife, even as Christ is the head of the church" (Eph. 5:22–23).

A small but persistent band of evangelical feminists has not let the implications of this message go unchallenged and have insisted that Paul's attitudes toward women stemmed more from his cultural background than from divine

[61] In making this point, I have no desire to oversimplify what in many ways is a complex issue; but it does seem to me that a focus on the negative response to feminist demands on the part of evangelical clergy and laity alike better accounts for both the timing and the direction of their activism than alternative explanations. An explanation emphasizing resource mobilization (as in Miller 1985) fails to explain the timing—that is, why so many hitherto passive evangelicals wanted to be mobilized in the late 1970s. On the other hand, an explanation stressing the way the evangelical "commitment to the preservation of traditional morality" became salient in a context of "the growing politicization of morality" (Wuthnow 1983, p. 179) fails to explain the specific content of that "morality." The evidence so far gathered strongly suggests that it was not the state of "morality" in general that aroused masses of evangelicals (what, for example, was the "evangelical" response to Watergate, or to subsequent revelations of the abuse of power and betrayal of the public trust?), but specific issues involving sex and gender, including abortion, which had been directly raised by the women's movement.

[62] For individual examples, see Fowler 1982, pp. 46–47, 54–55, 65–66, 74–75, 87–88, 170–77, 205–6.

inspiration. Their efforts have been largely unsuccessful because such an interpretation entailed the application of "the higher criticism" to Scriptural text, a method that many evangelical leaders thought they had banished when they broke with the modernists several generations ago.[63] The same commitment to Biblical inerrancy made evangelical leaders even more unyielding on the issue of homosexuality (Fowler 1982, 196–99; Jorstad 1981, 73–77). They consistently rejected revisionist efforts to reinterpret the lesson of Sodom and Gomorrah as referring "not to the inhabitants' sexual practices but to their intention to rape the visitors, as well as to the town's idolatry and lack of hospitality," or to read Paul's denunciation of "them that defile themselves with mankind" (1 Tim. 1:9–10) as condemning the specific use of boy prostitutes rather than same-sex relationships in general.[64]

The conservatism of the evangelical leadership on these cultural issues clearly influenced the laity.[65] The most relevant evidence was contained in the 1980 survey of evangelical attitudes conducted by the Gallup organization. Strictly defining "evangelical" as only those (1) who described themselves as "born-again Christians" or as having had a "born-again" experience, (2) who had encouraged others to believe in Jesus Christ, and (3) who believed in a literal interpretation of the Bible or accepted the absolute authority of the Bible, the researchers concluded that this group constituted about 19 percent of the total adult population, 28 percent of all Protestants, and a near-majority of denominations such as the Baptists. The Gallup organization found further evangelicals were less supportive of the proposed Equal Rights Amendment than were nonevangelicals, more likely to favor an antiabortion amendment, only half as willing to permit homosexuals to teach in the public schools, and far more supportive of *required* prayer in the public schools.[66]

[63] Fowler 1982, pp. 199–208; Jorstad 1981, pp. 60–67. In addition, as Fowler has pointed out, these women's decisions to make their feminist case from within a religious framework separated them from the militantly secularist mainstream of contemporary feminism (Fowler 1985).

[64] Walter Goodman, "Faiths Rely on Scripture in Homosexual Issues," *New York Times*, July 14, 1984, p. 10. The key text here is Letha Scanzoni and Virginia Ramey Mollenkott, *Is the Homosexual My Neighbor? Another Christian View* (New York: Harper and Row, 1978), especially pp. 54–72.

[65] The impact of this Biblically centered religion on attitudes toward women's roles is suggested in a study based on data drawn from the National Opinion Research Center surveys for 1974 and 1975. Those conducting it found that among fundamentalists religiosity (as measured by church attendance) correlated positively with "political sexism" (unwillingness to see women politically active or running for the presidency); among nonfundamentalists the correlations were negative (Peek and Brown 1980).

[66] Data drawn from *Gallup Opinion Index* 182 (December 1980): 4; and Dionne, "Poll Finds Evangelicals Aren't United Voting Bloc," p. 34. Data from the 1980 election study of the Center for Political Studies also lent support to the view of evangelicals as more conservative on cultural issues than the rest of the electorate, but not consistently so on economic issues (Smidt 1983, pp. 37–39).

On the other hand, a small-scale study of residents of Greene County, Missouri, conducted a

Those conducting the survey carefully pointed out that, especially on the major issues of the ERA and abortion, evangelicals were divided among themselves;[67] and they also noted that twice as many nonwhites considered themselves "evangelicals" as did whites. Given black opposition to its economic agenda, clearly not all evangelicals could be mobilized by the "new Christian right," or by the Moral majority in particular. Nevertheless, from the discussion so far, one can see the shape of the "potential constituency" Falwell hoped to reach. It was a constituency that significantly exceeded the actual size of his television audience and that included not only his fellow "fundamentalists" but many of those who saw themselves as "evangelicals." Because of their socioeconomic position evangelicals had not—contrary to a general impression—revealed distinctively conservative voting patterns in the past; but their cultural conservatism, particularly on issues related to women, sexuality, and the family, had by the late 1970s come into increasing tension with the feminist orientation of Democratic politicians.

It was clear, as the 1980 campaign began, that Falwell thought he could exploit that tension and mobilize these culturally conservative voters behind right-wing Republican candidates. It was also true, as the 1980 campaign progressed, that relatively few Americans either identified with or sympathized with the Moral Majority, probably no more than 8 or 9 percent of the adult population.[68] But translated into numbers, that percentage equals about 15 million potential voters, a bloc assuredly large enough to exert a decisive influence in individual states and on individual races. And beyond that, it was not inconceivable that individual men and women, either unsupportive of or ignorant about the Moral Majority as an organization, could yet be rallied behind politicians running on anti-ERA, antiabortion platforms. Did that happen? How influential was Jerry Falwell in mobilizing either these core supporters or evangelicals as a group? What was the impact of the Moral Majority—and indeed of the "new right" as a whole—on the 1980 election?

---

week before the 1980 election, found that the evangelical Christians in their sample tended to be more conservative on a variety of issues (fiscal policy and defense as well as abortion and the ERA) than were the nonevangelicals. These researchers emphasized, too, that their "born-again" religious identity was more significant in determining their attitudes than either their age or their educational level (Patel 1982).

[67] The major study using alternative definitions of "evangelical" also found comparable divisions on these issues; their evangelical sample was united only on the issue of school prayer (Rothenberg and Newport 1984, pp. 55–78).

[68] Compare the figures in *Gallup Opinion Index* 182, p. 4, with Buell and Sigelman 1985, p. 429.

Fourteen

The "New Right" and the 1980 Election: The Religious Factor Reconsidered

THE CONTEXT for mobilization in 1980—by the "new right" or any other group—was set both by the faltering economy, already wracked by inflation and then heading into a recession, and by the traumatic events abroad at the end of 1979: the seizure of the American embassy in Teheran and the Soviet invasion of Afghanistan. To many Americans those events symbolized the nadir of American power abroad just as the continuing economic stagnation symbolized governmental failure at home. At first it seemed that President Carter might be able to exploit the national anxiety over foreign affairs to his own political advantage: in early 1980 his popularity in the polls soared and he was able to turn aside Senator Edward Kennedy's challenge for the nomination. Still, even before Carter's overall popularity began to fall in the summer, Kennedy's primary victories in critical states such as New York, Pennsylvania, Michigan, and California revealed serious discontent over the economic situation; and the initial burst of enthusiasm for independent candidate Illinois Representative John Anderson suggested equally voter dissatisfaction with all the major candidates.

American political practice suggested that, however strong the challenges of Kennedy and Anderson, the ultimate beneficiary of dissatisfaction with Carter would be the Republican presidential candidate; and judging by the preference expressed by rank-and-file Republicans for the past several years, that candidate would be Ronald Reagan. Going into the first presidential primary in New Hampshire, however, seven men could be seriously considered potential Republican candidates; after that primary there were still four. In a situation not unlike that in 1964, Reagan's opponents subsequently so conducted themselves as to eliminate each other.[1] Anderson's liberalism on foreign policy and "cultural" issues limited his appeal among Republicans, and he failed to win a single primary. Eventually, he chose the third-party option, but in the short run he ran strongly enough in the crucial early contests to weaken the chances of the leading "moderate" candidate (in any other context a conservative, though not a right-wing spokesman like Reagan), ex-CIA di-

[1] My analysis here follows that in Pomper 1981a.

rector and former party chairman George Bush.[2] As both Bush and Anderson insisted on remaining in the race until near the end, a movement to draft ex-President Ford (an unlikely prospect in any case, considering Reagan's strength within the party) was simply out of the question.

Even as Reagan was moving down the road to the nomination, the various organizations associated with the "new right" were assuming major roles in the campaign. Fresh from what he claimed were NCPAC's 1978 victories in Iowa and New Hampshire, Terry Dolan had already begun his project "to get rid of five bad votes in the Senate"—specifically Democrats Birch Bayh of Indiana, Frank Church of Idaho, Alan Cranston of California, John Culver of Iowa, and George McGovern of South Dakota—through what he himself admitted would be a negative campaign. With what one senator's press secretary called an "unrelenting drumbeat" of radio and TV commercials starting in mid-1979, NCPAC attacked the senators' records without openly supporting any of their possible challengers. "In Indiana, a large baloney recently appeared on television screens. Abruptly, a cleaver sliced the baloney and a voice said, 'One very big piece of baloney is Birch Bayh telling us he's fighting inflation.' A price appeared on the sliced baloney: $46 billion. 'That's how much deficit spending Bayh voted for last year alone,' the voice said, pausing before concluding: 'So, to stop inflation, you'll have to stop Bayh first. Because if Bayh wins, you lose.' "[3]

The targets of the commercials charged that they were inaccurate and unfair: "One Idaho commercial was taped in front of an empty silo for intercontinental ballistic missiles, implying that Mr. Church was responsible for the void and 'has almost always opposed a strong national defense.' In fact, the Titan silo was empty because the weapons have been replaced by more advanced Minuteman missiles."[4] By the time the 1980 election was over, NCPAC had spent nearly $7.5 million, almost exclusively on such media spots. The figure was larger than that of any other political action committee, more than three times as much as the leading labor PAC, the United Auto Workers Voluntary Community Action Program, and more than five times as much as the leading liberal PAC, the National Committee for an Effective Congress.[5]

---

[2] Saloma has made the useful point that as a result of the rightward drift of the party, a conservative like Bush was perceived as "a moderate" and a moderate such as Anderson was seen as "too liberal" (Saloma 1984, pp. 95–96).

[3] Bernard Weinraub, "Million-Dollar Drive Aims to Oust 5 Senators," *New York Times*, March 24, 1980, city ed., p. B6.

[4] Weinraub, "Million-Dollar Drive Aims to Oust 5 Senators"; see also the interview with Frank Church in Flo Conway and Jim Sigelman, *Holy Terror: The Fundamentalist War on America's Freedoms in Religion, Politics, and Our Private Lives* (Garden City, N.Y.: Doubleday, 1982), pp. 27–33.

[5] Federal Election Commission data, reprinted in Adam Clymer, "Conservative Political Action Committee Evokes Both Fear and Admiration," *New York Times*, May 31, 1981, p. 26. For

Important as NCPAC appeared to be, it was soon overshadowed in the public's eyes by the "new Christian right," defined as those religious organizations associated with the "new right," especially the Moral Majority. The importance of the Moral Majority was due partly to its own organizational strength but even more to the attention it received from the mass media, which having previously slighted right-wing evangelicals now overcompensated by giving them an importance they did not warrant, and to Falwell's own considerable talent for self-promotion. These latter factors meant that the Moral Majority was increasingly perceived as the major agent of right-wing mobilization, actively registering nonvoters and, even though it claimed not to "endorse" candidates, organizing those already registered behind specific campaigns. Certainly Falwell could point to a number of local successes: in Alaska, where the state chapter dominated the state Republican convention; in Oklahoma, where Moral Majority efforts contributed to the victory of Don Nickles in the Senate primary; and most notably in the Alabama primaries where the state chapter helped Jeremiah Denton, a retired naval officer and former prisoner of war in Vietnam, defeat a better-known opponent for the Senate nomination, and Albert Lee Smith unseat moderate Representative John Buchanan. Thus Falwell was taken seriously when, looking toward the general election in November, he declared that he wanted to see six Democratic senators defeated: the five on Dolan's original list and Gaylord Nelson of Wisconsin as well.

By the time the 1980 Republican National Convention met in Detroit in July, the "new right" and the Republican party were converging in rhetoric and in goals; and Reagan himself was the major agent in this convergence. Though Weyrich and Viguerie had been cool toward a Reagan candidacy in 1980,[6] Reagan was the obvious candidate for the "new right" to support, and for reasons beyond his mastery of rhetoric and an affability no other right-wing politician could match. First of all, Reagan's past as a New Deal Democrat made him the ideal right-wing candidate, ironically enough, because he spoke the language of a vitally important constituency. Unlike Goldwater who always seemed to be chastising the public for wanting too much, Reagan exuded sympathy with their demands—with of course the corollary, which paralleled the "new right's" "populist" strategy, that it was the *government* bureaucracy that was thwarting individuals' aspirations. Second, even while some activists briefly contemplated a third party in the mid-1970s, Reagan never abandoned the goal of transforming the Republicans into a truly conser-

---

a review of NCPAC's spending, see Herbert E. Alexander, *Financing the 1980 Election* (Lexington, Mass.: Lexington Books, 1983), pp. 396–400.

[6] Paul Weyrich, "Reagan's Two Options," *Conservative Digest* 6 (May–June 1980): 6; Richard Viguerie, as quoted in Nick Kotz, "King Midas of 'The New Right,'" *Atlantic* 242 (November 1978): 60.

vative party. Here was one case where the activists were less steadfast than the politician.

Finally, there was the attractiveness of Reagan's religious views. Before he became governor of California, he was a man of irregular church attendance and unknown beliefs; but by the time of his presidential race in 1976, he had publicly announced that he was an evangelical.[7] His challenge to Ford may have failed but in the process he had gained the allegiance of right-wing evangelical leaders.[8] Now in 1980 Reagan was clearly reaching out to the constituency such leaders represented. At times in his speeches he made substantive appeals to such a constituency, as in his criticism of the way "the Government has increasingly tried to inject itself between parent and child" and his use as examples of sex education in the schools, federal court rulings prohibiting school prayer, and regulations permitting teenage girls to have abortions without their parents' knowledge.[9] At other times his rhetoric itself was suffused with religious imagery, as in his remarks that "this nation is hungry for a spiritual renewal—one nation, under God, indivisible," or in his evocation of the Revolutionary War minister who proclaimed, "There is a time to preach and a time to fight."[10]

It may be true that in strict intraparty terms Reagan, unlike Goldwater sixteen years before, was conciliatory in his victory—choosing the "moderate" Bush as his running-mate, retaining the party chairman, not attacking other Republicans, and so on[11]—but it is also true that the 1980 convention was a victory for the most conservative elements in the party, now allied with religious organizations such as the Moral Majority. One sign of the ascendancy of this right-wing alliance was the platform itself, which for the first time in a generation did not endorse an equal rights amendment, which called for one constitutional amendment permitting prayer in the public schools and another against abortion, and which suggested that opponents of abortion be given preference in federal judicial appointments.

In spite of this, a number of right-wing leaders remained dissatisfied, primarily because of Reagan's selection of Bush as his running-mate: Bush was the very model of the "country-club, preppy Republicans" the "new right"

[7] Ronald Reagan, as quoted in "Reagan on God and Morality," *Christianity Today* 20 (July 2, 1976): 39. For a penetrating discussion of Reagan's religious views and the context in which they evolved, see Garry Wills, *Reagan's America: Innocents at Home* (Garden City, N.Y.: Doubleday, 1987), pp. 7–26, 196–99, 382–88.

[8] On this point see especially Richard V. Pierard, "Reagan and the Evangelicals: The Making of a Love Affair," *Christian Century* 100 (December 21–28, 1983): 1182–85.

[9] Reagan, as quoted in David E. Rosenbaum, "Conservatives Embrace Reagan on Social Issues," *New York Times*, April 21, 1980, city ed., p. B12.

[10] Reagan, address in Victorville, California, May 26, 1980, as quoted in Elizabeth Drew, *Portrait of an Election: The 1980 Presidential Campaign* (New York: Simon and Schuster, 1981), p. 175.

[11] For this argument, see Jones 1981, pp. 88–90.

detested.[12] To rekindle right-wing enthusiasm, therefore, Reagan felt compelled to attend the Religious Roundtable's national affairs briefing in Dallas in August. In a conference dominated by the major figures of the "new right"—Helms, Schlafly, Phillips, and Weyrich among others, as well as ministers such as Falwell and Robison—Reagan succeeded in gaining their overwhelming support. First he stated at a press conference that the theory of evolution "has in recent years been challenged in the world of science and it is not yet believed in the scientific community to be as infallible as it once was believed."[13] Then, at the conference itself Reagan won over the audience by remarking, "I know this is a nonpartisan gathering and so I know you can't endorse me, but . . . I want you to know that I endorse you and what you are doing" (as quoted in Hadden and Swann 1981, 133). Finally, on the premise that actions speak louder than words, Reagan appointed Robert Billings, the director of the Moral Majority, as his religious liaison for the duration of the campaign. As the 1980 campaign moved into its final phase in the fall, the forces of the "new right"—NCPAC, the Moral Majority, and a great many Republican candidates—seemed to be advancing everywhere. The mounting alarm of liberals was tempered chiefly by the assurances of journalists and pollsters that the presidential race was still very close and major congressional upsets unlikely.

The results of the 1980 election thus came as a shock. Reagan won an absolute majority of the popular vote, and held a ten-point lead over Carter, a margin comparable (in two-party terms) to Eisenhower's margin over Stevenson in 1952. In the Senate the Democrats lost twelve seats, a loss so great that it gave Republicans control of the upper chamber for the first time since 1954, and especially devastating because it included among its victims Bayh, Church, Culver, McGovern, Nelson, and even old-timers like Washington's Warren Magnuson. Together with their thirty-three-seat gain in the House, these Senate and presidential victories gave the Republican party its greatest triumph since 1952, and possibly since 1928. At the very least the results revealed an unhappy electorate, one quite willing to hold the incumbent Democrats responsible for their unhappiness.

It was not surprising, in such a context, that some of the more enthusiastic Reagan supporters further interpreted the results as evidence of a critical realignment that was at last producing the long-awaited Republican majority. That argument, however, was greeted skeptically by most political scientists, even by those like Walter Dean Burnham who had been closely watching political developments for such evidence. A decade before, Burnham had seriously considered the possibility that 1968 was a critical election but had re-

---

[12] The phrase is Weyrich's, as quoted in Rosenbaum, "Conservatives Embrace Reagan on Social Issues," p. B12.

[13] Reagan, as quoted in Pierard, "Reagan and the Evangelicals," p. 1184.

jected it on the basis that partisan disaggregation—the incidence of ticket-splitting, the rise in self-designated Independents, and so on—was far too advanced for a 1930s-style realignment to occur. The 1980 results, stunning though they were, did nothing to change his mind: rather, he wrote, "the 1980 election was a landslide vote of no confidence in an incumbent administration," which like the landslides of 1920 and 1952 did not signal "the arrival of critical realignment."[14]

Even if the 1980 results did not indicate a critical realignment, the Republican sweep raised other, more immediate questions. Did, for example, the defeat of all those liberal senators indicate that the electorate had "swung to the right"? Or was it their fate to be linked to a president so uninspiring that only half the electorate bothered to vote? While these questions were being pondered by journalists and political scientists, those who saw themselves as contributing to the results came forward to express their satisfaction, among them the leaders of the "new right" and their religious allies. Falwell saw the election as reflecting the fact that "most of our people voted for traditional family values," and "these Christian people came out of the pews into the polls and caused this avalanche."[15] While he did not claim credit for "this avalanche," Viguerie and others were subsequently quite willing to give it to groups such as the Moral Majority.[16]

At first glance, the performance of the "new right" was indeed impressive, as a look at their Senate scorecard will show.[17] By the time the campaign had

---

[14] Burnham 1981, p. 127. A very similar view, including the analogy with 1952, is expressed in James L. Sundquist and Richard M. Scammon, "The 1980 Election: Profile and Historical Perspective," in Ellis Sandoz and Cecil V. Crabb, Jr., eds., *A Tide of Discontent: The 1980 Elections and Their Meaning* (Washington: Congressional Quarterly Press, 1981), pp. 19–44.

Even after Reagan's reelection landslide Burnham reiterated the point: "The 1984 Election and the Future of American Politics," in Sandoz and Crabb, eds., *Election 84: Landslide Without a Mandate?* (New York: New American Library, 1985), especially pp. 230–45. Such a conclusion, however, does not necessarily preclude the possibility that other kinds of realignment were occurring, more diffuse processes over several decades in which groups of voters gradually moved toward the Republicans: see, for example, John R. Petrocik, "Realignment: New Party Coalitions and the Nationalization of the South," *Journal of Politics* 49 (May 1987): 347–75.

[15] Jerry Falwell, as quoted in "Religious Right Goes for Bigger Game," *U.S. News & World Report* 89 (November 17, 1980): 42; and in "Anatomy of a Landslide," *Time* 116 (November 17, 1980): 31.

[16] Richard A. Viguerie, *The New Right: We're Ready to Lead* (Falls Church, Va.: Viguerie, 1981), p. 128.

[17] "New right" support of Senate candidates, as tabulated in Milton Ellerin and Alisa H. Kesten, "The New Right: What Is It?" *Social Policy* 11 (March–April 1981): 61. There is only one study of the impact of the "new right" on elections for the House of Representatives: Johnson and Bullock 1986. Taking the Christian Voice as their representative organization, they found that CV-supported challengers defeated incumbents in half (fourteen out of twenty-eight) of their "first priority" races, even though many of the incumbents had been considered safe, and CV-supported candidates won in eleven out of twelve open races. Johnson and Bullock term this record "remarkable," although they admit it is impossible to separate the "new right" contribu-

ended, NCPAC supported Republican challengers in eleven Senate races; eight of them won. The Moral Majority political action committees supported twelve challengers; eleven of them won. The Committee for the Survival of a Free Congress supported six challengers; four of them won. In five contests—the "big" ones—all three organizations contributed to the same challengers. In those five, four of the candidates—Stephen Symms who defeated Church, Dan Quayle who defeated Bayh, Charles Grassley who defeated Culver, and James Abdnor who defeated McGovern—won; Paul Gann who challenged Cranston was the only one to lose.

The "New Right" and the Presidential Election: The Question of Salience

The easiest way to begin to assess the impact of the "new right" on the 1980 election is with the best-documented question: to what extent was it successful in setting the agenda for the election, in having the election fought around the issues it stressed? Political scientists analyzing the survey data on why individuals voted the way they did in 1980 have generally concluded that economic issues were paramount and that the combination of persistent inflation and rising unemployment uniformly worked against the Democrats.[18] Foreign policy issues were of secondary importance, and there the public was more ambivalent, fearing military weakness under the Democrats but war under the Republicans.[19] To be sure, for several years before 1980 conservatives had charged policymakers with passivity in the face of Soviet adventurism and with fueling inflation through government spending; and that conservative offensive undoubtedly helped shape the mood of the electorate in 1980. But so many authoritative spokesmen—business leaders, former government officials, and prominent academics—had joined that critical chorus that the somewhat suspect "new right" activists can hardly be singled out as especially significant.

The "new right," as we have defined it, had decided, for both tactical and ideological reasons, to emphasize "cultural" issues. How salient were those issues in determining voters' choices? The simplest test of salience is asking

---

tion from that of either party organization or Reagan's coattails in accounting for these Republicans' victories.

[18] Schneider 1981, pp. 231–32; Pomper 1981b, pp. 87–88; also Stephen L. McDonald, "Economic Issues in the Campaign," in Sandoz and Crabb, eds., *A Tide of Discontent*, pp. 139–40; and Douglas A. Hibbs, "President Reagan's Mandate from the 1980 Elections: A Shift to the Right?" *American Politics Quarterly* 10 (October 1982): 387–420.

[19] Schneider 1981, pp. 233–34. See, however, the perceptive discussion in Stanley Kelley, Jr., *Interpreting Elections* (Princeton: Princeton University Press, 1983), pp. 190–216, which raises the question whether any *particular* issues were decisive in determining the outcome of the 1980 election.

voters what issues they consider important. The Center for Political Studies at the University of Michigan did exactly that; and they found that abortion came in fifth of nine issues in importance among Carter voters but ninth among Reagan voters, while the issue of "equality of women" came in third among Carter voters but only seventh among Reagan voters. The problem, however, is that even on an issue as fiercely debated as abortion, an issue on which Carter, Reagan, and their respective party platforms took clearly opposing stands, the majority of the voters remained uninformed. In the CPS survey, approximately half of the respondents admitted they did not know the parties' positions on the abortion issue; of the half who said they did, 40 percent thought the Democratic position was more restrictive than it actually was, and 32 percent thought the Republican position was more permissive than it actually was. Nor did the candidates fare much better: 41 percent of the respondents said they did not know Carter's position on abortion and 46 percent said they did not know Reagan's. Of those who said they did, only about half correctly recognized that Reagan's position was more restrictive than Carter's. In short, as far as abortion was concerned, not more than a quarter of the electorate could meet the minimum requirement for "issue-voting": being able correctly to identify the position of the candidates and parties on the issue in question (CPS data cited in Granberg and Burlison 1983, 234–35).

Presumably most of those who considered abortion salient correctly recognized the parties' and candidates' positions.[20] But did these voters then vote for the candidate who expressed their preference? Not necessarily. On behalf of ABC News the Louis Harris polling organization asked voters on Election Day to check off those issues on which they most *liked* the position of *their* candidate and those issues on which they most *disliked* the position of *any* of the candidates. Those who chose abortion as an issue on which they liked their candidate's stand (6 percent of the total) voted for Reagan (52 to 35 percent); but those who singled out Reagan's stand on abortion as something they *disliked* about him voted for him even more heavily (63 to 24 percent).[21] It is a nice question whether the abortion issue was not more significant because the electorate was ignorant or whether the electorate remained uninformed because it did not regard the issue as salient.

In contrast, public perception of the candidates' and parties' positions on the Equal Rights Amendment was much sharper. It has been argued that few other issue-positions so sharply differentiated Carter from Reagan voters (Granberg and Burlison 1983, 233). On closer examination, however, this cleavage may be due to a certain asymmetry in response: it would appear that

[20] One cannot say this with much assurance, however. The group of voters most likely to consider the abortion issue salient were those opposed to *all* abortions. Slightly more of this group voted for Carter than for Reagan; and of those of this group who voted for Carter, almost half believed their candidate agreed with them (Granberg and Burlison 1983, pp. 232, 234).

[21] ABC News–Harris poll cited in Schneider 1981, p. 235.

Carter voters as a whole were committed to passage of the proposed Equal Rights Amendment, and this was particularly true of those who regarded the ERA issue as salient; but the Reagan voters included not only the staunchest opponents of the ERA but also many of its supporters, some of whom regarded it as salient. Thus, according to the ABC News–Harris survey, those who checked ERA as an issue on which they liked their candidates' stand (18 percent of the total) voted heavily for Carter (69 to 18 percent); those who chose ERA as an issue on which they disliked a candidate's stand (29 percent of the total) were most likely to single out Reagan's opposition to it; but they voted for Reagan—47 to 39 percent (Schneider 1981, 236).

As far as the 1980 presidential election is concerned, then, what research we have indicates that "cultural" issues—even such hotly debated issues as abortion and the ERA—played a very minor role in shaping voters' choices.[22] True at the national level, this conclusion also held in social scientists' favorite microcosm, Muncie, Indiana (known to the academic world as "Middletown" ever since Robert and Helen Lynd first investigated it over half a century ago). Analyzing a sample of "Middletown" voters in 1980, two social scientists found that Reagan support there came from Republicans and even more from those concerned about the issue of inflation; the significance of "cultural" issues was marginal, and the impact of organizations such as the Moral Majority nowhere to be found (Johnson and Tamney 1982). It is therefore not surprising that even those analysts who saw the election results as reflecting conservative policy preferences—and many did not—tended to emphasize disenchantment with government activism rather than anxiety over challenges to traditional gender roles and family patterns.[23]

[22] In addition to the works cited above, see also Conover and Gray 1983, pp. 160–67, and Mueller 1983. It is because of the accumulated weight of the research supporting this conclusion that I find it difficult to accept John H. Simpson's argument that the "new Christian right" was influential in 1980 because it "politicized" issues such as abortion, which then redounded to Reagan's advantage at the polls. In addition, he offers no evidence that the majority of voters agreed with Reagan's position on either abortion or the ERA, the two most salient issues he analyzes (Simpson 1985b).

[23] For interpretations of the election that emphasize the public's desire for alternative policies, see *ABC News–Harris Survey* 2 (November 11, 1980): 2; and the analysis of CPS data in Warren E. Miller and J. Merrill Shanks, "Policy Directions and Presidential Leadership: Alternate Interpretations of the 1980 Presidential Election," *British Journal of Political Science* 12 (July 1982): 299–356.

In disagreement are those political scientists who argue that the 1980 results reflected the public's negative evaluation of Carter's performance as president, not its desire for alternative policies, a group that would include not only Hibbs, "President Reagan's Mandate from the 1980 Elections," but also Arthur H. Miller and Marvin Wattenberg in their reanalysis of CPS data: "Throwing the Rascals Out: Policy and Performance Evaluations of Presidential Candidates, 1952–1980," *American Political Science Review* 79 (June 1985): 359–72. Those who stress the public's ambivalence on key policy questions would also seem to disagree: see for example Ev-

The "New Right" and the Presidential Election:
The Question of Mobilization

But perhaps all these analysts were asking the wrong questions. It has frequently been maintained, for example, that "the 'new right' is not basically a proselytizing movement" and that "its chief concern is not to convert the unbelievers to the true faith" but "to activate people who are already 'true believers.' "[24] If, of course, the "new right" saw its purpose not as conversion but as mobilization, the important question becomes not whether they convinced the majority of the electorate that their issues mattered—if abortion is any indication, plainly they did not—but whether they persuaded that smaller but perhaps crucial portion of the electorate who already agreed with them that those issues were so salient that they should vote accordingly. It was generally agreed in 1980 that the primary targets for "new right" and particularly "new Christian right" efforts at mobilization were the evangelicals, the "born-again" Christians we have already discussed. According to the survey data gathered on behalf of the *New York Times* and CBS News, white evangelical Protestants did indeed vote heavily for Reagan (61 percent, to 34 percent for Carter). Given the efforts of the "new right" to mobilize these people through organizations such as the Moral Majority, it is not surprising that some commentators saw these results as reflecting evangelicals' widespread anxiety over "family/morality" concerns.[25]

The problem is that the figures for the vote cast by white evangelical Protestants in 1980 are almost identical to those for the vote cast by white Protestants as a whole (62 percent to 31 percent) and, for that matter, are not much different from the figures for the vote cast by white Americans as a whole (55 percent to 36 percent).[26] It is of course conceivable that evangelicals voted for Reagan for noneconomic reasons, while the others voted on the basis of economic issues; but remembering the relatively low socioeconomic position of most evangelicals this explanation seems doubtful. As Lipset and Raab remarked about their situation, "If there is an economic pinch, they are the ones who feel it most" (Lipset and Raab 1981, 25); and that assumption was partially confirmed by at least one small-scale study, of evangelicals in Missouri

erett Carll Ladd, Jr., "The Brittle Mandate: Electoral Dealignment and the 1980 Presidential Election," *Political Science Quarterly* 96 (Spring 1981): 1–25.

[24] Greg Denier, "A Shift to the Right? Or a Failure of the Left?" *Christianity and Crisis* 40 (December 20, 1980): 358.

[25] Albert Menendez, "Religion at the Polls, 1980," *Church and State* 33 (December 1980): 17; and (more ambiguously) *ABC News–Harris Survey* 2 (November 11, 1980): 1. For an elaboration of this point of view, see especially Kevin P. Phillips, *Post-Conservative America: People, Politics, and Ideology in a Time of Crisis* (New York: Random House, 1982), pp. 180–92.

[26] CBS News–*New York Times* data drawn from tabulations in *New York Times*, November 9, 1980, p. 28; and from Pomper 1981b, p. 70.

on the eve of the election. Researchers there found that those who said they had been "born again" in a religious sense were also far more likely than others (60 percent to 35 percent) to say that their economic situation had deteriorated over the past year (Patel 1982, 259). It would seem to be the case, therefore, that largely because of the stagnant economy Carter ran poorly among all segments of the white population. Comparing his overall performance in 1980 with that of 1976, Carter experienced far steeper declines in his support from both Catholics and Jews than from evangelical Protestants.[27]

The efforts of the "new right" to exploit cultural issues in 1980 may have played a role in determining the presidential results, but years later social scientists still had difficulty detecting it.[28] Surely, a critic might ask at this point, the Moral Majority must have had *some* kind of constituency, it must have been responsible for bringing *some* voters to the polls, and the perception of it as influencing the election could not have been *totally* the result of Falwell's manipulation of the media. Such a critic would have a point, and the role of the Moral Majority and similar groups in the 1980 election deserves closer analysis.

The most important effort to reconcile the journalists' impression that evangelical voters mobilized by the Moral Majority played a major role in defeating Carter with the predominant view of political scientists that no such development occurred was the study of Jeffrey Brudney and Gary Copeland (1984). The reason for the disagreement, they argued, was that researchers had never reached a consensus on which form of religious identification was politically significant, so that individuals were classified as "fundamentalist" and/or "evangelical" on the basis of either their denominational affiliation or their response to survey items (on Biblical inerrancy and so on). Brudney and Copeland suggested a third form of identification, "self-professed affinity with evangelical groups" as a whole. Testing all three measures against CPS data for 1980, they found that, while specific denominational affiliation was a poor predictor of either conservative policy preferences or Reagan support, and "evangelical" responses on survey items only somewhat better, their measure of "self-professed affinity" proved to be the best producer of all. Furthermore, those consciously identifying themselves with "evangelical groups" were more likely to vote than those merely affiliated with "evangel-

---

[27] This conclusion is based on the data in the CBS News–*New York Times* polls: *New York Times*, November 9, 1980, p. 28; and on the analysis in Lipset 1982, p. 55. Researchers using CPS data differ as to the evangelical shift away from Carter between 1976 and 1980; for an interpretation that found significant evangelical defection, see Smidt 1983, p. 45. Another team of political scientists using the same data minimized such defections and pointed out that Carter ran better among Southern Baptists than among any other Protestant denomination (Abramson 1982, p. 101).

[28] Note for example the conclusion of one analysis: "In sum, we have been unable to uncover any evidence that religion-related issues had a significant impact on the 1980 Presidential election" (Lopatto 1985, p. 55).

ical'' denominations. And, on the basis of other studies, one could conclude that these individuals' voting decisions—unlike those of most other voters, or even of most other evangelicals—were indeed influenced by their positions on issues such as abortion and the ERA.[29]

It was these self-conscious evangelical voters, who most clearly constituted Falwell's ''Christian people'' who ''came out of the pews and into the polls.'' But, in contradiction to Falwell's assumptions, there were not very many of them, Brudney and Copeland estimating that they constituted no more than 5 percent of the white population (Brudney and Copeland 1984, 1078). A more important reason for challenging Falwell's claims, however, involves these evangelicals' past voting behavior. The facts that 83 percent of them voted and that 86 percent of those who did voted for Reagan do not in and of themselves make the Moral Majority a major agent of political mobilization. For that to have happened, the Moral Majority would have had to persuade evangelicals who had not done so before (i.e., who had either not voted or voted Democratic) to now vote for Republican candidates. But there is relatively little evidence to suggest that that happened in 1980, and hardly any at all for the presidential election.[30] As Lipset and Raab pointed out, the drift of evangelicals to the Republican side in presidential elections had begun years before anyone outside of Lynchburg had heard of Jerry Falwell. And the only researchers who specifically investigated the voters who turned a narrow Republican loss in the presidential contest of 1976 into a landslide in 1980 concluded that these new Republican voters of 1980 were no more likely to be ''born again'' or to be intensely religious, and no more likely to be opposed to abortion or to the ERA, than those who had voted Republican four years before (Himmelstein and McRae 1984).

That last finding, along with conclusions from other studies, points to the possibility that the impact of the Moral Majority was as limited as it was because its most dedicated supporters were already voting Republican.[31] At first

[29] In drawing this conclusion I am referring to the findings of Miller and Wattenberg 1984: those in the ''most fundamentalist'' category in their sample were far more likely than others to see abortion as a major issue (pp. 311–12).

[30] The strongest claim for evangelical mobilization in 1980 has been made by Smidt. Using CPS data, he maintained that the election saw ''an influx of large numbers of newly registered evangelical Christians,'' so great an influx in fact that for the first time in recent political history evangelicals turned out to vote in higher proportions than nonevangelicals (Smidt 1983, pp. 41–43). If that is true, surely Falwell and the Moral Majority deserve much of the credit; but other political scientists working with the same data indicated no such mobilization occurred and that the role of the Moral Majority was overrated (Abramson 1982, p. 84).

[31] It should be noted in this connection that just as all those who agreed with its issue-positions did not actually support the Moral Majority, so those who did support it did not necessarily agree with all its issue-positions. The Dallas–Fort Worth supporters, for example, expressed overwhelming opposition to ''secular humanism'' in the abstract, but on its supposed manifestations against which Falwell had declaimed, sizable minorities went the other way. Over a third of these supporters did not think abortion was a sin, and about two-fifths supported either the Equal Rights

glance, that possibility seems startling, primarily because as social scientists traced the various circles over which Falwell hoped to extend his influence—the regular viewers of religious programming, those who agreed with some of the Moral Majority's positions on issues, and finally the evangelical community itself—they regularly uncovered similar constituencies: disproportionately elderly, female, low-income, poorly educated, southern, and not definably Republican. But as the 1980 campaign forced scholars to pay close attention to those who *actually* supported the Moral Majority, they uncovered a very different population.[32] The authors of one study, for example, found that on their "fundamentalism" scale, which included favorable evaluations of the Moral Majority as well as the usual religious measures, those occupying the "most fundamentalist" position were a "younger generation of well-educated conservatives" for whom support for the Moral Majority was "a politicized extension of religious beliefs."[33] This profile of Moral Majority supporters derived from the national CPS sample—relatively young, affluent, and educated—bore a close resemblance to that of supporters in "the buckle of the southern Bible Belt," the Dallas–Fort Worth area;[34] and the profiles drawn in both those studies closely resembled that of Ohioans who in fact joined the organization. With their "high levels of education and occupational prestige" and their Republican partisanship, the Ohio members resembled (in the words of the political scientist who studied them) the participants in the Christian Anti-Communist Crusade studied by Wolfinger and Koeppen twenty years before far more than they did the "lower SES fundamentalists of most media accounts."[35]

Amendment or sex education in the schools (Shupe and Stacey 1983, pp. 32–35). A similar divergence among Nebraska supporters is analyzed in Moore and Whitt 1986.

[32] For the very few studies that pointed in this direction, see those summarized in Pat Horn, "The New Middle-Class Fundamentalism," *Psychology Today* 10 (September 1976): 24–25; and in James L. Guth, "The Politics of the Christian Right," in Allan J. Cigler and Burdett A. Loomis, eds., *Interest Group Politics* (Washington: Congressional Quarterly Press, 1983), pp. 64, 81.

[33] Miller and Wattenberg 1984, pp. 308, 306. A study of those who gave to political action committees also found that "the tie between religiosity and conservative positions is most pronounced among younger and highly educated contributors" (Guth and Green 1987; quotation at p. 193). The relationship between fundamentalism and support for the Moral Majority, however, was more controverted. Shupe and Stacey, as we have seen, found a significant positive correlation between support and fundamentalism in the Dallas–Fort Worth area, but Tamney and Johnson found no such correlation in Middletown (Shupe and Stacey 1983, pp. 95–96; Tamney and Johnson 1983, pp. 151–53). In their analysis of the national CPS sample, Buell and Sigelman also found no correlation (Buell and Sigelman 1985, p. 431). Meanwhile, Wilcox had argued that adherence to fundamentalist doctrine was a better predictor of political behavior (including support for the Moral Majority) than membership in a fundamentalist denomination (Wilcox 1986b). He therefore criticized Buell and Sigelman for using the less adequate definition; and in their response they seem to have conceded his point (Wilcox 1987b; Buell and Sigelman 1987).

[34] Buell and Sigelman 1985, p. 431; Miller and Wattenberg 1984, pp. 307–8; Shupe and Stacey 1983, pp. 18–20.

[35] Wilcox 1987a, p. 56. His is the only published work on those who actually belong to the

The "New Right" and the Senate Elections

Analyzing only the presidential contest does not settle the question of the impact of the "new right" in general, or of the Moral Majority in particular, on the 1980 election. Granted that the repudiation of Carter was so massive that no one group could be regarded as critical, one might still raise the question of the defeat of all those Democratic senators. In a smaller constituency might not the kind of mobilization that Falwell and the others attempted prove decisive?[36] This argument gains considerable force when we look at the peculiarity of the 1980 Senate election results. Whether or not Reagan was given a "mandate" in the presidential election, Carter was indeed repudiated. It is, however, by no means clear that in the Senate elections the public as a whole repudiated Democrats; in fact, in 1980 approximately 5 million *more* voters cast their ballots for Democratic senatorial candidates than cast their ballots for Republican candidates.[37] The Republican sweep resulted from victories in a number of small states, so much so that a shift of only 50,000 votes would have changed the outcomes in seven races and allowed the Democrats to retain control of the Senate (Mann and Ornstein 1981, 293).

The massive victory of Republican conservatives in the 1980 Senate elections was in the first instance the result of a finely calculated political strategy—but on whose part? What, for example, was the actual impact on the "negative campaign" run by Dolan's National Conservative Political Action Committee? It is probably true that NCPAC's television spots, relentlessly attacking the incumbent Democrats and preceding the actual campaign of their Republican challengers, did have an effect in changing the former's image and making them more vulnerable.[38] Even though many voters found the spots offensive, the blame attached to NCPAC, not to the Republican candidate.[39] Several difficulties, however, face anyone trying to measure NCPAC's influence on the 1980 elections. Regarding himself as a "constitutional libertarian,"[40] Dolan tended to concentrate on economic and foreign policy issues,

---

Moral Majority and is based on questionnaires he submitted to members of the Ohio chapter in 1982. See also Wilcox 1986a; Wilcox 1987c; Wilcox 1987d.

[36] Miller and Wattenberg hint that supporters of the Moral Majority had a greater impact on the Senate elections than on the presidential contest, but their data preclude their saying where or how (1984, p. 313).

[37] This paradox was due to the winning margins accumulated by four Democrats in particular: incumbents Alan Cranston and John Glenn, who scored overwhelming victories in the populous states of California and Ohio; incumbent Russell Long, who was unopposed for reelection in Louisiana; and Alan Dixon, who won the open seat in Illinois by half a million votes.

[38] See the comments in Bill Keller, " 'New Right' Wants Credit for Democrats' Nov. 4 Losses But GOP, Others Don't Agree," *Congressional Quarterly Weekly Report* 38 (November 15, 1980): 3372–73; and the analysis in Robinson 1981, pp. 185–90.

[39] See the comments in Clymer, "Conservative Political Action Committee Evokes Both Fear and Adoration," p. 26.

[40] Terry Dolan, as quoted in Clymer, "Conservative Political Action Committee . . ."; but

precisely the same issues emphasized by the strategists in the Republican Senatorial Campaign Committee. It is not easy, then, to determine, for example, whether voters in Iowa were more likely to be persuaded that John Culver was "weak on defense" by NCPAC in the spring or by the Republican campaign in the fall. Republican strategists had some basis for complaining that in their postelection analyses the media gave far too much credit to the "new right" and far too little to their party organization.[41]

If NCPAC's role in the 1980 Senate elections is difficult to assess, what about that of groups such as the Moral Majority? To what extent did their mobilization of evangelical voters affect the outcomes in individual states? Throughout the year there had been mounting evidence of successful registration campaigns by local Moral Majority chapters, and the mobilization efforts in state primaries in Alabama and Oklahoma proved highly effective. Thus, when, in the general election, defeated incumbents agreed with Falwell and attributed their losses to such mobilization, many believed them. Here, for example, is Frank Church's testimony:

> Moral Majority, Christian Voice and the rest didn't move in until the last stage of the campaign. Then they closed ranks to reinforce everything the NCPAC had been doing. They took out advertisements that read, "Don't vote for Frank Church—Pray for him!" They leafleted the churches the Sunday before the election. They put literature on the cars. There was a terrific blitz at the end. The money behind it was immense. In the end I came within 1 percent of winning—that's only 4000 votes. But when a switch of 2500 might have swung the election, any one group alone probably did me enough damage to make the difference.[42]

Was Church correct? Did the efforts of the Moral Majority "and the rest" turn the tide? How can we find out?

In general, voting behavior in Senate elections receives little attention from social scientists, so little in fact that we have only the scantiest evidence on what determined voters' choices in 1980. Given the fragmentary nature of the data, questions about the impact of the Moral Majority on Senate elections cannot be answered conclusively. Using the survey data compiled by the Center for Political Studies, Corwin Smidt found that white evangelicals voted heavily Republican in the 1980 Senate contests (65.6 percent in the South, 59.7 percent outside the South) and were more likely to vote Republican than nonevangelicals in either region (7 percentage points more so in the South, 14 points elsewhere) (Smidt 1983, 47–48). Those figures might suggest a significant role for the Moral Majority, but we still cannot be sure.

One way of looking at the influence of the "new right" (and the Moral

---

Dolan also believed that abortion is murder and had no objection to local communities enforcing morality (Young 1982, pp. 144–45).

[41] Keller, " 'New Right' Wants Credit . . . ," pp. 3372–73; Jacob 1981, p. 123. For a different view, which hints at Republican–"new right" collusion, see Paige 1983, pp. 181–98.

[42] Frank Church, as quoted in Conway and Sigelman, *Holy Terror*, p. 30.

Majority in particular) on the Senate elections of 1980 is to consider specific issues.[43] During the campaign Falwell "stressed the issue of abortion above other issues";[44] thus evidence of the abortion issue as a determinant of voters' senatorial choices might reveal the impact of the Moral Majority. But the most exhaustive study of the abortion issue in the 1980 Senate races, by Donald Granberg and James Burlison, concluded that it had very little impact on the outcomes.

Granberg and Burlison investigated the seven Senate contests, including Iowa and South Dakota, in which in the general election the stands of the candidates were clearly marked, the Democratic candidate having been endorsed by the leading "prochoice" organization and the Republican candidate endorsed by the leading "prolife" organization. In those states, not surprisingly, voters divided over abortion, and also not surprisingly, those voting for the "prochoice" candidates were more likely to support abortion than those who voted for the "prolife" candidate. However, in order to prove that abortion was *the* issue that elected the Republicans, Granberg and Burlison argued, "it must also be shown that the attitudes of voters were in closer proximity to those of the winning candidate than to those of the loser." Yet when measured on a scale of abortion options (from 1 to 4) the average position of those voting for the "prochoice" candidates was remarkably similar to the average position of those voting for the "prolife" candidates (2.1 to 2.4). "If we assume," they concluded, "that the candidates had adopted the most liberal position (1.0) or the most restrictive (4.0), or a position equidistant from both extremes (2.5), it is hard to see in what way the abortion opponents could have gained an advantage from their position" (Granberg and Burlison 1983, 236–37). In these seven contests voters disagreed less over abortion than over the role of the Federal Government in providing social services, over defense spending—or even over the ERA, which attracted far less attention from journalists and social scientists than did abortion. Like those who had studied the 1978 midterm congressional elections, these researchers concluded that opponents of abortion were being elected to office not because they were against abortion but primarily because they were Republican challengers running against incumbent Democrats.[45]

---

[43] It might be noted in this connection that, in the only ecological analysis of the 1980 Senate elections, Robert Zwier found that in Iowa and South Dakota the issues pushed by the Moral Majority—issues such as abortion—appeared to have little impact on the voting behavior of members of evangelical denominations. But since Zwier's study relied on simple ecological correlations at the county level, its significance is limited (Zwier 1984, pp. 176–83).

[44] Fitzgerald 1981, p. 124. For a general analysis of the way various groups tried to use the abortion issue as a way of unseating liberal Democratic incumbents, see Paige 1983, pp. 198–217.

[45] Michael Traugott and Maris Vinovskis, "Abortion and the 1978 Congressional Elections," *Family Planning Perspectives* 12 (September–October 1980): 238–46; John E. Jackson and Vinovskis, "Public Opinion, Elections, and the 'Single-Issue' Issue," in Gilbert Y. Steiner, ed.,

In concluding this analysis of studies of the 1980 election, let us try to summarize the ways in which the cumulative conclusions of social scientists reinforced—or challenged—the widespread view that the Moral Majority played a major role. Those who studied the election did concur with that view on three important points. First, Ronald Reagan did run very well among white evangelicals; and, according to at least one study, so did Republican senatorial candidates. Second, evangelical voters were more likely to be conservative on cultural issues such as abortion, the Equal Rights Amendment, policies toward homosexuals, and school prayer. Third, religious groups linked to the "new right," such as the Moral Majority, were very active mobilizing evangelicals and stressing those cultural issues. But the existing studies do not demonstrate—even though the "new right" argued it, and many journalists and politicians agreed—that evangelicals voted for Reagan and the other Republicans *because* of their stance on cultural issues. Nor is there direct evidence from survey data to show that the mobilization efforts of groups such as the Moral Majority played a crucial role in the presidential contest; in the senatorial contests the evidence is contradictory and inconclusive.

After the Election: The "New Right," the Republicans, and the Future

If this was so, and journalists and politicians were misled in their overestimation of the impact of groups like the Moral Majority, then the question becomes: why was the Moral Majority's role in the election so small? There are several possible explanations. First, Falwell was correct in assuming that many Americans agreed with the Moral Majority's positions on various issues, and he was quite right in seeing evangelicals as the major part of his potential constituency; but, as we have seen, the issues he and the Moral Majority emphasized were simply not salient enough to determine the decisions of many voters. A second possible reason is that even as the media were portraying it as one of the major agents of right-wing mobilization, the Moral Majority received clearly negative reactions from the public. According to data collected by the Center for Political Studies, the public was less likely to "feel close to" what the pollsters labeled "evangelical groups active in politics, such as the Moral Majority" (5.9 percent) than to such suspect groups as "Hispanics" (7.4 percent), "big business" (8 percent) or "liberals" (12.8 percent). The public was also more likely to give "evangelical groups active in politics" unfavorable ratings than any other group listed—except for those two hardy perennials, "radical students" and "black militants."[46]

The Abortion Dispute and the American System (Washington: Brookings Institution, 1983), pp. 72–77.

[46] CPS data as summarized in Ralph Clark Chandler, "Worshipping a Past That Never Was," *Christianity and Crisis* 42 (February 15, 1982): 22.

More significantly, the Moral Majority was perceived negatively, by clergy and laity alike, in those areas of the country where supposedly it had its greatest strength. In one study, two-thirds of a sample of midwestern evangelical clergy had a "somewhat" to "very" unfavorable impression of the organization (Zwier 1984, 184); in another, half of a sample of Southern Baptist clergy considered themselves opponents, and only 3.3 percent were members (Guth 1983b, 119). In the Dallas–Fort Worth area, about twice as many (31 percent) of a white middle-class sample "opposed" the Moral Majority as "supported" it (16 percent).[47] The 1980 campaign thus ended on an ironic note: the candidates Falwell and the Moral Majority supported—Ronald Reagan and the Republican challengers in the Senate races—had steadily gained in public esteem; Falwell and the organization he helped create had not.

In the aftermath of the 1980 election, what seemed most likely was that the Moral Majority would remain an intensely committed minority of conservative evangelicals and fundamentalists. It was also likely that it would be as a pressure group rather than as an agent of electoral mobilization that it would exert its influence, contributing to what Burnham called "the snarly, intemperate, and blocked character of politics in contemporary America" (Burnham 1981, 138). But even considering the Moral Majority primarily as a pressure group, a look at its activities in the year after the election still raises questions as to how much influence it actually possessed. Part of its influence in 1981 came, not surprisingly, from the perception that it had already influenced the 1980 election. Having convinced the media that it was a power in the land, the Moral Majority went on to back a threatened boycott of companies sponsoring sexually titillating television programs, and in so doing gave the boycott an unexpected credibility. The boycott, organized in the spring of 1981 by Rev. Donald Wildmon of Tupelo, Mississippi, and his umbrella organization, the Coalition for Better Television, never took place, because it forced at least some producers to redesign their formats.[48] Yet even in the Bible Belt there was little evidence of a groundswell of opposition to such programs, and one poll (albeit sponsored by one of the networks) indicated that Moral Majority supporters were regular watchers of many of the programs the CBTV was condemning.[49]

Another reason that in this case the Moral Majority ultimately prevailed was that the most objectionable programs, the so-called "jiggle shows," had few

[47] Shupe and Stacey 1983, p. 30. Comparable findings were reported for Nebraska (13 percent of the total sample supporting, 29 percent opposing) and for "Middletown"—17 percent of the total sample supporting, 31 percent opposing (Moore and Whitt 1986, p. 429; Tamney and Johnson 1983, p. 150).

[48] This entire episode is most succinctly analyzed in Todd Gitlin, "The Reverend Wildmon's Crusade: When the Right Talks, TV Listens," *Nation* 237 (October 15, 1983): 333–40.

[49] Gitlin, "Reverend Wildmon's Crusade," p. 339; Tony Schwartz, "Studies by Two Networks Dispute Moral Majority," *New York Times*, June 19, 1981, city ed., p. C26.

defenders.[50] Apparently, there were equally few defenders of sodomy in the nation's capital. Thus, through a flurry of mass mailings Falwell was able, in the fall of 1981, to convince a large majority of the House of Representatives to reject a proposed revision of the District of Columbia criminal code that would have legalized homosexual acts between consenting adults. In an action closely approximating the requirements of the "symbolic politics" model, congressmen took a firm stand against "abominations" without significantly changing the private lives of gay men in Washington.[51] These victories against relatively vulnerable targets predicted nothing about the future success of the Moral Majority's agenda: it remained to be seen, for example, whether the necessary two-thirds congressional majority could ever be mustered behind constitutional amendments overturning the Supreme Court's decisions in the school prayer and abortion cases, both of which had powerful and articulate defenders on Capitol Hill.

It might be argued that the most effective work by the Moral Majority was being done not by the national organization but at the state and local level; by the end of 1981, however, it was becoming clear that a number of state and local chapters had overreached themselves. The media were full of entertaining items such as those involving the head of the Maryland chapter who wanted to ban the sale of anatomically detailed gingerbread cookies, the Santa Clara (California) spokesman who implied that homosexuals should be put to death, and the New York City activist who told reporters that "Jews have a God-given ability to raise money" and that Catholics "weren't Christians."[52] It is no wonder that shortly after these episodes Falwell confessed to one interviewer that the Moral Majority was still "trying to get organized" and admitted the necessity of "get[ting] those loose cannons out there under control."[53] Even where the state and local chapters were efficiently organized and under responsible leadership, however, their impact was hard to measure. In Indiana, for example, where the state chapter was headed by Falwell's old colleague Rev. Greg Dixon, the state and local chapters concentrated on modifying the child-abuse laws so that parents could administer physical punishment without fear of prosecution, on supporting legislation requiring physicians to notify a girl's parents before performing an abortion, and at the local level, on closing down adult bookstores in Indianapolis and Terre Haute. In all three cases, according to two close students of the organization, results favorable to the Moral Majority position were achieved; but, given the widespread support for "traditional values" in that state, it was hard for these

---

[50] Gitlin, "Reverend Wildmon's Crusade," p. 340.

[51] Terry Krieger, "Capital Sex," *New Republic* 185 (November 11, 1981): 10–11.

[52] Incidents cited in Jere Real, "What Jerry Falwell *Really* Wants," *Inquiry* 4 (August 3–August 24, 1981): 13–14.

[53] Interview with Falwell, *Christianity Today* 25 (September 4, 1981): 22.

analysts to see Dixon's organization as the decisive influence (Pierard and Wright 1984).

Admittedly, all this is easy to perceive a decade later, a decade that was not kind to the "new Christian right," its friends in Washington notwithstanding. As the 1980s drew to a close, Falwell had announced his withdrawal from politics and dissolved the Moral Majority; the blander and better-connected Rev. Pat Robertson had been unable to mobilize the viewers of his Christian Broadcasting Network into a force capable of sustaining him in the 1988 Republican presidential primaries; and other key figures in the "electronic ministry" were going down in a swamp of sexual escapades and financial malfeasance. But even on the basis of the evidence available soon after the election, it is doubtful that the Moral Majority warranted the attention paid to it. As a device for mobilizing "conservative Christians," it was probably less important in the long run than the earlier and more specific "profamily" movements against sex education, against the teaching of evolution, against the Equal Rights Amendment, and against abortion.

Those "profamily" movements also proved limited in their impact, however. It did not take exceptional foresight in 1980 to see that on educational issues their influence would be of relatively short duration and that sex education, Darwinian evolution, and even "modern" textbooks would ultimately prevail in American public schools. Their greater impact came in their apparent ability to block the legitimation of further changes in gender roles, as in their defeat of the proposed ERA and of ordinances to protect homosexuals from discrimination. Nonetheless, on the most controverted issue of them all, abortion, the most these forces were able to achieve was a cutoff of Medicaid payments at the federal level: abortion still remained legal, and a few states continued to subsidize abortions for poor women.

By the end of the decade it was even clearer that abortion would remain legal everywhere in the United States until the Supreme Court reversed its decision in *Roe v. Wade*. Such a development would be most likely to occur through appointments of "prolife" judges, and such appointments were indeed promised in the 1980 Republican platform. After January 20, 1981, however only Ronald Reagan was in a position to make such appointments, which prompts the thought that the forces of the "new right," including the Moral majority, had all along been more dependent on Reagan than he was on whatever mobilization the "new right" had been able to achieve.[54] That thought,

---

[54] In 1984 Reagan ran even better among white evangelical voters, both absolutely and proportionately, than he had in 1980. According to CBS News–*New York Times* exit polls, he received 81 percent of their vote, as opposed to 73 percent of the votes of white Protestants and 66 percent of the votes of all whites (data in Gerald M. Pomper, "The Presidential Election," in Pomper, ed., *The Election of 1984: Reports and Interpretations* [Chatham, N.J.: Chatham House, 1985], p. 68). Data collected by the Center for Political Studies show a comparable shift (Corwin Smidt, "Evangelicals and the 1984 Election: Continuity or Change?" *American Politics Quarterly* 15

in turn, leads to the larger conclusion that, in their attempt to measure the influence of the "new right," many of the political scientists and sociologists whose work we have reviewed may have been looking in the wrong place.

In the aftermath of the 1980 election it was certainly reasonable to conclude with Burnham that "the Republican Party is genuinely a party of the right," that it was headed by a president who "has long been a leading figure in the American right," and that it included many "in the executive, in Congress, and outside government . . . who have had continuous and close links to what we used to call not so long ago the 'radical right.' " But while a Republican victory in 1980 may, given Carter's troubles at home and abroad, have been inevitable, the right-wing ascendancy that accompanied it was not. The public mood in 1980, insofar as it can be ascertained, was not in all probability so very different from that in 1952; but the complexion of the Reagan administration would be significantly different from that of the Eisenhower administration twenty-eight years before. The differences between the two came less from shifts in public opinion than from shifts among Republican elites. In analyzing the factors behind these shifts too much attention has been given to the efforts of right-wing activists to make themselves heard, too little to the growing willingness of Republican leaders to listen to them. Too much scholarly effort has been spent trying to measure the degree of popular support the "new right," and especially the "new Christian right," could claim, and too little on what Burnham called "the remarkable consolidation around this right-wing ideological pole which has occurred within the Republicans' ranks."[55]

A consideration of the factors behind the Republicans' abandonment of the proposed Equal Rights Amendment illustrates the misplaced focus of much of the research we have been analyzing. The abandonment was unmistakable:

[October 1987]: 419–44). Fragmentary evidence suggests that cultural issues were more salient for white evangelicals in 1984 than in 1980: see the reanalysis of the CBS News–*New York Times* data in Adam Clymer, "Religion and Politics Mix Poorly for Democrats," *New York Times*, November 25, 1984, sec. 4, p. 2; Stephen D. Johnson and Joseph B. Tamney, "The Christian Right and the 1984 Presidential Election," *Review of Religious Research* 27 (December 1985): 124–33; James L. Guth, "Political Converts: Partisan Realignment Among Southern Baptist Ministers," *Election Politics* 3 (Winter 1985–86): 2–6; and Donald N. Granberg, "The Abortion Issue in the 1984 Elections," *Family Planning Perspectives* 19 (March–April 1987): 59–62.

Data from the 1986 midterm congressional elections reveal that seven out of ten white evangelicals voted for Republican candidates, a larger proportion than in any of the poll's categories—except for self-identified Republicans (data in CBS News–*New York Times* poll, in the *New York Times*, November 6, 1986, p. 15). But even if we assume that the strong Republican showing among these voters in 1984 and 1986 came from the party's stance against abortion and for school prayer, it seems likely that it was Reagan and other politicians—and not Jerry Falwell—who brought about that result. And even if (as some analysts argued) this shift constitutes a minor case of realignment, it was the Republican party and not the "new Christian right" that would be the ultimate beneficiary.

[55] Walter Dean Burnham, "Towards Confrontation?" in Seymour Martin Lipset, ed., *Party Coalitions in the 1980s* (San Francisco: Institute for Contemporary Studies, 1981), p. 382.

the 1976 convention nearly rejected it; in 1978 the majority of House Republicans voted against the extension of its ratification period; and in 1980 the national convention finally rejected it. Yet opinion polls showed public support for the amendment right up to the very end.[56] Even those analysts who question the breadth and depth of that support find it hard to argue that public opinion was the major factor behind the Republican reversal.[57]

For quite different reasons we can reduce the overall importance of Schlafly's anti-ERA movement, influential though it was in individual states. Unless we accept the rather naive assumption that all groups, even all organized groups, automatically receive attention from political elites, it would be wise not to place too much emphasis on Schlafly's organizational efforts as a factor in the Republican shift; in any case her feminist adversaries supporting the ERA were equally well-organized, certainly so at the national level. In the absence of any other compelling explanation, then, the simplest conclusion to draw would be that the Republican party came to abandon the amendment in the late 1970s primarily because more and more Republican leaders considered it bad public policy. Put another way, the Republican party was by 1980 increasingly dominated by those who because of their own right-wing ideology were so much in agreement with Schlafly's views that her mobilization efforts probably played a relatively minor role in influencing them.

This convergence between Republican politicians and the right-wing activists discussed in this book did not suddenly come about because of the perception of national decline in the late 1970s or because of the efforts of the "new right," though both surely helped accelerate the process. It began with the first stirrings for Goldwater in 1960 and only culminated in the Reagan campaign twenty years later. The ascendancy of the right wing within the Republican party is probably the most significant development in right-wing politics since World War II, but its story has not received very much attention from social scientists. They have largely left its full description and ultimate explanation to journalists—and, perhaps at some point in the future, to historians as well.

[56] See for example *Gallup Report* 203 (August 1982): 28–29; and the data analyzed in Mark R. Daniels, Robert Darcy, and Joseph W. Westphal, "The ERA Won—At Least in the Opinion Polls," *PS* 14 (Fall 1982): 578–84.

[57] One team of researchers, for example, has pointed out that opinion in the nonratifying states had been more negative toward the amendment than that in the ratifying states from the outset and that opposition grew disproportionately in the nonratifying states; but even their data show that it was not until 1980, near the end of the struggle, that opponents in those states equalled supporters (Bolce 1986, pp. 301–2). More generally, Jane Mansbridge has argued that even in the nation as a whole those who told pollsters they supported the ERA were often opposed to specific proposals granting equality to women. She also raises the possibility that on such an issue, about which the public is ambivalent, opinion surveys may not be the best predictors of behavior; and she cites as examples the defeat of state equal rights amendments in New York, New Jersey, Iowa, and Maine even though all had been supported in preelection polls (Mansbridge 1986, pp. 14–28). Still, she admits that it was not the ambivalence of its supporters but the intensity of its opponents that killed the proposed national amendment.

Part Five ———————————————————————

THE AMERICAN RIGHT WING IN PERSPECTIVE

Fifteen

Two Interpretations of the Right Wing:
Lipset and Rogin

THUS FAR WE have surveyed the scholarly work published by political scientists, sociologists, psychologists, and historians on the American right wing since World War II. Moving through the analyses of successive phenomena—support for Senator Joseph McCarthy, the "radical right" organizations of the early 1960s, the presidential candidacies of George Wallace, and the mobilization of the "new right" in the late 1970s—it is hard to avoid the sense that the scholarship as a whole is fragmented. This fragmentation almost certainly comes from the particular strategies researchers undertook. Most of the scholars whose work has been summarized in this book chose to study the right wing either by analyzing survey data on the support given particular candidates or by interviewing members of specific organizations. Focused on different individuals and groups scattered across time, the resulting published work has rarely conveyed any sense of a cohesive and influential right-wing movement operating over several decades. Perhaps because studying a handful of individuals is less methodologically rigorous than constructing a survey sample, few social scientists ever interested themselves in exploring the factors that held the right wing together over so long a time: its leaders and organizational networks, the financial resources at its disposal, and its links to politicians, businessmen, and national-security bureaucrats.[1]

It has largely fallen to journalists to make such connections, and it is they who have uncovered whatever continuities exist among McCarthy's defenders, the right-wing organizations of the early 1960s, the prenomination supporters of Barry Goldwater, the leaders of the "new right" in the late 1970s, and ultimately the personnel of the Reagan administration after 1981. The results of these journalistic investigations have been brought together, wherever possible, in this book in order to provide better historical documentation of the development of what might be called the right-wing infrastructure: the leaders, organizations, and networks that make it possible to speak of *a* right wing.

---

[1] The outstanding exception is the political scientist John S. Saloma III. Though designed for a popular audience and quite consciously written in an alarmist tone, his *Ominous Politics: The New Conservative Labyrinth* (Saloma 1984) offers a framework for understanding right-wing politics that, in my view, future researchers will be unable to ignore.

Social scientists may have missed much of the story, therefore, because they focused on public attitudes and members of organizations. But far more than journalists they were at least theoretically equipped to answer the question: to what extent has the American right wing been sustained by the larger social structure and political culture? In fact, however, few scholars attempted to answer this question. Of all those whose work we have surveyed, only Lipset has made a systematic attempt throughout his career to see right-wing politics on such a large scale. Of all the scholars covered in this book he casts the largest shadow: it would not be much of an exaggeration to say that the literature on the right wing has been, for the most part, an attempt in one way or another to confirm or refute Lipset's theories. Any attempt to grasp the right wing as a whole must begin, then, with an analysis of Lipset's interpretation. Precisely because his ideas have been challenged, however, a viable alternative interpretation is essential for purposes of comparison. Although far from being as systematic as Lipset's, that of Rogin comes closest. The discussion continues, therefore, with a complementary analysis of Rogin's interpretation, pointing to its largely ignored similarities with Lipset's as well as its more obvious differences. In the conclusion to this book, both Lipset's and Rogin's interpretations will be examined from a variety of perspectives; the point here is to compare their analyses of the American right wing.

Lipset: The Paradoxes of Egalitarian Values

Perhaps the easiest way to grasp Lipset's interpretation of right-wing politics in America is to begin with the general observation that as a sociologist he has devoted much of his effort to reconciling theories that "place a primary stress on values as the key source of action" (such as those of Weber and Parsons) with those that "emphasize the significance of interests" (such as those of Marx).[2] Whether or not he can be considered an "apolitical Marxist,"[3] in his work Lipset has emphasized "the significance of interests" far more than critics (including Rogin) have been willing to admit. He has consistently pointed out that the conflicts that arise from inequality are basic to all societies, including the democracies, which "remain highly stratified societies in which access to education, economic opportunity, culture, and consumption goods is grossly unequal" (Lipset 1968, 223). What distinguishes the democracies—what paradoxically is a source of their stability—is that their political systems facilitate the expression of protest against the inequalities their social and eco-

---

[2] Lipset 1963b, p. xx. As examples of his attempt to reconcile Marx, Weber, and Parsons, see particularly Lipset 1968, pp. 121–58, and Lipset 1985, pp. 11–44.

[3] Lipset has used this term (or something like it) to describe his approach, although—in a clear response to left-wing critics—he often adds that the designation was made by other scholars: compare, for example, Lipset 1963b, p. xxii, with Lipset 1970, pp. xi–xiii.

nomic systems engender (Lipset 1985, 4). For Lipset the most durable expression of that protest, what he has called "the democratic translation of the class struggle" (Lipset 1960, 220), is the competition between political parties. Thus, "more than anything else the party struggle is a conflict among classes," in which lower-income groups vote mainly for "parties of the left," which pledge to reduce those inequalities, while the upper-income groups vote mainly for "parties of the right," which seek to preserve the status quo (Lipset 1960, 223–24).

Since the dissatisfaction that social and economic inequalities engender finds expression in political demands, "there has been an inherent bias in favor of the extension of equality in all democratic societies" (Lipset 1968, 159). If that is so, how then can the antiegalitarian "parties of the right" hope to compete? One set of reasons of course has to do with the cultural and institutional dominance of those classes represented by the "parties of the right" (Lipset 1968, 160–63). While recognizing the role of these extrapolitical factors in furthering conservative political aims, however, Lipset has also called attention to right-wing political strategies, which in one way or another seek to deflect the electorate's attention from class-based issues:

> These efforts may take the form of (1) introducing national patriotic issues and nominating military heroes as candidates; (2) stressing noneconomic bases of cleavage such as religious or ethnic differences, or issues of morality; (3) the fostering of Tory socialism, that is, legislation designed to benefit the socioeconomic position of the lower strata; and (4) using a variant of pseudo-socialism and anti-elitism, a surrogate-exploiting scapegoat which will absorb antagonism to the societal elite. (Lipset 1968, 165)

On the one hand, then, Lipset has stressed the way in which, in all democratic societies, conservative politicians seek to deflect class-based demands for egalitarian policies. On the other hand, he has sought to underscore those factors that make American society different. As he deepened his comparative analysis, he found himself agreeing more and more with "the perspective taken by Max Weber which stresses the role of core values in influencing the institutional structure of a nation" (Lipset 1968, 20). He concurred with Hofstadter's comment that "culturally and anthropologically, human societies are cast in a great variety of molds, but once a society has been cast in its mold . . . the number of ways in which, short of dire calamity, it will alter its pattern are rather limited" (Hofstadter, as quoted in Lipset 1963c, 124).

In the American case, the "core values" have been "equality" and "achievement," values that "emerged from the interplay between the Puritan tradition and the Revolutionary ethos" at the time of the founding of "the new nation" and whose interaction has ever since been "a constant element in determining American institutions and behavior" (Lipset 1963c, 101). Although he usually brackets the two "core values," a close reading of his work suggests that Lipset has emphasized the consequences of "egalitarian" values on American political institutions and behavior far more than those that are "achievement"-oriented. The latter he reserves mainly as explanations for American optimism, materialism, preoccupation with success, and propensity for criminal activity.[4]

While he has focused on the impact of "egalitarian" values on American political life, it is essential to understand what Lipset has not said. Contrary to some of his critics' charges, he has never taken the position that the United States is now or ever has been an egalitarian society in any absolute sense: "It is obvious, of course, that the United States is not . . . if by egalitarian one means anything that approaches equality of results" (Lipset 1985, 349). Nor is American society more egalitarian than other societies on either of two commonly used indicators: he has pointed out that in the past upward social mobility here has been no greater than in Western Europe;[5] and that at present our national income distribution is in fact more skewed than in some of the European democracies (Lipset 1985, 349). Rather, what in Lipset's mind decisively differentiates American society is the near-universal commitment to egalitarian values. Insofar as they can be used by the disadvantaged to legitimize their claims, those values move the entire society in the direction of greater equality; and it is in that sense that American society has been moving in the direction of overcoming patterns of inequality.[6]

The American Revolution simultaneously gave the United States its national identity and made equality a core value: as a result, a commitment to equality has from the outset been an integral part of our national tradition, and that has put American conservatives at a severe disadvantage. At the same time, paradoxically, the same egalitarian influences have allowed right-wing movements to flourish, for at least two reasons. First, the lack of any legitimized social hierarchy makes many Americans unsure of their status in society so that they feel particularly threatened by those who seek upward mobility (Lipset 1963c, 112–13). Second, the parallel lack of deference to an established political elite means that, when such individuals rally behind leaders in movements to preserve their status, there are few elites with the authority to resist them and protect those under attack. Ironically, therefore, "civil liber-

---

[4] See for example his discussion in Lipset 1968, pp. 43–44. In fairness to him, it should be noted that in the essay he did link economic individualism and laissez-faire—which have played major roles in American politics—to "achievement"-oriented values (ibid.); and he further discussed the relationship in Lipset and Raab 1970, pp. 24–29. On the whole, however, he has not emphasized their political consequences as much as those arising from "egalitarian" values.

[5] This is an issue that Lipset has followed for a long time: for a more recent view, see especially Lipset 1977, pp. 103-10.

[6] Perhaps Lipset's strongest statement of this argument is in his discussion with Irving Louis Horowitz (Lipset and Horowitz 1966, p. 7).

ties for unpopular groups would seem to be stronger in elitist democracies [such as Britain and Canada] than in egalitarian ones" (Lipset 1968, 40).

In his major work on the subject, *The Politics of Unreason*, Lipset brings the two sides of right-wing politics together: conservative politicians seeking to broaden their electoral base by deflecting class-based demands, and individuals coming together in "backlash" movements that attempt to preserve their status by restricting the opportunity of those they see as threatening it. Given the massive amount of immigration to the United States and the way it has come to represent social and cultural change, these "backlash" movements have, as far as Lipset is concerned, expressed themselves chiefly in one or another kind of nativism: broadly anti-immigrant, often anti-Catholic and/or antiradical, and occasionally anti-Semitic. These movements have tended to mobilize those whose status seemed most directly threatened by that immigration or by change generally, the "lower strata" of society, the lower-middle and working classes. For Lipset the story of right-wing politics since the Civil War is thus largely the story of the relationship between these nativist "backlash" movements and politicians in the "conservative," Republican party. Unable to break the two-party monopoly, these movements nonetheless "succeed in failure" because some of their demands are incorporated in Republican platforms and at least partially implemented. If, however, their "monistic" demands for ethnic and cultural uniformity or their violations of democratic procedures exceed the tolerance of the respectable core of the party and challenge the pragmatism of Republican leaders, the movements' dynamism is halted and they soon collapse.[7]

Clearly any model as sweeping as this has greater explanatory power for some historical episodes than for others. Insofar as it contains three components—a movement aimed at preserving status, advocacy of an overtly nativist agenda, and incorporation by the Republican party—it would seem to work best for two periods, the 1880s and the 1920s. In the former period anti-Catholic organizations successfully persuaded Republican politicians to oppose public funding for parochial schools, in the latter the revived Ku Klux Klan (which outside the South operated through the Republican party) saw many of its demands enacted, most notably prohibition and immigration restrictions. For two other periods the model is somewhat more problematic. The 1970s also saw the demands of a "preservatist" movement incorporated by the Republicans, when the Nixon administration tried to coopt George Wallace's appeal by taking a punitive approach toward student and antiwar demonstrators and by trying to weaken administrative and judicial efforts to achieve racial integration. The Wallace movement can only with difficulty be considered politically nativist, however. It was much more obviously politically rac-

[7] Lipset and Raab 1970, pp. 47; 29–30, 50–59, 82–88, 123–31, 171–78, 362–67, 379–87; 91–92, 235–36.

ist; and while for some purposes the social impact of black migration to northern cities is comparable to that of European immigrants, American nativism and American racism have had quite different origins and far different degrees of durability. In the fourth case, the 1950s, Senator McCarthy and the Republicans generally certainly exploited the antiradical component of nativism; but as Lipset himself noted, McCarthyism did not constitute a movement, was neither anti-Catholic nor anti-Semitic, and appeared to draw its strength from those *rising* in status.[8]

These qualifications notwithstanding, the overall view Lipset conveys is that the dynamics of right-wing politics in America involve the interaction of Republican politicians, their core constituency of affluent conservatives, and lower-middle and working-class "backlash" movements. What is notable, however, is that within this general framework Lipset has increasingly placed his emphasis on the third group rather than the first two. A significant reevaluation of Republican politicians results. Far from self-interestedly looking for new issues to deflect the electoral majority from voting their "class" interests, they now assume a more statesmanlike role, deflecting the passions of "backlash" movements (Lipset and Raab 1970, 498–504).

Rogin: The Psychic Costs of a Liberal Society

Although he has moved from one emphasis to another in his work, Lipset has consciously tried to develop a theory that explains right-wing politics in American. While Rogin too, has had much to say on the subject, it is not clear that he has ever deliberately attempted to develop such a theory. To juxtapose Rogin to Lipset, therefore, it is first necessary to recognize that although Rogin has offered explanations for individual cases—whether German-Americans in Wisconsin or suburbanites in southern California—he has come to be less interested in discovering which groups are predisposed to right-wing behavior or under what circumstances than in interpreting American culture and society from his own critical perspective. It is up to us to deduce from Rogin's evolving interpretation those concepts that aid in understanding right-wing politics.

There is a further difficulty in comparing Lipset and Rogin. Whatever his emphasis, Lipset has at least been writing much the same kind of political sociology during the whole of his scholarly career. Rogin, on the other hand, has by his own admission shifted his approach from the relatively conventional "study of group politics and social movements . . . to a radical psychoanalysis of politics that is wholly outside the discipline" (Rogin 1987, xix). Though as a result of this shift he has been exceptionally eclectic in his scholarship, his perspective on right-wing politics throughout his career has consis-

---

[8] Lipset and Raab 1970, pp. 73–83, 141–45, 421–24, 220, 210–14.

tently been shaped by the work of the political scientist Louis Hartz. In two enormously suggestive books, Hartz set forth the argument that the political culture of the United States is a "fragment culture," separated from the European parent at precisely that moment that liberalism was emerging to challenge the ancien régime.[9] What was a "bourgeois" liberalism in conflict with an "aristocratic" feudalism (and later, a "proletarian" socialism) in the European context became in America the *only* political tradition, embracing all classes, though—a point of the utmost significance in Rogin's analysis—not necessarily all races.

Hartz's insistence that (white) Americans were "born equal" (a phrase he adapted from Tocqueville) certainly resembles Lipset's argument that equality has been one of the "core values" that have subsequently shaped American institutions and behavior. A closer reading, however, uncovers enough differences between the two authors to enable us to understand how Rogin could build upon Hartz to develop an interpretation different from Lipset's. The first difference lies in Hartz's implication that, while the values of what Americans call "democratic capitalism" (the name they give to their "fragment culture") may be sustainable at the societal level, the unending competition those values inculcate exacts a fearful psychic cost on individuals. One can interpret Hartz as saying that it is these "achievement"-oriented values of capitalism, and not the influence of "egalitarianism," that have produced the insecurity and frustration that concern Lipset.[10] The second difference between the two comes from Hartz's observation that with time all "fragment cultures" acquire a nationalist veneer; since attacks on the fragment are perceived as attacks on the nation's source of identity, within the fragment lie the seeds of repression (Hartz 1964, 13–14). So in America, before McCarthy, before even the Bolshevik Revolution, critics of "democratic capitalism" found themselves branded as "un-American."

Finally—again from a comparative perspective—Hartz emphasized the ways fragment cultures find all "alien" elements, ethnic as well as ideological, peculiarly threatening: the most durable "aliens" in American life have been the two racial groups excluded at the outset from what he called "the 'American' club: the Indian and the Negro" (Hartz 1964, 93). Here the contrast between Hartz and Lipset is strongest: in his book on right-wing politics Lipset does not discuss antiblack racism as a factor in shaping either right-wing attitudes or American consciousness generally until he reaches the

[9] Hartz 1955; Hartz 1964. Readers familiar with recent trends in the writing of American history will notice the absence in this analysis of any mention of "republicanism," the currently fashionable concept invoked to explain much of eighteenth- and nineteenth-century American political development. In my view, the extension of the concept to explain more and more phenomena deprives it of its original utility and renders it vulnerable to the same kind of criticism that followed the overextension of Hartz's "liberal fragment" model. More to the point, Rogin himself appears to have doubts about its applicability, especially to the problems he is analyzing (Rogin 1987, pp. 281, 283).

[10] On this point, contrast Lipset 1963c, pp. 110–16, with Hartz 1955, pp. 219–25.

1960s,[11] but for Hartz the presence of enslaved Africans and their descendants—and, even more significantly, the suppressed Indian aborigines—has helped determine the evolution of our fragment since its very beginning (Hartz 1964, 16–20, 58–63, 94–103).

From insights such as these Rogin built his model of American society and culture which, even if he has not consistently intended it as such, can be used to interpret the right wing. Rogin restates Hartz's thesis to argue that since "America had no feudal past," the European colonists "were confronted with no alternatives to liberal uniformity save the psychically charged presences of [what James Madison had referred to as] 'the black race within our bosom . . . [and] the red on our borders' " (Rogin 1975, 7). From its inception, "this was a society of individualists" who aimed at "mastery of the environment, with success the result of individual effort not special privilege" (Rogin 1967, 36). One early manifestation of the anxieties "alien" races could induce in these "individuals" was the effort of Andrew Jackson and his supporters to remove the Indian from their tribal lands.

As he investigated the matter further, Rogin found that these confident Jacksonians who aimed to master their environment by driving out the original inhabitants were basically lonely men. Tocqueville had noted at the time that the lack of an ascriptive social hierarchy and a powerful religious establishment—the absence of the entire corporate order of the ancien régime in America—had made white men not only "equal" but "separate," each in isolation pursuing an unattainable goal of success.[12] Rogin adds that they were not only cut off from one another but from part of themselves. Underneath all the talk of "civilization" and "savagery" that accompanied the process of Indian removal lay regressive impulses blocked by the dominant liberalism: "Indians were in harmony with nature; lonely, independent liberal men were separated from it, and their culture lacked the richness, diversity, and traditional attachments necessary to sustain their independence. Liberalism generated a forbidden nostalgia for childhood—for the nurturing, blissful, primitively violent connection to nature that white Americans had to leave behind." The rage resulting from these thwarted impulses expressed itself in the violent subjugation of the Indians: by uprooting, "civilizing," even killing them, whites "reunited themselves with nature" and "created a uniquely American identity" (Rogin 1975, 8, 9).

What, the reader may be asking at this point, does Andrew Jackson's Indian

---

[11] Although in *The Politics of Unreason* Lipset briefly touched on black migration to northern cities during and after World War I as a factor in producing urban support for the Klan (Lipset and Raab 1970, pp. 118, 120), he did not really bring blacks on as major figures—even as targets of prejudice—until his discussion of the John Birch Society (ibid., pp. 267–69) and then, more significantly, in connection with George Wallace and his supporters (ibid., pp. 338ff.).

[12] Alexis de Tocqueville, *Democracy in America*, ed. Phillips Bradley, 2 vols. (New York: Knopf, 1945) 2:104, 147.

policy have to do with the contemporary American right wing? One obvious response would be to note the central role the settlement of the West—a process that the subjugation of the Indians made possible—has had in right-wing mythology. Right-wing politicians tend, for example, to see themselves as "sheriffs" single-handedly imposing "law and order" and their countrymen as God-fearing "pioneers" surrounded by "savages." To return more directly to Rogin, where else in his work does one come across lonely strivers whose apparent success masks their inauthentic existence, and whose frustrations can have politically significant consequences? The answer, as the reader may recall, is in southern California, whose right-wing voting behavior Rogin explains in terms of its distinctive cultural patterns. Again, he begins his analysis with a restatement of Hartz: "Suppose we look at southern California as a distended fragment of the American fragment, magnifying certain aspects of liberal, bourgeois culture." If we do, he continues, we will find in exaggerated form "the cycle of optimism, restlessness, longing, and dissatisfaction" that for Tocqueville characterized American life.[13]

Successful and affluent, southern Californians have indeed mastered their environment—they have created a "man-made synthetic universe"—but they have never been able to realize their deeper longings for "unconditional love and security." Nor, more immediately, have they been able to eliminate "alien" threats to their "fragment of a fragment": in fact, with the rising tide of student protest and black insurgency in the 1960s, the "aliens" seemed to be multiplying. White Americans had always believed that "groups so different from the bourgeois liberal fragment had to be incorporated or mastered, cured or imprisoned, made safe or destroyed." For white southern Californians in the late 1960s those groups included not only the original "aliens," the blacks, but also radicals, hippies, and all those who "seem to express relations of sensuality, rebellion, and acknowledged dependence" and thereby threaten the integrity of the liberal fragment. "The Negro threat to property values, the students' rejection of property, and the Communists' desire to take it away— all metaphorically threaten ownership and control of the self, that is, self-government, self-mastery, and protection against the world of significant objects." To protect the fragment from these threats, southern Californians elected Ronald Reagan governor (Rogin 1970b, 193, 188, 198–99, 200).

By the end of the eighteenth century—so Rogin's thesis would seem to run—the self-control demanded by the culture of the liberal fragment was already almost impossible for individuals to sustain. By the end of the nine-

---

[13] Rogin 1970b, pp. 185, 187. This essay, "Southern California: Right-Wing Behavior and Political Symbols," represents the turning point in Rogin's intellectual development. It looks back to his studies of group politics and voting behavior, as represented in "Progressivism and the California Electorate" (Rogin 1970a) and before that, in *The Intellectuals and McCarthy* (Rogin 1967). It looks forward to his "radical psychoanalysis of politics" exemplified in *Fathers and Children* (Rogin 1975) and in the essays in *"Ronald Reagan," the Movie* (Rogin 1987).

teenth century the optimism underlying "democratic capitalism," the conviction that material success was possible through individual self-mastery, was
becoming less and less relevant to the realities of an industrialized, bureaucratized society. By the latter part of the twentieth century, the American liberal
fragment was forced to confront an increasingly "alien" world of assertive
nonwhites and revolutionary socialists. At each point angry, frustrated, and
frightened Americans looked for scapegoats and thus became the consumers
for what Rogin calls "political demonology." Throughout our history, he argues, political and intellectual leaders have transformed threatening groups
into inflated, stigmatized, and dehumanized "monsters." Thus, Indians and
blacks became cannibals and rapists, radical labor leaders were transformed
into bomb-throwing anarchists, and Communists were portrayed as conspiratorial agents of the Kremlin (Rogin 1987, xiii and, in general, 44–80).

Those who over time have created these "demonological" images constitute what Rogin calls "a countersubversive tradition," and it is a tradition
that—unlike Hofstadter's "paranoid style"—"occupies not the political margins of America but its mainstream." In the twentieth century, that tradition
has been maintained not so much by the written word as by images on film.
Rogin has underscored the crucial role of the movies in several recent essays.
One reminds us of the importance of D. W. Griffith who (especially in his
racist masterpiece, *The Birth of a Nation*) "shifted the locus of the real in
America . . . by crystallizing demological images and placing them on film."
By "tapping collective fantasies" he "created a conviction of truth beyond
history," replacing conflicting interpretations of the past with a compelling
representation of it on the screen. From the great director who presided over
the birth of the movies it is but a short distance to the movie actor who became
president. Ronald Reagan, Rogin submits, had an identity crisis that was resolved only through his career as an actor: "he found out who he was through
the roles he played," and, moreover, he played those roles—at least the major
ones—in the morally simplistic and politically conformist movies made during
World War II and the early Cold War years. Like Griffith, Reagan was able to
crystallize demonological images for the wider public, in a rhetoric that like
Griffith's images on the screen, soars above reality. If as Rogin suggests the
rage induced by the lonely independence of life in the liberal fragment has
been sufficient over the years to elect Andrew Jackson and Ronald Reagan,
and the "countersubversive tradition" that began as a justification for a war
against "savage" Indians has culminated in a justification for a war against
the "Communist" government of Nicaragua, then his critique may indeed
have something to tell us about the origins and development of the American
right wing.[14]

Since about 1970, it is true, Rogin has not specifically labeled those he has

---

[14] Rogin 1987, pp. xiv, 5, 228, 3, 11–13, 29–42, xiv–xvi.

studied as "right-wing." One has to deduce it, therefore, from the parallels he draws—between, for example, the Jacksonians and southern California suburbanites. That particular analogy may stun those still under the spell of Arthur M. Schlesinger, Jr.'s, laudatory *The Age of Jackson*, but Rogin is by no means alone among contemporary scholars in emphasizing Jackson the defender of slavery and the architect of Indian removal; in an intellectual milieu sensitized to the historic oppression of racial minorities, Jackson emerges as a very different figure than he did forty years ago.[15] Rogin, of course, is making a much broader argument, and it may not be much of an exaggeration to conclude that, especially in his recent work, he sees American political culture as a whole as "right-wing" both in its traditional commitment to "white supremacy" and in its continuing commitment to "free enterprise."

The Convergence of Lipset and Rogin: The Sources of Right-Wing Behavior

Since the differences between Lipset's interpretation and Rogin's will become obvious (and have in any case been emphasized by Rogin), in order to grasp the contribution of both men it is necessary to point out the degree to which their models of right-wing behavior do in fact converge. One specific area of analysis, for example, on which they concur is that the core of the American right wing consists of white Protestants. That Lipset takes this position is fairly obvious: as he wrote in the mid-1960s, one of the major consequences of twentieth-century politics has been the increasing degree to which "the ideal-typical Republican Protestant, God-fearing, deeply religious, moral, middle-class, living in a stable, nonurban community" sees himself "losing control of the society which his father had dominated and which he had learned to expect as his birthright" (Lipset 1968, 307). The "backlash movements" analyzed in *The Political of Unreason* are simply examples of this larger development. The parallel conclusion has to be inferred from Rogin's work, but certainly those he studied in Indiana who voted for Goldwater, as well as the persistently right-wing voters in southern California, were disproportionately Protestant (Rogin 1969, 36; Rogin 1970b, 173–74). Neither Rogin nor Lipset are able to ignore the facts that leap out from the survey data: Catholics were more likely to support McCarthy than Protestants[16] and outside the South about as likely to support Wallace in 1968 (Lipset and Raab 1970, 387). Still, one comes away from both authors with the sense that white Protestant support

---

[15] For the relevant scholarship on Jackson and the Indians, see the citations in Rogin 1975; for that on Jackson and slavery, a good place to begin is Leonard R. Richards, "The Jacksonians and Slavery," in Lewis Perry and Michael Fellman, eds., *Antislavery Reconsidered: New Perspectives on the Abolitionists* (Baton Rouge: Louisiana State University Press, 1979), pp. 99–118.

[16] Lipset and Raab 1970, pp. 231-32; Rogin 1967, pp. 238–39.

for these right-wing politicians represented a durable base: midwestern-con-
servative in the case of McCarthy, southern-segregationist in the case of Wallace. Catholic support, on the other hand, was more the result of immediate
concerns, whether the recent extension of Soviet control over Eastern Europe
in the first case, or urban riots and rising crime in the second.[17]

There is also a convergence in the approach both men take toward explaining right-wing behavior. Now over the years Rogin has maintained the contrary, and he has insisted that he differs from Lipset in his interpretation of the
motivations that induce individuals to support right-wing candidates or join
right-wing organizations. In a recent essay, for example, he distinguishes between two general approaches to the problem: one, which he calls "realist,"
stresses "interests" and sees political actors pursuing rational objectives; the
other, which he calls "symbolist," stresses "anxieties" and sees political actors as unconscious of their motivations. He charges social scientists of Lipset's generation with emphasizing the latter to the exclusion of the former and
calls for a new integration of both approaches (Rogin 1987, 272–81). There
are problems with Rogin's analysis here. His dichotomy is too sharply drawn,
and in some cases he misrepresents those he intends to categorize—including,
among others, Lipset. He completely overlooks the scholars who, building on
Gusfield's work, have argued that both the defense of values and "lifestyles"
and the decision to engage in "symbolic politics" are as conscious, as fully
"rational," as the pursuit of economic interests. Most important of all, a review of Rogin's own work indicates that his analysis of motivation resembles
Lipset's in a significant number of ways.

Critics of Lipset's work, including Rogin, are surely correct to point out the
way he has emphasized "anxiety" as the major source of right-wing behavior;
Lipset himself insists upon it. Throughout *The Politics of Unreason*, for example, he stresses the way "customs, mores, sexual habits, styles of life" are
"cultural baggage," accompanying but not creating "backlash" movements.
One such example of "cultural baggage," in Lipset's view, is "religious fundamentalism," which often accompanies "people or groups who are the objects rather than the beneficiaries of change" but does not itself "create right-
wing extremism." Another is nativism: "right-wing extremist movements
have not sprung up out of a nativist bigotry: they have sprung up out of a backlash against change which invented or reinvented nativist bigotry" (Lipset and
Raab 1970, 488, 118, 491). It would be hard to assert more strongly the proposition that the motivation leading to right-wing political behavior is not a
specific concern—whether over groups perceived as threatening, or challenges

---

[17] This, admittedly, is an impression, but one based on comments scattered throughout both
authors' work. See, for example, Lipset 1955, pp. 201–6; Lipset and Raab 1970, pp. 509–12;
Rogin 1966, p. 107; Rogin 1968, pp. 310–12.

to traditional values—but a general anxiety over change, which in turn springs from a loss of status.

In what ways does Rogin differ from this line of analysis? Just as much as Lipset he sees the right wing as motivated by anxiety. He simply relocates the sources of that anxiety. If Lipset focuses on the inability of a particular group to maintain its status in a society suffused with egalitarian-democratic values, Rogin emphasizes the malformation of individual personality in a society dominated by a liberal-capitalist ethos.

Like Lipset, furthermore, Rogin does not imply that the entire right wing is driven by anxiety. He, too, has another way of explaining motivations for right-wing political activity, as indicated by his discussion of a "realist" approach as an alternative to a "symbolist" one. What does he mean by such a "realist" approach, and to what kind of individuals does he see it as applicable? The fact that the first book he cites as exemplifying the "realist" approach is Charles Beard's classic *An Economic Interpretation of the Constitution* (Rogin 1987, 273, 350n) both informs us that "realists" study elites pursuing their "interests" and suggests the problems with the "realist" approach. When Beard decided to look behind the framers' publicly professed patriotism and explore the way their financial holdings would benefit from a change in government, he became a major intellectual figure; but in his analysis he left crucial questions unresolved. As Hofstadter pointed out, at a fundamental level Beard was simply unclear as to whether he meant that "the Founding Fathers were trying to line their own pockets" or that "they saw public issues as they did because they had certain kinds of interests."[18] Because Beard was one of the shapers of twentieth-century political science in the United States, his influence—including this ambiguous view of motivation—has been profound. Many of those Rogin calls "realists" have followed in Beard's footsteps: they too have studied elites and have rather easily been able to show that in many cases altruistic rhetoric covers material interests. What they have not been able to determine is whether this correlation comes from conscious duplicity and manipulation, as Beard's "muckraking" contemporaries would have assumed, or whether, as Marxists would argue, it reflects the way their view of the world is shaped by their position in the social structure.

The question of conscious duplicity, raised but not resolved by Beard and successive "realists," has particular resonance for any analysis of the American right wing, for two reasons. There is, first of all, as a variety of observers have noted over the years, the tendency of right-wing activists to lose a sense of proportion. Consider, for example, the McCarthyites' fixation with the ineffectual American Communist party and the tiny number of Communists in

[18] Hofstadter, *The Progressive Historians: Turner, Beard, Parrington* (New York: Knopf, 1968), p. 213, and generally pp. 212–18.

the foreign policy apparatus in the 1940s; or the conviction of anti-ERA activists in the 1970s that the amendment would legitimize homosexual marriages. Inevitably, journalists and social scientists alike have wondered how the sophisticated businessmen and politicians funding and endorsing these activists could believe these things. Second, on most of the occasions covered in this book, the institutional agent of right-wing reaction has been the Republican party, which has put Lipset in the awkward position of having to explain why the party representing the better educated—those who according to survey data are more cosmopolitan, more liberal on noneconomic issues including tolerance for dissent and alternative gender roles[19]—has also been the party of the "backlash." His solution has been to make Republican politicians the key figures in reconciling their "cosmopolitan" party with "backlash" movements among the less educated but gives us no clue as to what these politicians actually believed (Lipset 1968, 306–7, 320–21).

Rogin's response to the question of elite duplicity and manipulation has gone through several phases. As first he leaned toward the "realist," Beardian perspective which had become dominant in political science. Following the insights of his mentor at the University of Chicago, Grant McConnell,[20] Rogin argued in *The Intellectuals and McCarthy* that elites use the rhetoric of "grass roots democracy" not because they actually favor "democratic participation and popular control" but because it is politically effective (Rogin 1967, 50–51). Where Lipset and the other contributors to *The New American Right* went wrong in his estimation was in taking this "populist" rhetoric at face value, not realizing that it often "functions to protect the power and conservative interests of locally powerful groups"—in McCarthy's case, of the "local elites . . . based in the conservative small towns and small cities of the Middle West," who were defending their power against the New Deal and the labor movement (Rogin 1967, 215). Rogin implied that those local elites who were McCarthy's initial supporters and, more clearly, the Republican politicians at the national level had agendas extending beyond the investigation of supposed Communists in the State Department. But like Beard and the other "realists," Rogin failed to make clear the extent to which these elites believed their own rhetoric: did they accept McCarthy's charges or simply regard him as a useful tool against their opponents in the Democratic party and the unions? If, as

[19] Lipset 1960, pp. 101–5, 298–301; Lipset and Raab 1970, pp. 432–49.

[20] Grant McConnell, *The Decline of Agrarian Democracy* (Berkeley and Los Angeles: University of California Press, 1953); McConnell, *Private Power and American Democracy* (New York: Knopf, 1966). McConnell's influence on Rogin is most evident in the latter's essays on the ideology and organization of the American Federation of Labor: "Voluntarism: The Political Functions of an Antipolitical Doctrine," *Industrial and Labor Relations Review* 15 (July 1962): 521–35; and "Nonpartisanship and the Group Interest," reprinted in Rogin 1987, pp. 115–33. For evidence of a more general influence, compare McConnell, *Private Power and American Democracy*, pp. 352–57, with Rogin 1967, pp. 268–72.

Rogin seems to imply, their "populism" was little more than a public-relations ploy, how deep was their "anticommunism"?

Rogin's next series of studies of the American right wing was of those who voted for George Wallace in the 1964 primaries, but—unless one counts the personal aides whom the governor was able to patch together as a campaign organization as an elite—no elites were involved. Then, for unknown reasons, Rogin chose to deemphasize elites in his essay on southern California. By the time he returned to the study of elites his entire approach to politics had been transformed, and he had become convinced that Freudian theory was closer to the language of these men than the political scientists' favored categories of "pragmatism, behaviorism, and materialism." With this new critical tool he now believed that he could overcome what he saw as "a peculiarly split view of human existence in which symbolizations of meaning operate in a closed universe of their own, divorced from the 'real' facts of historical causation."[21]

Rogin's attempt to understand the motivation of elite figures by applying psychoanalytic theories to their rhetoric and their lives produced a number of brilliantly written essays—on Jackson, on Griffith, on Nixon, and on Reagan[22]—that suggest both what Rogin has achieved and the limits of his achievement. Whatever the broader utility of psychobiography, he has certainly made an effective case that unconscious "anxiety" affects elite behavior as much as that of rank-and-file activists or members of the general public. The inner demons that pursue Rogin's Jackson are as powerful as those that (according to Lipset) lead individuals into "backlash" movements and are far more vividly delineated. At the same time, however, Rogin's attempts to tie these anxieties to more substantial "interests" are too loosely drawn to fulfill his larger objective. The "interest" of Jackson's supporters in territorial expansion and economic development is so obvious as to make their "anxieties" seem superfluous (Rogin 1975, esp. 75–110, 165–205, 296–313). Nor are Rogin's attempt to connect Griffith's anxieties about racial minorities to the politics of the Wilson administration, and his implication that somehow the enthusiasm for *The Birth of a Nation* reflected contemporary elite "interest" in a subordinate labor force, particularly persuasive (Rogin 1987, 192–98).

In the course of their scholarly careers Lipset and Rogin have each tried to analyze the motivations that lead men and women to vote for right-wing candidates or join right-wing organizations; they have ended with remarkably similar conclusions. Initially, both scholars proceeded from "realist" assumptions, and stressed the way in which elites created or at least sustained right-wing movements for their own purposes. For Lipset this was the case with

[21] Rogin 1975, p. 12. A decade later he was considerably more confident about his approach, writing that "American political demonologists speak a sexually charged, familial political language; no Freud is required to uncover it" (Rogin 1987, p. 287).

[22] On Jackson, Griffith, and Reagan, see the citations above; on Nixon, see Rogin 1987, pp. 100–14.

Republican politicians generally as they searched for new electoral cleavages to exploit; for Rogin it was the case for local elites in the Midwest when, operating through the Republican party, they sought to regain national power in the late 1940s and early 1950s.

Then, Lipset began to emphasize a theme he had already developed, the "anxieties" that led individuals negatively affected by social change to participate in "backlash" movements that sought to preserve their status. About the time Lipset worked through this line of analysis in *The Politics of Unreason*, Rogin also began abandoning his earlier emphasis on "interests." Supplementing Hartz's interpretation not with Beard and McConnell but with psychoanalytic theory, he now decided to focus on the content of political and cultural leaders' rhetoric, emphasizing the way their use of a particular "set of symbols" sprang from "partly conscious and partly unconscious . . . sources in human personality and in liberal culture" (Rogin 1975, 12). Most recently, he appears to be attempting to reintegrate his earlier concern with "interests"; his criticism of Lipset and others on that score may possibly indicate a personal decision to reconsider his own emphasis on "anxiety."[23]

Through all their shifting emphases on "anxiety" and "interest," both Lipset and Rogin have, most of the time, been unwilling to accept the stated goals of right-wing activity as offered by the participants themselves. For both scholars, unconscious "anxieties" (though they explain their origins very differently) and a certain kind of "interest" suggesting elite duplicity (which neither of them fully explains) have been the key categories of motivation. This sets them—and indeed the scholarly literature they have influenced, which dominates this book—apart from those social scientists who in the past few years have insisted on the relative autonomy of values (worldviews, ideologies) and have emphasized the extent to which they cannot be reduced to either the projection of unconscious "anxieties" or the rationalization of material self-"interest."[24]

[23] Note for example his reference to his own work in the 1970s which "bore unacknowledged resemblances to the approach I had originally opposed" (Rogin 1987, p. 274).

[24] As the analysis in the following chapter should make clear, I am myself sympathetic to interpretations of political behavior that emphasize the relative autonomy of values. But unless very carefully framed, such "cultural" interpretations can raise more issues than they resolve; and there are questions they cannot answer.

One influential critique, for example, of the tendency of social scientists to "explain" attitudes (issue-positions, worldviews, "ideologies") through "interest theories" or "strain theories" has been that of Clifford Geertz. In his call to scholars to see "ideologies" primarily as mapping devices in which humans try to comprehend a "problematic social reality," he has certainly not lacked disciples. But some of those who claim to have followed him seem to have missed his point that "the demand for a nonevaluative concept of ideology is not a demand for the nonevaluation of ideologies" (Geertz, *The Interpretation of Cultures: Selected Essays* [New York: Basic Books, 1973], p. 200n). The epistemological modesty resulting from this oversight, one that characterizes some of the most recent social science scholarship, can be seriously misleading. To take a current example: feminists complain that they are victimized by a "patriarchal" order in

The Divergence of Lipset and Rogin: The Right Wing in Social Structure and in Historical Development

Lipset and Rogin do genuinely disagree, however, on two important issues. They disagree over the right wing's location in the American social and institutional structure, with Lipset seeing the right wing as peripheral and Rogin seeing it as central.[25] And they disagree over its position in the course of American history: for Lipset the right wing represents the past, for Rogin the present and quite possibly the future.

To say that Lipset sees the right wing as peripheral is not to say that he sees it as inconsequential. However much a minority or however transient the anxieties that motivate them, his "backlash" movements can have a profound effect on public policy. In his very first essay on the subject, "The Sources of the 'Radical Right,' " he drew an analogy between the mid-1950s and the mid-1920s when "the Klan died and the anti-radical hysteria subsided, but the quota restrictions based on the assumption of Nordic supremacy remained. Clearly the recent defeat of Senator McCarthy and the seeming decline of radical right support have not resulted in an end or even a modification of many of the measures and administrative procedures which were initiated in response to radical right activity" (Lipset 1955, 218–19).

---

which fundamentalists are but the most aggressive representatives; Falwell and his allies charge that they are confronted by a dominant "secular humanist" establishment that relentlessly pushes the feminist agenda. Both sides may be wrong but they cannot both be right; and for the scholar to present both sides and end the discussion there seems to me an abdication of intellectual responsibility. The dominant tendency in twentieth-century American social science (shared by both Lipset and Rogin) at its worst has tended toward reductionism of one kind or another, but its central insight—that it is the scholar's task to look behind the "rhetoric" to perceive the "reality"—still seems to me essential.

There are also problems with Geertz's approach itself. It has frequently been observed that he is better at explaining how "ideologies" function than in explaining what causes them and what motivates individuals to act upon them. Those questions remain unanswered, but they are of particular relevance to this book. Certainly Geertz helps one understand how the activists opposing the Equal Rights Amendment could, having constructed a symbolic world that dictated a specific order of gender relationships, so easily believe that the ERA would require unisex toilets. His approach provides no guidance, however, as to the motivations of those who fabricated this rumor—which brings us back to the conscious manipulation assumed under at least one version of the "interest theory." Geertz and his disciples are quite right to note that such a theory is limited; but in the age of "spin control," "negative campaigns," and "disinformation," it is also invaluable.

[25] My use of the terms "center" and "periphery" is compatible with that proposed by Edward A. Shils, who sees the "center" as both "the center of the order of symbols, of values and beliefs, which govern society" and the center of the "structure of activities, of roles and persons, within the network of institutions" upholding those symbols and values. The problem here of course is that Lipset and Rogin disagree on what the "central" values and institutions actually are. For Shils's definitions, see his essay, "Center and Periphery," in *Center and Periphery: Essays in Macrosociology* (Chicago: University of Chicago Press, 1975), pp. 3–16.

Rather, for Lipset the "backlash" movements are peripheral both because their participants—mainly lower-middle class and working-class individuals—are remote from the centers of power and, even more, because "backlash" movements by definition are reactions to larger, ongoing processes of societal transformation. In a recent essay he has written that "the recurrent emergence of right-wing, that is preservatist, movements . . . is endemic in the processes labeled as development" because such processes necessitate "changes in values, in concepts of moral rectitude, as well as in the status accorded to different activities and roles." Thus, it is not surprising that "the most developed nation," the United States, has produced a proliferation of "backlash" movements (Lipset 1985, 253, 276). What has prevented these movements from achieving even more of their goals has been not so much public opposition (though this has varied over time) as American political institutions, especially the party system. "The sheer practicalities of American coalition politics have often militated against the acceptance of all-out monistic politics by 'respectable' national political leaders or the 'respectable' practice of national politics" (Lipset and Raab 1970, 501).

On this issue Rogin has consistently challenged Lipset. At first he concentrated on trying to show that voters supporting right-wing candidates—surely one aspect of participation in a "backlash" movement—came from higher social strata than Lipset had indicated. This was the approach he followed in his study of McCarthyism, when he noted the role of local midwestern elites in backing McCarthy, pointed out the way the senator's electoral support in Wisconsin paralleled the traditional Republican vote, and played down whatever broader patterns of support could be extracted from survey data as largely irrelevant to explaining McCarthy's success. Rogin's next study of right-wing behavior—of those who voted for George Wallace in the 1964 primaries—also included a focus on Wisconsin, where he found the core of Wallace's support in the upper-middle-class suburbs. These Wallace voters, who on the basis of ecological data, "appear to be educated, successful, upwardly mobile professional men and corporate executives," suggested to him that "extremist behavior may be more integrated into modern American institutions and social life than many commentators would like us to believe" (Rogin 1966, 106–7).

That larger thesis received a blow, however, when it became clear that this configuration of Wallace support was unique to Wisconsin in 1964. Neither in the Indiana and the Maryland primaries that year nor anywhere in the general election of 1968 were middle-class voters more likely than working-class voters to vote for Wallace. Although, as Richard Hamilton suggested, the differences in the vote Wallace received from the two classes may not have been especially significant, in no way was the center of gravity where Rogin initially thought it was. Perhaps because of these difficulties, Rogin began to deemphasize class factors and bring race and culture to the fore: what we remember about the backgrounds of his right-wing southern California suburbanites is that they were white Protestants.

When Rogin shifted his attention to the rhetoric and personality of American political and cultural leaders, of course, the case for his subjects' centrality was obvious and he was spared having to locate them in the social and institutional structure. In the specific case of anticommunism, he seems to be saying in his recent work that "political demonology" was manufactured at the center and spread to the periphery. He makes the point most clearly in his discussion of the explicitly anticommunist films of the early 1950s—movies such as *I Was a Communist for the FBI* and *My Son John*—which "represent the feelings Hollywood wanted the rest of us to mirror as our own." Contrary to the analyses of Lipset and others, "such movies are not evidence for a mobilized, popular anticommunism" but examples of the way institutions themselves "formed a public opinion fearful of unorthodox political ideas and quiescent at their suppression" (Rogin 1987, 262).

In addition to differing over whether the right wing occupies a "central" or a "peripheral" position in the social structure, Lipset and Rogin also disagree over how to place it in the perspective of American historical development. Lipset has consistently seen the right wing as representing values that, however widely shared in the past, are now held by a dwindling minority. Nowhere else, it might be added, does his background in the left-wing politics of the 1930s reveal itself so clearly as in his "progressive" orientation toward history. Writing in the late 1960s, for example, at a time when Wallace was emerging as a national figure, Lipset made a point of emphasizing the degree to which "the politics of the 'backlash,' whether religious-cultural, economic, or racially motivated, is a consequence of the fact that the United States is becoming more liberal" (Lipset 1968, 324). Again, in the first year of the Reagan administration, when other commentators were making much of the political impact of the Moral Majority and similar organizations, he dissented. "What is most striking about the right-wing backlash movements . . . during the last decade," he wrote—whether the "single-issue movements" opposing abortion and the ERA or the "widespread efforts to mobilize fundamentalist Christians"—"is not the fact that they exist, but their weakness," particularly when compared to earlier "backlash" movements (Lipset 1985, 276, 284).

Rogin, of course, would differ: the very fact that he can find a persistent "countersubversive tradition" running from the colonial era to Ronald Reagan indicates that he is far more skeptical about the inevitability of progress in America; and, as in the case of Lipset, Rogin's view may well reflect his own generational experience, with the almost millennial hopes engendered and then shattered in the 1960s.[26] Their differences over the extent to which Amer-

---

[26] My analysis of the way Lipset's and Rogin's different views of progress reflect their generational backgrounds is indebted to the very similar distinction Gene Wise has made between the

ica really is moving toward tolerance and acceptance of diversity separates the two scholars, and in turn shapes their perception of the right wing and the cultural and institutional support it receives.

These interpretations of the American right wing as developed by Lipset and Rogin are hardly the only ones imaginable; but they do represent the only ones that have actually encompassed the American right wing as a whole. As such they help overcome the fragmentation—the organization-by-organization, issue-by-issue analysis—that has characterized so much of the existing scholarship on the subject. More than is commonly recognized, these interpretations converge: not only do both men see the core of the American right wing as consisting of white Protestants, but they typically locate the sources of right-wing behavior either in terms of unconscious psychological tensions or all-too-conscious manipulation.

Where Lipset and Rogin differ is in the way they locate the right wing in the larger social and institutional structure and in the course of American historical development. In this debate Rogin would at first glance appear to have the better argument: the right wing is socially and institutionally less peripheral, and historically less the product of a succession of group anxieties, than Lipset would imply. Its centrality over time undoubtedly has been due, as Rogin would be quick to point out, to its connections with elites. But the right wing's relationship with elites has been a far more complicated affair than Rogin intimates; and its strength has also come from the degree to which the creed its spokesmen have expounded has engaged the loyalties of millions of Americans, not all of them reducible to the category of "white Protestants."

Before we can begin to place the right wing in perspectives other than those that Rogin's framework permits, and before we can retrieve what is still valuable in Lipset's interpretation, however, it is essential that we review, for the last time, what the accumulated scholarship has or has not told us about the American right wing since World War II. The conclusion that follows, therefore, will begin with a summary of that scholarship and then go on—reworking the insights of Rogin and Lipset—to place the right wing in a broader historical perspective.

---

optimism of "Progressive" historians and the pessimism of the "New Left." Wise, *American Historical Explanations: A Strategy for Grounded Inquiry* (Homewood, Il.: Dorsey Press, 1973), pp. 85–86.

Sixteen

Conclusion: The American Right Wing in Perspective

THOSE WHO LIKE their conclusions neat and their summations tidy will be disappointed with the scholarly studies of the American right wing. The steady accumulation of research on each of the major aspects of the right wing since World War II—support for Senator Joseph McCarthy, the "radical right" organizations of the early 1960s, the presidential campaigns of George Wallace, and the mobilization of the "new right" in the late 1970s—has resolved many, but by no means all, of the relevant issues. In fact many of the scholarly debates have never really been concluded, leaving the rest of us with a whole series of unanswered questions and significantly qualified conclusions. Before we can make any attempt to see the American right wing as a whole and place it in a broader perspective, we have to see just which issues have been resolved by scholars in the past thirty years and which have not.

A Summary of the Research So Far

The first right-wing development that scholars analyzed—and indeed the one that provoked many of the arguments that would be debated through the 1980s—was the rise of Senator Joseph McCarthy. Today it is easy to identify McCarthy's career with the wider national obsession with domestic Communists and their ostensibly "subversive" activities which marked the early Cold War years. Those writing at the time were aware, however, that the two phenomena were in important ways distinct. Many prominent Americans concerned with the problem of "subversion" strongly opposed McCarthy's rhetoric and his tactics, while McCarthy himself had a surprisingly narrow focus, concentrating almost totally on what he viewed as "subversion" in the foreign policy apparatus of the United States Government. Because of the polarization he created, the question of who supported McCarthy seemed at the time to be an important one. In retrospect this may not have been the most important question to ask but (the point cannot be made too often) it was the question scholars asked at the time.

McCarthy's foreign policy preoccupations provided one point of departure. The pioneering investigations of the journalist Samuel Lubell had suggested that McCarthy might have used the foreign policy defeats of the early Cold War years to exploit the residual "isolationism" of German- and Irish-Americans who had resented America's alliance with Britain in two world wars. At the same time, the enthusiastic support the senator received from Texas oil men seemed to indicate that his attacks on Harvard and the State Department might be especially appealing to the newly wealthy who felt excluded from the established citadels of wealth and respectability. Those possible interpretations, along with others, were incorporated in the most influential book ever written on the sources of McCarthy's support (and indeed on the contemporary American right wing): *The New American Right*, which appeared in 1955.

The contributors to that collection of essays offered two broad explanations for the base that made McCarthy's ascendancy possible. The first, offered straightforwardly by Richard Hofstadter and in a more modulated manner by Seymour Martin Lipset, was that McCarthy's strident "Americanism" fed upon the anxieties of those whose position in society was insecure: those from the old-stock upper class who were downwardly mobile, but even more those (often of recent-immigrant backgrounds) who were upwardly mobile. Because the contributors to *The New American Right* who emphasized this kind of "status politics"—Daniel Bell, David Riesman, and Nathan Glazer, along with Hofstadter and Lipset—never precisely defined what they meant by it, except that it was broadly noneconomic in nature, their arguments became almost impossible to confirm. Two empirical studies that did attempt to correlate attitudes toward McCarthy with "status" and other variables reached inconclusive results. Thereafter, "status" anxieties were seldom invoked as explanations of support for McCarthy, although as a concept "status politics" would take on a life of its own.

The second hypothesis offered in *The New American Right* was considerably more productive of controversy and raised issues that to this day have not been completely resolved. Primarily the contribution of Peter Viereck (who subsequently expanded his argument in *The Unadjusted Man*), it took off from Lubell's observation that, like McCarthy a generation later, Wisconsin's great insurgent senator Robert LaFollette had also drawn significant German-American support because of his opposition to American entry in World War I. Viereck then argued that, like LaFollette, McCarthy too had denounced eastern "pro-British" elites, and was thus in some sense his political heir, and beyond that of a midwestern insurgent tradition going back to the Populists of the 1890s. Viereck's argument soon met with dissent from historians and even more notably from the historically oriented political scientist Michael Rogin. In *The Intellectuals and McCarthy* (1967) Rogin pointed to important differences between the socioeconomic base of the constituencies supporting LaFollette and other insurgents and those later supporting McCarthy, and in the kind of "isolationism" they represented. To some extent his primitive methodology weakened his conclusions, particularly his attempts to trace the voting behavior of constituencies over time. Nonetheless, since the appearance of his book the putative Populist-LaFollette-McCarthy connection made in the 1950s, most notably by Viereck, has found few scholarly adherents.

Beyond challenging that specific connection, Rogin also doubted that any of the explanations offered in *The New American Right* was really useful, because McCarthy's career could more economically be explained as the result of partisan maneuvers. The voters may have been afraid of Communist "subversives," he argued, but their fear was not intense enough to decisively effect their voting behavior, let alone sustain the power of one senator. Building upon the insights of fellow political scientist Nelson Polsby, Rogin emphasized the way McCarthy's career was decisively advanced by factors other than popular support: by the prerogatives he possessed as a senator, by journalists either openly sympathetic or credulous enough to reprint his charges without examining them, and most of all by other Republican politicians who (at least until 1953–54) thought they could use him as a weapon with which to bludgeon the incumbent Democrats. In Rogin's view, it was the action of these strategically placed elites, and not the diffuse anxieties of the mass public, that best explained the McCarthy phenomenon. Beyond the opportunities that these elites provided McCarthy, his real support—and here Rogin's conclusions paralleled those of political scientist Earl Latham—came from midwestern conservatives within the Republican party, opposed to the New Deal, increasingly frustrated at their exclusion from power, and able to seize upon the most obvious foreign policy setback, the Communist victory in China, to advance their goals. As with his refutation of the idea that McCarthy came out of the midwestern insurgent tradition, so Rogin's interpretation of McCarthy's rise as the result of partisan elite frustration and not mass anxiety seems to have carried the day within the scholarly community.

But whatever else he accomplished Rogin had not eliminated the possibility that McCarthy represented a broader "populist" impulse, which could take right-wing as well as left-wing forms. Both Viereck and Edward Shils in *The Torment of Secrecy* had argued that McCarthy stood squarely in a "populist" tradition going back to the American Revolution, which distrusted intellectual as well as economic elites, emphasized direct democracy, and was impatient with procedural restraints. Rogin had engaged this argument by noting that since the early nineteenth century practically every politician, no matter how conservative, has claimed to represent "the people" against "the elite."

In the 1970s, however, a new interpretation of this "populist" impulse appeared, which could also be used to interpret support for McCarthy, due largely to the influence of the historian Robert Wiebe. Perceiving much of the last century of American history as revolving around the efforts of what he called "island communities" to retain their autonomy against the centralizing forces wrought by capitalist industrialization, Wiebe documented the wide variety of forms ("left-wing" and "right-wing") these efforts would take: the Farmers' Alliances and the Knights of Labor at one point, the revived Ku Klux

Klan and the movements led by Father Coughlin and Huey Long at another. McCarthy's kind of anticommunism, he argued, also drew on the fears of locally oriented Americans, who saw in "subversion" all that threatened their traditional way of life. For Wiebe and those influenced by him the impulses behind McCarthy could thus be seen as "populist"—but unlike that postulated by Viereck and Shils, a "populism" not so much aggressively majoritarian as defensively localist.

Although Wiebe tended to see united communities where others saw conflict, his interpretation had two great strengths. One was that it underscored the role of culture, not clearly reducible to economic interests, in shaping support for McCarthy. It may be, as Michael Miles suggested, that McCarthy's appeal was not so much to Republicans in general as to the less-educated Republicans in the small towns in the hinterland who were far more upset by the erosion of their Anglo-Saxon Protestant cultural dominance than by government restrictions on business. The other strength of Wiebe's perspective was that, by emphasizing the diffuse fears of change to which McCarthy appealed, it pointed toward the future; far better than Rogin's, it explained why McCarthy's most avid supporters could go on to become the core of the contemporary American right wing.

McCarthy's demise did not doom his supporters to political obscurity. On the contrary, the years immediately after his death in 1957 saw the first major phase of organization-building on the part of the contemporary right wing, most notably the creation of the John Birch Society, the Christian Anti-Communist Crusade, the Young Americans for Freedom, the New York Conservative party, and as a kind of culmination the Goldwater-for-President movement. In varying degrees these organizations revealed their McCarthyite connections by emphasizing the continued menace of an internal Communist conspiracy. Unlike McCarthy, however, they had positive agendas, which, in view of their demands for the restoration of laissez-faire and states' rights at home and total victory over Communism abroad, might be (and indeed were) called "radical."

Since the authors of *The New American Right* had been interested in McCarthy as a catalyst for larger social forces more than as a figure in his own right, it was not surprising that, in the context of all this right-wing activity, they updated and reissued their book as *The Radical Right* in 1963. The added essays were even more diverse than those in the first edition had been, but scholars largely failed to investigate the hypotheses advanced in those by Bell and Riesman, in many ways the most original and illuminating of all the contributions. Bell saw the united force behind the expansion of right-wing activity as the anxieties of those he termed "the dispossessed." In this category he placed residents of small towns, often of fundamentalist religious backgrounds, who saw the structures of the modern world challenging their commitment to individual effort and responsibility. That observation did indeed

attract scholarly attention, but Bell also considered "dispossessed" elites—
small in number but substantially more powerful than the activists within the
organizations—who played key roles in the apparently growing influence of
the right wing: middle-level managers threatened not only by government and
organized labor but by technicians within their own firms, and professional
military officers similarly losing influence over policy to specialists in international relations, management experts, and nuclear physicists.

Riesman was among the first to raise the possibility that the bellicosity of
the right wing drew upon the same sense of frustration that produced the
sweeping foreign policy commitments of the Kennedy administration, and that
the right wing's chief effects might be to reinforce the administration's interventionist tendencies in Cuba, Vietnam, and elsewhere in the world. Concurrent journalistic investigations substantiated many of these observations of
Bell and Riesman, adding that the firms underwriting the right wing's expansion included some of the country's largest, and that in foreign policy it was
no longer so clear where military influence ended and civilian influence began. But in retrospect the striking fact is that practically no social scientists
tried to investigate this emerging pattern of continuing interaction between the
right wing and important segments of both the business community and the
national-security bureaucracy.

Instead the overwhelming majority of those conducting empirical research
on the right wing in the early 1960s chose to study members of organizations,
their backgrounds and their attitudes. Because of the various methodological
limitations of these studies, the conclusions drawn must of necessity be qualified, which is doubly unfortunate since they are the only such studies that will
ever be undertaken. Of the relevant background variables, two clear conclusions emerged: these activists were all white and overwhelmingly Republican.
In addition, they were not likely to be Jews; further, the preponderance of
evidence suggests that if they were Protestant they were (as Bell had suggested) disproportionately from fundamentalist backgrounds. Their socioeconomic backgrounds varied significantly, however, as did their psychological
and attitudinal profiles.

These activists turned out in short to be surprisingly diverse; and so the
obvious next question was: what brought them all together? One solution was
to look for those cultural factors that might bring individuals from such different backgrounds into common cause, and the most obvious common denominator appeared to be the values associated with fundamentalist religious
groups that still adhered to Weber's model of "ascetic Protestantism." Some
preliminary research had already suggested that attendance at fundamentalist
churches pulled lower-class individuals (who might otherwise support government programs) in a politically conservative direction. Since the issue has
been misconstrued, it is important to emphasize that no scholar ever claimed
that the right-wing activists of the era were predominantly fundamentalists.

What they did notice was that there were too many right-wing activists whose commitments could not be reduced to simple economic interest. Many of the empirical studies, furthermore, did in fact reveal a fundamentalist correlation; and one suspects that if additional studies had been made of some of the more overtly fundamentalist groups (Billy James Hargis's Christian Crusade, for example) the correlation would have been clearer still.

All this is preparatory to summarizing the most influential concepts to come out of the era's research, those formulated by Hofstadter in his essays in *The Paranoid Style in American Politics* (1965). Ever since *The New American Right* ten years before, he had been reworking some of his ideas about the sources of the right wing. Then he had tried to account for support for McCarthy in terms of the suppressed rage of the children of recent immigrants against their parents which they displaced onto the elites whom McCarthy attacked. Now he was not so sure such a psychoanalytic approach was particularly productive and he began to consider cultural factors. In the years since *The New American Right* he had become increasingly convinced that American political culture had been shaped by the impulses of early modern Protestantism: in fact what he called "the paranoid style in American politics" represented a secularization of the saints' continual struggle against the deceitful agents of Satan. Finally, the appearance of Joseph Gusfield's study of the temperance movement, *Symbolic Crusade*, enabled Hofstadter to define "status politics" in far more specific terms. Gusfield had insisted that "status politics" involved a conflict over the allocation of prestige and over whose values would be legitimized, and far from being a projective rationalization (as Hofstadter had argued in 1955) was as rational a conflict as that over the allocation of economic goods.

As a result of these developments, by the time he wrote his essays in *The Paranoid Style*, Hofstadter was able to link the right wing to "status politics" through the medium of religion and of a broadly defined fundamentalism in particular. In this model the traditional values upheld by fundamentalists were increasingly rejected by dominant leaders and institutions, and so those who were most committed to these values looked for new leaders in the emerging "radical" right-wing organizations of the era.

The most significant right-wing development for which Hofstadter had to account was of course the Goldwater nomination of 1964. Although he could fairly easily place the man himself in his larger framework (the Goldwater campaign was less concerned with winning voters' support than with lecturing them on the superiority of the "fundamental" values they apparently had abandoned), he had greater difficulty explaining the men and women who actually made the Arizona senator the Republican presidential candidate. Had they been in some significant way "fundamentalist," his thesis would have been greatly strengthened; but, unfortunately, of the very few studies of the actual delegates none asked the question. Unconfirmed though part of Hofstadter's thesis is, it accounts for the breadth of the right wing of the era better than many of the competing explanations; and, more important, it remains a useful way of understanding certain strains in the broader American political culture that could crystallize in right-wing politics.

Along with many other commentators, Hofstadter assumed that Goldwater's defeat would mark the decline of right-wing influence and the beginning of an era of consensus presided over by Lyndon Johnson. In reality, Johnson's was the most divisive presidency in recent American history. Out of the conflicts over black demands, campus protest, and protracted war in Southeast Asia the right wing surged once again. Its most notable initial expression, however (the independent presidential candidacy of George Wallace in 1968), presented scholars with a puzzle. On the economic issues that had distinguished the right wing from its liberal opponents since the New Deal, the Alabama governor was far more clearly on the New Deal, liberal side. Yet, at the same time, his campaign was run by right-wing activists, notably those belonging to the John Birch Society, men and women who unlike the majority of Goldwater activists were alienated from the Republican party.

What then made it possible for these right-wing activists to work for a man whose economic positions were those of a New Deal liberal, and what does that tell us about the changing dimensions of the American right wing? The most obvious answer was that Wallace placed very little emphasis on economic issues in 1968: he was best known for his unrelenting attack on the Federal Government. Those who chose to look more closely found that behind his defense of states' rights lay his unyielding segregationist record as governor of Alabama, his condemnation of civil rights legislation in his 1964 primary challenge to President Johnson, and his consistent refusal to criticize the most blatant expressions of white-supremacist sentiment. Far more than any major politician before him, Wallace could be seen as a right-wing "populist," in his case a "populism" best subsumed under Wiebe's model as a determination of local communities to defend their way of life against alien and distant centers of power.

Social scientists investigating the Wallace candidacy tried to find out who in the public indicated support for Wallace in the summer and/or voted for him in the fall, and then suggest hypotheses as to why they did so. Half of Wallace's 13.5 percent of the vote came from the eleven ex-Confederate states, and only in the South was he a major candidate, carrying five states and coming in second in three. Given his segregationist record and his appeal to racial resentments, it seemed plausible that he might find the most favorable response within the South from those whites living in greatest proximity to blacks. The methods of ecological analysis usually used to test such a hypothesis were already under attack as unsound and misleading; but those scholars who insisted on the importance of "the politics of place" persisted in their efforts, refined their methods, and generally confirmed that pattern. Mean-

while, analyses of survey data produced a profile of the southern Wallace supporter that surprised no one. He was most likely to be a young man, employed
either as a worker or a farmer, resident of a small town, with relatively little
education, and often with fundamentalist religious views. He was already
hostile to the national Democratic party, having either voted for Goldwater in
1964 or not voted at all; he was opposed to civil rights legislation and had
negative attitudes toward blacks; and he was convinced that "Communists"
and "the Federal Government" were responsible for the trouble in the country.

   The situation outside the South was very different and raised the question:
were the motivations of pro-Wallace northern whites the same and if so why?
Survey data revealed that like his southern counterpart the northern Wallace
supporter was likely to be a poorly educated young man engaged in broadly
defined "manual labor," who in 1964 had either voted for Goldwater or not
voted at all, and as far as can be ascertained had views on issues comparable
to his southern counterpart. But unlike his southern counterpart he was more
likely to live in a large city than in a small town, and quite possibly he was a
Catholic rather than a Protestant. He was, in other words, far removed from
the rural fundamentalist milieu of Wallace support in the south. Why then
were his attitudes so similar?

   The most probing analysis of the northern urban working-class Wallace
voter came from the research team of Thomas Pettigrew, Robert Riley, and
Reeve Vanneman. Using the "relative deprivation" model already developed
by sociologists, they argued that these individuals voted for Wallace as a way
of expressing their anger at those around them who seemed to be making gains
they were not, professionals and white-collar workers as well as the increasingly militant blacks. Their feelings of deprivation, Pettigrew, Riley and
Vanneman continued, came not from their situation as individuals but from
their situation as a group, suggesting a relatively high degree of "class consciousness."

   The scholars' location of the core of the northern Wallace vote within the
urban working class was soon followed by the journalists' conclusion that
these workers had now become part of a "middle America" lashing back at
campus and ghetto protests, a great conservative upheaval that would redound
to the advantage of the Nixon administration. But this was a conclusion that
not all those studying the Wallace constituency accepted. For some, Robert
Kennedy's appeal to many of those northern workers who ended up voting for
Wallace demonstrated that their anxieties—their feelings of "relative deprivation," their sense that the government had forgotten them—could be
addressed in an enlightened manner. A more ambitious response was to challenge the journalists' basic premise and to argue instead that northern working-
class support for Wallace had been exaggerated; that racial motivations were
less significant in shaping this support than had been expected; and that in a

highly volatile political situation the single act of voting might not be the best way of indicating deeper patterns of support. J. Michael Ross, Vanneman, and Pettigrew undertook their own study and found that when asked to evaluate Wallace, middle-class Republicans were far more positive than might otherwise have been believed; that Wallace's northern support had more to do with his calls for victory in Vietnam and for forcible repression of disorder than with opposition to civil rights; and that the votes of northern whites upset by the pace of racial integration went preponderantly to Nixon, not to Wallace. The significance of these findings, it should be emphasized, came not from what they said about those who actually voted for Wallace nor from any disagreement over the generally right-wing nature of his appeal. Rather they helped turn attention away from the working class to the more affluent middle class as a possible repository of racist and repressive sentiments.

No scholar studying the Wallace phenomenon was more interested in exploring right-wing tendencies among the middle class than Rogin. Unlike other scholars, he did not spend much time investigating the Wallace vote in 1968, but instead analyzed the support Wallace had received in his first run in 1964 and the politics of southern California where right-wing Republicans exploited very similar anxieties. In his analysis of the 1964 primaries Rogin portrayed a middle class that not only had racist and repressive attitudes but was far more likely than the working class to act upon those attitudes in response to distant and abstract threats. In the case of southern California he broadened his analysis to argue that voters generally in that distinctively synthetic environment were likely to lose contact with reality and respond to such threats. Rather than abandon their dream, they turned their frustrations against the militant blacks and dissident youths who seemed to threaten it by voting for right-wing candidates such as Ronald Reagan.

The political contours of the late 1960s, Rogin noted, were very different from those of the early 1950s he had already studied. Then McCarthy had appealed primarily to Republicans and had pushed an issue that did not engage masses of Americans; but race had a reality that the Communist issue lacked and now partisan identification was breaking down. Wallace had run poorly in southern California because right-wing Republicans had already co-opted his issues, and Rogin surmised that nationally someone like Reagan could attract many Wallace voters by appealing to the same dreams and conjuring up the same symbolic threats he had done in California. Rogin's essay on right-wing behavior in southern California was insufficiently specific and in some ways overstated. Yet more than anyone else he made it possible to understand how, reacting to symbolic threats, Americans could be susceptible to right-wing appeals regardless of their socioeconomic background.

The potential breadth of Wallace's appeal was also the subject of the major attempt to put his candidacy in comparative historical perspective. The political scientist Walter Dean Burham chose to make the most frightening analogy possible, America in the 1960s with Germany in the 1920s and Wallace with Hitler. What particularly concerned him was why in Germany the trade unions and the Social Democratic party with which they were allied remained bulwarks against the Nazi surge, while in America the Democrats suffered massive defections in the South and the best the leadership of organized labor could do in the major industrial states was to hold their membership's vote for Wallace down to the level of that of nonunionized workers. The reason, he submitted, was that neither American unions nor parties provided their adherents with worldviews that would immunize them against political extremism. In Germany, the old middle-class parties were (unlike the Marxist Social Democrats) incapable of such immunization, and so their former members were particularly susceptible to the Nazi appeal. But while in Germany such middle-class liberalism was only one political tendency, in the United States it was the only political tendency.

A middle-class political culture such as the American, especially one within a fragmented governmental system, was in Burnham's view incapable of responding easily and creatively to massive social and economic change. In the American experience the only way the system could readjust was through critical realignments, series of elections in which old majorities dissolved and new ones lasting a generation or more were created. This had happened in the mid-1850s, in the mid-1890s, and in the early 1930s. In each case the realignment had been preceded by the appearance of third parties, and Burnham thought that Wallace's American Independent party might play such a role. Whether or not that happened—or whether realignment was still possible given the erosion of political partisanship—remained to be seen. But since the dislocations wrought by social and economic change persisted (most notably the migration of poor rural blacks into the central cities) and the dominance of middle-class values precluded a left-wing alternative, Burnham remained convinced that some kind of right-wing victory, in which Wallace voters would play a major role, would occur in the near future. He reached those conclusions in 1970; from that point on, every four years political commentators waited to see if the victory had been achieved.

Wallace would try again for the presidency in 1972 and 1976 but the issues that had engaged his supporters, and that Nixon as president had successfully exploited, were losing their salience. The ghettoes and campuses were once again somnolent, and both the containment of Communism in Southeast Asia and the elimination of racial segregation at home were increasingly regarded as the overcommitments of the 1960s. But placid though they may seem in retrospect, the mid-1970s were years of growing anxiety: the country was economically stagnant, plagued with inflation and recession; and the consequent erosion of American economic power in the world was accompanied by a widespread perception of military decline vis-à-vis the nation's adversaries. Taking advantage of those perceptions, conservative forces—in the business

community, among intellectuals, and within the national-security bureaucracy—took the offensive, going on to achieve an influence unprecedented in
the last half century. What attracted the most comment at the time, because
they had the most intense commitments and because many of them reached
down to the grass roots, were the movements and organizations subsumed
under the "new right." Although the "new right" had economic and foreign
policy agendas, what kept its troops in the field was their opposition to a whole
series of cultural developments that in some way challenged traditional concepts of sexuality and the family: the teaching of Darwinian evolution, modern
literature, and sex education in the public schools; the widespread availability
of pornography; the legalization of abortion; the resurgence of feminism; and
the rise of homosexual militancy. Though local activists remained preoccupied with individual issues, "new right" leaders were able to portray these
developments as "weakening America" and in doing so able to gain important
support from business and political elites.

Social science research tended to focus on the "profamily" activists fighting changes in the curriculum and the demands of the women's and gay liberation movements. From the accumulated studies two conclusions stood out.
First, the socioeconomic profile of these activists, especially as compared to
their feminist adversaries, was nowhere as significant as their overwhelming
religiosity, whether fundamentalist Protestant or Catholic. Second, the ongoing research revealed the essentially noneconomic nature of these conflicts:
many of them were over whether public policies should legitimize certain lifestyles (ordinances prohibiting discrimination against homosexuals, for example) or whether in doing so they would "dishonor" others (the Equal Right
Amendment's ostensible exaltation of the career woman at the expense of the
housewife). As a result of these conclusions, many scholars went back to the
battered but still durable concept of "status politics."

Though apparently without much utility in explaining Wallace support,
Gusfield's reformulation of the concept in the early 1960s—as encompassing
conflicts over the allocation of prestige, conflicts as basic and as rational as
that over the allocation of goods—seemed to offer the most useful model for
understanding the current struggles over sexuality and family-related issues.
As the concept began to be used again, however, it was further revised, so that
what emerged by 1980 as "the politics of lifestyle concern" bore only a faint
resemblance to the "status politics" offered by the contributors to *The New
American Right* a quarter century before. While the original formulators of
"status politics" had seen individuals' struggle to preserve their prestige as
primary and their defense of lifestyles or worldviews as secondary, in the late
1970s social scientists reversed the emphasis. Now the primary conflict was
seen as being over the prestige that should be attached to a particular lifestyle
or worldview; the issue of the prestige of specific individuals was derivative
from that. The "status" component in the conflicts over abortion and the

ERA, for example, arose not over the prestige that should be given individual women but over the legitimacy that should be accorded a religiously based worldview or one avowedly secular. As the 1970s ended, it became increasingly obvious that those who saw their traditional religious views under attack provided much of the impetus behind the movements against abortion, gay rights, and sex education.

The creation of the "new right" as an organizational structure—the network connecting these grass-roots "profamily" activists with major financial contributors, political strategists, and policy intellectuals—was the work of key individuals such as Richard Viguerie, Howard Phillips, Terry Dolan, and Paul Weyrich. The organizations these men created—Viguerie's direct mail operation, the National Conservative Political Action Committee, the Conservative Caucus, the Committee for the Survival of a Free Congress, the Heritage Foundation—were, like the similar first wave of organization-building in the early 1960s, largely ignored by social scientists. Their strategic goal—of uniting the "profamily" activists with economic and foreign policy conservatives in a broad movement that would take over the Republican party— attracted somewhat more scholarly attention. It became clear that it was their defense of the prerogatives of local communities to retain their traditional norms against the intervention of outside elites that justified their designation as "populists"; in contrast, their various connections with corporate sponsors dictated a far more orthodox economic agenda. By calling for the reduction of *federal* power, however, they could hold together both the "profamily" activists opposed to Supreme Court decisions and entrepreneurs seeking repeal of the new wave of environmental, safety, and antidiscrimination regulations.

Of far greater interest to social scientists was the effort of "new right" leaders to form links with the leaders of the evangelical Protestant community, a community whose quantitative growth and rising political consciousness attracted much comment in the mid-1970s. Although the politics of the evangelical rank-and-file was not yet clear, their most aggressive spokesmen— those expanding religious broadcasting, beginning "Christian" schools, and engaging in politics—were distinctly on the conservative side. The coming together of "new right" leaders and the politically active evangelical clergy at the end of the 1970s resulted in two new organizations that would serve both as pressure groups and political-action committees: Christian Voice and the Moral Majority. It would not be much of an exaggeration to say that the Moral Majority and its founder, Jerry Falwell, became for social scientists the center of attention.

The first wave of research established that while those actually watching Falwell's TV program and "the electronic ministry" generally did tend to be supportive of the Moral Majority there were far fewer of them than Falwell and his allies had claimed. Researchers then turned to analyses of Falwell's "potential" constituency and found that though many Catholics agreed with him on issues, the constituency consisted primarily of Protestant evangelicals. Previous analyses had revealed no overall correlation between religious and political conservatism among the general population; but the data underlying this analysis preceded the conflicts over women, sexuality, and the family. Evidence gathered during the 1970s indicated that evangelicals were more likely to oppose the ERA, legal abortion, and equal opportunity for homosexuals.

The massive victory of Ronald Reagan over incumbent President Jimmy Carter and the Republican recapture of the Senate in 1980 suggested not only to right-wing activists but to many journalists as well that the issues pushed by the "new right" and the mobilization of evangelicals on the part of groups such as the Moral Majority had a decisive effect on the outcome. The great majority of social scientists studying the election disagreed. Both survey data at the national level and local studies indicated that economic issues were paramount in 1980, with foreign policy issues occupying a secondary role. The issues that the "new right" in general and the Moral Majority in particular had emphasized—abortion, the Equal Rights Amendment, and the rest—on the other hand were of decisive importance for very few voters. Other data indicated that while white evangelical voters were more likely to vote Republican in the Senate contests, there was little evidence to indicate that even there Falwell's issues were decisive.

Did all this mean that the Moral Majority had no constituency whatsoever? Not quite. One problem that had made a resolution of that question so difficult was that researchers used different measurements of "evangelical": some used denominational affiliation, others response to survey items (on Biblical inerrancy, etc.). But a third possible definition—self-professed identification with evangelical groups—might have very different consequences. Researchers using that measure found that those who did so identify were not only more likely to vote for Reagan but to do so on the basis of their opposition to the ERA and abortion, thus closely approximating the model of those who were supposed to be mobilized by the Moral Majority. In contrast to Falwell's assumptions (and those of much of the media), however, the voters who fell into that category constituted only about 5 percent of the white population. And, although the evidence is not as unambiguous as it might be, there are strong indications that these individuals had already been voting Republican, which would help explain the finding that the new Reagan voters of 1980 were no more likely to be evangelical than those who had voted for Ford four years before.

Furthermore, contrary to the general profile of the broader ("potential") evangelical constituency—largely elderly, low-income, poorly educated—those in the public who actually supported the Moral Majority were quite different: young, affluent, and educated. Clearly, whatever the situation had been before, by the 1980s being upper-middle-class and fundamentalist were no longer inconsistent. To be sure, as the 1980s progressed other white evangelicals (most probably from more modest background) also moved over to the conservative Republican side; whether the long-awaited realignment had occurred (and Burnham for one believed it had not), something of the sort may well have taken place among white evangelicals. But if so it was almost certainly more the achievement of Ronald Reagan as president rather than of Jerry Falwell in 1980, in part because the Moral Majority remained suspect even among evangelicals who might otherwise have been supportive.

On the evidence now available, it is reasonable to conclude that the Moral Majority did not warrant the attention paid to it by social scientists. In that sense it was another example of the scholarly tendency over the years to limit the question of right-wing influence to analyzing the sources of support within the public for a few major figures and organizations: McCarthy, the John Birch Society, Wallace, and the Moral Majority. These analyses of mass support were of course interspersed with studies of right-wing activists, most notably in the early 1960s and again in the late 1970s. But for reasons that are difficult to comprehend, studies of public support and of individual activists were seldom undertaken concurrently. The resulting scholarly literature is thus skewed in unexpected and, at least from a historian's perspective, almost eccentric directions. We know, for example, far more about the men and women who belonged to the John Birch Society than we do about those who actually nominated Barry Goldwater for president in 1964.

But even if it has often produced uneven coverage and is sometimes bewilderingly fragmented, the alternation of social science research between studies of public support and studies of activists has given us a far fuller view of the American right wing than otherwise might be possible. Studies of right-wing activists over the years suggest a greater continuity in attitudes and values than might otherwise be suspected: in moving from the economic and foreign policy agenda of the Goldwater movement to the "profamily" emphases of the "new right," Phyllis Schlafly was by no means alone. Studies of public support over the years reveal the way the right wing has continually been searching for (and often finding) new issues to exploit: Communism in the early 1950s, the extension of federal power in the early 1960s, civil rights and black unrest in the late 1960s, changing concepts of women's roles and of sexuality in the late 1970s. And at various points right-wing candidates have attracted constituencies—workers, southerners, evangelicals—far removed from the upper-middle-class background of most of their initial supporters.

But the insistence of social scientists on locating either right-wing activists or supportive segments of the public in precise socioeconomic (or religious) categories has its limits. To see how the right wing developed and to explain its persistence over time, one must place it in some kind of broader historical perspective.

Toward a Further Understanding of the
American Right Wing

The two scholars, Lipset and Rogin, who have most persistently attempted to see the right wing as a whole, present divergent views. While both see the core of the American right wing as consisting of white Protestants, they differ in their estimation of its place in the larger social and institutional structure and in the course of American historical development. One reading of the differences between them would be to say that for Lipset the right wing draws its support from peripheral segments of the population trying to protect their "status" from the impact of larger societal changes, while for Rogin the right wing gains its strength both from the support given it by elites within major institutions and—a quite different argument—from its defense of values central in American political culture. To more fully understand the American right wing, however, it is necessary to see the ways in which Lipset's and Rogin's interpretations (and by extension those of other social scientist they have influenced) are not necessarily exclusive, to redefine some of the categories they use, and ultimately to move beyond them.

Rogin is quite right to stress the central role of elites in shaping the right wing, but to confine the debate within his framework is ultimately fruitless because many of his categories in fact represent irrelevant dichotomies. In a recent essay, for example, he contrasts two views of the McCarthy era: one (with which he appears to agree) that sees repression moving "out into the countryside from Washington" and other centers of power, and one (which he attributes to Lipset) that sees "provincials from the hinterlands attacking cosmopolitan values and groups" (Rogin 1987, 273). Actually, we have to choose between them only if the two views are contradictory, with *either* an "elite" that dominates the "masses" *or* "masses" that threaten an "elite." Without denying the utility of an elite/mass dichotomy in other areas of research, the insistence of many social scientists on making such a distinction in analyzing the American right wing has distorted much of the work we have reviewed. These scholars need to be reminded, as the British political scientist Margaret Canovan has put it, that far from there being "*one* people (whether massively barbarous or united in simple common sense) and *one* elite (whether enlightened and heroic or snobbish and fraudulent," in fact "any actual confrontation is likely to be more complex than that." "In real life there are generally members of the elite on both sides of a conflict," and " 'the people' . . . are generally even less homogeneous than the elite" (Canovan 1981, 258). In short, there are many conflicts—including most of those covered in this book—in which "elites" and "masses" both divide, with segments of each interacting with those among the other with whom they agree.

With that caveat in mind, let us return to Rogin's contrast between "Wash-

ington'' and "provincials from the hinterlands.'' Why do we have to accept
the contrast in the first place? Thirty years before Rogin's essay appeared,
after all, Edward Shils had seen Washington as dominated by "provincials
from the hinterlands.'' His error was to locate them all in Congress (Shils
1956, 105, 125, 140, 143) and in doing so to overlook those segments of the
bureaucracy that articulated right-wing values and served as agents of what
Rogin calls "political repression.'' To understand why the American right
wing continues to confound scholars who insist on distinctions between the
elite and the masses or who contrast the center and the periphery, it is essential
to investigate the social origins, professional careers, and ideologies of central
figures in the federal bureaucracy. Such an investigation would require another book, but a brief look at one figure—J. Edgar Hoover, a right-wing idol
and arguably the most important bureaucrat in the twentieth century—will
suggest the relevance of an analysis of these "provincial bureaucrats'' to the
understanding of the American right wing.

Now it is true that, as a number of recent studies make clear,[1] Hoover's
career was dominated by his total identification with the Federal Bureau of
Investigation. The priority he attached to the protection of the Bureau made
him cautious, willing to learn from past mistakes and eager to avoid unnecessary political risks. It thus produced reactions—most notably in his doubts
about the need to intern Japanese-American citizens during World War II and
in his skepticism about the Nixon administration's master surveillance plan
(the so-called Huston Plan) of 1970—not otherwise predictable. The same
commitment to "his'' Bureau dictated support for those presidents who supported him and determined personal relationships—such as his consistent loyalty to Roosevelt or his prickly relations with the Nixon White House—not
explicable on the basis of ideology alone. Those qualifications admitted, however, Hoover did have a consistent ideology that shaped the FBI's operations;
and it bears a marked resemblance to the views of the right-wing politicians,
activists, and voters analyzed in this book.

From the very beginning of his bureaucratic career, in the Justice Department during World War I, Hoover revealed a preoccupation with the beliefs
of individuals. As time went on, the problems with which the FBI was asked
to deal—crime in the 1930s, "subversion'' in the late 1940s and 1950s, protest and disorder in the 1960s—assumed in Hoover's mind cultural dimen-

---

[1] My discussion of Hoover is partly based on specialized studies, notably Kenneth O'Reilly,
Hoover and the Un-Americans: The FBI, HUAC, and the Red Scare (Philadelphia: Temple University Press, 1983), and David J. Garrow, *The FBI and Martin Luther King, Jr.* (New York:
Norton, 1981). Even more, however, I have been influenced by the interpretation in Richard Gid
Powers's biography, *Secrecy and Power: The Life of J. Edgar Hoover* (New York: Free Press,
1987). Unlike many of the other contributors to the growing Hoover literature, Powers seeks to
understand the man rather than simply condemn him; and, unless otherwise noted, my discussion
follows his.

sions, examples of a more general failure to obey immutable moral laws; and he continually urged his audiences to remember that "the basic decline of all civilizations in the past has been the debauchery of law and order." The institutions that had in the past served as bulwarks of these moral laws were in his mind steadily being weakened by the corrosive forces of intellectual skepticism: a generation before the advent of the "new right," Hoover warned against those who attacked parental authority in the belief that "youth should be self-directed," and he was found of describing Communism as "secularism on the march." In his mind of course Communism was the greatest threat of all; and even beyond his official charge of protecting national security, his view of it came to resemble Hofstadter's "paranoid style." For Hoover, Communism was "a way of life—an evil and malignant way of life. It reveals a condition akin to a disease that spreads like an epidemic and like an epidemic a quarantine is necessary to keep it from infecting the nation."[2]

The ideology that he bequeathed to the Bureau reflected his own background, which itself resembled the profile of right-wing activists uncovered by many of the scholars discussed in this book. Born in 1895 to a middle-class family of civil servants in Washington, D.C., Hoover preserved—as one biographer has noted—"a turn-of-the-century vision of America as a small community of neighbors, proud of their achievements, resentful of criticism, fiercely opposed to change." It was therefore not surprising that a man who maintained that vision so easily gained the support of masses of "old-stock Americans . . . who had traditionally defined themselves through invidious comparisons to outsiders" and who saw "the New Deal's indiscriminate sense of community" as "un-American."[3]

Unlike those whose rhetoric Hofstadter chose to investigate, Hoover was hardly marginal: in fact one historian has suggested that the FBI was the primary institutional force behind the anticommunist frenzy of the late 1940s and early 1950s.[4] On the other hand, the ultimate frustration of Hoover's vendetta against Dr. Martin Luther King, Jr., reveals the limitations of his power, and should remind us that what Rogin calls "a repressive politics that moves out of Washington" was never monolithic but rather, as Wiebe astutely pointed out, represented temporary convergences between "cosmopolitan" and "local" ("provincial") elites and constituencies. When, as in the late 1940s and the 1950s, Hoover could ally himself not only with congressional representatives of conservative local elites but enjoy universally favorable press coverage and receive the support of sympathetic presidents such as Eisenhower, he was at the height of his influence. But in the 1960s he was forced to maneuver in a more cosmopolitan environment—one increasingly committed, among

[2] Hoover, as quoted in Powers, *Secrecy and Power*, pp. 213, 261, 311, 289.

[3] Powers, *Secrecy and Power*, pp. 3, 308.

[4] O'Reilly, *Hoover and the Un-Americans*, p. x.

other things, to racial equality—than that to which he had been accustomed. Whatever concerns about "subversion" John and Robert Kennedy shared with him (concerns sufficient to authorize wiretaps on King's phone), Hoover's subsequent obsession with the civil rights leader's private life left most of official Washington unmoved. Paradoxically, even though he retained his popularity in "the hinterlands," a popularity that probably exceeded King's, his attempt to destroy the civil rights leader's reputation was thwarted by other elites in Washington, especially in the media: no *public* campaign against King ever materialized.

The power Hoover amassed and the support he enjoyed from so many ordinary Americans help clarify the way in which, far from being either an "elite" or "mass" phenomenon, either at the center or on the periphery, the American right wing has at various points been both—which suggests that, at least in this case, the dichotomies constructed by social scientists need to be refined. The story of Hoover's life, on the other hand—his ascent from middle-class origins even as his view of the world remained frozen in time— brings us to the second problem social scientists have had in analyzing the right wing: the problem of placing it in the perspective of American historical development.

Part of the problem here comes from the ambiguity of the concepts, crucial in the case of Lipset's work, though less so in the case of Rogin's, of "status" and "status politics." Whatever "status politics" entails, it can only be measured historically: if membership in a group is regarded as prestigious (or its members see themselves as so regarded) at one point in time but not at later points, only then can we say that the group has declined in status. The question of the applicability of "status" models to the American right wing, a question that engaged the attention of many of the historians and social scientists reviewed in this book, is thus directly related to the larger issue of the right wing's place in American historical development. If right-wing activists and voters come disproportionately from groups declining in status, then (as Lipset has always assumed) the right wing should steadily have been losing power and authority. This is a permissible reading of recent American history but hardly the only one; and insofar as the right wing seemed to gain power and authority in the years to between Goldwater's defeat and Reagan's election, that advance requires explanation. Perhaps the problem lies in the way Lipset and others developed the concept of "status politics" in the first place.

As the reader of this book will recall, the major problem of the "status politics" concept has been its imprecision, one of the legacies of its original formulation in *The New American Right*. Putting aside the literature on "status inconsistency" (which involves a somewhat different definition of "status"), at least three distinctive meanings have been given the concept. "Status politics" can refer to the political behavior resulting from an individual's social mobility upward or downward—or, more probably, from the mobility of the ethnic or religious group of which he or she is a member. "Status politics" can also refer to the behavior resulting from the increasing or decreasing prestige given a group with narrowly defined, often occupational, boundaries. Examples would include the late-nineteenth-century ministers and lawyers portrayed by Hofstadter in *The Age of Reform* and the military professionals after World War II portrayed by Bell in *The Radical Right*: in those cases (the concept implies) the group's political behavior was a response to their loss of prestige. Finally, "status politics" can refer to the prestige accorded a particular set of values with which various groups identify: the estimation in which these values are held by opinion leaders in the larger society determines whether these groups feel that their own prestige has been enhanced or threatened. It is in this last framework that social scientists have recently tried to understand the conflicts between "profamily" activists and their opponents as a primarily cultural dispute, as what has been called "the politics of lifestyle concern."

As far as the application of the original "status politics" model in *The New American Right* is concerned, one point cannot be repeated often enough because it has been so often overlooked: the essays in that book overwhelmingly focused on the "status politics" of the *upwardly* mobile. Hofstadter's "pseudoconservatives," Riesman's and Glazer's "discontented classes," and most of all Viereck's resentful coalition of Texas millionaires and Boston Irish—all fall into that category. Then, however, Hofstadter abandoned this line of argument and went off in a different direction, exploring in his books and essays the way old-stock Protestants' support of the right wing reflected their anxiety over the diminishing prestige their values were receiving from the larger society. Since he carried other analysts with him, one result of his shift in focus was that the relationship between "status politics" and social mobility he and others had originally posited was now identified with the relationship between "status politics" and conflicts over values. Even critics ignored the distinction, as when Rogin argued that those Wisconsin voters who supported Wallace in the 1964 primary "in no sense represent the declining values and lifestyles said to explain support for right-wing extremists" and then tried to substantiate his argument by pointing to their upwardly mobile careers (Rogin 1969, 106). Few of the scholars whose work we have reviewed seriously explored the possibility that it is upward mobility and the defense of traditional values which may be connected, that this may account for the attraction right-wing politics has had not only for the "new rich" but for segments of the middle class, and that it is this association with those of rising (not declining) status that helps makes the right wing so durable.

In this connection one cannot help noticing the odd way the strategic assumptions of the contemporary "new right" parallel Hofstadter's initial observations of over three decades ago. The most obvious case is that of Kevin Phillips, by far the most sophisticated right-wing political analyst of recent years. In the mid-1960s, even before the 1968 election results appeared to vindicate him, he had already concluded that "the great political upheaval of the 1960s" was not among the groups—radicalized students, angry blacks, antiwar liberals—that were receiving the attention of the media. Rather, it was "a revolt of the American masses who have been elevated by prosperity to middle-class status and conservatism. *Their* revolt is against the caste, policies, and taxation of Establishment liberalism." Who were these people who constituted what he than saw as "the emerging Republican majority"? In the East, clearly, they were "the sons and daughters" of immigrants: "Irish, Italians, and Germans" moving "up the ladder to middle-class status."[5] As far as the rest of the country was concerned, Phillips strongly implied a parallel development among old-stock migrants to the burgeoning metropolitan areas in the South and the West, the area he was among the first to call "the Sunbelt." By the early 1980s, he was speculating that the "revolt" of these upwardly mobile southerners and westerners arose from causes beyond their increased affluence and he now gave attention to the middle-class character of the evangelical-fundamentalist resurgence.[6]

The implications of Phillips's linkage between right-wing politics, on the one hand, and religiosity, upward mobility, and regional growth, on the other, deserve further comment. As those who have read my analysis of studies of the Moral Majority and the 1980 election will recall, he was hardly alone in attaching political significance to the increasing affluence of fundamentalists and evangelicals. But the potential impact of those findings on the way we look at the right wing should be emphasized because they challenge one of the most pervasive assumptions of scholarly analysis of the subject: namely, that the right wing is basically a coalition of two differently situated—and differently motivated—socioeconomic groups. Even Hofstadter, far more sensitive to the religious variable than many others, nevertheless concluded that the right wing drew its support from an upper middle class that "responds to ultraconservative economic issues as well as to militant nationalism and anti-communism" *and* from a lower middle class "somewhat less educated and less charmed . . . by old-fashioned economic liberalism but even more fearful of communism, which it perceives rather abstractly in the light of a strong evangelical-fundamentalist cast of thought."[7] Adding only "profamily" concerns to that purported lower-middle-class worldview, Hofstadter's characterization would be echoed in scholarly portrayals of the "new right" two decades later, with the result that the upper-middle-class segment of the right wing continued

[5] Kevin P. Phillips, *The Emerging Republican Majority* (New Rochelle, N.Y.: Arlington House, 1969), pp. 470; 29, 158; 260, 273, 281, 396, 433, 444.

[6] Kevin P. Phillips, *Post-Conservative America: People, Politics, and Ideology in a Time of Crisis* (New York: Random House, 1982), pp. 180–92, especially pp. 182–83.

[7] Hofstadter 1965b, p. 72. In fairness, it should be noted that he did say that at points the two groups overlapped, a qualification others have ignored.

to be explained in terms of economic interest, and the lower-middle-class segment by one or another of the "status politics" models.

If, however, evangelicals and fundamentalists are increasingly entering the upper middle class, then the internal dynamics of the right wing become very different and new ways of understanding it emerge. Insofar as those of similar religious orientations have come to constitute a large part (if not indeed the core) of the right wing, so that one can see Amway executives, Orange County homeowners, and the elderly viewers of "The Old-Time Gospel Hour" on the same side, then scholars can move beyond the narrowly conceived "interest" or "anxiety" models reviewed in the previous chapter. Second, to the extent that evangelical Protestantism has over the years justified both economic libertarianism and moral traditionalism (a point to which we will return), then one can more easily see the underlying coherence of the right wing and doubt (as many analysts insist on believing) that it is about to run aground on the shoals of internal ideological conflict. Finally, insofar as theological and political conservatism may finally have come together, it is a process that has taken years to reach fruition. The political behavior of evangelicals and fundamentalists at any one point in time is largely irrelevant; it is the trend that matters. We know that white evangelicals did not disproportionately vote for Goldwater in 1964 but that they did disproportionately vote for Reagan twenty years later. It would be interesting to investigate the way right-wing activism itself has reflected a parallel shift in the direction of evangelical-fundamentalist dominance.[8]

Phillips's analysis thus reopens the possibility that there are connections between upward mobility and right-wing politics, in this case upward mobility, a particular kind of religiosity, and right-wing politics. He also brings us back to a second issue that engaged both Lipset and Rogin but that neither scholar ever adequately resolved: the relationship of right-wing politics to economic and demographic growth. Influenced by the general theory that individuals join such movements as a way of coping with the disorganization of their environments, particularly so in the case of those moving to a new location, Lipset tried to apply this theory to the specific case of southern California. However, the subsequent finding that neither new arrivals to the state nor those moving around in it were disproportionately right-wing cast doubt on its applicability. Rogin then tried, without much success, to salvage it by arguing that while "simple short-run population growth in a relatively stable region need not produce right-wing sentiment . . . mobility and restlessness are cultural experiences in southern California" that "will affect not only those who move but also those who remain fixed while all is flux around them" (Rogin

[8] I would be the first to admit that, with Joseph McCarthy at one end, Phyllis Schlafly and Paul Weyrich at the other, and the Buckleys in between, the Catholic role in the contemporary right wing has been an important one. Nevertheless, it does seem to me that as it has evolved since World War II the right wing has taken on a far more recognizably evangelical-fundamentalist tone.

1970b, 208n). Intriguing though it was, that suggestion was simply beyond the reach of empirical confirmation.

Lipset, meanwhile, was using the example of California to develop a quite different explanation for the apparent correlation of right-wing activity and rapid growth, one that suggests more promising possibilities for future research. "New, rapidly expanding centers of population," he wrote, typically "lack a leadership structure accustomed to the responsibilities of running community institutions, reducing community tensions, and supporting the rights of various groups to share in community decisions and authority." This was preeminently the case in the Los Angeles of the mid-1960s, where the wealthy were "largely *nouveaux riches*" and "political and cultural sophistication has been slow to develop among [this] southern California economic elite" (Lipset 1968, 318). Lipset's introduction of elites into the discussion thus raises another possible explanation for the association between right-wing politics and areas of growth, which substantiates the various suggestions (from Hofstadter through Phillips) that right-wing attitudes are somehow linked to upward mobility. Elites not only possess power; they are also objects of emulation, especially for the upwardly mobile. The attitudes of the upwardly mobile in a given region may, therefore, be partially determined by—because they attempt to reflect—the attitudes of the region's elites.[9]

The potentially significant role of regional elites in shaping the attitudes of the rest of the population, particularly in the context of economic growth, is perhaps best indicated by the case of the contemporary South. The South continues to draw as much scholarly attention as it does because, the pressure of homogenizing economic and cultural forces notwithstanding, it retains its regional distinctiveness. To explain that distinctiveness, two broad interpretations now compete for influence among analysts of southern development. One emphasizes the abiding influence of the "folk culture"[10] among ordinary southerners, a complex of attitudes that includes the attachment to the land characteristic of a rural society, the special importance attached to kinship networks, and the adherence of the overwhelming majority of the population to one or another form of low-church Protestantism, often of an evangelical or fundamentalist variety. That "folk culture" has over the years produced men and women both traditionalist in their opposition to new lifestyles and values and localist in their opposition to centralized authority.

The other explanation for the distinctiveness of southern development fo-

---

[9] Although no scholar has followed this specific line of inquiry, one who comes close, pointing out the way right-wing activists in Houston picked up the cues offered by local elites, is Don E. Carleton, *Red Scare! Right-Wing Hysteria, Fifties Fanaticism, and Their Legacy in Texas* (Austin: Texas Monthly Press, 1985), especially pp. 6–18, 64–100.

[10] My use of the term is adapted from David M. Potter's essay "The Enigma of the South," reprinted in Potter, *The South and the Sectional Conflict* (Baton Rouge: Louisiana State University Press, 1968), pp. 15–16.

cuses on political and economic elites and starts from a very different basis: more than other regions of the United States, the South has historically been dominated by a succession of "labor-repressive systems," in which the labor from agricultural workers is by one means or another coerced.[11] The obvious case is slavery; but for many scholars the productive relations that arose after emancipation—tenant farming, sharecropping, and the rest, in what was still largely a plantation economy—also contained significant coercive elements. The racial aspect of these southern "labor-repressive systems" is hard to miss; but as the subsequent exploitation of white tenant farmers and the harassment of those who championed them suggest, blacks were by no means the only objects of this kind of coercion.

Some historians thus see the years of the Depression and World War II as the decisive turning points in southern history, even more than those of Civil War and Reconstruction, because they marked the beginning of the end of the plantation economy.[12] The consolidation and mechanization of southern farming and the departure of masses of poor whites and blacks from the countryside obviated the need for "labor-repressive" systems in agriculture. The economic and social trends accelerating after 1945—the arrival of new industries and the influx of northern professionals, the spurt in urban growth, the rise of a native middle class not tied to the agricultural sector—also challenged the traditional "folk culture." Insofar as all those changes may in some indirect way have facilitated the abolition of legal segregation in the 1960s, this transformation was of major importance. Yet in spite of this, one cannot help noticing the degree to which the South has not been transformed or transformed in unexpected ways.[13]

What seems to have happened since 1945 is that the southern economic boom has produced a growth psychology among many of the region's leaders that duplicates attitudes among comparable northerners in the generation after

[11] One of the first, and certainly one of the most influential, uses of this concept was by Barrington Moore, Jr., in his *Social Origins of Dictatorship and Democracy: Lord and Peasant in the Making of the Modern World* (Boston: Beacon Press, 1966). In referring to "labor-repressive systems of which slavery is but an extreme type," Moore identified such systems with agricultural societies and argued that they relied primarily on legal controls (including physical coercion) to keep the work force subservient, rather than on the economic fears more typically exploited by industrial capitalists (ibid., pp. 434–35). In a sympathetic review of the literature using "labor-repressive" models, Dwight B. Billings and Kathleen M. Blee make the useful point that modernization theories based on the development of the northern United States and Western Europe may be irrelevant to societies, such as the South, with a history of such systems. Billings and Blee, "Bringing History Back In: The Historicity of Social Relations," *Current Perspectives in Social Theory* 7 (1986): 51–68.

[12] Gavin Wright, *Old South, New South: Revolutions in the Southern Economy Since the Civil War* (New York: Basic Books, 1986), pp. 236–41.

[13] In the analysis that follows, I have been particularly influenced by the concluding argument in James C. Cobb, *Industrialization and Southern Society, 1877–1984* (Lexington: University Press of Kentucky, 1984), pp. 135–64.

the Civil War. Reading the pronouncements of these men, one political scientist remarked in the early 1970s, "one frequently feels that he has transmigrated into the McKinley era. Added to the unrelenting emphasis on the capacity of free enterprise and social Darwinism to provide a naturalistic solution to almost all the problems of a contemporary centralized society is an attitude which seems almost to deny the need for any regulative public institutions or even any concern for the *general* as opposed to the private welfare."[14] At almost exactly the same point in time, Samuel Lubell was reaching similar conclusions about southern attitudes, except that the individuals he interviewed hardly qualified as members of an elite. Nevertheless, he too found white southerners driven by what he called a "competitive economic individualism and harsh 'work ethic' " and increasingly "suspicious of government and resentful of taxes."[15] These combined observations suggest that elite attitudes had worked their way down through much of the rest of the white population. By the mid-1980s survey data made it clear that, on questions ranging from general assessments of the role government assistance should play in helping an individual achieve economic success to specific policy issues, there was relatively little difference in attitudes expressed by southern whites, whether middle-class or working-class.[16]

Indigenous elites have played a crucial role in shaping the South's political climate over the past century. From the 1870s onward, these politicians and businessmen deliberately created a low-tax, low-wage, nonunion environment in order to attract outside investment. The failure of generations of southern insurgents to alter these priorities appreciably convinced many observers that only sustained economic growth would produce a changed political climate. Such sustained growth did indeed occur after 1945, but its attendant ethos of "McKinleyism" seems on balance to have helped southern Republicans more than the region's progressive forces. At the same time, the South continues to maintain its position as the most culturally conservative part of the country. The resulting adherence to both economic laissez-faire and to cultural traditionalism has sustained and been reinforced by the region's fundamentalist and evangelical preachers and has played a major role in the success of politicians like Jesse Helms and the regional popularity of presidential candidates like

[14] William C. Havard, "The South: A Shifting Perspective," in Havard, ed., *The Changing Politics of the South* (Baton Rouge: Louisiana State University Press, 1972), p. 25.

[15] Samuel Lubell, *The Future While It Happened* (New York: Norton, 1973), pp. 43, 62.

[16] Earl Black and Merle Black, *Politics and Society in the South* (Cambridge, Mass.: Harvard University Press, 1987), pp. 57–72. Part of this apparent conservatism on the part of the southern white working class undoubtedly comes from their sense—which George Wallace was able to exploit so effectively—that many government programs are designed primarily to benefit blacks. Yet that explanation cannot for the sizable hostility expressed by these working-class respondents to groups such as the "women's liberation movement," and more notably "unions," not normally associated with blacks.

Ronald Reagan.[17] On specific issues it is hard to determine where economic influences end and cultural factors begin. Only two southern state legislatures, for example, ratified the Equal Rights Amendment. Like the very similar southern rejection fifty years before of a constitutional amendment prohibiting child labor, that can be explained either by the importance attached to family in the "folk culture" of the masses or, probably with even greater persuasiveness, by the persistence of the elite's desire for an easily controllable work force (Wohlenberg 1980; Nice 1986).

The influence of "McKinleyism" on southern white attitudes suggests the role regional elites can play in shaping attitudes, particularly in a context of economic growth with which those elites can be identified, and the right-wing politics that follows. Far from proving a source of resistance to this growth psychology, furthermore, southern "folk culture" has proved quite compatible with it,[18] and states with "traditionalist" political cultures have been disproportionately represented among those with the fastest economic and demographic growth.[19] At this point in the discussion it should be obvious that something is missing from any analysis (such as Lipset's) that locates the American right wing on the periphery. Not only the existence of national elite figures such as Hoover, but even more the association of right-wing politics with upward mobility and with economic and demographic growth, and the success of political and business leaders in such areas in conveying their "boosterism" to the rest of the population would all suggest a different model. The thought has therefore occurred to a number of observers that there is something about American development that actively creates a right wing, and that far from being a relic soon to be consigned to the dustbin of history the right wing has a durability transcending today's and tomorrow's reactions.[20]

The existence of a South that continues to be traditionalist even as it becomes increasingly urban and industrial challenges the belief of many social scientists that large-scale processes of social change affect all areas of life, so

[17] Black and Black, *Politics and Society in the South*, pp. 269–75, 312–16. For a somewhat different reading of the future of southern politics, see Alexander P. Lamis, *The Two-Party South* (New York: Oxford University Press, 1984); but Lamis's conclusion, that the Democratic party can transform itself into an interracial lower-class coalition and as such effectively challenge the region's increasingly Republican elites (pp. 229–32), seems to me contradicted by most of the evidence he presents in his book.

[18] Black and Black, *Politics and Society in the South*, pp. 213–31.

[19] For a classification of states by political culture and a review of the relevant literature, see John H. Kincaid, introduction to Kincaid, ed., *Political Culture, Public Policy, and the American States* (Philadelphia: Institute for the Study of Human Issues, 1982), pp. 1–23.

[20] I have in mind here particularly Alan Wolfe's "Sociology, Liberalism, and the Radical Right" (Wolfe 1981). Even though I do not share his view that the right-wing resurgence of the late 1970s could have been avoided if liberals in power over the years had been *less* committed to stimulating economic growth at home and pursuing an anticommunist foreign policy abroad, I have found his essay enormously stimulating.

that at a comparable stage of economic development the politics and culture of Miami or Dallas would come to resemble that of Boston or New York.[21] For many scholars, particularly in the late 1950s and early 1960s, this belief was formalized in the premises of "modernization theory," which held that "the processes of modernization in the different institutional spheres—economic, political, or social organization—tended to go together and to coalesce in relatively similar patterns," and that, once established, "they would lead to the development of similar irreversible structural and organizational outcomes in other spheres and to the general process of sustained growth and development."[22] As the 1960s progressed, however, critics increasingly questioned whether this model adequately grasped the complexity of the transformations actually undergone by past or present societies.[23]

Social scientists' use of modernization theory also raises another issue that is of greater relevance here. Conceptualizations of modernization have typically taken one of two forms: either they equate modernization with one or more specific variables—industrialization, urbanization, increasing education, and so on—or they posit a "traditional-modern" dichotomy in which modernization is the process by which societies and individuals move from being "traditional" to being "modern."[24] In the former case the modernization process is open-ended (urbanization continues, for example) and the most recent of the stages in the process is the most "modern." The latter formulation has very different implications. If modernization is the process by which a "traditional" society becomes "modern," than at some point the process is completed. What is "modern" is therefore not simply what is most recent but the specific values, institutions, and social structures that resulted from that process of change.

It is this latter, dichotomous form of modernization theory that has had the greatest impact on the writing of American history in recent years, particularly in the work of the scholar who has applied the concept the most systematically, Richard D. Brown.[25] Although recognizing that "traditional" and "modern" society are "ideal types" that simplify a more complex reality, he nevertheless sees modernization as that process by which the one becomes the other. In traditional societies, he writes, "present, past, and future are essen-

[21] Billings and Blee, "Bringing History Back In"; Cobb, *Industrialization and Southern Society*, pp. 144–45, 157–59.

[22] S. N. Eisenstadt, *Tradition, Change, and Modernity* (New York: Wiley, 1973), pp. 15–16.

[23] The most concise review of the critical literature is Dean C. Tipps, "Modernization Theory and the Comparative Study of Societies; A Critical Perspective," *Comparative Studies in Society and History* 15 (March 1973): 199–226.

[24] I borrow here from Tipps, "Modernization Theory and the Comparative Study of Societies," pp. 203–5.

[25] Richard D. Brown, "Modernization and the Modern Personality in Early America, 1600–1865," *Journal of Interdisciplinary History* 2 (Winter 1972): 201–28; Brown, *Modernization: The Transformation of American Life, 1600–1865* (New York: Hill and Wang, 1976).

tially the same''; communication is primarily ''word-of-mouth, face-to-face'';
''human and animal power are the only energy sources''; social structure and
political organization ''rely on ascriptive hierarchy and deference''; ''social
roles are not highly specialized''; and ''the prevailing outlook . . . is one of
acceptance or resignation toward life as it is.'' In modern societies, in contrast,
time becomes ''a scarce commodity proceeding rapidly into the future''; ''in-
animate sources of energy like wind, water, and fuel are harnesses''; literacy
becomes a necessity; ''social status is functional rather than ascriptive''; social
roles are sharply differentiated; political organization emphasizes mass participation and is formally egalitarian; and the dominant outlook is characterized
by ''rational manipulation combined with expanding aspirations.''[26] In the approximately two and a half centuries between the launching of the first English
settlement at Jamestown and Lee's surrender at Appomattox, so Brown argues, American society moved from being a traditional society to a modern
one.

Whatever the problems with modernization theory in general, Brown's particular model offers a way to bring together much of the evidence we have
discussed and place it in a historical context. Specifically, it leads us to consider the important ways the American right wing represents the fulfillment of
modernization rather than, as Lipset's formulation would imply, a reaction to
it. In the first place, the profile of Brown's ''modernizers'' bears a remarkable
similarity to Lipset's and Rogin's right wing: they are predominantly white
Protestants. For Brown, furthermore, they are northerners, so much so that he
argues that it was because of their differing responses to modernization that
the North and South drifted apart.[27] By the eve of the Civil War the political
home for most northern white Protestants had become the Republican party,
and there they would remain ever after. Brown's party of ''modernization'' is
thus Lipset's party of ''backlash.''

Brown further suggests that northern Protestants' hostility to immigration
was closely linked to their perception of themselves as the conscious transmit-
ters of the ''modern'' values of ''thrift, self-discipline, and improvement for
the sake of future rewards.'' Their nativist responses to the waves of immigrants—most of them transplanted peasants, ''traditionalists'' with very different attitudes toward time, self-discipline, and progress—arose not only out
of simple prejudice but from what Brown calls ''the values of a modern citi-
zenry.''[28] The official Republican response to these newcomers would over
the years alternate between support for benevolent cultural assimilation—advocated by party leaders in the Civil War era and again under McKinley and
Theodore Roosevelt—and harsher expressions that culminated in the exclu-

[26] Brown, *Modernization*, pp. 9–10, 13–14.
[27] Brown, *Modernization*, pp. 141–46, 161–74.
[28] Brown, *Modernization*, pp. 199, 153.

sionism of the Harding-Coolidge years. Throughout the entire period of large-scale immigration the implicit belief in "Anglo-Saxon" superiority, however defined, remained part of this larger complex of "modernizing" attitudes. These attitudes, moreover, were shared not only by those recognizably middle class in terms of occupation or income, but by significant segments of the native-born working class as well.[29]

For approximately a century after the Irish began to arrive in significant numbers, probably the most durable objects of hostility for these Republicans—and here we are speaking of the rank-and-file of the party, not of the magnates who funded it—were Catholic immigrants and their descendants. After World War II, however, it had become clear to all but the most benighted that, far from being subversive, these individuals were themselves bulwarks of stability and staunch defenders of God, the family, and "the American way of life." One consequence was that the postwar right wing, though initially operating out of a Republican base, would be characterized by a degree of cooperation between Protestants and Catholics that is extraordinary when measured against a past of mutual hostility.

This postwar reconciliation not only makes the contemporary right wing possible but allows the individuals within it to concentrate their energies on other targets. Heirs of the nineteenth-century "modernizers," their ideal has remained an America composed of self-governing individuals; and so their major enemy in the years since 1945 has been the elites and institutions representing "collectivism." One manifestation of this "collectivism" was "the new national state" created by Franklin Roosevelt.[30] To Hartz, as well as to left-wing observers then and now, the New Deal was only a series of minor adjustments within the ongoing liberal-capitalist framework; but to many Americans it represented the first direct intrusion of the Federal Government into their lives, the imposition of regulations in practically all areas of economic activity, and the principle, however haphazardly applied, of redistributive taxation, in which the tax dollars of the "deserving" went to the "undeserving."

A second, even more obvious manifestation of "collectivism" was the rise of the Soviet Union to superpower status after 1945. The forces of foreign radicalism, which had haunted the imaginations of much of the American public since the 1870s and had been the potential instrument of Russian foreign policy since 1917, were victorious in China, Cuba, and Vietnam, representing

---

[29] One application of the "traditionalist-modernist" dichotomy to the working class in the early industrial era that is directly applicable here is by Alan Dawley and Paul Faler: "Working-Class Culture and Politics in the Industrial Revolution: Sources of Loyalism and Rebellion," *Journal of Social History* 9 (Summer 1976): 466–80.

[30] The phrase is that of Theodore J. Lowi, in "Europeanization of America? From United States to United State," in Lowi and Alan Stone, eds., *Nationalizing Government: Public Policies in America* (Beverly Hills: Sage Publications, 1978), p. 18.

(for the right wing at least) the further encroachment of Soviet power. More ominously from the right-wing perspective, the "collectivism" established in the United States after 1933 was spreading throughout the world with—so the Hiss case and the "loss of China" seemed to show—the connivance of the same leaders in the Federal Government.

A third right-wing concern emerging after World War II involved black Americans, the major "alien" group (in Hartz's sense) in the United States. Its critics have probably overestimated the degree of racial prejudice in the right wing; but neither should one underestimate it, particularly after the early 1960s when the right wing began reaching out to disaffected southern segregationists. The more important conclusion to be drawn, however, is that, even if racial prejudice did not exist, there would still be grounds for hostility between the right wing and the majority of black Americans—first, because from the 1860s through the 1960s the protection of black civil rights has always involved significant extensions of federal power; and second, because, even before Jesse Jackson emerged as a major political figure, it was clear that their economic circumstances made black Americans the chief constituency for what in another environment would be called "social-democratic" policies. In either case, whether on issues of civil rights or of economic policy, blacks had become the chief American advocates of the "collectivism" that the right wing in principle opposed.

To summarize the situation of the contemporary right wing in this way is to suggest the degree to which it continues to reflect many of the values of nineteenth-century "modernizers," like them aiming at a society of self-governing individuals but forced to do so in an increasingly "collectivist" world. The most visible recent manifestations of right-wing activity have, however, been the "new right's" involvement in issues concerning the family and sexuality; and to understand that involvement in terms of modernization models is a more complicated task.

For many analysts the abortion issue represents a clear-cut conflict between "traditional" and "modern" views. In this interpretation one side accepts conception as "the will of God" and asserts "the rights of the extended kin group as paramount over those of the individuals" within it; the other sees "choice and planning . . . as basic human characteristics" and strongly affirms, as a matter of individual rights, a woman's freedom "to exercise control over the uses to which her body is put."[31] Certainly the interviews with activist on both sides of the controversy by Luker and others would seem to confirm this "traditionalist-modernist" polarity. That may be so, however, because the participants in antiabortion organizations have been disproportionately

---

[31] Barbara Hargrove, "The Church, the Family, and the Modernization Process," in William V. D'Antonio and Joan Aldous, eds., *Families and Religions: Conflict and Change in Modern Society* (Beverly Hills: Sage, 1983), p. 39.

Catholics: for them opposition to abortion is "traditional," at least in the sense that it reflects the Church's long-standing position and possibly too in the sense that it reflects some of the fatalist and corporatist attitudes of the "premodern" European cultures from which their families came. (For the ways in which opposition to abortion is *not* traditionalist, see Cavanaugh 1986.)

Other ways of looking at the opposition to abortion, however, suggest a "modernist" component, one that better explains the role of evangelicals in the "prolife" movement and the salience of the issue to the contemporary right wing as a whole. To see this "modernist" element in the antiabortion movement, it is necessary to go back to Brown's conclusion that the modernization process in America was substantially completed with the northern victory in the Civil War and thus, from a comparative perspective, in the context of Anglo-American "Victorian" culture. He has made the connection explicit in one essay, writing of "the Victorian climax of modernization";[32] and another historian has pointed out that Victorian values were "specifically linked to the modernization process" insofar as they "taught people to work hard, to postpone gratification, to repress themselves sexually, to 'improve' themselves, to be sober, conscientious, even compulsive." The need to disseminate these values had very different implications for women than for men. Since men were typically preoccupied with asserting themselves in business, politics, or the professions, it was women's function to transmit those values: this was the underlying rationale for the Victorians' "cult of domesticity" and their "exaltation of motherhood."[33] Given the anxieties induced by the race for success, which, long before Hartz or Rogin, Tocqueville had seen as dominating the middle class, it is not too much to say that the burden of preserving the American moral and social order rested largely on the shoulders of women.[34]

By so separating work from domestic life and giving women the primary responsibility for the latter, the Victorians believed that they had freed women from the "traditional" power of men as heads of households. This concept of "separate spheres" was not only accepted by many of the middle-class women who entered public life at the end of the nineteenth century, but exploited by their leaders as they sought to further expand women's influence. "We hear 'A woman's place is at home,' " temperance crusader Carry Nation

[32] Brown, "Modernization: A Victorian Climax," in Daniel Walker Howe, ed., *Victorian America* (Philadelphia: University of Pennsylvania Press, 1976), pp. 29–44.

[33] Daniel Walker Howe, "Victorian Culture in America," in Howe, ed., *Victorian America*, pp. 17, 25–26.

[34] Note, in this connection, Phyllis Schlafly's remark: "It is on its women that civilization depends—on the inspiration they provide, on the moral fabric they weave, on the parameters of behavior they tolerate, and on the new generation that they breathe life into and educate." Schlafly, *The Power of the Positive Woman* (New Rochelle, N.Y.: Arlington House, 1977), p. 139.

wrote in her autobiography. "That is true, but what and where is home? Not the walls of a house. Not furniture, food, or clothes. Home is where the heart is, where our loved ones are. If my son is in a drinking place, my place is there. If my daughter, or the daughter of anyone else, my family, or any other family is in trouble, my place is there."[35] The demands of female reformers for civil and political rights for women was in many cases simply an extension of Nation's argument, marking not a break with but a continuation of women's generally accepted role as guardians of order. The often-noted individualism of "modern" nineteenth-century Americans was real enough, but it was limited to men and it centered on economic activity. Indeed, it can be argued that "the climax of modernization" was absolutely dependent on a family structure in which the overwhelming majority of women were not and could not become independent individuals.

The women's movement of the 1970s operated on the quite different assumption that society should encourage women to develop themselves as individuals and not merely as future wives, mothers, or defenders of the home.[36] The intended consequence—women defining their own roles, whether in terms of legal status, economic opportunity, or sexual behavior—directly challenged the "cult of domesticity" and "exaltation of motherhood" which the Victorians had seen as so essential to maintaining cohesion in a "modernizing" society. In retrospect it is not surprising that the feminist drive for the Equal Rights Amendment met with the opposition of those who believed that the roles prescribed for women by an earlier generation were still essential for social stability.[37]

The sharpest reaction, however, came over the feminist insistence that women be given freedom of sexual choice, an insistence that lay at the heart of the demand that abortion be solely the "choice" of the individual woman. It did not take long before opponents of abortion pointed out that the crucial "choice" was not whether to abort but whether to engage in sexual intercourse in the first place; in response feminists began to move beyond the rhetoric of "family planning" to defend abortion as a means of securing the freedom of all sexually active women, single adolescents as well as married adults. In the eyes of their opponents, feminists were thus seen as not only extending the

[35] Carry Nation, as quoted in Carl N. Degler, *At Odds: Women and the Family in America from the Revolution of the Present* (New York: Oxford University Press, 1980), p. 281.

[36] My formulation here follows that of Sheila M. Rothman, *Woman's Proper Place: A History of Changing Ideals and Practices, 1870 to the Present* (New York: Basic Books, 1978), pp. 6, 260.

[37] The persistence within the evangelical community of the belief that women's "natural" altruism complements men's careerism and the consequent rejection of demands for abortion rights as "selfish" are stressed in Fowler 1985, pp. 12–20. For the historical context in which this belief arose, see especially Barbara Leslie Epstein, *The Politics of Domesticity: Women, Evangelism, and Temperance in Nineteenth-Century America* (Middletown, Conn.: Wesleyan University Press, 1983).

premises of individualism to women, thereby undercutting the integrity of the family but, like the parallel gay liberation movement, wrongly identifying individualism with expressions of sexuality. For many Americans, demands for sexual freedom were more evidence of a corrupting hedonism that threatened the emphasis on self-control and the postponement of gratification so important to Victorian "modernizers"; and that emphasis continued to play an important role in, for example, evangelical and fundamentalist opposition to abortion.[38]

If Brown is correct, that the modernization process in America was over by the last third of the nineteenth century, then it was consummated in a society that carefully restricted women's roles in order to provide stability for their competitive husbands and guidance to their children and thus raise the moral level of society as a whole. If that was "modern" society, then how do we describe a society far more tolerant of the expressions of women's individuality, including sexual expression? The logical answer, which historian Richard Jensen has provided, is to call these emerging trends in contemporary society "postmodern." Centered in the affluent, educated upper middle class, the bearers of "postmodern" values, he argues, challenge the values associated with "modernization," both because "they downplay the ideals of progress, efficiency, and growth for growth's sake in favor of a search for more personal freedom," and because their search for freedom entails the abandonment of "much of the intense self-discipline so characteristic of modernity." He regards "charge-account life-styles, the quest for luxury and new experiences, freer sexual standards, full-time careers for women, and a lesser concern with efficiency" as all manifestations of these "postmodern values.[39]

[38] One social scientist analyzing survey data found that while "respect for life," as measured by opposition to euthanasia, was a better predictor of opposition to abortion for Catholics than was "sexual conservatism," as measured by opposition to premarital sex, sex education in the schools, or the dissemination of birth control, for fundamentalist Protestants the reverse was true. Ted. G. Jelen, "Respect for Life, Sexual Morality, and Opposition to Abortion," *Review of Religious Research* 25 (March 1984): 220–31.

[39] Richard J. Jensen, *Illinois: A History* (New York: Norton, 1977), pp. xv, xvi, xviii. Jensen's typology helps reconcile the conclusions of other scholars working on similar questions. In *The Making of the Modern Family* (New York: Basic Books, 1973), for example, the historian Edward Shorter differentiated the "postmodern" from the "modern family" throughout the western world on the basis of three general trends: the ascendancy of the peer group as the agency of the socialization of the young; the awareness (reflected in rising divorce rates) that "romantic love" is insufficient to sustain a marriage; and the large-scale entry of women into the work force (ibid., especially pp. 227–28, 269–70, 278–79). At the same time, political scientists have described the rise of a "postmaterialist" segment in the publics of advanced industrial societies, notably Ronald J. Inglehart in *The Silent Revolution: Changing Values and Political Styles Among Western Publics* (Princeton: Princeton University Press, 1977).

Lipset has used this latter to explain a wide variety of contemporary conflicts. On one side are those, based primarily in the universities, the professions, and the public-sector bureaucracy, who (in his words) desire "a less impersonal, cleaner, more cultured society, a freer personal life and

Jensen applies his model to recent cultural conflicts which, far from involving the resurgence of "traditional" values that others have seen, represent for him a "conservative reaffirmation of modern values . . . against the postmoderns." He sees the fight over the ERA, for example, as at bottom a symbolic conflict between "conservative women clinging to the modernist ideal of separate spheres for men and women" and "postmodern" feminists trying to dissolve it.[40] Jensen's interpretation undoubtedly draws the cleavages over the ERA too neatly and leaves unanswered questions: precisely how, for example, is one to distinguish in this day and age between the "modernist" defense of "separate spheres" and a "traditionalist" defense of undiluted patriarchy? But he does help explain the apparent riddle of the "profamily" activists: far from being as inconsistent as their feminist adversaries have charged, they like their nineteenth-century predecessors have entered politics to defend home and family against what they see as external corruptions. Theirs is an activism that only "modernism" makes possible; were they truly "traditionalist" women, they probably would not be participating in public life at all.

Whatever the validity of his general terminology, Jensen's model (like that of Brown) serves to remind us that insofar as modernization can be conceived as a finite process, it occurred during a particular era of American history and was associated with specific values. Perceiving its connection with this historically bound process of modernization helps explain the durability of the right wing. Since at least 1776, Americans have tended to reject "tradition," and the right-wing commentator who said that "the average American is modernist in his bones" grasped something essential about the evolving relationship of the right wing to the American people.[41] His observation is even more compelling if with Brown we regard the modernization of American society as a process consummated by the latter third of the nineteenth century. It is hard not to catch the distinctly Victorian flavor of so many of today's right-wing positions or the appeal that turn-of-the-century America—now seen as a golden age of small-town harmony, entrepreneurial freedom, and the vigorous assertion of American power in the world—has for so many right-wing politicians and activists.

At the same time, Brown's use of the concept of "modernity" helps us understand the sources of the right wings activism. It makes sense of one key

---

democratization of political work and community life." On the other are the more conventional middle- and working-class individuals who remain primarily concerned with a higher standard of living, a stable family life, and the maintenance of public order. (For Lipset's use of the concept, see particularly Lipset 1985, pp. 195–205; the quotation is from p. 195.)

[40] Richard J. Jensen, "The Last Party System: The Decay of Consensus, 1932–1980," in Paul Kleppner, ed., *The Evolution of American Electoral Systems* (Westport, Conn.: Greenwood, 1981), p. 229.

[41] Jeffrey Hart, "The Intelligent Woman's Guide to Modern American Conservatism," in Robert W. Whitaker, ed., *The New Right Papers* (New York: St. Martin's, 1982), p. 39.

element in the original concept of the ''radical right'': whatever the case with conservative movements in other times and other places, the American right wing since World War II has wanted to transform the world, surely one of the most characteristic of ''modern'' attitudes. A passive acceptance of history has not characterized the right wing, nor—and this is where studies of isolated intellectuals can mislead—has a consistent pessimism been dominant. It is not accidental that the first genuinely right-wing President in over fifty years liked to quote Thomas Paine: ''We have it in our power to begin the world over again.''[42]

Putting the relevant data together, it therefore seems appropriate to take a new look at the anger with which so many right-wing activists have tended to respond to the wider world. It would be more useful to deemphasize feelings of personal failure or membership in groups declining in status and stress the fact that many of them are successful: they see themselves and are seen by their families and their communities as models of achievement. Convinced that their adherence to a Victorian morality has been instrumental in their own success, they are shocked to discover that major national institutions—the universities, segments of the media, and the public-sector bureaucracy—not only define success differently but are far more permissive about its prerequisites. The contributors to *The New American Right* who continued their analyses of the right wing, not only Lipset but Hofstadter and Bell, were quite right to sense this shock.

Insofar as these right-wing activists see themselves as successful (their actual income level and occupational prestige may be less important than their subjective perception), they have embraced liberal-capitalist values. Those values may, Lipset notwithstanding, be more pervasive in our society than democratic-egalitarian ones. It is at this point that the Brown-Jensen ''modernization'' model converges with Hartz's and Rogin's idea of the ''liberal fragment'': both perspectives emphasize the commitment to an intense individualism, a determination to achieve economic success and upward mobility, and an insistence on maintaining self-control on the part of significant segments of the public. These would include not only the right-wing activists but also the constituencies (largely but not wholly ''middle class'') that they have attempted to mobilize by portraying government regulation as the major obstacle to economic success.

For many of these constituencies (especially but not exclusively evangelical Protestants) religion can play a crucial role in reinforcing right-wing attitudes, a phenomenon of considerable importance in what, in Lipset's words, ''is still the most religious country in the western world, with the exception of Ireland'' (Lipset 1985, 286). Liberal-capitalist values in America, as Garry Wills has

---

[42] Ronald Reagan, as quoted in Blumenthal 1986, p. 253. The original is in Paine's appendix to *Common Sense*.

persuasively argued, have been sustained less by invocations of the authority of economists, whether Adam Smith or Ludwig von Mises, than by religious appeals. Competition in the marketplace, as he puts it, has long been regarded as "a school of moral formation," and so behind "the Horatio Alger ethic" stand "Methodist morals and Baptist fervor and Puritan rhetoric."[43] (It is the importance of self-control in this complex of attitudes, it seems almost unnecessary to point out, that has so easily allowed the right wing to add to its appeals the antiabortion, anti-gay-rights, and anti-sex-education agendas of the "profamily" activists.)

The persistence of these religious underpinnings of economic individualism, from the Victorian era to the present, indicates once again the pervasiveness of the values that the right wing upholds. In retrospect, it seems obvious that social scientists studying the right wing should have devoted more attention to investigating those factors—continuity in leadership, the developing organizational infrastructure, access to funding—that have been able to keep it going even when the issues it attempts to exploit lose their salience. Nonetheless, the accumulated scholarly efforts to develop profiles of right-wing activists and uncover the constituencies for right-wing politicians have the great virtue of leading us to the conclusion that, ultimately, the sources of the durability of the right wing lie within the wider American political culture. No matter how well-funded or well-organized, the right wing could not have survived, or had any influence on public life, without significant support from different segments of the American public. Millions of Americans continue to believe that a society of economically autonomous individuals without extensive government intervention is feasible, that family cohesion and strict morality are compatible with advanced capitalism and technological change, that the external world is amenable to American purposes, and that whatever difficulties exist in achieving those goals come from "alien" forces such as "collectivism" and "secularism." As long as these ideas are as widely believed as they are, the right wing will endure. For the right wing to disappear, those beliefs would also have to lose their hold; and that would require a cultural and social transformation of a magnitude greater than anything America has experienced. In the absence of such a transformation, the prudent conclusion is that the right wing will persist, waxing and waning over time, but remaining a permanent presence in American public life.

---

[43] Garry Wills, *Nixon Agonistes: The Crisis of the Self-Made Man* (Boston: Houghton Mifflin, 1971), pp. 549, 564. From another perspective, Walter Dean Burnham has noted the way American religiosity, with its "dominant emphasis on the personal salvation of the individual," has reinforced the secular liberal-capitalist components of our political culture by leading individuals to see their success or failure in personal rather than structural terms (Burnham 1981, pp. 110–11, 134–36).

Bibliography

Listed here are those scholarly works that in one way or another proved central to the analysis or argument of this book. Cited in abbreviated form in the text and footnotes, they are given full citation here. Books and articles that engage the analysis or argument only tangentially are cited in full in the footnotes.

Abcarian, Gilbert. 1971. "Political Deviance and Social Stress: The Ideology of the Radical Right." In John Paul Scott and Sarah F. Scott, eds., *Social Control and Social Change*, pp. 131–61. Chicago: University of Chicago Press.

Abcarian, Gilbert, and Sherman M. Stanage. 1965. "Alienation and the Radical Right." *Journal of Politics* 27 (November): 776–96.

Abramson, Paul, John H. Aldrich, and David W. Rohde. 1982. *Change and Continuity in the 1980 Election*. Washington: Congressional Quarterly Press.

Adorno, T. W., Else Frenkel-Brunswick, Daniel J. Levinson, R. Nevitt Sanford. 1950. *The Authoritarian Personality*. New York: Harper.

Anderson, Donald N. 1966. "Ascetic Protestantism and Political Preference." *Review of Religious Research* 7 (Spring): 167–71.

Arrington, Theodore S., and Patricia A. Kyle. 1978. "Equal Rights Amendment Activists in North Carolina." *Signs: Journal of Women in Culture and Society* 3 (Spring): 666–80.

Barker, Edwin N. 1963. "Authoritarianism of the Political Right, Center, and Left." *Journal of Social Issues* 19 (April): 63–74.

Bartley, Numan V. 1970. *From Thurmond to Wallace: Political Tendencies in Georgia, 1948–1968*. Baltimore: Johns Hopkins University Press.

Bartley, Numan V., and Hugh D. Graham. 1975. *Southern Politics and the Second Reconstruction*. Baltimore: Johns Hopkins University Press.

Bell, Daniel. 1955. "Interpretations of American Politics." In Bell, ed., *The New American Right*, pp. 3–22. New York: Criterion Books.

———. 1962. "The Dispossessed—1962." *Columbia University Forum* 5 (Fall): 4–12.

———. 1963. "The Dispossessed." In Bell, ed., *The Radical Right*, pp. 1–38. Garden City, N.Y.: Doubleday.

Bennett, Stephen E. 1971. "Modes of Resolution of a Belief Dilemma in the Ideology of the John Birch Society." *Journal of Politics* 33 (August): 735–72.

Berenson, William M., Robert D. Bond, and J. Leiper Freeman. 1971. "The Wallace Vote and Political Change in Tennessee." *Journal of Politics* 33 (May): 515–20.

Black, Earl. 1973. "The Militant Segregationist Vote in the Post-*Brown* South: A Comparative Analysis." *Social Science Quarterly* 54 (June): 66-84.

Black, Earl, and Merle Black. 1973a. "The Demographic Basis of Wallace Support in Alabama." *American Politics Quarterly* 1 (July): 279–304.

———. 1973b. "The Wallace Vote in Alabama: A Multiple Regression Analysis." *Journal of Politics* 35 (August): 730–36.

Bland, Richard, and Roy Wallis. 1977. "Comment on Wilson and Zurcher's 'Status Inconsistency and Participation in Social Movements.' " *Sociological Quarterly* 18 (Summer): 426–29.

Blumenthal, Sidney. 1986. *The Rise of the Counter-Establishment: From Conservative Ideology to Political Power*. New York: Times Books.

Bolce, Louis, Gerald de Maio, and Douglas Muzzio. 1986. "ERA and the Abortion Controversy: A Case of Dissonance Reduction." *Social Science Quarterly* 67 (June): 299–314.

Boles, Janet K. 1979. *The Politics of the Equal Rights Amendment: Conflict and the Decision Process*. New York: Longman.

Brady, David W., and Kent L. Tedin. 1976. "Ladies in Pink: Religious and Political Ideology in the Anti-ERA Movement." *Social Science Quarterly* 56 (March): 564–75.

Brandmeyer, Gerard A., and R. Serge Denisoff. 1969. "Status Politics: An Appraisal of the Application of a Concept." *Pacific Sociological Review* 12 (Spring): 5–11.

Brogan, D. W. 1952. "The Ilusion of American Omnipotence." *Harper's* 205 (December): 21–28.

Broyles, J. Allen. 1963. "The John Birch Society: A Movement of Social Protest of the Radical Right." *Journal of Social Issues* 19 (April): 51–62.

———. 1964. *The John Birch Society: Anatomy of a Protest*. Boston: Beacon Press.

Bruce, Steve. 1987. "Status and Cultural Defense: The Case of the New Christian Right." *Sociological Focus* 20 (August): 242–46.

Brudney, Jeffrey L., and Gary W. Copeland. 1984. "Evangelicals as a Political Force: Reagan and the 1980 Religious Vote." *Social Science Quarterly* 65 (December): 1072–79.

Buell, Emmett H., and Lee Sigelman. 1985. "An Army That Meets Every Sunday? Popular Support for the Moral Majority in 1980." *Social Science Quarterly* 66 (June): 426–34.

———. 1987. "A Second Look at 'Popular Support for the Moral Majority in 1980: A Second Look.' " *Social Science Quarterly* 68 (March): 167–69.

Burnham, Walter Dean. 1968a. "American Voting Behavior and the Election of 1964." *Midwest Journal of Political Science* 12 (February): 1–40.

———. 1968b. "Election 1968—An Abortive Landslide." *Trans-Action* 6 (December): 18–24.

———. 1970. *Critical Elections and the Mainsprings of American Politics*. New York: Norton.

———. 1972. "Political Immunization and Political Confessionalism: The United States and Weimar Germany." *Journal of Interdisciplinary History* 3 (Summer): 1–30.

———. 1981. "The 1980 Earthquake: Realignment, Reaction, or What?" In Thomas Ferguson and Joel Rogers, eds., *The Hidden Election: Politics and Economics in the 1980 Presidential Campaign*, pp. 98–140. New York: Pantheon.

———. 1982. *The Current Crisis in American Politics*. New York: Oxford University Press.

Burnham, Walter Dean, and John D. Sprague. 1970. "Additive and Multiplicative

Models of the Voting Universe: Pennsylvania, 1960–1968." *American Political Science Review* 64 (June): 471–90.

Burris, Val. 1987a. "Business Support for the New Right: A Consumer's Guide to the Most Reactionary Corporations." *Socialist Review* 17 (January–February): 33–63.

———. 1987b. "The Political Partisanship of American Business: A Study of Corporate Political Action Committees." *American Sociological Review* 52 (December): 732–44.

Canfield, James Lewis. 1985. *A Case of Third-Party Activism: The George Wallace Campaign Worker and the American Independent Party*. Lanham, Md.: University Press of America.

Canovan, Margaret. 1981. *Populism*. New York: Harcourt, Brace, Jovanovich.

Carlson, Jody. 1981. *George C. Wallace and the Politics of Powerlessness: The Wallace Campaigns for the Presidency, 1964–1976*. New Brunswick, N.J.: Transaction Books.

Carney, Francis. 1971. "A State of Catastrophe." *New York Review of Books* 17 (October 7): 30–36.

Carver, Joan S. 1982. "The Equal Rights Amendment and the Florida Legislature." *Florida Historical Quarterly* 60 (April): 455–91.

Cavanaugh, Michael A. 1986. "Secularization and the Politics of Traditionalism: The Case of the Right-to-Life Movement." *Sociological Forum* 1 (Spring): 251–83.

Chesler, Mark, and Richard Schmuck. 1963. "Participant Observation in a Super-Patriot Discussion Group." *Journal of Social Issues* 19 (April): 18–30.

———. 1969. "Social-Psychological Characteristics of Super-Patriots." In Robert A. Schoenberger, ed., *The American Right Wing: Readings in Political Behavior*, pp. 164–92. New York: Holt, Rinehart, and Winston.

Chester, Lewis, Godfrey Hodgson, and Bruce Page. 1969. *An American Melodrama: The Presidential Campaign of 1968*. New York: Viking.

Clabaugh, Gary K. 1974. *Thunder on the Right: The Protestant Fundamentalists*. Chicago: Nelson-Hall.

Clawson, Dan, Allen Kaufman, and Alan Neustadtl. 1985. "Corporate PACs for a New Pax Americana." *Insurgent Sociologist* 13 (Summer–Fall): 63–77.

Clawson, Dan, Maureen J. Karson, and Allen Kaufman. 1986a. "The Corporate Pact for a Conservative America: A Data Analysis of 1980 Corporate PAC Donations in Sixty-Six Conservative Congressional Elections." *Research in Corporate Performance and Policy* 8: 223–45.

Clawson, Dan, Alan Neustadtl, and James Beardon. 1986b. "The Logic of Business Unity: Corporate Contributions to the 1980 Congressional Elections." *American Sociological Review* 51 (December): 797–811.

Cleghorn, Reese. 1968. *Radicalism Southern Style: A Commentary on Regional Extremism of the Right*. Atlanta: Southern Regional Council.

Conover, Pamela Johnston. 1983. "The Mobilization of the New Right: A Test of Various Explanations." *Western Political Quarterly* 36 (December): 633–49.

Conover, Pamela Johnston, and Virginia Gray. 1983. *Feminism and the New Right: Conflict Over the American Family*. New York: Praeger.

Constantini, Edmond, and Kenneth H. Craik. 1969. "Competing Elites Within a Political Party: A Study of Republican Leadership." *Western Political Quarterly* 22 (December): 879–903.

Converse, Philip E., Warren E. Miller, Jerrold G. Rusk, and Arthur C. Wolfe. 1969. "Continuity and Change in American Politics: Parties and Issues in the 1968 Election." *American Political Science Review* 63 (December): 1083–1105.

Conway, M. Margaret. 1968. "The White Backlash Reexamined: Wallace and the 1964 Primaries." *Social Science Quarterly* 49 (December): 710–19.

Cosman, Bernard. 1966. *The Case of the Goldwater Delegates: Deep South Republican Leadership*. University, Ala.: University of Alabama Press.

Crass, Philip. 1976. *The Wallace Factor*. New York: Mason/Charter.

Crawford, Alan. 1980. *Thunder on the Right: The "New Right" and the Politics of Resentment*. New York: Pantheon.

Crespi, Irving. 1965. "The Structural Base for Right-Wing Conservatism: The Goldwater Case." *Public Opinion Quarterly* 29 (Winter): 523–43.

———. 1971. "Structural Sources of the George Wallace Constituency." *Social Science Quarterly* 52 (June): 115–32.

Crosby, Donald F. 1978. *God, Church, and Flag: Senator Joseph R. McCarthy and the Catholic Church*. Chapel Hill: University of North Carolina Press.

Cummings, Scott, Richard Briggs, and James Mercy. 1977. "Preachers vs. Teachers: Local-Cosmopolitan Conflict over Textbook Censorship in an Appalachian Community." *Rural Sociology* 42 (Spring): 7–21.

Danzig, David. 1962. "The Radical Right and the Rise of the Fundamentalist Minority." *Commentary* 33 (April): 291–98.

Davis, L. J. 1980. "Conservatism in America." *Harper's* 261 (October): 21–26.

Deutchman, Iva E., and Sandra Prince-Embury. 1982. "Political Ideology of Pro- and Anti-ERA Women." *Women and Politics* 2 (Spring–Summer): 39–55.

Dudman, Richard. 1962. *Men of the Far Right*. New York: Pyramid Books.

Ehrenhalt, Alan. 1978. "The Right in Congress: Seeking a Strategy." *Congressional Quarterly* 36 (August 5): 2022–28.

Eitzen, D. Stanley. 1970. "Status Inconsistency and Wallace Supporters in a Midwestern City." *Social Forces* 48 (June): 493–98.

Ellsworth, Ralph E., and Sarah M. Harris. 1962. *The American Right Wing*. Washington: Public Affairs Press.

Elms, Alan C. 1969. "Psychological Factors in Right-Wing Extremism." In Robert A. Schoenberger, ed., *The American Right Wing: Readings in Political Behavior*, pp. 143–63. New York: Holt, Rinehart, and Winston.

———. 1970. "Those Little Old Ladies in Tennis Shoes Are no Nuttier Than Anyone Else, It Turns Out: Pathology and Politics." *Psychology Today* 3 (February): 27ff.

Epstein, Benjamin R., and Arnold Forster. 1967. *The Radical Right: Report on the John Birch Society and Its Allies*. New York: Random House.

Falik, Marilyn. 1983. *Ideology and Abortion Policy Politics*. New York: Praeger.

Feigert, Frank B. 1972. "Conservatism, Populism, and Social Change." *American Behavioral Scientist* 17 (November–December): 272–78.

Felsenthal, Carol. 1981. *Sweetheart of the Silent Majority: The Biography of Phyllis Schlafly*. Garden City, N.Y.: Doubleday.

Fitzgerald, Frances. 1981. "A Disciplined, Charging Army." *New Yorker* 57 (May 18): 53–141.

Forster, Arnold, and Benjamin R. Epstein. 1964. *Danger on the Right*. New York: Random House.

Fowler, Robert Booth. 1982. *A New Engagement: Evangelical Political Thought, 1966–1976*. Grand Rapids, Mich.: Eerdmans.

———. 1985. "The Feminist and Antifeminist Debate Within Evangelical Protestant-ism." *Women and Politics* 5 (Summer/Fall): 7–39.

Frady, Marshall. 1968. *Wallace*. New York: New American Library.

Frankl, Razelle. 1987. *Televangelism: The Marketing of Popular Religion*. Carbon-dale: Southern Illinois University Press.

Frankl, Razelle, and Jeffrey K. Hadden. 1987. "A Critical Review of the Religion and Television Research Project." *Review of Religious Research* 29 (December): 111–24.

Freeman, Bonnie Cook. 1983. "Antifeminists and Women's Liberation: A Case Study of a Paradox." *Women and Politics* 3 (Spring): 21–38.

Fried, Richard M. 1976. *Men Against McCarthy*. New York: Columbia University Press.

Gabennesch, Howard. 1972. "Authoritarianism as World View." *American Journal of Sociology* 77 (March): 857–76.

Gargan, John J. 1975. "Conservative Success in Liberal New York." In Louis Maisel and Paul Sacks, eds., *The Future of Political Parties*, pp. 165–92. Beverly Hills: Sage Publications.

Ginsburg, Faye. 1984. "The Body Politic: The Defense of Sexual Restriction by Anti-Abortion Activists." In Carole S. Vance, ed., *Pleasure and Danger: Exploring Female Sexuality*, pp. 173–88. New York: Routledge and Kegan Paul.

Glazer, Nathan. 1953. "The Method of Senator McCarthy: Its Origins, Its Uses, and Its Prospects." *Commentary* 15 (March): 244–56.

Glazer, Nathan, and Seymour Martin Lipset. 1955. "The Polls on Communism and Conformity." In Daniel Bell, ed., *The New American Right*, pp. 141–65. New York: Criterion Books.

Gordon, Linda, and Allan Hunter. 1977. "Sex, Family, and the New Right: Anti-Feminism as a Political Force." *Radical America* 11–12 (November 1977–February 1978): 9–25.

Granberg, Donald N. 1981. "The Abortion Activists." *Family Planning Perspectives* 13 (July–August): 157–63.

Granberg, Donald N., and Donald Denney. 1982. "The Coathanger and the Rose." *Society* 19 (May–June): 39–46.

Granberg, Donald N., and James Burlison. 1983. "The Abortion Issue in the 1980 Elections." *Family Planning Perspectives* 15 (September–October): 231–38.

Grasmick, Harold G. 1974. "Rural Culture and the Wallace Movement in the South." *Rural Sociology* 39 (Winter): 454–70.

Green, John C., and James L. Guth. 1984. "The Party Irregulars." *Psychology Today* 18 (October): 46–52.

Griffith, Robert. 1970. *The Politics of Fear: Joseph R. McCarthy and the Senate*. Lexington: University Press of Kentucky.

Grupp, Fred W. 1969. "The Political Perspectives of John Birch Society Members." In Robert A. Schoenberger, ed., *The American Right Wing: Readings in Political Behavior*, pp. 83–118. New York: Holt, Rinehart, and Winston.

Grupp, Fred W., and William M. Newman. 1973. "Political Ideology and Religious Preference: The John Birch Society and the Americans for Democratic Action." *Journal for the Scientific Study of Religion* 12 (December): 401–14.

Gurney, Joan N., and Kathleen J. Tierney. 1982. "Relative Deprivation and Social Movements: A Critical Look at 20 Years of Theory and Research." *Sociological Quarterly* 23 (Winter): 33–47.

Gusfield, Joseph. 1963. *Symbolic Crusade: Status Politics and the American Temperance Movement*. Urbana: University of Illinois Press.

————. 1978. "Proposition 6: Political Ceremony in California." *Nation* 227 (December 9): 633–35.

Guth, James L. 1983a. "The New Christian Right." In Robert C. Liebman and Robert Wuthnow, eds., *The New Christian Right: Mobilization and Legitimation*, pp. 31–45. Chicago: Aldine.

————. 1983b. "Southern Baptist Clergy: Vanguard of the Christian Right?" In Liebman and Wuthnow, eds., *The New Christian Right*, pp. 117–30.

Guth, James L., and John C. Green. 1986. "Faith and Politics: Religion and Ideology Among Political Contributors." *American Politics Quarterly* 14 (July): 186–200.

————. 1987. "The Moralizing Minority: Christian Right Support Among Political Contributors." *Social Science Quarterly* 68 (September): 598–610.

Hadden, Jeffrey K. 1984. "Televangelism and the Future of American Politics." In David G. Bromley and Anson Shupe, eds., *New Christian Politics*, pp 151–65. Macon, Ga.: Mercer University Press.

————. 1987. "Religious Broadcasting and the Mobilization of the New Christian Right." *Journal for the Scientific Study of Religion* 26 (March): 1–24.

Hadden, Jeffrey K., and Charles E. Swann. 1981. *Prime-Time Preachers: The Rising Power of Televangelism*. New York: Addison-Wesley.

Hadden, Jeffrey K., and Razelle Frankl. 1987. "Star Wars of a Different Kind: Reflections on the Politics of the Religion and Television Research Project." *Review of Religious Research* 29 (December): 101–10.

Hamilton, Richard F. 1972. *Class and Politics in the United States*. New York: Wiley.

————. 1975. *Restraining Myths: Critical Studies of U.S. Social Structure*. New York: Wiley.

Harper, Charles L., and Kevin Leicht. 1984. "Religious Awakenings and Status Politics: Sources of Support for the New Christian Right." *Sociological Analysis* 45 (Winter): 339–54.

Harrington, Mona. 1986. *The Dream of Deliverance in American Politics*. New York: Knopf.

Hartz, Louis. 1955. *The Liberal Tradition in America*. New York: Harcourt, Brace.

————. 1964. *The Founding of New Societies: Studies in the History of the United States, Latin America, South Africa, Canada, and Australia*. New York: Harcourt, Brace, and World.

Himmelstein, Jerome L. 1983. "The New Right." In Robert C. Liebman and Robert

Wuthnow, eds., *The New Christian Right: Mobilization and Legitimation*, pp. 13–30. Chicago: Aldine.

———. 1986. "The Social Basis of Antifeminism: Religious Networks and Culture." *Journal for the Scientific Study of Religion* 25 (March): 1–15.

Himmelstein, Jerome L., and James A. McRae, Jr. 1984. "Social Conservatism, New Republicans, and the 1980 Election." *Public Opinion Quarterly* 48 (Fall): 592–605.

Hofstadter, Richard. 1955a. "The Pseudo-Conservative Revolt." In Daniel Bell, ed., *The New American Right*, pp. 33–55. New York: Criterion Books.

———. 1955b. *The Age of Reform: From Bryan to F.D.R.* New York: Knopf.

———. 1963a. "The Pseudo-Conservative Revolt: A Postscript." In Daniel Bell, ed., *The Radical Right*, pp. 81–86. Garden City, N.Y.: Doubleday.

———. 1963b. *Anti-Intellectualism in American Life*. New York: Knopf.

———. 1964. "Goldwater and His Party: The True Believer and the Radical Right." *Encounter* 23 (October): 3–13.

———. 1965a. "The Goldwater Debacle." *Encounter* 24 (January): 66–70.

———. 1965b. *The Paranoid Style in American Politics and Other Essays*. New York: Knopf.

———. 1970. "Reflections on Violence in the United States." In Hofstadter and Michael Wallace, eds., *American Violence: A Documentary History*, pp. 3–43. New York: Knopf.

Hogan, J. Michael. 1984. "Wallace and the Wallaceites: A Reevaluation." *Southern Speech Communication Journal* 50 (Fall): 24–48.

Hoover, Stewart M. 1987. "The Religious Television Audience: A Matter of Significance or Size?" *Review of Religious Research* 29 (December): 133–51.

Hottois, James, and Neal A. Milner. 1975. *The Sex Education Controversy: A Study of Politics, Education, and Morality*. Lexington, Mass.: Lexington Books.

Howard, Perry, William H. Long, and Gene A. Zdrazil. 1971. "An Ecological Analysis of Voting Behavior in Baton Rouge: From Strom Thurmond to George Wallace." *Social Forces* 50 (September): 45–53.

[Huberman, Leo, and Paul Sweezy]. 1954. "The Roots and Prospects of McCarthyism." *Monthly Review* 5 (January): 417–34.

Hunt, Larry, and Robert G. Cushing. 1970. "Status Discrepancy, Interpersonal Attachment, and Right-Wing Extremism." *Social Science Quarterly* 51 (December): 587–601.

Hunter, Allan. 1981. "In the Wings: New Right Ideology and Organization." *Radical America* 15 (Spring): 113–38.

Hunter, James Davidson. 1983. *American Evangelicalism: Conservative Religion and the Quandary of Modernity*. New Brunswick, N.J.: Rutgers University Press.

Hyman, Herbert H. and Paul B. Sheatsley. 1954. " 'The Authoritarian Personality'— A Methodological Critique." In Richard Christie and Marie Jahoda, eds., *Studies in the Scope and Method of "The Authoritarian Personality,"* pp. 50–122. Glencoe, Ill.: Free Press.

Jacob, Charles E. 1981. "The Congressional Elections." In Gerald M. Pomper et al., *The Election of 1980: Reports and Interpretations*, pp. 119–41. Chatham, N.J.: Chatham House.

Janson, Donald, and Bernard Eismann. 1963. *The Far Right*. New York: McGraw-Hill.

Jenkins, J. Craig. 1983. "Resource Mobilization Theory and the Study of Social Movements." *Annual Review of Sociology* 9: 527–53.

Jenkins, J. Craig, and Teri Shumate. 1985. "Cowboy Capitalists and the Rise of the New Right: An Analysis of Contributors to Conservative Policy Formation Organizations." *Social Problems* 33 (December): 130–45.

Johnson, Benton. 1962. "Ascetic Protestantism and Political Preference." *Public Opinion Quarterly* 26 (Spring): 35–46.

———. 1964. "Ascetic Protestantism and Political Preference in the Deep South." *American Journal of Sociology* 69 (January): 359–66.

———. 1966. "Theology and Party Preference Among Protestant Clergymen." *American Sociological Review* 31 (April): 200–208.

———. 1967. "Theology and the Position of Pastors on Public Issues." *American Sociological Review* 32 (June): 433–42.

Johnson, Benton, and Richard H. White. 1967. "Protestantism, Political Preference, and the Nature of Religious Influence: Comment on Anderson's Paper." *Review of Religious Research* 9 (Fall): 28–35.

Johnson, Loch, and Charles S. Bullock III. 1986. "The New Religious Right and the 1980 Congressional Elections." In Benjamin Ginsberg and Alan Stone, eds., *Do Elections Matter?*, pp. 148–63. Armonk, N.Y.: Sharpe.

Johnson, Stephen D., and Joseph B. Tamney. 1982. "The Christian Right and the 1980 Presidential Election." *Journal for the Scientific Study of Religion* 21 (June): 123–30.

Jones, Charles O. 1981. "Nominating 'Carter's Favorite Opponent': The Republicans in 1980." In Austin Ranney, ed., *The American Elections of 1980*, pp. 61–98. Washington: American Enterprise Institute.

Jorstad, Erling. 1970. *The Politics of Doomsday: Fundamentalists of the Far Right*. Nashville: Abingdon.

———. 1981. *Evangelicals in the White House: The Cultural Maturation of Born-Again Christianity*. New York: Edwin Mellen Press.

Kessel, John H. 1968. *The Goldwater Coalition: Republican Strategies in 1964*. Indianapolis: Bobbs-Merrill.

Key, V. O. 1949. *Southern Politics in State and Nation*. New York: Knopf.

Kirscht, John P., and Ronald C. Dillehay. 1967. *Dimensions of Authoritarianism: A Review of Research and Theory*. Lexington: University of Kentucky Press.

Klatch, Rebecca E. 1987. *Women of the New Right*. Philadelphia: Temple University Press.

Knoke, David, and Natalie Kyriazis. 1977. "The Persistence of the Black-Belt Vote: A Test of Key's Hypothesis." *Social Science Quarterly* 57 (March): 899–905.

Koeppen, Sheilah [Rosenhack]. 1969a. "The Radical Right and the Politics of Consensus." In Robert A. Schoenberger, ed., *The American Right Wing: Readings in Political Behavior*, pp. 48–82. New York: Holt, Rinehart, and Winston.

———. 1969b. "The Republican Radical Right." In American Academy of Political and Social Science *Annals* 382 (March): 73–82.

Kolkey, Jonathan Martin. 1983. *The New Right, 1960–1968. With an Epilogue, 1969–1980*. Washington: University Press of America.

Ladd, Everett Carll, Jr. 1966. "The Radical Right: White-Collar Extremists." *South Atlantic Quarterly* 65 (Summer): 314–24.

Latham, Earl. 1966. *The Communist Controversy in Washington: From the New Deal to McCarthy*. Cambridge, Mass.: Harvard University Press.

Leahy, Peter, and Allan Mazur. 1986. "A Comparison of Movements Opposed to Nuclear Power, Fluoridation, and Abortion." *Research in Social Movements, Conflict, and Change* 1: 143–54.

Lehnen, Robert G. 1970. "Stability of Presidential Choice in 1968: The Case of Two Southern States." *Social Science Quarterly* 51 (June): 138–47.

Lenski, Gerhart. 1954. "Status Crystallization: A Non-Vertical Dimension of Social Status." *American Sociological Review* 18 (August): 405–13.

Liebman, Robert C. 1983. "Mobilizing the Moral Majority." In Liebman and Robert Wuthnow, eds., *The New Christian Right: Mobilization and Legitimation*, pp. 57–69. Chicago: Aldine.

Lienesch, Michael. 1982. "Right-Wing Religion: Christian Conservatism as a Political Movement." *Political Science Quarterly* 97 (Fall): 403–25.

———. 1983. "The Paradoxical Politics of the Religious Right." *Soundings* 66 (Spring): 70–99.

Lipset, Seymour Martin. 1955. "The Sources of the 'Radical Right.' " In Daniel Bell, ed., *The New American Right*, pp. 166–233. New York: Criterion Books.

———. 1960. *Political Man: The Social Bases of Politics*. Garden City, N.Y.: Doubleday.

———. 1963a. "Three Decades of the Radical Right: Coughlinites, McCarthyites, and Birchers." In Daniel Bell, ed., *The Radical Right*, pp. 313–77. Garden City, N.Y.: Doubleday.

———. 1963b. Introduction to the Anchor edition. *Political Man*, pp. xix–xxxvi. Garden City, N.Y.: Anchor Books.

———. 1963c. *The First New Nation: The United States in Historical and Comparative Perspective*. New York: Basic Books.

———. 1964. "Beyond the Backlash." *Encounter* 23 (November): 11–24.

———. 1968. *Revolution and Counterrevolution: Change and Persistence in Social Structures*. New York: Basic Books.

———. 1970. Preface to the Anchor edition. *Revolution and Counterrevolution*, pp. vii–xx. Garden City, N.Y.: Anchor Books.

———. 1977. "Why No Socialism in the United States." In Seweryn Bialer and Sophia Sluzar, eds., *Radicalism in the Contemporary Age: Sources of Contemporary Radicalism*, pp. 31–149. Boulder, Colo.: Westview.

———. 1982. "Failures of Exremism." *Society* 20 (November–December): 47–58.

———. 1985. *Consensus and Conflict: Essays in Political Sociology*. New Brunswick, N.J.: Transaction Books.

Lipset, Seymour Martin, and Earl Raab. 1969. "The Wallace Whitelash." *Trans-Action* 7 (December): 23–35.

———. 1970. *The Politics of Unreason: Right-Wing Extremism in America, 1790–1970*. New York: Harper and Row.

Lipset, Seymour Martin, and Earl Raab. 1981. "The Evangelicals and the Election." *Commentary* 71 (March): 25–31.

Lipset, Seymour Martin, and Irving Louis Horowitz. 1966. "The Birth and Meaning of America: A Discussion of *The First New Nation*." *Sociological Quarterly* 7 (Winter): 3–20.

Lo, Clarence Y. H. 1982. "Countermovements and Conservative Movements." *Annual Review of Sociology* 8: 107–34.

Lopatto, Paul. 1985. *Religion and the Presidential Election*. New York: Praeger.

Lorentzen, Louise J. 1980. "Evangelical Life Style Concerns Expressed in Political Action." *Sociological Analysis* 41 (Summer): 144–54.

Lubell, Samuel. 1952. *The Future of American Politics*. New York: Harper.

———. 1956. *The Revolt of the Moderates*. New York: Harper.

———. 1970. *Hidden Crisis in American Politics*. New York: Norton.

Luker, Kristin. 1984. *Abortion and the Politics of Motherhood*. Berkeley and Los Angeles: University of California Press.

Mann, Thomas E., and Norman J. Ornstein. 1981. "The Republican Surge in Congress." In Austin Ranney, ed., *The American National Elections of 1980*, pp. 263–302. Washington: American Enterprise Institute.

Mansbridge, Jane J. 1986. *Why We Lost the ERA*. Chicago: University of Chicago Press.

Markson, Stephen L. 1985. "The Roots of Contemporary Anti-Abortion Activism." In Paul Sachdev, ed., *Perspectives on Abortion*, pp. 33–43. Metuchen, N.J.: Scarecrow Press.

Marsden, George M. 1983. "Preachers of Paradox: The Religious New Right in Historical Perspective." In Mary Douglas and Stephen Tipton, eds., *Religion in America: Spiritual Life in a Secular Age*. Boston: Beacon Press.

Marshall, Susan E. 1984. "Keep Us on the Pedestal: Women Against Feminism in Twentieth-Century America." In Jo Freeman, ed., *Women: A Feminist Perspective*, pp. 568–82. 3d. ed. Palo Alto, Calif.: Mayfield.

———. 1985. "Ladies Against Women: Mobilization Dilemmas of Antifeminist Movements." *Social Problems* 32 (April): 348–62.

Marshall, Susan E., and Anthony M. Orum. 1986. "Opposition Then and Now: Countering Feminism in the Twentieth Century." *Research in Politics and Society* 2: 13–34.

Marty, Martin E. 1976. *A Nation of Behavers*. Chicago: University of Chicago Press.

Mathews, Donald G., and Jane De Hart Mathews. 1982. "The Cultural Politics of ERA's Defeat." Organization of American Historians *Newsletter* 10 (November): 13–15.

McCarthy, John D., and Mayer Zald. 1977. "Resource Mobilization and Social Movements: A Partial Theory." *American Journal of Sociology* 82 (May): 1212–39.

McClosky, Herbert, Paul J. Hoffman, and Rosemary O'Hara. 1960. "Issue Conflict and Consensus Among Party Leaders and Followers." *American Political Science Review* 54 (June): 406–27.

McEvoy, James T. III. 1969. "Conservatism or Extremism: Goldwater Supporters in the 1964 Election." In Robert A. Schoenberger, ed., *The American Right Wing:*

Readings on Political Behavior, pp. 241–79. New York: Holt, Rinehart, and Winston.

―――. 1971. *Radicals or Conservatives? The Contemporary American Right*. Chicago: Rand McNally.

McEvoy, James T. III, Mark Chesler, and Richard Schmuck. 1967. "Content Analysis of a Super-Patriot Protest." *Social Problems* 14 (Spring): 455-63.

McIntyre, Thomas J. (with John C. Obert). 1979. *The Fear Brokers: Peddling the Hate Politics of the New Right*. Boston: Beacon Press.

McNall, Scott G. 1975. *The Career of a Radical Rightist: A Study in Failure*. Port Washington, N.Y.: Kennikat.

Meyer, John W., and James G. Roth. 1970. "A Reinterpretation of American Status Politics." *Pacific Sociological Review* 13 (Spring): 95–102.

Miles Michael. 1980. *The Odyssey of the American Right*. New York: Oxford University Press.

Miller, Arthur H., and Marvin D. Wattenberg. 1984. "Politics from the Pulpit: Religiosity and the 1980 Election." *Public Opinion Quarterly* 48 (Spring): 301–17.

Miller, Margaret I., and Helene Linker. 1974. "Equal Rights Amendment Campaigns in California and Utah." *Society* 11 (May–June): 40–53.

Miller, Wesley E., Jr. 1985. "The New Christian Right and Fundamentalist Discontent: The Politics of Lifestyle Concern Revisited." *Sociological Focus* 18 (October): 325–36.

Mintz, Frank P. 1985. *The Liberty Lobby and the American Right Wing: Race, Conspiracy, and Culture*. Westport, Conn.: Greenwood.

Moen, Matthew C. 1984. "School Prayer and the Politics of Life Style Concern." *Social Science Quarterly* 65 (December): 1065–71.

Moore, Helen A., and Hugh P. Whitt. 1986. "Multiple Dimensions of the Moral Majority Platform: Shifting Interest Group Coalitions." *Sociological Quarterly* 27 (Fall): 423–39.

Mottl, Tahi. 1980. "The Analysis of Countermovements." *Social Problems* 27 (June): 620–35.

Mueller, Carol. 1983. "In Search of a Constituency for the 'New Religious Right.' " *Public Opinion Quarterly* 47 (Summer): 213–29.

Mueller, Carol, and Thomas Dimieri. 1982. "The Structure of Belief Systems Among Contending ERA Activists." *Social Forces* 60 (March): 657–75.

Murphy, Charles J. V. 1954a. "McCarthy and the Businessman." *Fortune* 49 (April): 156ff.

―――. 1954b. "Texas Business and McCarthy." *Fortune* 49 (May): 100ff.

Neitz, Mary Jo. 1981. "Family, State, and God: Ideologies of the Right-to-Life Movement." *Sociological Analysis* 42 (Fall): 265–76.

Nice, David. 1986. "State Opposition to the Equal Rights Amendment: Protectionism, Subordination, or Privatization?" *Social Science Quarterly* 67 (June): 315–28.

O'Brien, Michael. 1980. *McCarthy and McCarthyism in Wisconsin*. Columbia, Mo.: University of Missouri Press, 1980.

Oldendick, Robert, and Stephen E. Bennett. 1978. "The Wallace Factor: Constancy and Cooptation." *American Politics Quarterly* 6 (October): 469–84.

Orum, Anthony M. 1970. "Religion and the Rise of the Radical White: The Case of

Southern Wallace Support in 1968." *Social Science Quarterly* 51 (December): 674–88.

Oshinsky, David M. 1976. *Joseph McCarthy and the American Labor Movement*. Columbia, Mo.: University of Missouri Press.

———. 1983. *A Conspiracy So Immense: The World of Joe McCarthy*. New York: Free Press.

Page, Ann L., and Donald A. Clelland. 1978. "The Kanawha County Textbook Controversy: A Study of the Politics of Life Style Concern." *Social Forces* 57 (September): 265–81.

Paige, Connie. 1983. *The Right-to-Lifers: Who They Are, How They Operate, Where They Get Their Money*. New York: Summit Books.

Parsons, Talcott, 1955. "Social Strains in America." In Daniel Bell, ed., *The New American Right*, pp. 117–40. New York: Criterion Books.

Patel, Kent, Denny Pilant, and Gary Rose. 1982. "Born-Again Christians in the Bible Belt: A Study in Religion, Politics, and Ideology." *American Politics Quarterly* 10 (April): 255–72.

Peek, Charles W., and Sharon Brown. 1980. "Sex Prejudice Among White Protestants: Like or Unlike Ethnic Prejudice?" *Social Forces* 59 (September): 169–85.

Peele, Gillian. 1984. *Revival and Reaction: The Right in Contemporary America*. Oxford: Clarendon Press.

Petcheskey, Rosalind Pollack. 1981. "Antiabortion, Antifeminism, and the Rise of the New Right." *Feminist Studies* 7 (Summer): 206–46.

Pettigrew, Thomas F., and Robert T. Riley. 1971. "The Social Psychology of the Wallace Phenomenon." In Pettigrew, *Racially Separate or Together?*, pp. 231–56. New York, McGraw-Hill.

Pettigrew, Thomas F., Robert T. Riley, and Reeve D. Vanneman. 1972. "George Wallace's Constituents." *Psychology Today* 5 (February): 47ff.

Pierard, Richard V. 1970. *The Unequal Yoke: Evangelical Christianity and Political Conservatism*. Philadelphia: Lippincott.

Pierard, Richard V., and James L. Wright. 1984. "No Hoosier Hospitality for Humanism: The Moral Majority in Indiana." In David C. Bromley and Anson Shupe, eds., *New Christian Politics*, pp. 195–212. Macon, Ga: Mercer University Press.

Pohli, Carol Virginia. 1983. "Church Closets and Back Doors: A Feminist View of Moral Majority Women." *Feminist Studies* 9 (Fall): 529–58.

Polsby, Nelson W. 1960. "Towards an Explanation of McCarthyism." *Political Studies* (October): 250–71.

———. 1966. "Strategic Considerations." In Milton C. Cummings, ed., *The National Election of 1964*, pp. 82–110. Washington: Brookings Institution.

Pomper, Gerald M. 1981a. "The Nominating Contests." In Pomper et al., *The Election of 1980: Reports and Interpretations*, pp. 1–37. Chatham, N.J.: Chatham House.

———. 1981b. "The Presidential Election." In Pomper et al., *The Election of 1980*, pp. 65–96.

Quebedeaux, Richard. 1978. *The Worldly Evangelicals*. New York: Harper and Row.

Quinney, Richard. 1964. "Political Conservatism, Alienation, and Fatalism: Contingencies of Social Status and Religious Fundamentalism." *Sociometry* 27 (September): 372–81.

Redekop, John Harold. 1968. *The American Far Right: A Study of Billy James Hargis and Christian Crusade*. Grand Rapids, Mich.: Eerdmans.

Reeves, Thomas C. 1976. "McCarthyism: Interpretations Since Hofstadter." *Wisconsin Magazine of History* 60 (Autumn): 42–54.

———. 1982. *The Life and Times of Joe McCarthy*. New York: Stein and Day.

Reinhard, David W. 1983. *The Republican Right Since 1945*. Lexington: University Press of Kentucky.

Richardson, James T. 1984. " 'The Old Right' in Action: Mormon and Catholic Involvement in an Equal Rights Amendment Referendum." In David C. Bromley and Anson Shupe, eds., *New Christian Politics*, pp. 213–33. Macon, Ga.: Mercer University Press.

Richardson, John G., and Julia E. Cranston. 1981. "Social Change, Parental Values, and the Salience of Sex Education." *Journal of Marriage and the Family* 43 (August): 547–88.

Riesman, David. 1963. "The Intellectuals and the Discontented Classes: Some Further Reflections." In Daniel Bell, ed., *The Radical Right*, pp. 115–34. Garden City, N.Y.: Doubleday.

Riesman, David, and Nathan Glazer. 1955. "The Intellectuals and the Discontented Classes." In Daniel Bell, ed., *The New American Right*, pp. 56–90. New York: Criterion Books.

Robinson, Michael J. 1981. "The Media in 1980: Was the Message the Message?" In Austin Ranney, ed., *The American Elections of 1980*, pp. 177–211. Washington: American Enterprise Institute.

Rodgers, Harrell R., Jr. 1975. "Prelude to Conflict: The Evolution of Censorship Campaigns." *Pacific Sociological Review* 18 (April): 194–205.

Rogin, Michael Paul. 1966. "Wallace and the Middle Class: The White Backlash in Wisconsin." *Public Opinion Quarterly* 30 (Spring): 98–108.

———. 1967. *The Intellectuals and McCarthy: The Radical Specter*. Cambridge, Mass.: M.I.T. Press.

———. 1968. "The Wallace Catharsis." *Commonweal* 89 (November 29): 310–12.

———. 1969. "Politics, Emotion, and the Wallace Vote." *British Journal of Sociology* 20 (March): 27–49.

———. 1970a. "Progressivism and the California Electorate." In Rogin and John L. Shover, *Political Change in California: Critical Elections and Social Movements, 1890–1966*, pp. 35–61. Westport, Conn.: Greenwood.

———. 1970b. "Southern California: Right-Wing Behavior and Political Symbols." In Rogin and Shover, *Political Change in California*, pp. 153–212.

———. 1975. *Fathers and Children: Andrew Jackson and the Subjugation of the American Indian*. New York: Knopf.

———. 1987. *"Ronald Reagan," the Movie and Other Episodes in Political Demonology*. Berkeley and Los Angeles: University of California Press.

Rogin, Michael Paul, and John L. Shover. 1970. Preface. *Political Change in California: Critical Elections and Social Movements, 1890–1966*, xiii–xviii. Westport, Conn.: Greenwood.

Rohter, Ira S. 1969. "Social and Psychological Determinants of Radical Rightism."
In Robert A. Schoenberger, ed., *The American Right Wing: Readings in Political
Behavior*, pp. 193–237. New York: Holt, Rinehart, and Winston.

———. 1970. "The Genesis of Political Radicalism: The Case of the Radical Right."
In Roberta A. Sigel, ed., *Learning About Politics: A Reader in Political Socialization*, pp. 626–51. New York: Random House.

Rokeach, Milton. 1960. *The Open and Closed Mind: Investigations into the Nature of
Belief Systems and Personality Systems*. New York: Basic Books.

Ross, J. Michael, Reeve D. Vanneman, and Thomas F. Pettigrew. 1976. "Patterns of
Support for George Wallace: Implications for Racial Change." *Journal of Social
Issues* 36, 2: 69–91.

Rothenberg, Stuart, and Frank Newport. 1984. *The Evangelical Voter: Religion and
Politics in America*. Washington: Institute for Government and Politics of the Free
Congress Research Association.

Rubin, Eva Z. 1982. *Abortion, Politics, and the Courts: Roe v. Wade and Its Aftermath*. Westport, Conn.: Greenwood.

Rush, Gary B. 1967. "Status Consistency and Right-Wing Extremism." *American
Sociological Review* 32 (February): 86–92.

St. Angelo, Douglas, and Douglas Dobson, 1975. "Candidates, Issues, and Political
Estrangement: A Research Note on 1968 Political Activists." *American Politics
Quarterly* 3 (January): 45–49.

Saloma, John S., III. 1984. *Ominous Politics: The New Conservative Labyrinth*. New
York: Hill and Wang.

Schiff, Lawrence F. 1964. "The Obedient Rebels: A Study of College Conversions to
Conservatism." *Journal of Social Issues* 20 (October): 74–95.

———. 1966. "Dynamic Young Fogies—Rebels on the Right." *Trans-Action* 4 (November): 31–36.

Schneider, William. 1981. "The November 4 Vote for President: What Did It Mean?"
In Austin Ranney, ed., *The American National Elections of 1980*, pp. 212–62.
Washington: American Enterprise Institute.

Schoenberger, Robert A. 1969. "The New Conservatives: A View from the East." In
Schoenberger, ed., *The American Right Wing: Readings in Political Behavior*, pp.
280–98. New York: Holt, Rinehart, and Winston.

Schoenberger, Robert A., and David R. Segal. 1971. "The Ecology of Dissent: The
Southern Wallace Vote in 1968." *Midwest Journal of Political Science* 15 (August):
583–86.

Scott, Wilbur J. 1985. "The Equal Rights Amendment as Status Politics." *Social
Forces* 64 (December): 499–505.

Shannon, David A. 1961. "Was McCarthy a Political Heir of LaFollette?" *Wisconsin
Magazine of History* 45 (Autumn): 3–9.

Sherrill, Robert. 1968. *Gothic Politics in the Deep South*. New York: Grossman.

Sherwin, Mark. 1963. *The Extremists*. New York: St. Martin's.

Shils, Edward A. 1954. "Authoritarianism: 'Right' and 'Left.' " In Richard Christie
and Marie Jahoda, eds., *Studies in the Scope and Method of "The Authoritarian
Personality,"* pp. 24–49. Glencoe, Ill.: Free Press.

————. 1956. *The Torment of Secrecy: The Background and Consequences of American Security Policies*. Glencoe, Ill.: Free Press.

Shupe, Anson, and John Heinerman. 1985. "Mormonism and the New Christian Right: An Emerging Coalition?" *Review of Religious Research* 27 (December): 146–57.

Shupe, Anson, and William A. Stacey. 1983. *Born-Again Politics and the Moral Majority: What Social Surveys Really Show*. New York: Edwin Mellen Press.

Simpson, John H. 1983. "Moral Issues and Status Politics." In Robert C. Liebman and Robert Wuthnow, eds., *The New Christian Right: Mobilization and Legitimation*, pp. 187–205. Chicago: Aldine.

————. 1984. "Support for the Moral Majority and Its Sociomoral Platform." In David C. Bromley and Anson Shupe, eds., *New Christian Politics*, pp. 65–68. Macon, Ga.: Mercer University Press.

————. 1985a. "Status Inconsistency and Moral Issues." *Journal for the Scientific Study of Religion* 24 (June): 155–62.

————. 1985b. "Socio-Moral Issues and Recent Presidential Elections." *Review of Religious Research* 27 (December): 115–23.

Smidt, Corwin. 1983. "Born-Again Politics: Political Behavior of Evangelical Christians in the South and Non-South." In Tod A. Baker, Robert P. Steed, and Lawrence W. Moreland, eds., *Religion and Politics in the South: Mass and Elite Perspectives*, pp. 27–56. New York: Praeger.

Sokol, Robert. 1968. "Power Orientation and McCarthyism." *American Journal of Sociology* 73 (January): 443–52.

Spitzer, Robert J. 1987. *The Right to Life Movement and Third Party Politics*. Westport, Conn.: Greenwood.

Stacey, William A., and Anson Shupe. 1984. "Religious Values and Religiosity in the Textbook Adoption Controversy in Texas, 1981." *Review of Religious Research* 25 (June): 321–33.

Staggenborg, Suzanne. 1987. "Life-Style Preferences and Social Movement Recruitment: Illustrations from the Abortion Conflict." *Social Science Quarterly* 68 (December): 779–97.

Stone, Barbara J. 1974. "The John Birch Society: A Profile." *Journal of Politics* 36 (February): 184–97.

Summers, Gene F., Doyle P. Johnson, Richard L. Hough, and Kathryn A. Veatch. 1970. "Ascetic Protestantism and Political Preference: A Re-examination." *Review of Religous Research* 12 (Fall): 17–25.

Tamney, Joseph B., and Stephen D. Johnson. 1983. "The Moral Majority in Middletown." *Journal for the Scientific Study of Religion* 22 (June): 145–57.

————. 1984a. "Support for the Moral Majority: A Test of a Model." *Journal for the Scientific Study of Religion* 23 (June): 183–96.

————. 1984b. "Religious Television in Middletown." *Review of Religious Research* 25 (June): 303–13.

Tatalovich, Raymond, and Byron W. Daynes. 1981. *The Politics of Abortion: A Study of Community Conflict and Public Policy Making*. New York: Praeger.

Taylor, Marylee C. 1980. "Fraternal Deprivation and Competitive Racism: A Second Look." *Sociology and Social Research* 65 (October): 37–56.

Tedin, Kent L. 1978. "Religious Preference and Pro/Anti Activism on the Equal Rights Amendment Issue." *Pacific Sociological Review* 21 (January): 55–66.

Tedin, Kent L., David W. Brady, Mary E. Buxton, Barbara M. Gorman, and Judy L. Thompson. 1977. "Social Background and Political Differences Between Pro- and Anti-ERA Activists." *American Politics Quarterly* 5 (July): 395–408.

Tilly, Charles. 1978. *From Mobilization to Revolution*. Reading, Mass.: Addison-Wesley.

Trow, Martin. 1958. "Small Businessmen, Political Tolerance, and Support for McCarthy." *American Journal of Sociology* 44 (November): 270–81.

Vanneman, Reeve D., and Thomas F. Pettigrew. 1972. "Race and Relative Deprivation in the Urban United States." *Race* 13 (April): 461–86.

Viereck, Peter. 1955. "The Revolt Against the Elite." In Daniel Bell, ed., *The New American Right*, pp. 91–116. New York: Criterion Books.

———. 1956. *The Unadjusted Man: A New Hero for Our Time*. Boston: Beacon Press.

Warren, Donald I. 1974. "The Middle American Radicals." *Nation* 219 (August 17): 107–10.

———. 1976. *The Radical Center: Middle America and the Politics of Alienation*. Notre Dame, Ind.: University of Notre Dame Press.

Wasserman, Ira M. 1979. "A Reanalysis of the Wallace Movement." *Journal of Political and Military Sociology* 7 (Fall): 243–56.

Wasserman, Ira M., and David R. Segal. 1973. "Aggregation Effects in the Ecological Study of Presidential Voting." *American Journal of Political Science* 17 (February): 177–81.

Westby, David L., and Richard G. Braungart. 1970. "The Alienation of Generations and Status Politics: Alternative Explanations of Student Political Activism." In Roberta A. Sigel, ed., *Learning About Politics: A Reader in Political Socialization*, pp. 476–89. New York: Random House.

Westin, Alan F. 1963. "The John Birch Society." In Daniel Bell, ed., *The Radical Right*, pp. 201–26. Garden City, N.Y.: Doubleday.

Wie, Yung, and H. R. Mahood. 1971. "Racial Attitudes and the Wallace Vote: A Study of the 1968 Election in Memphis." *Polity* 3 (Summer): 532–49.

Wiebe, Robert H. 1967. *The Search for Order, 1877–1920*. New York: Hill and Wang.

———. 1975. *The Segmented Society: An Introduction to the Meaning of America*. New York: Oxford University Press.

———. 1977. "Modernizing the Republic, 1920s to the Present." In Bernard Bailyn et al., *The Great Republic: A History of the American People*, pp. 1053–1267. Lexington, Mass.: Heath.

Wilcox, Clyde. 1986a. "Evangelicals and Fundamentalists in the New Christian Right: Religious Differences in the Ohio Moral Majority." *Journal for the Scientific Study of Religion* 25 (September): 355–61.

———. 1986b. "Fundamentalists and Politics: An Analysis of the Effects of Differing Operational Definitions." *Journal of Politics* 48 (November): 1041–51.

———. 1987a. "America's Radical Right Revisited: A Comparison of the Activists in Christian Right Organizations from the 1960s and the 1980s." *Sociological Analysis* 48 (Spring): 46–57.

————. 1987b. "Popular Support for the Moral Majority in 1980: A Second Look." *Social Science Quarterly* 68 (March): 157–66.

————. 1987c. "Religious Orientations and Political Attitudes: Variations Within the New Christian Right." *American Politics Quarterly* 15 (April): 274–96.

————. 1987d. "Religious Attitudes and Anti-Feminism: An Analysis of the Ohio Moral Majority." *Women and Politics* 7 (Summer): 59–77.

————. 1987e. Popular Backing for the Old Christian Right: Explaining Support for the Christian Anti-Communist Crusade." *Journal of Social History* 21 (Fall): 117–32.

Wildavsky, Aaron. 1965. "The Goldwater Phenomenon: Purists, Politicians, and the Two-Party System." *Review of Politics* 27 (July): 386–413.

Will, Jeffry, and Rhys Williams. 1986. "Political Ideology and Political Action in the New Christian Right." *Sociological Analysis* 47 (Summer): 160–68.

Wilson, Kenneth L., and Louis A. Zurcher, Jr. 1976. "Status Inconsistency and Participation in Social Movements: An Application of Goodman's Hierarchical Modeling." *Sociological Quarterly* 17 (Autumn): 520–33.

————. 1977. "Status Inconsistency and Participation in Social Movements: A Rejoinder to Bland and Wallis' Comments." *Sociological Quarterly* 18 (Summer): 430–35.

Wohlenberg, Ernest H. 1980. "Correlates of Equal Rights Amendment Ratification." *Social Science Quarterly* 60 (March): 676–84.

Wolfe, Alan. 1981. "Sociology, Liberalism, and the Radical Right." *New Left Review* 128 (July–August): 3–27.

Wolfinger, Raymond E., Barbara Kaye Wolfinger, Kenneth Prewitt, and Sheilah Rosenhack. 1969. "America's Radical Right: Politics and Ideology." In Robert A. Schoenberger, ed., *The American Right Wing: Readings in Political Behavior*, pp. 9–47. New York: Holt, Rinehart, and Winston.

Wolfinger, Raymond E., and Fred I. Greenstein. 1968. "The Repeal of Fair Housing in California: An Analysis of Referendum Voting." *American Political Science Review* 62 (September): 753–69.

————. 1969. "Comparing Political Regions: The Case of California." *American Political Science Review* 63 (March): 74–85.

Wood, Michael, and Michael Hughes. 1984. "The Moral Basis of Moral Reform: Status Discontent vs. Culture and Socialization Explanations of Anti-Pornography Social Movement Adherence." *American Sociological Review* 49 (February): 86–99.

Woodward, C. Vann. 1960. "The Populist Heritage and the Intellectual." *American Scholar* 29 (Winter): 55–72.

Wright, Gerald C., Jr. 1976. "Community Structure and Voting in the South." *Public Opinion Quarterly* 40 (Summer): 201–15.

————. 1977. "Contextual Models of Electoral Behavior: The Southern Wallace Vote." *American Political Science Review* 71 (June): 497–508.

Wrinkle, Robert D., and Charles Elliott. 1971. "Wallace Party Activists in Texas." *Social Science Quarterly* 52 (June): 197–203.

Wrinkle, Robert D., and Jerry L. Polinard. 1973. "Populism and Dissent: The Wallace Vote in Texas." *Social Science Quarterly* 54 (September): 306–20.

Wrong, Dennis H. 1954. "Theories of McCarthyism—A Survey." *Dissent* 1 (Autumn): 385–92.

Wuthnow, Robert. 1973. "Religious Commitment and Conservatism: In Search of an Elusive Relationship." In Charles Y. Glock, ed., *Religion in Sociological Perspective*, pp. 117–32. Belmont, Calif.: Wadsworth.

———. 1983. "The Political Rebirth of American Evangelicalism." In Robert C. Liebman and Wuthnow, eds., *The New Christian Right: Mobilization and Legitimation*, pp. 167–85. Chicago: Aldine.

Yinger, J. Milton, and Stephen J. Cutler. 1984. "The Moral Majority Viewed Sociologically." In David C. Bromley and Anson Shupe, eds., *New Christian Politics*, pp. 69–90. Macon, Ga.: Mercer University Press.

Young, Perry Deane. 1982. *God's Bullies: Native Reflections on Preachers and Politics*. New York: Holt, Rinehart, and Winston.

Zurcher, Louis A., Jr., R. George Kirkpatrick, Robert G. Cushing, and Charles K. Bowman. 1971. "The Anti-Pornography Campaign: A Symbolic Crusade." *Social Problems* 19 (Fall): 217–38.

———. 1973. "Ad Hoc Anti-Pornography Organizations and Their Active Members: A Research Summary." *Journal of Social Issues* 29, 3: 69–94.

Zurcher, Louis A., Jr., and R. George Kirkpatrick. 1976. *Citizens for Decency: Antipornography Crusades as Status Defense*. Austin: University of Texas Press.

Zwier, Robert. 1982. *Born-Again Politics: The New Christian Right in America*. Downers Grove, Ill.: InterVarsity Press.

———. 1984. "The New Christian Right and the 1980 Elections." In David C. Bromley and Anson Shupe, eds., *New Christian Politics*, pp. 173–94. Macon, Ga.: Mercer University Press.

Index

Abcarian, Gilbert, 90n
abortion, 179, 191–96, 220, 256, 260, 264, 265, 267, 268, 303, 321–24
Abramson, Paul, 259n, 260n
Acock, Alan C., 161n
Adorno, T. W., 12n, 85n, 87n
Agnew, Spiro, 148
Alexander, Herbert E., 251n
alienation: and "profamily" activists, 205; and "radical right" activists of early 1960s, 89–91; and Wallace supporters, 134–35
Allen, Howard W., 34n
Almy, Timothy, 161n
Altman, Dennis, 179
Amann, Peter H., xiin
Ambrose, Stephen F., 8
American Independent Party, 116–18, 188. *See also* Wallace
Anderson, Donald N., 243
Anderson, Totton J., 159n
anticommunism. *See* Communism
Apple, R. W., 215n, 216n
Apter, David, 169n
Arrington, Theodore S., 191
"authoritarianism," 85–87; and McCarthy supporters, 12, 14–15; and "profamily" activists, 205; and "radical right" activists of early 1960s, 87–88, 94–95; and Wallace supporters, 135
Ashbrook, John, 54
Ayres, R. Drummond, 215n

Baker, Susan S., xxn
Balswick, Jack O., 243n
Barker, Edwin N., 87
Bartley, Numan V., 124, 127n, 128n, 132, 136–37, 146, 172
Bartos, Patricia E., 243n
Beard, Charles, 285, 288
Beck, Paul A., 131n
Behn, Dick, 215n
Bell, Charles G., 159n
Bell, Daniel, xi, xx, 9, 61, 181n, 218n; on

fundamentalism, xxvi, 63–64; on "radical right" of early 1960s, 62–68, 72, 78, 93, 296–97; on sources of "McCarthyism," 11, 48, 294; on "status politics," 80, 311, 326
Bennett, David H., xivn
Bennett, Stephen E., 117n, 216n
Benson, George S., 68–70
Berenson, William M., 127n
Bernstein, Barton J., 32n
Bibby, Reginald W., 228n
Billings, Dwight B., 315n
Billings, Robert, 232, 233, 253
Billington, Ray A., 18n
Black, Earl, 119n, 126, 316n, 317n
Black, Merle, 119n, 316n, 317n
Bland, Richard, 198n
Blee, Kathleen M., 315n
Bloom, Alexander, xxn
Blumenthal, Sidney, 180n, 216, 226
Bolce, Louis, 190n, 270n
Boles, Janet K., 188, 190, 191n
Boylan, James, 25n
Brady, David W., 191n
Brandmeyer, Gerard A., 12n, 203
Braungart, Richard G., 81–82
Breasted, Mary, 187
Brick, Howard, xxn
Briggs, Kenneth A., 229n
Bright, Bill, 230
Brinkerhoff, Merlin, 228n
Brinkley, Alan, xiin, 43, 225
Broder, David S., 213
Brogan, D. W., 6
Brown, Richard D., 318–20, 322, 324–26
Brown, Roger, 87n
Brown, Sharon, 247n
Broyles, J. Allen, 70n, 76, 78, 88, 91n
Bruce, Steve, xivn, 233n
Brudney, Jeffrey, 259–60
Bryant, Anita, 197, 207
Brye, David L., 31
Buckley, William F., Jr., xvi, xvii, 46, 56, 222n, 313n